中国科学院规划教材

英美文学教程(英国卷)

A Course of British and American Literature
(British Literature)

主　编　李正栓　姬生雷　冯　梅

副主编　白凤欣　田金平　韩美竹

参　编　刘剑英　李　丽　季　敏

　　　　马春兰　申玉革　张媛媛

科学出版社

北　京

内 容 简 介

本书运用学界最新的研究成果和观点，吸纳现代教学理论和方法，结合现代文学批评理论，将文学史、作品选读和文学知识纳入同一本书。本书按照文学式样的不同划分而采用了一种独特的编写体例，共包括四部分：按体裁划分：诗歌、小说、戏剧和散文。各部分均有发展脉络概说、作家生平与作品介绍、选文、注释和思考题。同一作家根据其作品分类出现在不同体裁部分，但讲解侧重点有所不同。本书按历史时期划分，其中文学史部分和作家生平部分文字浅显，易读易懂，可最大程度地帮助学生清晰文学发展的脉络，领悟文学作品的内涵，欣赏文学杰作的美韵。

本书既可作为高等院校或者自学考试英语专业学生的教材，也可供英语专业研究生和广大英语爱好者阅读参考。

图书在版编目(CIP)数据

英美文学教程(英国卷)= A Course of British and American Literature (British Literature)/李正栓，姬生雷，冯梅主编．—北京：科学出版社，2009
(中国科学院规划教材)

ISBN 978-7-03-025421-4

Ⅰ. 英… Ⅱ. ①李…②姬…③冯… Ⅲ. ①英语-阅读教学-高等学校-教材②文学史-英国 Ⅳ. H319.4：I

中国版本图书馆 CIP 数据核字（2009）第 150211 号

责任编辑：相 凌 王 芳/ 责任校对：张 琪
责任印制：徐晓晨/ 封面设计：鑫联必升

科学出版社出版
北京东黄城根北街 16 号
邮政编码：100717
http://www.sciencep.com

北京虎彩文化传播有限公司印刷
科学出版社发行 各地新华书店经销

*

2009 年 9 月第 一 版 开本：787×1092 1/16
2019 年 1 月第八次印刷 印张：24 1/2
字数：568 000

定价：59.00 元

（如有印装质量问题，我社负责调换）

前言

近几十年来，我国的高等教育迅猛发展，英语专业的发展势如破竹，发展之快如雨后春笋。近千所大学都设有英语系。与此同时，与英语有关(或者说，脱胎于英语专业而另图发展)、更直接为社会经济发展服务的翻译专业或方向和商务英语专业也如火如荼。英语教学在中国的发展大有“前无古人，后无来者”之势。

近年来，相关部门和专家对专业建设和课程建设进行调查，发现一些学校在英语专业建设上仍存在差距。一些地方没有完全按教育部英语专业教学大纲规定开设一些专业知识必修课，如语言学和英美文学。有些地方削减文学必修课的课时、简化课程。一些学校的英语专业负责人认为：美国历史太短，美国文学没有必要；有些地方干脆不开这些课程。实际上，这一切现象都暴露出英美文学师资的短缺，师资短缺严重影响了课程建设和专业建设。

英美文学教学历来是我国英语教学的重要组成部分。过去，许多大学有“外文系”，而不是“外语系”，更不是现在统称的“外国语学院”。“外文系”这一名称充分体现了对文学的重视，至今，复旦大学仍保留“外文系”。有些学校的英语专业开设欧洲文学或欧洲文学史课程；有些学校的英语专业开设亚非文学讲座；有些学校的英语专业开设中国文学与文化大讲堂；有些学校的英语专业开设世界文学简史。我国老一辈英语专家们都是通过阅读文学原著掌握其精髓，都是在中西文学王国中自由“徜徉”的学者。今天，我们要追逐前辈之伟大，恐极为不易，但对优秀的文学作品，我们还是应当掌握。这是培养合格外语人才和建设者所必需的。因为文学作品提供了人类最美好的语言，提供了丰富多彩的世界，提供了多样的人文素养。这也是英语专业教学大纲中要求的重要板块。

可喜的是，越来越多的专家学者充分认识到英美文学课的重要性，呼吁并正在实现英语专业建设中传统课程的回归。我们欣喜地注意到，翻译专业和商务英语两个新建专业都把英美文学课程列入其中。这说明，无论是英语专业、翻译专业，还是商务英语专业，都意识到在培养合格专业人才中文学所起到的基础作用和高级功能。

近年来，英美文学教材建设也取得巨大成就，成果很多，甚至出现了细化到讲解英语诗歌知识的教材，如高等教育出版社出版的《英语诗歌教程》，还出版了多种诗歌注释和选读读本，各种戏剧选读读本和小说选读读本也纷纷涌现。据悉，英语散文方面的教材正在出版过程中。英美文学教材真是异彩纷呈，为学生们学习英美文学提供了丰盛的菜单和自由的选择。然而，由于学时有限，各地办学条件不一，学生家境不同，经济承受能力有别等原因，大量采购阅读英美文学图书是不现实的。因此，编者研究决定推出这一版本教材，旨在让学生们在有限的学时内和经济能力能承受的情况下完成英美文学的学习。编者把文学史、作品选读和文学知识纳入同一本书，文学史部分和作家生平介绍部分文字浅显、易读易懂，学生可以自己读,教师亦可以适当讲解,教师应当重点讲解作品部分。本书所选作品如多于教学学时所要求的数量,教师则可以从众多作品中挑选自己认为最应该让学生学会的,学生也可以在有时间时自己多读一些作品,无须另外买书。

根据这一指导思想,本书的编写体例是:全书共四部分,分别是诗歌、小说、戏剧和散文。每种体裁均有发展脉络概说、作家生平与作品介绍,之后是选文、注释和思考题。同一作家根据其作品分类出现在不同体裁部分,讲解侧重点不一样。本书按历史时期划分,不按作品流派划分。

在编写本书时,编者充分采用学界最新的研究成果和一些新观点,诸如谁是英国第一个小说家等问题,还充分利用现代叙事学理论加强小说部分的选文、注释和思考题的设计。小说的节选最大限度地体现不同时期、不同作家的写作风格,体现英美小说叙事技巧的脉络流变,给学生提供多样的叙事审美体验。我们还吸收了许多知识讲解和文学批评常识。

在设计编写提纲时,本书吸收了一些现代教学理论和教学方法。编者认为,书中内容有一些应该是以多种形式留给学生去读,有一些应该让教师重点讲解,有一些应该在课堂上加强互动,有一些应该让学生课下掌握。本书既倡导拓宽视野,包括同一国家内作家间的比较,也倡导广大师生在使用本书时加强英美作家与世界作家的比较与分析。任何一个国家的文学,只有放在世界文学范围内才能独显其魅力,才能显示各国文学之间的相互交流、发展与繁荣。

本书集诗歌、小说、戏剧和散文为一书,但授课教师未必是同一教师,可以分成几个时段由不同教师共同承担此课,各自发挥特长,此建议仅供参考。本书入选作品较多,因为这些作品很优秀,不选太遗憾。对于有些作品,学生可以自己学习,遇到问题可以向教师请教,也可以上网或去图书馆查找译文、评论或赏析。

本书是学校统一规划教材,与科学出版社共同开发建设。它既是学校规划教材建设的重要组成部分,也是英美文学与文化教学团队的成果之一,还是对河北省级精品课程"英美诗歌欣赏"的重要补充。本书由李正栓统一协调负责,英国卷由李正栓、姬生雷、冯梅主编,美国卷由冯梅、李正栓、姬生雷主编。在编写过程中,吸收了华北地区山西和内蒙古几所高校的教师参加编写,壮大了学术力量。

本书的编写得到科学出版社的大力支持,并且,在编写过程中,编者参考网上一些资料和一些学者的同类书籍以及一些学术观点,在此一并致谢。

由于水平和学识有限,纰漏之处在所难免,敬请指出,以便改正。

编　者

2009年7月

Drama

Essay

Poetry

Part One
Early and Medieval Period
(to 1485)

The medieval period in English literature covers more than 800 years, beginning from Caedmon's *Hymn* at the end of the 7th century to *Everyman* at the end of the 15th century. The English Medieval Ages embraced the Old English (or Anglo-Saxon) and the Middle English, sharply divided by the Norman's conquest in 1066. Both English culture and the English language changed radically in the years following this event, and English literature embodied a new spirit. The medieval period covers the following periods: Anglo-Saxon, Anglo-Norman, the 14th century and the 15th century.

Chapter 1 Anglo-Saxon Poetry

The ancestors of today's Englishmen are Anglo-Saxons. Their conquest of Britain in the 5th century marks the beginning of the history of English literature. The Anglo-Saxon invaders who occupied Britain actually consisted of three Germanic tribes, the Angles, the Saxons, and the Jutes, coming from the northern part of the European continent. The Anglo-Saxons lived a stern barbarous life, characterized by power of endurance, seriousness of thought, and belief in fatalism. They showed their heroic ideals in love of glory, allegiance to lord or king, reverence for womanhood, love of personal freedom, open-handed hospitality of lord to squires, honoring of truth, and repression of sentiment. All these things can be seen clearly in the literature of Anglo-Saxon period. The Anglo-Saxons were heathen people, believing in the old mythology of northern Europe. They were Christianized in the 7th century. The introduction of Christianity exerted a great influence upon the English literature, not only enriching the language with many ecclesiastical terms, but also stimulating contacts with a richer culture and providing a haven for literary composition as well as for the copying of manuscripts.

Anglo-Saxon Poetry. Anglo-Saxon Poetry falls into two groups: Pagan and Christian. Before the Anglo-Saxons were converted, the Anglo-Saxon literature had experienced a Bookless Age. English Literature of that period was almost exclusively a verse literature in oral form. The literary survivals from that period are only specimens of poetry, whose origin was in the Germanic legends. The former was the marker of the poetry while the latter was the reciter of poetry. The English poetry produced before the conversion of the Anglo-Saxons was pagan poetry. The good examples of pagan poetry are *Beowulf*, the greatest of Germanic epics and some other poems such as *Widsith*, *The Wanderer*, *The Seafarer*, *Deor's Lament and The Battle of Maldon*.

Christian poetry came into being after the Anglo-Saxons became Christians. The vast bulk of Anglo-Saxon poetry is specifically Christian, devoted to religious subjects. Among the old English poets (most of whom are nameless), Caedmon and Cynewulf towered above the rest.

***Beowulf*.** Beowulf is the most important example of Anglo-Saxon literature and the oldest surviving epic of any Germanic people. It was composed by the Anglo-Saxons before they invaded England. They brought it to their new home. It had been passed from mouth to mouth hundreds of years before it was written down by an unknown religious scholar. The long epic consists of more than 3000 lines. Its stories come from the folk legends of the primitive Germanic tribes. The scenes of the stories are descriptive of Denmark and South Sweden, not of England. The participating figures are Danes, Geats, Franks, and Frisians, not Britons. The whole poem is essentially pagan in spirit and matter, but has biblical elements and Christian reflections provided by the Christian author.

The Story of *Beowulf*. The whole poem falls into two parts. The first part deals with Beowulf's victory over the monster Grendel and his slaying of Grendel's mother in her lair. The second part describes Beowulf's victory-in-death, fifty years later, over the Firedrake.

Hrothgar, king of the Danes, has built a splendid hall named Heorot near the sea. Every night, the king and his thanes (squires) come to the hall to feast and listen to the songs of his gleemen. One night, misfortune befalls them. A frightful monster called Grendel breaks into the hall and kills thirty warriors. The appalling visit repeats for 12 years. Fear and death reign in the hall, and"becomes deserted and silent." Beowulf is the nephew of Hygelac, king of the Geats. When the sad news of the Danes comes to him, he offers to rid Hrothgar of the monster. So he sails to Denmark with 14 warriors. After a feast of welcome, Beowulf and his companions lie down in the hall for the night. Then Grendel comes and devours one of Beowulf's companions. When he is going to attack Beowulf, Beowulf has a hand-to-hand fight with him. Finally, with his big strength, Beowulf wrenches off one of Grendel's arms. Then Grendel runs back to his den to die. The next night, Grendel's mother descends upon the hall to avenge her son's death and carries away Hrothgar's dearest friend. Beowulf and his companions follow the bloody trail of the she-monster to the edge of a lake. Beowulf plunges into the water, finds the she-monster and follows her into her liar under the waves. In the desperate struggle with the she-monster, he happens to find a big sword wrought by the ancient giants, with which he slays her. There, too, he finds Grendel's corpse. Then he cuts off Grendel's head and the head of his mother, and comes back triumphantly. Loaded with treasures given by the

Danes, Beowulf and his companions return to their kingdom in glory. Later, Beowulf becomes king and has reigned for 50 years. Then a fire dragon begins to devastate the land, because he is robbed of a golden cup from an immense gold hoard which he has guarded for 300 years. The aged king goes to the dragon's barrow with 11 chosen warriors. The fighting is a hard one. All his companions seek for safety in flight except his nephew Wiglaf. With the aid of this kinsman, Beowulf kills the dragon at last. But he is fatally wounded. Before he dies, he names Wiglaf his successor. His body and the treasures are placed on a funeral pile, and twelve warriors ride around the great mount to show their love and respect for the bravest, gentlest and most generous king.

Features of *Beowulf*

1. It emphasizes stress. Number of stresses, not number of syllables, is important. Normally, there are four stressed syllables in each line, and at least three of these syllables alliterate.

2. Each line is divided into two halves. Each half has two strongly accented syllables, at least one of the stressed syllables in the first half-line must alliterate with the first accented syllable in the second half-line.

3. A lot of metaphors and understatements are used in the poem, for example, the sea is referred to as the whale-road or the swan-road; the soldiers are described as the shield-men; the chieftains are named the treasure-keepers; human-body is portrayed as the bone-house; God is described as the wonder-wielder; the monster is called soul-destroyer. The epic presents an all-round picture of the tribal society. One can see the social conditions and customs of that period. In this sense, the epic is also a poem of great social significance.

Christian Poetry. Anglo-Saxon Christian poetry is represented by the religious poetry produced by Caedmon and Cynewulf.

Caedmon, the first English known poet, has been called the father of English songs. His life story and how he composed his first famous poem are vividly described in Venerable Bede's *Historic Ecclesiastica*. Caedmon is mainly famous for his first poem which is entitled *Hymn*. In the nine-line poem, he highly praises the Creator. Later on, by using the biblical material, he composed some other poems.

Cynewulf lived in the early 9th century. He was the greatest Anglo-Saxon poet and the expected composer of *Beowulf*. He was probably a Northumbrian ecclesiastic and scholar. His work was more lyrical and personal than Caedmon. It was not until 1840, more than a thousand of years after his death, that his name became known. The only signed poems by Cynewulf are *Christ*, *Juliana*, *the Fates of the Apostles and Elene*.

Chapter 2 Anglo-Norman Poetry

The Norman Conquest. The Normans were originally a hardy race of sea rovers living in Scandinavia. In the 10th century, they conquered a part of Northern France, which has since been called Normandy, and settled down there. They adopted French as their language and believed in Christianity. They were renowned for their adaptability, martial spirit and organizing ability. The Duke of Normandy William was an able general and statesman. In 1066, he led the Norman army to invade England, defeated the English army at Hastings and became the King of England. After the conquest, the English social life greatly changed. Feudal system was established in England. The king became the supreme ruler and below him were his noblemen, such as barons and knights. The Anglo-Saxons sank to the position of slaves. The Norman Conquest brought a great change to the English language. For three hundred years after the conquest, three tongues were spoken in England: Norman-French, the official language of the Conquerors, Latin, the learned language of the clergy and English, and the tongue of the great mass of the people. The Conquest enriched the English vocabulary. French terms of warfare and chivalry, art and luxury, science and law began to enter the English language. After the Conquest, French culture dominated the English language and literature for three hundred years. With the Norman Conquest, the most cultured ways of Continental Europe were introduced into England. The body of customs and ideals known as chivalry, linked with feudal obligations, was introduced by the Normans. The knightly code, the romantic interest in women, a religious exaltation bordering on erotic mysticism, and a mingled tenderness and reverence paid to the Virgin Mary were reflected in the literature.

The Romance. In the Anglo-Norman period, the feudal system promoted the growth of the romance of chivalry. So, Romance became the prevailing literary form and prospered for about three hundred years (1200—1500). The essential features of the Romance are as follows.

1. There is a lack of verisimilitude. For example, the lack of general resemblance to truth or reality is shown by an exaggeration of the vices of human nature and an idealization of virtues, or by an imagination of adventures more or less remote from ordinary life.

2. There is an emphasis upon supreme devotion to a fair lady. A sentimental woman-worship arises from the Virgin cult.

3. Scenes are laid in the past, with the manners and morals representing some aspect or aspects of the contemporary ideal of Chivalry.

4. There is a presence of a quest, in one form or another.

5. There is the appearance of either a religious or a supernatural element, or both.

6. The characters are analyzed according to the type, not to the individual.

Three Matters of the Romance. The Subject-matters of the Romance were drawn from the common stock of three main storehouses. They are The Matter of France, The Matter of Rome and The Matter of Britain.

1. The Matter of France.

This group of romances deals with the matter of France, centering around Charlemagne and his twelve peers. The oldest and most notable of the Romances in this group is *The Chanson de Roland* (11th-12th century).

2. The Matter of Rome.

This group of romances deals with the exploits of Alexander the Great (13th century), tales of Trojan War and tales of Thebes.

3. The Matter of Britain.

The legendary tales about King Arthur and the Knights of the Round Table provide much material for this group of Romances. The important Characters in the stories are Guinevere, Sir Lancelot, Sir Kay, Sir Galahad, Tristram and Iseult, and Sir Gawain. The most notable romance in this group is *Sir Gawain and the Green Knight*.

Sir Gawain and the Green Knight (c. 1370). A verse-romance of 2,530 lines, derived from Celtic legend. The story goes like this:

On New Year's day, King Arthur and his knights are holding a feast. A giant in green enters the banquet-hall on horseback with a battle-axe in his hand. The big man comes to challenge any knight of King Arthur to give him a blow with the battle-axe. The condition is that a return stroke be given a year later at the Green Chapel. At first no knight dares to accept the challenge. Seeing this, the king becomes angry and wants to accept the challenge himself. Just then, Arthur's nephew Gawain stands up and takes up the challenge. With one blow he sends the giant's head rolling through the hall. Then the green knight, who is evidently a terrible magician, picks up his head and mounts his horse. He holds out his head and the ghastly lips warn Gawain to be faithful to his promise and to come to see him next New Year's day at the Green Chapel, where he will return the blow.

The next year, before the New Year's day comes, Sir Gawain leaves Arthur's court to look for the Green Chapel and the green knight. He goes through a lot of adventures and dangers on his journey. But he cannot find the chapel and the knight. On Christmas eve, he is lost in a vast forest. Then he offers prayers to Mary. Suddenly a big green castle appears on the hill before him. He goes up and knocks the door. He is warmly received by the host and the hostess. He is told that the Green Chapel is not far away and he is asked to have a three-day rest in the castle.

Sir Gawain stays in the castle for three days. The host makes a compact with him. According to the compact, the host goes out hunting each day, while Gawain stays in the castle to entertain the beautiful hostess, and in the evening, they exchange what they have got during the day. On the first day, the host goes out hunting, and Gawain stays in the castle. The beautiful hostess tries to seduce Gawain, but is refused. Finally, she gives her guest a kiss. In the evening, the host gives Sir Gawain the game he has killed, and Gawain gives him the kiss back which he has got from the hostess. On the second day, the same thing happens. Gawain gets a kiss from the lady, but in the evening, he returns the kiss to the host. On the third day, the hostess not only gives Sir Gawain a kiss but also gives him a ring and a magic girdle. She tells Gawain the green girdle will protect him from death if he wears it. Gawain rejects the ring, but accepts the girdle. He makes a promise to the lady that he will say nothing about the girdle to anybody. When the host comes back in the evening, Gawain returns the kiss, but says nothing about the girdle.

On the fourth day, Gawain is taken to the Green Chapel by the host. As soon as they come before the chapel, the host disappears. Sir Gawain finds the chapel is a terrible place. When he approaches it, he hears a big sound. The Green Knight is sharpening his new axe. When the Knight comes out with an axe in his hand, Gawain offers his neck for the blow. Twice, he was not injured, and when the third blow falls upon his shoulder, he is slightly wounded. Then the Green Knight tells Gawain that he is the host of the Green Castle. He explains to Gawain that the first two swings have not inflicted any injury on him because he was true to the compact and twice he returned the kiss. The last blow has wounded him because he did not return the girdle. Full of shame, Gawain throws back the girdle to atone for his deception. But the Green Knight wants him to keep the girdle as a gift.

When Sir Gawain is back to his kingdom, his story becomes widely known. King Arthur orders that each of his knights wear a green girdle in order to keep Gawain's story in memory. *Sir Gawain and the Green Knight* is the first great romance in English literature. In form, it is an interesting combination of French and Saxon elements. It is characterized by sophisticated and chivalrous emotion, delicate description of landscape, sympathetic understanding of human feeling. It is written in an elaborate stanza combining meter and alliteration. At the end of each stanza, there is a rhyming refrain.

Chapter 3 Poetry in the Age of Chaucer

Geoffrey Chaucer (1340—1400) lived in the 14th century. His writings brought about the first harvest in English poetry. He towers above all the other writers of this century. So, the 14th century has been traditionally called the Age of Chaucer. English poetry flowered in the writings of three great poets: William Langland, Geoffrey Chaucer, and John Gower.

William Langland's achievement in *Piers Plowman* is important both in literature and in history, since he faced squarely the great religious and social issues of his day. It takes a powerfully disciplined mind to comprehend infinite variety in a single artistic vision. Such a mind was Chaucer's. While he was entirely rooted in the soil of the Middle Ages and tried his hand at a large number of medieval genres, his art is so fully realized as to carry him out of the Middle Ages and make him one of the two or three greatest poets in English literature.

John Gower, one of Chaucer's friends, has not proved much of a threat to Chaucer's predominance. He seems a far more typical medieval writer than Chaucer. He wrote three works which summarized the English Middle Ages: one in Latin, one in Norman French, and one, *Confessio Amantis* (*The lover's Confession*), in English. Were it not for its proximity to Chaucer's, this last would probably be rated somewhat higher than it has been, for it is a work of considerable skill and interest. And it is certainly infinitely superior to anything produced by the English poets of the following century.

William Langland and His *Piers Plowman*

William Langland (1330－1387) was probably born in the Western Midland and was educated in the school of a monastery at Malvern. Then he took minor orders, but never rose to a higher position in the church. Later, he moved to London and made a scanty living by singing for the masses, copying legal documents and doing some other odd jobs. Around 1362, he began writing his famous poem *Piers Plowman*. This poem was repeatedly revised. Now, it exists in three versions, which scholars refer to as the A, B, C Texts. The first, about 2,400 lines long, stops at a rather inconclusive point in the action; the second (generally agreed to be the best form of the poem) is a revision of the first plus an extension of more than 4,000 lines; and the third is a revision of the second. The poem was avidly read and studied by a great many people, and enjoyed great popularity.

Piers Plowman has the form of a dream vision. It is perhaps the greatest of English allegories. It takes the form of a whole series of visions, separated by brief intervals when the narrator is awake. The first passage, which is the prologue to the poem, introduces the famous first vision of the Field of Folk. In this part, the narrator says that on a May morning on Malvern Hills, he fell asleep. Then he had a curious dream. He saw a fair field full of people from all walks of life, the poor and rich, working and wandering as the world requires. The laborers were working full hard, ploughing and sowing in the field, but their laboring fruit was taken away and wasted by the proud idlers. The corrupted bishops, deacons, cardinals, friars, monks, and hermits did nothing but cheat the poor. Yet, a lot of gold came into their pockets, while the laboring people lived in hunger and poverty.

In this part, one can see a satiric picture of the 14th-century England drawn in the heart of an individual 14th-century Christian. When he found that Christianity failed in reforming society because of the corruption of the church, he described the 14th-century English society in terms of its failure to represent an ideal society living in accordance with Christian principles. He pours out savagely indignant satire toward the corruption of the church and churchmen. And he is equally angry with the failure of the wealthy laity to alleviate the sufferings of the poor. That is the very reason why his poem became so popular with the peasant rebels of 1381.

The political situation is summed up by the poet when he tells that he saw a group of rats rush upon the scene in his dream. They discussed how to get rid of a court cat. One rat proposed that their enemy should be killed. But another one pointed out that, even if this cat was killed, another would succeed to its place. So, finally all the rats agreed, "Let That Cat Be. "

After his vision of the Field of Folk in the Prologue, the narrator saw Lady Holy Church in his next vision. Lady Holy Church, who represented Truth, explained to him the fundamental principles of Christianity. He asked to be shown the false, and Holy Church told him to witness the marriage of a personified False to Lady Meed (Bribery). Lady Meed is portrayed as an alluring wealthy woman. Her many rascally followers recognized her as bribery, but Theology considered her the reward God had promised to give to true men, and objected to her proposed marriage to False. As a result of this objection, Meed and False, accompanied by a vast train of dishonest members of society, proceeded to London to get the legal opinion on the validity of their marriage. The king was informed of their coming and sent officers to arrest Meed. All the remainder of the company ran away. Though under arrest, Meed was warmly welcomed in the royal court, because she at once started to corrupt functionaries with money and promises of influence. The king proposed that she marry one of his knights named Conscience, to which she gladly assented. But when Conscience appeared, he refused to marry her, and she and he had a long debate about the true meaning of her name Meed. She tried to describe herself as merely payment for services rendered or things purchased, but Conscience would allow her no licit role in society. He declined to obey the king's command to become reconciled with her, unless Reason advised him to do so. Reason was summoned and, aided by Meed's flagrant attempts to corrupt the king's justice, succeeded in persuading the king and his subjects that Meed should not be condemned.

Here the dreamer awakes for the first time, but after a very short interval he falls asleep again and dreams that Reason preaches a sermon to the entire kingdom. At the end of this, the people confess their sins, an action which Langland describes by personifying the seven deadly sins, each one relating to how he behaves in society. These confessions display most clearly Langland' social realism. In this part, one can see clearly that the poet tries to whip the corruption of the court with bitter satire. In contrast with the corruption of the court and the Church, the poet describes the miserable condition of the poor peasants.

The next part of the poem describes the pilgrimage of people of various social positions in search of Truth. The narrator saw in his dream a lot of people set off to search for Truth. But they said that they could never find Truth without a guide. Then Piers Plowman appeared on the scene. Before taking the people to look for Truth, he said that he had to have his half acre of land ploughed. He explained to the pilgrims that the best way in search of Truth was to labor. So he set all of the pilgrims to work in his field.

Here, one can see that the dignity of honest labour is highly praised. The author points out that the laboring people are the nearest to Truth.

Geoffrey Chaucer

In the period of Medieval English, literature found its best expression mainly in poetry. The most famous and the greatest poet of the time was Geoffrey Chaucer (1343—1400), who is often called the father of English poetry although there were many poets before him. John Dryden (1631—1700) said that Chaucer, as the father of English poetry, was the perpetual fountain of good sense.

Geoffrey Chaucer was born in London. His father was a wine merchant. At 17, he became a page in a nobleman's house. At 19, he went to France for one of the campaigns of the Hundred Years' War. There he was taken prisoner. Later he was ransomed by the king. On his return, he became connected with the noble through marriage. John of Gaunt, the Duke of Lancaster, became his patron.

He went to the European Continent several times on diplomatic missions, which took him to France and Italy, where he was greatly influenced literarily. Then he was appointed controller of Customs at London and performed good duties. He was M. P. for Kent in 1386. He liked reading and writing in his spare time. His library of sixty books was quite a large one at the time.

Chaucer had a good knowledge of Latin, French and Italian. He was versed in French and Italian literature. His rich life experiences and his knowledge of the world equipped him socially and intellectually for his future career in English poetry.

After his death, he was buried in Westminster Abbey, thus founding the "Poets' Corner". Chaucer's literary career coincided with his life experiences, falling into three periods: the first being one of translation from French (e. g. *The Romaunt of the Rose*), the second being one of adaption from the Italian (e. g. *Troilus and Criseyde*), the third being one of creation in purely English with *The Canterbury Tales* as the masterpiece of his whole literary career. On this monumental work he spent 15 years, beginning from 1386.

In the first period, Chaucer tried his hand at meter, language and subject. In the second period, he borrowed foreign themes but showed his own creativeness. In the third period, he had his own choice of subject, depiction of characters, diction and plot. As John

Dryden put it, Chaucer could take"into the compass of his *Canterbury Tales*"the various manners and humours of the whole English nation, in his age. Not a single character has escaped him. All his pilgrims are clearly distinguished from each other, not only in their inclinations, but in their very physiognomies and personalities. Dryden called *The Canterbury Tales* "God's plenty".

The Canterbury Tales. The *Canterbury Tales* total about 17,000 lines—about a half of Chaucer's entire literary production.

The whole poem is a collection of tales and stories strung together according to a simple plan, which shows the influence of Boccaccio's *Decameron*. One spring day, the poet is in the Tabard inn in Southwark at the south end of London Bridge. He joins the other pilgrims bound for Canterbury. The host of the inn suggests that they tell stories to kill time during the journey. All agree. The host acts as the judge. Each is to tell two stories while going and two while returning. There are 30 people in the company, which meant that there would be 120 stories, but actually only 24 were written. The tales cover all the major types of medieval literature: romances of knights and ladies, folk tales, animal stories, stories of travel and adventure, and others. Perhaps the"marriage group"are most worth reading. All but two of these tales are in verse. And the Prologue needs careful reading. The Prologue provides a framework of this long poem. Like the host's comments on and steering of the story-telling, the Prologue also serves to connect the individual stories. In this Prologue are included vivid sketches of typical medieval figures. The prologue is a miniature of the English society of Chaucer's time. In order to have a good understanding of the whole poem, it is advised that one should refer frequently to the Prologue. Owing to the true-to-life depiction of characters and the broad reflection of the whole society, Chaucer was praised by Gorky as "founder of English realism".

The Canterbury Tales has its social significance in several ways. First, it represents the spirit of the rising bourgeoisie. People's right to pursue earthly happiness is affirmed by Chaucer. Second, the ideas of humanism are shown in Chaucer's praising of man's energy, intellect, wit and love of life. Third, Chaucer exposed and satirized the evils of the time. Fourth, the corruption of the Church is vigorously attacked. Fifth, Chaucer showed sympathy for the poor to some extent. Lastly, Chaucer established the language of literature. The language he used is vivid and smooth, which, together with the rhymed couplet, makes a very easy and good reading.

Chaucer's contribution to English poetry is that he greatly enriched the rhyme schemes by introducing from France rhymed stanzas. The rhymed couplet of iambic pentameter is the form he was most at home with. Alliterative verse of the Old English period was to give way to new poetic forms.

The Canterbury Tales

The General Prologue[1]
(excerpt)

When the sweet showers of April fall and shoot
Down through the drought of March to pierce the root,
Bathing every vein[2] in liquid power
From which there springs the engendering[3] of the flower,
When also Zephyrus[4] with his sweet breath
Exhales an air in every grove and heath
Upon the tender shoots, and the young sun
His half-course in the sign of the Ram has run[5],
And the small fowls are making melody
That sleep away the night with open eye
(So nature pricks[6] them and their heart engages)
The people long to go on pilgrimages
And palmers[7] long to seek the stranger strands
Of far-off saints, hallowed in sundry[8] lands,
And specially, from every shire's end[9]
In England, down to Canterbury[10] they wend[11]
To seek the holy blissful martyr[12], quick
In giving help to them when they were sick
    It happened in that season that one day
In Southwark[13], at The Tabard[14] as I lay
Ready to go on pilgrimage and start
For Canterbury, most devout at heart,
At night there came into that hostelry[15]
Some nine and twenty in a company
Of sundry folk happening then to fall
In fellowship, and they were pilgrims all
That towards Canterbury meant to ride.
The rooms and stables of the inn were wide[16],
They made us easy[17], all was of the best.
And shortly, when the sun had gone to rest,
By speaking to them all upon the trip
I was admitted to their fellowship
And promised to rise early and take the way
To Canterbury, as you heard me say.

But none the less, while I have time and space,
Before my story takes a further pace[18],
It seems a reasonable thing to say
What their condition was, the full array[19],
Of each of them, as it appeared to me,
According to profession and degree[20],
And what apparel[21] they were riding in;
And at a knight I therefore will begin.

Notes

1. The excerpt taken here is the first 42 lines of the Prologue. What follows it is the introduction to the individual pilgrims. This is a modern verse translation by Nevill Coghill who faithfully preserved Chaucer's original form-the heroic couplet (lines of iambic pentameter in rhymed couplet). Please read some original lines and compare Coghill's translation: Whan that April with his showeres soote/The droughte of March has perced to the roote/And bathed every reine in swich licour/Of which vertu engendred is the flowr.
2. vein—rib of a leaf.
3. engendering—budding or springing up.
4. Zephyrus—the west wind.
5. the young sun/His half—course in the sign of the Ram has run—It is the time after eleventh of April.
6. pricks—stimulates.
7. palmers—pilgrims to foreign countries.
8. sundry(archaic)—diverse, different.
9. from every shire's end—from the farthest place in every shire (county).
10. Canterbury—a town southeast of London; on the road to Dover. Canterbury became a shrine after Thomas à Becket was murdered.
11. wend (archaic)—go.
12. the holy blissful marty—Thomas à Becket, a close friend of Henry II before becoming the archbishop of Canterbury. He later quarreled with king Henry II who wanted to deprive the church courts of some power. At the hint of Henry II, four knights went to Canterbury and murdered Thomas. Thomas was later regarded as a martyr and saint. His tomb at Canterbury became a shrine.
13. Southwark—a suburb of London.
14. The Tabard—an inn at Southwark.
15. hostelry—an inn.
16. wide—spacious.

17. easy—feel comfortable.
18. take a further array—proceeds or goes further.
19. the full array—dress and appearance.
20. degree—social rank.
21. apparel (archaic)—clothing.

For Study and Discussion

1. What's the rhyme pattern of this poem? Do we have such poetic rhyme pattern? Name some works if you can.
2. Read these lines aloud repeatedly. Say something about your feeling. Are they smooth and easy?

Chapter 4 The Fifteenth Century Poetry

The 15th century was a period of general unrest. People's major attention was absorbed by a series of wars, and many nobles, who had been the patrons of art and literature, were killed on the battlefield. Thus, the development of literature was greatly affected. There were no great names in poetry except a group of Chaucerians (Chaucer's followers). But it is a period in which folk literature, especially ballads, flourished.

Chaucerians. The following poets are often considered as Chaucerians.

John Lydgate (1370—1449) was the most prolific follower of Chaucer and the most voluminous poet between Chaucer and Spenser. His chief works are translations and compilations. He was once considered Chaucer's equal, but he resembled Chaucer only in versatility. His works include beast fables, saints' lives, and popular poems.

John Skelton (1460—1529) was the poet-laureate of his day and a satirist. He was the most original and vivacious English Chaucerian. He mainly wrote doggerel, but his poems are deep in meannings. Humor and pathos are often seen in his poems.

James I (1394—1437) was the king of Scotland from 1406—1437. For 18 years, he was detained as a prisoner in England. He was well-educated. He has been famous for his poem *The King's Quair*. The story of the poem tells that from the prison window of the English Castle, the imprisoned prince saw Lady Jane walking in the garden below. She was so beautiful that he fell in love with her at the first sight. Then in a dream at night, the prince was carried to the palace of Venus, where the Goddess sent him to The Goddess of Good Hope, who guided him to see the goddess of Fortune. This goddess made the prince climb upon her ever-revolving wheel. When he woke up, a message came to him. He was told that his proposal was accepted by the beautiful lady.

The poem was written in seven-line pentameter stanza, riming ababbcc, henceforth called"rime royal" in honor of king James.

William Dunbar (1460—1530) was a wandering preacher, king's messenger, and the poet-laureate of his day. He has been called Chaucer of Scotland. His representative poems are *The Lament for the Makers* and *Poems on London*.

Popular Ballads. Ballads belong to the domain of folk literature.

A ballad is a story told in song, usually in 4-line stanzas, with the second and fourth lines rhymed. As the ballad-singers sang, the audience joined in the refrain which usually follow each stanza. Ballads followed the tradition of folk songs which existed long before the Norman Conquest (1066).

Around the 15th century, ballads were widely spread among the common people. But as a matter of fact, ballads already existed in the 12th and 13th centuries.

The ballads were composed collectively by the people and constantly revised as they were handed down from mouth to mouth. They were written down and recorded in the 18th century by Thomas Percy (1729—1811) in his *Reliques of Ancient English Poetry* in 1765 and by Walter Scott (1771—1832) in his *Minstrelsy of the Scottish Border in* 1802—1832 and others. But the greater collection of ballads is that of F. J. Child, *The English and Scottish Popular Ballads*, first published in 1882.

The ballads usually adopt various English and Scottish dialects. They have a variety of themes, including the struggle of young lovers against feudal families, the conflict between love and wealth, the cruel effect of jealousy, the border wars between England and Scotland, and matters of class struggle, etc. The contents of ballads cover historical events, folktales, mythology and legends, common life and event, etc. Some ballads are highly lyrical, some very humorous, giving the reader a feeling of simplicity and freshness.

Ballads were found all over Europe in the Middle Ages. But a particularly fertile soil was the border area between England and Scotland, for once there were many bloody battles fought between the English and the Scots there.

Ballads of Robin Hood. The most famous cycle of the English ballads deal with the stories of a legendary outlaw named Robin Hood. In English history, Robin Hood is a partly real and partly legendary figure. Some historical books say that he lived during the reign of Richard I. He was the leader of a group of outlaws, and they lived in a big forest. They often attacked the rich, waged wars against the bishops and archbishops, but helped the poor people. They were constantly hunted by the sheriffs. The rebellious spirit of Robin Hood and his companions often inspired the English people in the struggle against their oppressors.

Get Up and Bar the Door[1]

It fell about the Martinmas time[2]
And a gay time it was then,
When our goodwife[3] got puddings to make,
And she's boild[4] them in the pan.

The wind sae cauld[5] blew south and north,
And blew into the floor,
Quoth our goodman[6] to our goodwife,
'Gae[7] out and bar the door.'

'My hand is in my hussyfskap[8],
Goodman, as ye[9] may see;
An it should nae be barred[10] this hundred year,
It's no be barred for[11] me.'

They made a paction[12] tween[13] them twa[14],
They made it firm and sure,
That the first word whaeer[15] should speak,
Should rise and bar the door.

Then by there came two gentlemen,
At twelve o'clock at night,
And they could neither see house nor hall,
Nor coal nor candle-light.

'Now whether is this a rich man's house,
Or whether is it a poor?'
But neer[16] a word wad[17] ane o them[18] speak,
For barring of the door.

And first they ate the white pudding,
And then they ate the black;
Tho muckle[19] thought the goodwife to hersel[20],
Yet neer a word she spake.

Then said the one unto the other,
'Here, man, tak ye[21] my knife;
Do ye tak aff[22] the auld[23] man's beard,
And I'll kiss the goodwife.'

'But there's nae water in the house,
And what shall we do than?'[24]
'What ails ye at the pudding-broo[25],

That boils into the pan?'

O up then started our goodman,
An angry man was he,
'Will ye kiss my wife before my een[26],
And scad me wi pudding-bree?'[27]

Then up and started our goodwife,
Gied[28] three skips on the floor:
'Goodman, you've spoken the foremost word[29],
Get up and bar the door.'

Notes

1. The ballad metre here is stanzaic form.
2. Martinmas time—November 11th, the time of feast of St. Martin.
3. Good wife—housewife, the mistress of the house.
4. boild—boiled.
5. sae cauld—so cold.
6. Good man—the master of the house.
7. Gae—go.
8. hussyfskap—housework, here referring to the pudding-making.
9. ye—you.
10. An it should nae be barred—if it should not be barred.
11. for—by.
12. paction—agreement.
13. tween—between.
14. twa—two.
15. whaeer—whoever.
16. neer—never.
17. wad—would.
18. ane o them—one of them (husband and wife).
19. Tho muckle—though much.
20. hersel—herself.
21. tak ye—you take.
22. tak aff—take (shave) off.
23. auld—old.
24. than—then.
25. 'What ails ye at the pudding-broo...?'—What paints you if you use the pudding broth as shaving water?
26. een—eyes.

27. scad me wi pudding-bree—scald me with pudding-broth.
28. Gied—gave.
29. you've spoken the foremost word—you've spoken first.

For Study and Discussion

1. What is expressed in this poem?
2. What kind of ballad is this?
3. How are the lines rhymed?

Part Two
The Sixteenth Century

Chapter 1 The Renaissance in England

The 16th century is the Renaissance period in England. The Renaissance, a European phenomenon, is an intellectual movement that embraced the reawakening of scholarship, the recovery of the ancient learning, the rise of the spirit of religious and scientific inquiry, and self-emancipation of the individual from the thralldom of institutions. By subverting feudalism, the intellectual tyranny of scholasticism, and of the church in secular matters, the transition from medieval to modern methods of study and thought occurred.

The Renaissance had its origin in north Italy in the 14th century, and spread northward to other European countries—to France, to Germany, to the Low Countries, and lastly to England. It revived the study of Roman and Greek classics, and marked the beginning of the bourgeois revolution. During the Renaissance period, England enjoyed stability and prosperity. It gradually became the strongest power in Europe. Reformation of the church was carried out completely by Henry VIII in England. As a result, the English church broke with the church of Rome. Protestantism was established in England, and the English king became the supreme ruler of the state and the church.

Humanism became the keynote of the English Renaissance. The English scholars and educators called themselves Humanists, who emphasized the capability of the human mind and the achievements of human culture, in contrast to the medieval emphasis on God and contempt for the things of the human world.

The English Renaissance went through three periods: The Beginning, The Flowering (also called Age of Elizabeth), and The Decline.

The Prosperity of English Poetry. English poetry in the Renaissance period had one of its highlights. It achieved original beauty and exuberance, especially in the Age of Elizabeth. Elizabethan poetry is remarkable for its variety, freshness, youthfulness, and romantic ardor. A group of excellent poets appeared, and a large number of noble poetic works were produced. In the Age of Elizabeth, writing poetry became a vogue. Almost all educated people could write poems, and England became "a nest of singing birds". The queen herself was a poet. She suggested topics for poets to write and rewarded poets. Her ministers and courtiers obeyed her example and tried to rival one another in shaping beautiful verses.

The verse forms used by the Elizabethans range from the extremely simple four-line ballad stanza through the rather complicated form of the sonnet to the elaborate and beautiful 18-line stanza of Spenser's *Epithalamion.*

The sonnet, the most common Italian poetic form, was introduced by Thomas Wyatt. Henry Howard, Earl of Surrey, invented the English sonnet, which was practiced by Shakespeare and other sonneteers. There also appeared many variations of the sonnet form. Henry Howard also introduced blank verse into English, which became the major instrument in the hands of the playwrights.

The six-line and the seven-line stanza (rhyme royal), both practiced by Chaucer, survived into the 16th century. Shakespeare used the former in *Venus and Adonis* and the latter in *The Rape of Lucrece*. An innovation was Spenser's nine-line stanza, "Spenserian stanza", named after him. This form serves the large descriptive and narrative requirements of *The Faerie Queene* so well.

The major genres and conventions in poetry adopted by the Elizabethans are the following: pastoral poems, e. g. Spenser's *Shepheardes Calenders*, mythological-erotic poems, e. g. Shakespeare's *Venus and Adonis* and Marlowe's *Hero and Leander*, complaint poems, and love sonnets, which reached the height of its vogue in the last decade of the 16th century, depended upon a convention established by Petrarch and followed by his many imitators in Italy and France. In this tradition the poet complains of his lady's coldness. He describes the contrary states of feeling the lover experiences, and he writes sonnets on the conventional themes of sleep, absence, originality, renunciation, and others. There were also satirical poems and heroic poems. Spenser's *Faerie Queen* is the prime example of the heroic poems.

Chapter 2 Sir Thomas Wyatt

Sir Thomas Wyatt (1503—1542), together with Henry Howard, Earl of Surrey, was generally regarded as the founder of the golden age in English poetry under the reign of Elizabeth I. Wyatt was born at Arlington Castle in Kent, and educated at St. John's College, Cambridge. He spent most of his life as a courtier and diplomat. On diplomatic missions, he had travelled to Spain, France and Italy. Influenced greatly by especially Italian literature, he translated the poems of Petrarch, Sannazaro, Alamanni and others. He imitated these Italian sonneteers. At the same time, he wanted to show that, through his own writings, English could also be a reflexible and elaborate language.

Wyatt tried his hand on various rhythms and rhymes, but his greatest contribution to English literature is that he introduced into England the sonnet, a 14-Line poem with a complicated rhyme scheme. The most common rhyme scheme in Wyatt's sonnets is abba abba cddc ee. The usual Italian structure of an octave (first eight lines) is followed, after a turn in the sense, by a sestet (last six lines). This rhyme scheme was beginning to break down in the "English" structure for the sonnet (three quatrains and a couplet). The sonnets of Shakespeare are English-structure invented by Henry Howard, usually rhyming abab cdcd efef gg.

On the one hand, Wyatt was a forerunner of the Elizabethan poetry, on the other hand, his poems were different from those of his contemporaries like Sidney, Spenser and others. Wyatt's poems are characterized by the directness, simplicity and the emotion toward Nature while the poems of others move people with rich diction and imagery. Wyatt was rather like Chaucer and Chaucer's contemporaries. So, in a sense, Wyatt and Surrey built the bridge between the Middle Ages and the Elizabethan Age. Wyatt was twice arrested, but on both occasions, he was fortunate enough to regain King Henry Ⅷ's favor and receive a pardon. Wyatt also wrote a large portion of non-sonnet poems. His temperament and disposition were shown more clearly in these poems. The lover in the Petrarchan sonnet is usually in a mood of doleful despair. The typical poem is essentially a complaint, though the interest lies in following the elaborately worked out "conceits" or comparisons. The lover is the lady's slave. The lady's coldness is a perpetual torture to him. That is why we call such poems male complaint poems. But in his non-sonnet poems, a rather gay, manly independence is the characteristic note.

Farewell, Love[1]

Farewell, Love, and all thy laws forever,
Thy baited hooks shall tangle[2] me no more;
Senec and Plato[3] call me from thy lore[4],
To perfect wealth my wit[5] for to[6] endeavor.
In blind error when I did persever,
Thy sharp repulse, that pricketh[7] ay[8] so sore[9],
Hath taught me to set in trifles no store
And 'scape[10] forth since liberty is lever[11],
Therefore farewell, go trouble younger hearts,
And in me claim no more authority;
With idle youth go use thy property,
And thereon spend thy many brittle darts[12]
For hitherto though I have lost all my time,
Me lusteth[13] no longer rotten boughs to climb[14].

Notes

1. love—not lover, but cupid or the abstract love.
2. tangle—seize; take hold me.
3. Senec and Plato—Senec (BC4-AD65) , Roman politician, philosopher and author; Plato (BC427-BC347), Greek philosopher. Here they represent the classic learning of ancient Greece and Rome.
4. lore—teaching, referring to the romance stories.
5. wit—intellect.
6. for to—to.
7. pricketh—pricks.
8. ay—aye, ever, always.
9. sore—sorely, painfully.
10. 'scape—escape.
11. lever—more pleasing, dearer.
12. brittle darts—sharp arrows of Cupid
13. me lusteth—I care.
14. rotten boughs to climb—to climb rotten boughs. The rotten boughs refer to the romance of the Middle Ages.

For Study and Discussion

1. What is the rhyme scheme of this poem?
2. How many syllables are there in each line?
3. To whom is the poet bidding farewell? To his lover?
4. What is the main idea of this poem?

Chapter 3 Henry Howard, Earl of Surrey

Henry Howard, Earl of Surrey (1517－1547), together with Sir Thomas Wyatt, was called the founder of the golden Elizabethan poetry. He was versed in Italian and French poetry. In his works, he also tried to show that English was, like other languages, reflexible, elaborate and good for writing poetry. He tried his hand on various metres and forms. Like Sir Thomas Wyatt, he served as a bridge between the Middle Ages and the

Elizabethan Age. Surrey was the eldest son of the Duke of Norfolk. He was descended from kings on both sides of his family. He was brought up with Henry VIII's illegitimate son, the Duke of Richmond, who married Surrey's sister.

Surrey was an able soldier and went to fight whenever called upon. Surrey's importance as a poet rests upon two facts. The first one is that he continued the practice of the sonnet in English as instituted by Wyatt. The second one is that he was the first one to use blank verse—unrhymed iambic pentameter—a verse form that flourished in the succeeding four centuries, which Shakespeare and Milton used masterfully in their drama and non-dramatic works. Surrey used the blank verse in his translation of part of Virgil's "Aeneid". As a courtier poet, he was interested in circulating his poems in manuscript rather than in printing them. But he did publish the bulk of his poetry in *Tottel's Miscellany*. Apart from his greatest contribution to English literature by introducing blank verse into it, his development of the sonnet should be his second greatest contribution. It is he who changed the Italian form (an octave and a sestet) into a form of three quatrains plus a couplet, which is called English sonnet and often mistakenly called Shakespearean sonnet as if it were invented by Shakespeare.

Surrey's poems are more fluent and musical. His poetic diction is clear and consistent. In many ways, Surrey indicated the direction in which the main stream of English verse would flow. Yet he often seemed less vivid and vigorous than Wyatt.

It is not easy to estimate how he and Wyatt influenced the succeeding generations, but they did popularize court poetry and paved the way for Sidney, Spenser and others.

Love, That Doth Reign and Live Within My Thought[1]

Love that doth reign and live within my thought,
And built his seat within my captive breast,
Clad in the arms wherein with me he fought,
Oft in my face he doth his banner rest.
But she that taught me love and suffer pain,
My doubtful hope and eke[2] my hot desire
With shamefast[3] look to shadow and refrain,
Her smiling grace converteth[4] straight to ire
And coward love, then, to the heart apace
Taketh[5] his flight, where he doth lurk and plain[6]
His purpose lost , and dare not show his face.
For my lord's guilt thus faultless bide I pain,
Yet from my lord shall not my foot remove:
Sweet is the death that taketh end by love.

Notes

1. The rhyme scheme of this poem is abab cdcd efef gg. The last 2 lines are eye rhyme.
2. eke—also.
3. shamefast—modest.
4. converteth—converts.
5. taketh—takes.
6. plain—complain.

For Study and Discussion

1. Compare the rhyme scheme of this poem with those of Wyatt's sonnets. Count the syllables of each line.
2. How did the poet describe love?
3. What is the main idea of this poem?

Chapter 4 Sir Philip Sidney

Sir Philip Sidney (1554—1586) was regarded by Spenser as "the noble and virtuous gentleman most worthy of all titles both of learning and chivalry". When he died in battle at the age of 32, the whole country mourned his death.

Sidney was born into a prominent aristocratic family who lived in Kent (also the native country of Sir Thomas Wyatt). His father was Sir Henry Sidney, thrice Lord Deputy of Ireland. His mother's brother was Robert Dudley, Earl of Leicester, the most spectacular and powerful of all the queen's subjects. He attended Oxford University, but left without taking a degree and completed his education by traveling on the Continent, where he had opportunities to meet many famous people including writers, educators, heads of state and religious leaders. When he returned to England, he passionately committed to the Protestant cause. He also learned a lot from the main literary and artistic developments of the late Renaissance in Italy, France, and northern Europe.

After he returned to England, he lived the life of a prominent courtier, diplomat and casual man of letters, active in political and religious interests and actively encouraging young writers, most importantly the young Edmund Spenser, who dedicated *The*

Shepheardes Calender to him.

When he incurred the queen's displeasure by opposing her projected marriage to the Duke of Anjou, he was dismissed from court for a time. It was in Wilton, the estate of his beloved sister Mary, Countess of Pembroke, at her request and for her entertainment that he wrote *Arcadia*, a pastoral romance. Sometime during the early 1580s he wrote *The Defence of Poesy* , the finest piece of Elizabethan literary criticism to counterattack an extremist Puritan attack against poetry and plays. In this essay, he said the real defence of the poet depends not upon what he has been but upon what he does, and all arts depend upon works of nature, but the poet, supreme among artists, can make another nature, new and more beautiful. His greatest contribution in *The Defence of Poesy* is that he developed the ideas of classical theories by saying that poetry not only delights and instructs, but also moves.

Sidney's greatest contribution to English poetry is his *Astrophel and Stella* (*Starlover and Star*), the first of the great Elizabethan sonnet sequences of Petrarch and other Italian and French poets of the Renaissance. He also used the form ending with a couplet created by Wyatt and Surrey. The series of 108 sonnets reflect an actual autobiographical situation—Sidney's love for and eventual engagement to Penelope Devereux who eventually married Lord Rich. Through the interplay of argument and feeling in *Astrophel and Stella*, Sidney developed both an analysis and demonstration of how to write subtly and impressively about love.

Sidney's sonnet cycle was the chief inspiration for many other such cycles in the 1590's. Apart from being a brilliant and sophisticated love poet, Sidney was a man of deep moral conviction, famous for his beauty, courage, wit, learning and noble character. He died when fighting at Zutphen for the Dutch Protestant against the Catholicon Spanish in 1586.

Leave Me, O Love[1]

Leave me, O love which reachest but[2] to dust
And thou, my mind, aspire to higher things;
Grow rich in that which never taketh[3] rust,
Whatever fades but[4] fading pleasure brings.
Draw in thy beams, and humble all thy might
To that sweet yoke where lasting freedoms be;
Which breaks the clouds and opens forth the light
That doth both shine and give us sight to see.
O take fast hold; let that light be thy guide
In this small course which birth draws out to death,
And think how evil becometh him to slide,
Who seeketh heav'n, and comes of heav'nly breath[5].
Then farewell, world; thy uttermost I see;
Eternal Love, maintain thy life in me.

Notes

1. The rhyme scheme is abab cdcd efef gg. This is one of Sidney's best sonnets. This sonnet, not included in either *Arcadia* or *Astrophel and Stella*, describes the refusal of love.
2. but—only.
3. taketh—takes.
4. but—only merely.
5. And think how evil becometh him to slide,/Who seeketh heav'n, and comes of heav'nly breath—and think how evil it is for one who is seeking heaven and has a divine spirit or soul in him to descend to earthly things.

For Study and Discussion

1. Why was the poet asking love to leave him? What kind of love was he seeking?
2. Please comment on the last two lines.

Chapter 5 Edmund Spenser

The greatest nondramatic poet of the English Renaissance, Edmund Spenser (1552—1599), is regarded as "the poet's poet" because of his great influence on later poets. Spenser was born and educated in London. He attended Cambridge University, where he performed certain useful duties to cover the college expenses, where he read the classics and Italian poets, where he became friends with other young writers interested in applying the forms and the standards of classical poetry to English poetry.

After he left Cambridge in 1576, he took a series of positions in the service of prominent English noblemen, including Dr. John Young, Bishop of Rochester, the Earl of Leicester, the Queen's favourite, and finally, Lord Gray of Wilton, Lord Deputy of Ireland. While he was in the service of Earl of Leicester, he made friends with Sir Philip Sidney, with whom he often discussed literature and exchanged poems, to whom he dedicated *The Shepheards Calendar* in 1579. They were interested in promoting a new English poetry.

The Shepheards Calendar was Spenser's first major work, a series of pastoral poems arranged according to the months of the year. It consists of twelve pastoral eclogues, one for each month. The eclogue was a classical form, practiced by Virgil and others. It represents, usually in dialogue between shepherds, the moods and feelings and attitudes of the simple life. The pastoral eclogue sometimes criticizes the world and sometimes becomes didactic or satirical. In form it is a dialogue between the shepherds, but in fact, the eclogues are the author's and his friends' comments on the contemporary affairs.

That same year, Spenser went to Ireland to serve Lord Grey. He spent the rest of his life there, except for two visits to England.

In 1589, at the suggestion of Sir Walter Raleigh, he went to London to publish the first three books of his great romantic epic *The Faerie Queene* , which was published in 1590 and made Spenser "the prince of poets in his time". This "greatest poet" of England continued to work on this epic during the 1590's. In 1596, three additional books of *The Faerie Queene* came out. In 1594, when he was over 40, he married Elizabeth Boyle, the lady in his sonnet sequence *Amoretti* (1595). He also wrote two marriage poems *Prothalamion* and *Epithalamion* (1591—1595).

His masterpiece *The Faerie Queene* (1590—1596) consists of six books. (He planned to write twelve books but only finished a half of the project.) According to the plan, the Fairy Queen (signifying Queen Elizabeth) holds a feast of twelve days, and on each day a stranger in distress appears to ask for help. A knight is assigned to each stranger, and the twelve books were to write about twelve adventures. Each knight represents a virtue such as Holiness, Temperance, Chastity, Friendship, Justice and Courtesy. The opponents are their contrary vices. So this poem is an allegory. The knights as a whole symbolize England. The evil figures symbolize her enemies. The dominating thoughts of this long poem are nationalism (see the celebration of Queen Elizabeth), humanism (see from the strong opposition to Roman Catholicism), and Puritanism (shown in its moral teachings).

Spenser's contribution to English literature lies not only in what he wrote, but also in how he wrote. He created new poetic forms. The 9-line stanza form, called Spenserian stanza, rhymed abab bcbc c is one of his inventions. The first eight are iambic pentameter lines, and the last line is an iambic hexameter line.

The sonnet form he invented, based on an intricate pattern of interlocking rhymes, also contributes to his highly formal, undramatic approach to the lyric. He often used such rhyme scheme as abab bcbc cded ee.

He tried his hand on different forms and meters. Apart from the above-mentioned ones, there are thirteen different meters in *The Shepheardes Calendar* alone: three kinds of couplet, three kinds of four-line stanza, three kinds of six-line stanza, stanzas of eight, nine and ten lines, and a sestina.

Spenser holds a very high position in English literature. First, the publication of *The Shepheardes Calendar* marked the budding of the Renaissance flower in England. Second, Spenser was the first master to make English (Modern English) the natural music of his poetic effusions. Third, his sonnets in *Amoretti*, together with Shakespeare's sonnets and Sidney's *Astrophel and Stella* were, and still are, regarded as the most famous sonnet sequences of the Elizabethan Age. Fourth, he influenced many later poets. In the 19th century alone his influence may be seen in Shelley's *Revolt of Islam*, Byron's *Childe Harold's Pilgrimage*, Keats' *Eve of St. Agnes*, and Tennyson's *The Lotos Eaters*. Spenser's last few years were darkened by the Irish uprisings. In an uprising in 1599, his house at Kilcoman was burnt down. He had to return to London, where he died on January 13, 1599. He was buried near Chaucer, his great medieval forerunner, in Westminster Abbey.

The Faerie Queene[1]

(**excerpt**)

1

A Gentle Knight was pricking[2] on the plaine,
Ycladd in mightie armes and silver shielde,
Wherein old dints of deepe wounds did remaine,
The cruell markes of many a bloudy[3] fielde;
Yet armes till that time did he never wield[4]:
His angry steede did chide his foming bitt,
As much disdayning to the curbe to yield:
Full jolly[5] knight he seemd, and faire did sitt,
As one for knightly giusts[6] and fierce encounters fitt.

2

But on his brest[7] a bloudie Crosse he bore,
The deare remembrance of his dying Lord,
For whose sweete sake that glorious badge he wore,
And dead as living ever him adored:
Upon his shield the like was also scored,
For soveraine hope, which in his helpe he had:
Right faithfull true he was in deede and word,
But of his cheere[8] did seeme too solemne sad[9];
Yet nothing did he dread, but ever was ydrad[10],

3

Upon a great adventure he was bond,
That greatest Gloriana to him gave,
That greatest Glorious Queene of Faerie Land,
To winne him worship, and her grace to have,
Which of all earthly things he most did crave;
And ever as he rode, his hart[11] did earne[12]

To prove his puissance[13] in battell brave
Upon his foe, and his new force to learne;
Upon his foe, a Dragon horrible and stearne.

4

A lovely Ladie rode him faire beside,
Upon a lowly Asse more white than snow,
Yet she much whiter, but the same did hide
Under a vele[14], that wimpled[15] was full low,
And over all a blacke stole she did throw,
As one that inly mournd: so was she sad,
And heavie sat upon her palfrey slow:
Seemed in heart some hidden care she had,
And by her in a line a milke white lambe she lad[16].

5

So pure an innocent, as that same lambe,
She was in life and every vertuous lore,
And by descent from Royall lynage came
Of ancient Kings and Queenes, that had of yore
Their scepters stretcht from East to Westerne shore,
And all the world in their subjection held;
Till that infernall feend with foule uprore
Forwasted all their land, and them expel:
Whom to avenge, she had this Knight far compeld[17].

6

Behind her farre away a Dwarfe did lag,
That lasie seemd in being ever last,
Or wearied with bearing of her bag
Of needments at his backe. [18] Thus as they past,
The day with cloudes was suddeine overcast,
And angry Jove an hideous storme of raine
Did poure into his Lemans[19] lap so fast,
That every wight[20] to shrowd[21] it did constrain,
And this faire couple eke [22] to shroud themselves were fain.

7

Enforst to seeke some covert nigh at hand,
A shadie grove not far away they spide,
That promist ayde the tempest to withstand:
Whose loftie trees yclad with sommers pride,
Did spred so broad, that heavens light did hid

Not perceable with power of any starre:
And all within were pathes and alleies wide,
With footing worne, and leading inward farre:
Faire harbour that them seemes; so in they entred arre.

8

And foorth they passe, with pleasure forward led,
Joying to heare the birdes sweete harmony,
Which therein shrouded from the tempest dred,
Seemed in their song to scorne the cruell sky.
Much can[23] they prayse the trees, so straight and hy[24],
The sayling Pine, the Cedar proud and tall,
The vine-prop Elme, the Poplar never dry,
The builder Oake, sole king of forrests all,
The Aspine good for staves, the Cypresse funeral.

9

The Laurell, meed[25] of mightie Conquerours
And Poets sage, the Firre that weepeth still,
The Willow worne of forlorne Paramours,
The Eugh obedient to the benders will,
The Birch for shaftes , the Sallow for the mill,
The mirrhe sweete bleeding in the bitter wound
The warlike Beech, the Ash for nothing ill,
The fruitfull Olive, and the Platane round,
The carver Holme, the Maple seeldom inward sound.

10

Led with delight, they thus beguile the way,
Untill the blustring storme is overblowne;
When weening[26] to returne, whence they did stray,
They cannot finde that path, which first was showne,
But wander too and fro in wayes unknowne,
Furthest from end then,' when they neerest weene,
That makes them doubt, their wits be not their owne:
So many pathes, so many turnings seene,
That which of them to take, in diverse doubt they been.

Notes

1. The stanzas chosen here are from Canto Ⅰ of book Ⅰ.
2. pricking—cantering.

3. bloudy—bloody.
4. wield—Redcross wears the armor of the Christian man to stand against the wiles of the devil. The armor bears the dents of every Christian's fight against evil; Redcross himself is as yet unretired.
5. jolly—ouragaeous.
6. giusts—tourneys, jousts.
7. brest—breast.
8. cheere—facial expression.
9. solemne sad—serious.
10. ydrad—dreaded, feared.
11. hart—heart.
12. earne—yearn.
13. puissance—ability.
14. vele—veil.
15. wimpled—folded.
16. a milke white lambe she lad—The lady will be called by name in line 405; She is Una, short for Una Vera Fides, "The One True faith" (if it is true it can only be one). But like other figures, she may bear other roles and attributes. Therefore she may also be the Church of England, with whom Redcross, in his role as Britain (St. George) will be united. Her parents typify all mankind—originally lords of Eden, now fallen. She is veiled because fallen man cannot see the one truth but only fragments thereof, and she is sad because man is fallen. The lowly Asse is a figure of humility, the "lambe" is that of innocence.
17. compeld—summoned.
18. the Dwarfe is sometimes taken as Redcross's conscience—useful in emergencies, otherwise forgotten or lost. In addition, or alternatively, the Dwarfe may represent common sense or common prudence.
19. Lemans—His lover, i. e, the earth.
20. Wight—creature.
21. shrowd—cover.
22. eke—also.
23. can—did.
24. hy—high, tall.
25. meed—reward.
26. weening—upposing.

For Study and Discussion

Identify the rhyme scheme of each stanza. Count the syllables of each line.

Sonnet 34[1]

Lyke as[2] a ship that through the ocean wyde[3],
By conduct of[4] some star doth make her way,
Whenas[5] a storme hath dimd[6] her trusty guyde[7],
Out of her course doth wander far astray.
So I whose star, that wont[8] with her bright ray
Me to direct,[9] with clouds is overcast,
Doe [10] wander now in darknesse and dismay,
Through hidden perils round about me plast[11].
Yet hope I well, that when this storme is past
My Helice[12] the lodestar[13] of my lyfe
Will shine again, and looke on me at last,
With lovely light to cleare my cloudy grief.
Till then I wander carefull[14] comfortlesse,
In secret sorrow and pensivenesse.

Notes

1. This sonnet is chosen from"Amoretti" (little love poems).
2. like as—as.
3. wyde—wide.
4. by conduct of—under the guidance of; guided by.
5. whenas—when.
6. hath dimd—has darkened.
7. guyde—guide.
8. wont—be accustomed to
9. that wont with her bright ray. /Me to direct,—that wont to direct me with her bright ray.
10. doe—do.
11. round about me plast—placed round about.
12. Helice—The Big Dipper or North Star.
13. lodestar—North Star.
14. carefull—full of cares.

For Study and Discussion

1. Identify the rhyme scheme of this sonnet. Compare with the rhyme scheme of previous poets.

2. What did the poet compare his love to? How important was her love to him?

Chapter 6 Sir Walter Ralegh

Sir Walter Ralegh (1552—1618) was brilliant and versatile. He was a soldier, courtier, poet, philosopher, explorer and colonizer, student of science and historian.

He was the founder of Virginia and the introducer of tobacco into Europe. But in his own time, he was only known for his skeptical mind, his great favor with the Queen, his hatred of Spain. To Edmund Spenser and others, he was only known for his poetry.

Among all the court poets, Ralegh's position was next only to Spenser's and Sidney's. He pursued the style of conciseness, thinking of poetry as an elaborate and graceful art, written for amusement. Not many of his poems survived. Some of his shorter poems were very popular. His reply to Marlowe's *Passionate Shepherd* is only one of such answers. His *Farewell, False Love* is an early poem, which was set to music by the composer William Byrd in 1588. His popular short poems were often printed in anthologies or songbooks.

He also wrote a long poem to the queen called *Cynthia*, which was never printed and only a few stanzas in manuscript remained. He wrote some discovery books. He also wrote an unfinished *History of the World* confining itself to the earliest times only.

From 1603 to 1618, Ralegh was imprisoned in the Tower of London by King James, except for a period in 1617 when he made his ill-fated last voyage to Guiana. *History of the World* was written in prison. In 1618, he was executed.

The Nymph's Reply to the Shepherd[1]

If all the world and love were young[2],
And truth in every shepherd's tongue,
These pretty pleasures might me move
To live with thee and be thy love.

Time drives the flocks from field to fold
When rivers rage and rocks grow cold,
And Philomel [3] becometh dumb;
The rest complains of cares to come.

The flowers do fade, and wanton fields
To wayward winter reckoning yields;

A honey tongue, a heart of gall,
Is fancy's spring, but sorrow's fall.

Thy gowns, thy shoes, thy beds of roses,
Thy cap, thy kirtle[4] and thy posies
Soon break, soon wither, soon forgotten—
In folly ripe, in reason rotten.

Thy belt of straw and ivy buds,
Thy coral clasps and amber studs,
All these in me no means can move
To come to thee and be thy love.

But could youth last and love still breed,
Had joys no date[5] nor age no need,
Then these delights my mind might move
To live with thee and be thy love.

Notes

1. This is a reply to Marlowe's *The Passionate Shepherd to His Love*. See Marlowe's poem below.
2. This poem consists of six 4-line stanzas, each having the rhyme scheme of aabb.
3. Philomel—the nightingale.
4. kirtle—skirt, outer petticoat.
5. date—ending.

For Study and Discussion

1. Compare this poem with Marlowe's *The Passionate Shepherd to His Love*. What assumption made by Marlowe's shepherd does Ralegh's nymph begin by attacking? How does she follow up this attack?
2. What's the main idea of this poem?

Chapter 7 Christopher Marlowe

Christopher Marlowe (1564—1593) was born two months before William Shakespeare. He was murdered in 1593.

His father was a shoemaker. In 1580, he went to Corpus Christi College, Cambridge. There he studied for six years and took the Master of Arts degree.

Marlowe is chiefly remembered for his plays such as *Tamburlaine*, *The Jew of Malta and Doctor Faustus* (see the drama section). Marlowe is regarded as the greatest of the pioneers in English drama, first making blank verse the principal instrument of English drama. Some people say Marlowe's works paved the way for plays of the greatest English dramatist Shakespeare.

Apart from his plays, Marlowe also wrote some lyrics.

In 1591, he was living in London with the playwright Thomas Kyd, who later accused Marlowe of atheism and treason. On May 30, 1593, at the inn of the Widow Bill, in an argument over the bill he was killed. Modern scholars have pointed out that he was murdered deliberately because the Privy Council had already released a warrant to arrest Marlowe. It is a great pity that he died too young at the age of only 29. With all he had written, when he died in 1593, he had established an immortal place for himself in English drama and poetry. If Shakespeare also had died at the same age, he would scarcely be known today.

The Passionate Shepherd to His Love[1]

Come live with me and be my love,
And we will all the pleasures prove[2]
That valleys, groves, hills, and fields,
Woods, or steepy mountain yields[3].

And we will sit upon the rocks,
Seeing the shepherds feed their flocks
By shallow rivers to whose falls
Melodious birds sing madrigals[4].

And I will make thee beds of roses
And a thousand fragrant posies,

A cap of flowers, and a kirtle[5]
Embroidered all with leaves of myrtle[6];

A gown made of the finest wool
Which from our pretty lambs we pull;
Fair lined slippers for the cold,
With buckles of the purest gold;

A belt of straw and ivy[7] buds,
With coral clasps[8] and amber studs:
And if these pleasures may thee move,
Come live with me, and be my love.

The shepherds' swains[9] shall dance and sing
For the delight each May morning.
If these delights thy mind may move,
Then live with me and be my love.

Notes

1. This pastoral lyric of invitation is one of the most famous of Elizabethan songs, and a few lines from it are sung in Shakespeare's *Merry Wives of Windsor*. Many poets have written replies to it. The finest reply is by the great Elizabethan romantic Sir Walter Raleph. See his *The Nymph's Reply to the Shepherd*.
2. prove—test ,experience.
3. yields—gives.
4. madrigals—love songs.
5. kirtle—skirt.
6. myrtle—a kind of plant, Venus's sacred thing.
7. ivy—the sacred thing of Bacchus.
8. clasps—buttons.
9. swains—lovers.

For Study and Discussion

1. What does the shepherd offer his love to make his world sound attractive and desirable? What things does he offer to her?
2. Lines 19 and 20 almost repeat the poem's opening lines. What effect is created by this near repetition? Instead of ending with this refrain like repetition, the shepherd goes on for another stanza. Does the promise of the final stanza add anything new to the promises made earlier? If so, what does it add?

3. What is the central idea of this poem?
4. How are the lines rhymed?

Chapter 8 William Shakespeare

William Shakespeare (1564—1616), the greatest figure of English literature, was born in Stratford-on-Avon, a charming little village in Warwickshire. His father, John Shakespeare, was a fairly prominent citizen of the town who dealt in wool, hides and leathern articles before eventually becoming an alderman and bailiff.

At seven, Shakespeare went to the local grammar school where he studied for six years, reading widely and learning a "small Latin and less Greek". He also read some European ancient poetry and plays. When he was 14, he left school and probably became a country school teacher, to help support his family. When he was 18, he married a farmer's daughter Ann Hathaway. They had a daughter in 1583, and a boy and a girl, in 1585. Shakespeare arrived in London in 1586 or 1587, when he was 22 or 23. At the time when he arrived in London, drama was rapidly gaining popularity among people. It is said that he kept horses for gentlemen outside the play-houses. He must have gone through many hardships and undertaken many odd jobs before becoming acquainted with certain theatrical companies. Then he became an actor playing minor parts. He did not seem to have distinguished himself as an actor, but he must have learned much of the technique of dramatic art from his personal experience with the stage. He later became a share holder of a troupe.

By 1592 he was both an actor and a playwright. In this year he was attacked in writing by a resentful rival. In 1593, London theatres were closed because of an outbreak of the plague. He got the support of the Earl of Southampton, a wealthy young nobleman, to whom he dedicated two long narrative poems: *Venus and Adonis* (1593) and *The Rape of Lucrece* (1594).

It was after the theatres were reopened that Shakespeare became an actor of the most successful company called "the Lord Chamberlain's Men". He became a shareholder in this company and its principal playwright. In 1599, Shakespeare's company built the famous Globe Theater, where his best known plays were performed. His company was often called by Queen Elizabeth to put on performances for her at court. In 1603, James I took over the company as his own acting company and renamed it The King's Men. By this time, Shakespeare's status as the greatest dramatist of his day was securely established.

In his whole life, he wrote 37 plays (see the drama section), 2 long poems and 154 sonnets.

His sonnets, apparently written over a long period at the beginning of his career and printed in 1609, were mainly dedicated to a "W. H." and many others about "a dark lady" who is thought to be the poet's ideal woman.

In 1611, he retired to his native town. In 1616, Shakespeare died on April 23, his fifty-second birthday.

Sonnet 18[1]

Shall I compare thee[2] to a summer's day?
Thou art[3] more lovely and more temperate:
Rough winds do shake the darling buds of May,
And summer's lease hath all too short a date[4]:
Sometime[5] too hot the eye of heaven[6] shines
And often is his gold complexion dimmed;
And every fair[7] from fairs[8] sometimes declines,
By chance or nature's changing course[9] untrimmed[10];
But thy eternal summer shall not fade,
Nor lose possession of that fair thou ow'st[11];
Nor shall Death brag [12] thou wander'st in his shade,
When in eternal lines to time thou grow'st[13]:
So long as men can breathe, or eyes can see,
So long lives this, and this gives life to thee[14].

Notes

1. Shakespeare's sonnets were published in 1609, though written much earlier in the 1590's. They rhyme uniformly abab cdcd efef gg. The 154 sonnet suggest a "story". The first 126 are addressed mainly to a young man of great beauty and promise. This young man is mysterious. Some people suggest that he was Shakespeare's patron. The speaker addresses his affection and admiration for the young man, urges him to get married and perpetuate his virtues through children, and warns him about the destructive power of time, age and moral weakness. Sonnet 78—86 are concerned with a rival poet who has also addressed to the young man. Sonnet 127—152 are addressed to a lady with dark hair, eyes, and complexion. Both the young man and the speaker seem to be involved with her romantically.
2. thee—you.
3. thou art—you are.
4. date—a limited period of time.
5. sometime—sometimes.

6. the eye of Heaven—the sun.
7. every fair—every beautiful object or person or thing.
8. fair—beauty.
9. By chance or nature's changing course—either by fortune or by the normal course of change in the natural world.
10. untrimmed—stripped of beauty.
11. thou ow'st—thou ownest, you own, you possess.
12. brag—boast.
13. to time thou grow'st—you grow to time.
14. this—this poem.

For Study and Discussion

1. What is the relationship in Lines 1-8 between the young man's loveliness and temperateness and that of a "summer's day"?
2. What is the relationship in lines 9-12 between the young man's "eternal summer" and the "eternal lines" of the speaker's verse?
3. In what sense can the speaker make the young man eternal through poetry?
4. Analyse the development of thought in this sonnet.
5. Identify the rhyme scheme of this sonnet.
6. What's the main idea of this sonnet?
7. Learn the sonnet by heart.

Chapter 9 Ben Jonson

Ben Jonson (1572—1637) was one of the most outstanding figure in the literary world of the early 17th century. He was a man of versatility, a soldier, actor, playwright, poet and poet laureate, scholar, critic, translator, man of letter, and head of a literary "school", the so-called "sons of Ben". In short, he was a giant.

His father died before he was born. He was brought up by a bricklayer and educated by the great classical scholar William Camden. After he returned from Flanders where he as a soldier fought against the Spaniards, he became an actor and playwright in 1595. His learning helped him to be pardoned after he killed a fellow actor. He had other troubles but rode them out. He grew mellower as he grew older and became in fact the unofficial literary dictator of London, the King's pensioned poet, a favorite around the court, and the good friend of men like Shakespeare, Donne, Francis Beaumont, John Selden, Francis Bacon, dukes, diplomats and distinguished folk generally.

Jonson's main dramatic works include *Every Man in His Humor* (1598), a comedy of humors, *Sejanus* (1603) a classical tragedy, *Volpone* (1606) and *The Alchemist* (1610), two supreme satiric comedies of the English stage.

His poetry can be divided into five groups: poems of festive ceremony, poems in imitation of Horace with English tonality, elegies and epitaphs, compliments and tributes, and epigrams.

Ben Jonson was also a very important critic. He advocated classicism, modeling on the old Greek and Roman masters, taking a firm stand for the three unities "in play-writing" (see the part of Drama).

Ben Jonson, with his *Epitaph on S. P.*, *My Picture Left in Scotland*, *A Hymne to God the Father* and others, was also listed as one of the Metaphysical Poets.

Song: To Celia[1]

Drink to me only with thine eyes,
And I will pledge with mine;
O leave a kiss but in the cup,
And I'll not look for wine.
The thirst that from the soul doth rise,
Doth ask a drink divine:
But might I of Jove's nectar[2] sup,
I would not change for thine.

I sent thee late a rosy wreath,
Not so much honoring thee,
As giving it a hope, that there
It could not withered be.
But thou thereon[3] did'st only breathe,
And sent'st it back to me;
Since when[4] it grows and smells, I swear,
Not of itself, but thee.

Notes

1. This is a patchwork of five separate passages in the "Epistles of Philostratus", a Greek sophist of the 3rd century A. D. Jonson reworded the phrases into this classic lyric, in the ballad meter—alternate 8-syllable and 6-syllable lines of iambic metre and with alternate rhymes.

2. Jove's nectar—the drink of gods.
3. thereon—on it.
4. when—then.

For Study and Discussion

1. What kind of love does the speaker describe it as?
2. How precious is Celia's wine?
3. How does the speaker expect Celia to drink to him? Can we say such imagination is conceit?

Part Three
The Seventeenth Century

Chapter 1 Revolution and Restoration

The 17th century covers two historical periods: the period of the English bourgeois Revolution and the period of the Restoration. When the Tudor dynasty was brought to a close by the death of Elizabeth in 1603, James Ⅵ of Scotland, the son of Mary Stuart, Protestant, and descendant of Henry Ⅷ of England, ascended the throne as James I. With the accession of the first Stuart King, James I ruled England for 22 years (1603—1625). This period is known as Jacobean Age.

When the son of James Ⅰ, Charles ascended the English throne in 1625, social conflicts and contradictions were inflamed. By 1640 they were ready to flare into a full-scale revolution. Then a civil war broke out in England. As a result, the bourgeois class under the leadership of Oliver Cromwell defeated the king, and established the military dictatorship under the name of the Commonwealth. This period is known as the period of bourgeois revolution. It is also called the Puritan Age because most of the bourgeois revolutionaries believed in Puritanism.

The so-called Commonwealth collapsed after the death of Cromwell. In 1660 Charles Ⅱ (the son of Charles) was recalled from exile. The absolute monarchy was restored. The period from 1660 to 1688, is known as the period of Restoration. In 1688 James II was expelled from throne and William III, a Dutchman, was named as his successor. This event is known as the Glorious Revolution.

General View of the English Poetry. Poetry was the major literary form in the English literature of the 17th century. Jacobean Age (1603—1625), like the Elizabethan Age, was particularly rich in literary activity. The king, James I, published two books on poetry. The most active poets of this period were John Donne and his followers. Later, they were given the name of Metaphysical Poets. Poetry took new and startling forms in their hands.

During the reign of Charles I (1625—1649), also known as Caroline Period, while the metaphysical poets were still producing poems, the Cavalier Poets became popular for their elegant lyrics. John Milton wrote his lyrics and most of his sonnets in this period. He showed his great poetic talent in these poems. For Milton, with his deep sense of moral imperative, his heroic ambitions for poetry, his proud Englishness, all the fashionable verses of his contemporaries must have seemed unbearably constricting. Like any great poet, Milton was capable of profiting from the study of craftsmen whom he had no intention of imitating. He did profit by a study of Donne, Johnson and Spenser.

During the 20 years of Puritan rule at mid-century, besides Milton's voice in his sonnets, there were almost no great poets. But in the Restoration period, another important poet appeared.

The Restoration period between 1660 and 1688 was remarkably vigorous. Dryden was the dominant figure writing in all the important contemporary forms—occasional verse, comedy, tragedy, heroic play, ode, satire, translation, and critical essay. The variety of Dryden suggests the variety of his age. Both his example and his precepts had great influence. That is why the Restoration period has been traditionally regarded as Age of Dryden. The poetry of the Restoration was dominated by neo-classic traits. The lyrical spirit was marked by charm and skill. It was, however, often artificial in thought and deficient in originality. Except for Dryden, only the court poets merit much consideration. The ode was a favorite form, and Dryden was the master of this poetic form. The most spectacular type was the satire. The heroic couplet made an outstanding development. The Restoration did not break wholly with the immediate past. It retained the Renaissance admiration for the typically aristocratic heroic ideal expressed in the "heroic poem" or epic. John Milton, modeling upon the structure and conventions of ancient epic poetry, produced his masterpiece *Paradise Lost*, and other two major poetical works: *Paradise Regained* and *Samson Agnistes*. Generally speaking, Milton's contribution is greater than that of Dryden in English poetry. Milton's poetry is noted for sublimity of thought and majesty of expression. His blank verse is rich in every poetic quality and never monotonous. His dominant influence was strongly felt in the whole century, especially in the first half. So, the Age of Milton is often used to describe that period.

Chapter 2 Metaphysical Poets

Metaphysical poets are a group of poets writing in the first half of the 17th century. Its major members are John Donne, Carew, George Herbert, Richard Crashaw, Henry Vaugham, Andrew Marvell, John Cleveland and Abraham Cowley. The marks of the metaphysical poetry in the 17th century were arresting and original images and conceits, wit, ingenuity, dexterous use of colloquial speech, considerable flexibility of rhythm and meter, complex themes, a liking for paradox and dialectical argument, a direct manner, a caustic humor, a keenly felt awareness of mortality, and a distinguished capacity for elliptical thought and tersely compact expression. But for all their intellectual robustness the metaphysical poets were also capable of refined delicacy, gracefulness and deep feeling, passion as well as wit.

The metaphysical poets represented by John Donne have made a profound influence on the course of English poetry in the 20th century.

John Donne

John Donne(1572—1631) was born into an old and devout Roman Catholic family. When young, he received his education in a Catholic atmosphere. His father died when John was only 4 years old. Because of the relationship with the Catholicism on his mother's side, his family members were persecuted. At a time when anti-Catholic feeling in England was near its height, his faith in Catholicism barred him from career, let alone success. He studied at Oxford and Cambridge Universities as well as Lincoln's Inn for 6 years, but he was never given any academic degrees because of his religious background. His early life passed in dissipation and roguery. But later he turned saintly.

John Donne quietly abandoned Catholicism some time during the 1590's. But he did not become an Anglican until 1615 when Donne finally overcame his scruples and entered ministry.

John Donne read enormously in divinity, medicine, law and the classics. He wrote to display his learning and wit. He made his way in the world by wit, charm, learning, valor, and above all favour.

His traveling also enriched his experiences. He traveled on the continent, esp., to Spain. With Ralegh and Essex he took part in two hit-and-run expeditions against Cadix and the Azores.

In 1598, John Donne was appointed private secretary to Sir Thomas Egerton, the Lord Keeper. He could sit in Elizabeth's last parliament and move in court circles: he seemed to march well worldly. But in 1601 he secretly married Lady Egerton's niece, Ann More, who was then 16 years old. Sir George More had John Donne imprisoned and dismissed from his post.

For about a dozen of years, he struggled at a series of make-shift employments to support his growing family. The middle years of Donne's life were a period of searching, uncertainty, and unhappiness.

In 1615, Donne took divine orders and was promptly appointed Reader in Divinity at Lincoln's Inn. He soon became a great preacher. In 1621, he was made Dean of St. Paul's Cathedral. He wrote very good sermons and continued to write sacred poetry until the very end of his life.

The poetry of Donne represents a sharp shift from that written by his predecessors and contemporaries. Much Elizabethan verse is decorative and flowery in its quality. Its images adorn; its meter is mellifluous. Images harmonize with images, and line swells almost predictably into line. Donne's poetry, on the other hand, is written very largely in conceits—concentrated images which involve an element of dramatic contrast, of strain, or of intellectual difficulty. In Donne's love poetry, one cannot see the traditional flower images, cannot encounter bleeding hearts, cheeks like roses, lips like cherries, teeth like pearls or Cupid shooting the arrows of love. Donne's conceits in particular leap continually in a restless orbit from the personal to the cosmic and back again.

Donne's rhythms are colloquial and various. He likes to twist and distort not only ideas, but metrical patterns and grammar itself, especially in the satires. But in the lyrics, elegies and sonnets, the verse can always display a complex and memorable melody.

Donne and his followers are known in literary history as the "metaphysical school" of poets. We now generally use the term "metaphysical poetry", though it is a misnomer.

Metaphysical poetry revived after H. J. C. Grierson published Donne's complete poems (1912). Grierson did a great deal to make Donne's poetry more available to the modern reader. Almost at once it started to exert an influence on modern poetic practice. T. S. Eliot and many other critics helped a lot to construct Donne as an acknowledged master.

The Flea

Mark but this flea, and mark in this,
How little that which thou deniest[1] me is;
Me it sucked first, and now sucks thee,
And in this flea our two bloods mingled be
Thou know'st that this cannot be said
A sin, or shame, or loss of maidenhead,
Yet this enjoys before it woo,
And pampered swells with one blood made of two,
And this, alas, is more than we would do[2].

Oh, stay, three lives in one flea spare,
Where we almost, nay more than married, are.
This flea is you and I, and this
Our marriage bed and married temple is;
Though parents grudge, and you, we are met,
And cloistered in these living walls of jet,
Though use[3] make you apt to kill me
Let not to that, self-murder added be,
And sacrilege, three sins in killing three.

Cruel and sudden, hast thou since
Purpled thy nail, in blood of innocence[4]?

Wherein could this flea guilty be,
Except in that drop which it sucked from thee?
Yet thou triumph'st, and say'st that thou
Find'st not thy self nor me the weaker now;
'Tis true, then learn how false fears be;
Just so much honor, when thou yield'st to me,
Will waste, as this flea's death took life from thee.

Notes

1. thou deniest—you deny.
2. this, alas, is more than we would do—we, alas, don't dare to hope for this consummation of our love, which the flea freely accepts. This idea of swelling suggests that of pregnancy.
3. use—Custom.
4. L. 19-20—Donne's mistress has slaughtered the innocent, and is now clothed in imperial purple.

For Study and Discussion

1. Can you identify the rhyme scheme of this poem?
2. Do you think it's natural to connect love with a flea?
3. What's special about this image? How is it different from that of other love poems? Make some comparisons if you can.

George Herbert

George Herbert (1593—1633) was from an ancient and distinguished Welsh family. His father died when he was young. He was brought up by his mother, Magdalen Herbert, a friend of John Donne's, and a lady eminent both for her piety and her love of letters.

George Herbert took his degrees with distinction at the University of Cambridge. His distinguished achievement in study resulted in his being elected Public Orator of the University which put him in a position to rise to high public office or to a prominent place at court. But he did not use his position as a stepping stone, but decided instead to become a minister. In 1626 he took a minor office in the church. In 1629 he married Jane Danvers. In 1630 he accepted the living of Bemerton near Salisbury. In 1633 he died there of consumption. Shortly after his death his volume of poems known as *The Temple* which he editted during the three years of his ministry was published by the friend to whom it had been left. His fame rests on this volume.

At Bemerton, he preached eloquent sermons to the farmers and villagers, poor and rich, visiting the poor, consoling the sick, sitting by the bed of the dying and administering true pastoral care to his congregation. When he died, he was mourned by parishioners intensely loyal to this learned, aristocratic man who had given up a life of fame and prominence to serve them.

Herbert's poetry is quiet, graceful and neat. His argument and imagery are less dazzling than Donne's. His religious verse is full of resignation, humility and wise obedience. Herbert frequently makes use of emblematic images—verbal pictures or figures with a long tradition of moral or religious meaning attached to them. Herbert is never flashy, nor even strongly dramatic. The ancient forms are Herbert's chief delight; His poetry is always fresh, rich in traditional designs, which open for the humblest and simplest person to enter.

Virtue

Sweet day, so cool, so calm, so bright,
The bridal of the earth and sky:
The dew shall weep thy fall tonight;
For thou must die.

Sweet rose, whose hue, angry and brave[1],
Bids the rash gazer wipe his eye:
Thy root is ever in its grave,
And thou must die.

Sweet spring, full of sweet days and roses,
A box where sweets[2] compacted lie;
My music shows ye have your closes[3],
And all must die.

Only a sweet and virtuous soul,
Like seasoned timber, never gives;
But though the whole world turn to coal[4],
Then chiefly lives.

Notes

1. angry—having the hue of anger, red; brave-splendid. Both adjectives indicate the arrogant yet pathetic defiance of beauty in the face of time.
2. sweets—perfumes.
3. closes—concluding cadences. This expresses that Herbert intended his poem to be

sung—as it has, often in fact been.

4. turn to coal—be reduced to a cinder at the Last Judgment.

For Study and Discussion

1. The first two stanzas are devoted to the "Sweet day" and the "Sweet rose". How are these aspects of the natural world treated in the first two lines of these stanzas? How does the imagery of the third stanza related to that of first and second stanzas?
2. What words or phrases in the first three stanzas suggest a personification of nature? How is the act of personification related to the theme of death?
3. In the last stanza, the poet compares the "sweet and virtuous"soul to"seasoned timber". Why is this image an effective one for the soul?
4. How is this image related to the images of the rose and the spring used earlier in the poem?

Andrew Marvell

Andrew Marvell (1621 — 1678) was born at Winead in Holderness, Yorkshire. Later his family moved to Hull. He attended Hull Grammar School and then went on to Cambridge University. After graduation with the degree B. A. in 1638, he travelled in Europe for some years.

Around 1650 he began to tutor young Mary Fairfax, daughter of Sir Thomas Fairfax, Lord General of Oliver Cromwell's Parliamentary army. In this period he wrote some lyrics including *The Garden*.

In 1657, Marvell was appointed assistant to John Milton who was blind then, and in his quiet way, he seemed to have been responsible for saving Milton from imprisonment and possible execution after the Restoration. In 1659, he was elected MP for Hull, and remained as MP for Hull until his death. He was devoted to the interests of Hull.

He wrote a lot of lyrics and satires. His "serious "verse was only published three years after his death, by his house-keeper Mary Palmer, who gave herself out to be his widow. Marvell's is the most major minor verse in English. Playful, casual, and witty in tone, always light on its metrical feet and exact in its diction, it displays depth and intellectual hardness in unexpected places; its texture is extraordinarily rich. One needs only glance at the famous *To His Coy Mistress* to see these qualities exemplified. At first it looks like a dozen other poems on the carpe diem theme, slight, sing-song, and semi-serious, it urges on the lady enjoyment of the present hour. But soon the four-beat couplet is made to sound deep and hollow, is made to reverberate like a bell as well as pattering like a nursery rhymes and a vision of the grinning grave and the deserts of eternity rises out of Marvell's gallant compliments to a pretty girl.

All of Marvell's lyric poems were written by the early 1650's, although they were not published until 1681, when they seemed old-fashioned and out-of-date.

Like Donne, Marvell was largely forgotten during the 18th and 19th centuries. It was not until after the First World War, with Grierson's *Metaphysical Lyrics* and T. S. Eliot's *Andrew Marvel* that the modern high evalnation of his poetry began to prevail. Eliot saw that Marvell's wit and magniloquence joined together the two great strands of the 17th-century poetry.

To His Coy Mistress

Had we but world[1] enough, and time,
This coyness, lady, were no crime.
We would sit down, and think which way
To walk, and pass our long love's day.
Thou by the Indian Ganges' [2] side
Shouldst rubies find; I by the tide
Of Humber[3] would complain[4]. I would
Love you ten years before the flood[5],
And you should, if you please, refuse
Till the conversion of the Jews[6].
My vegetable[7] love should grow
Vaster than empires and more slow;
A hundred years should go to praise
Thine eyes, and on thy forehead gaze;
Two hundred to adore each breast,
But thirty thousand to the rest;
An age[8] at least to every part
And the last age should show your heart.
For, lady, you deserve this state[9],
Nor would I love at lower rate[10].

But at my back I always hear
Time's winged chariot hurrying near;
And yonder all before us lie
Deserts of vast eternity.
Thy beauty shall no more be found.
Nor, in thy marble vault, shall sound
My echoing song; then worms shall try
That long-preserved virginity,
And your quaint[11] honor[12] turn to dust,
And into ashes all my lust[13]:

The grave's a fine and private place,
But none, I think, do there embrace.
    Now therefore, while the youthful hue
Sits on thy skin like morning dew,
And while thy willing soul transpires
At every pore with instant fires[14],
Now let us sport us[15] while we may,
And now, like amorous birds of prey,
Rather at once our time devour
Than languish in his slow-chapped [16] power.
Let us roll all our strength and all
Our sweetness up into one ball,
And tear our pleasures with rough strife
Thorough[17] the iron gates of life:
Thus, though we cannot make our sun
Stand still, yet we will make him run[18].

Notes

1. world—space.
2. the Indian Ganges—a big river in India.
3. Humber—Ha river in the poet's home town Hull. It is in the England. The poet's father died in it while trying to cross it in January in 1641.
4. complain—sing songs of plaintive love.
5. the flood—the flood God made to get rid of the evil people. It's commonly known as the Flood of Noah. See Genesis 6-9.
6. the conversion of the Jews—according to popular chronology, the Jews were to be converted just before the last Judgment. Here it is implied that to make the Jew convert is impossible. People have to wait a very long time.
7. vegetable—slow like the growth of.
8. age—a long period of time.
9. state—dignity.
10. at lower rate—with emotion less than this.
11. quaint—fastidious.
12. honor—purity, chastity.
13. lust—desire, passion.
14. instant fires—immediate, present enthusiasm.
15. sport us—divert ourselves, make ourselves happy.
16. slow-chapped—slow-jawed. Time is envisaged as slowly chewing up the world and the people in it.

17. Thorough—Through.
18. In the final lines, lover and mistress triumphantly reverse their relation to time, eating it avidly like birds of prey instead of being eaten by it, forcing the sun to race after them instead of fruitlessly imploring it to stand still.

For Study and Discussion

1. What is the theme of this poem?
2. Compare this poem with Robert Herrick's *To the Virgins, to Make Much of Time*. Tell how they are similar and different respectively.
3. Comment on Marvell's images he chooses and develops in the poem. And tell how the speaker tries to persuade his mistress. Is his method efficient? What would you do, if you were the mistress?
4. T. S. Eliot said the poet expressed the passionate feeling with a tough reasonableness beneath the slight lyric grace. How do you understand this statement?

Chapter 3 Cavalier Poets

The Cavalier poets are a group of English lyric poets who were active, approximately, during the reign of Charles I. This group includes Richard Lovelace, Sir John Suckling, Robert Herrick, Thomas Carew, and Waller. These poets virtually abandoned the sonnet form which had been the favoured medium for love poems for a century. They were considerably influenced by Ben Jonson. Their lyrics are light, witty, elegant and, for the most part, concerned with love. They show much technical virtuosity. Good representative examples are: Suckling's *Why so Pale and Wan, Fond Lover*? Herrick's *Delight in Disorder*; Lovelace's *To Althea, from Prison*.

Robert Herrick

Robert Herrick (1591 — 1674), son of a prosperous London goldsmith, whose personal history was not much known, is thought to be the happiest of English poets. He attended Cambridge University where he received his B. A. in 1617 and his M. A. in 1620. He liked literature better than anything else, preferring to talk literature and drink with Ben Jonson while polishing his verses. But under social pressure, he took orders in the church and moved unwillingly to Devonshire in the rough West Country.

He secreted poems as a hen laid eggs, making playful verses out of his pets, pleasures and momentary peeves. Paganism, which the Puritans did not quite notice at first, was a recurrent theme in his verses. At the top of his poetic bent, in *Corinna's Going A-Maying*, Herrick produced a major lyric on the central theme of his life, the happy reconciliation between nature and nature's god.

In the storm of the Civil War, the Puritans dispossessed him. Then he came to London and published his poems in 1648. For the secular poems he entitled them as *Hesperides*, and for the sacred ones *Noble Numbers*. Because of the fatness of this volume containing 1200 poems, it was neglected, not to be restored to English literature till the 19th century. When King Charles Ⅱ came to power in 1660, his religious position was restored, which brought him back to Dean Prior, where he first went and finally lived out his last years quietly until his death at the age of 83.

He invented dozens of imaginary mistress, hectic, bewitching creature with exotic names. But the maid who kept house for him was prophetically named Prudence.

For him as well as Ben Jonson, life was a sacrament. Herrick brought to that sometimes portentous view of things a modesty and sense of proportion that are uniquely his own. Herrick was not directly concerned with the deeper questions of life. He customarily took up a light, even whimsical subject, and articulated his response to it with a delicate warmth and sureness of touch. The refinement of his poetic craftsmanship always reminds one of his early association with the art of the jewler and the goldsmith. His best poems are like richly worked miniatures—they give us that special pleasure of contemplating the small thing incomparably well.

To the Virgins, to Make Much of Time

Gather ye rosebuds while ye may,
    Old time is still a-flying;
And this same flower that smiles today
    Tomorrow will be dying.

The glorious lamp of heaven, the sun,
    The higher he's a-getting,
The sooner will his race be run,
    And nearer he's to setting.

That age is best which is the first,
    When youth and blood are warmer;
But being spent, the worse, and worst
    Times still succeed the former.

Then be not coy, but use your time,
    And, while ye may, go marry;
For, having lost but once your prime,
    You may forever tarry.

For Study and Discussion

1. The theme of this poem, "live for today", belongs to a tradition known as "seize the hour" that was typically Cavalier. Which lines in this poem best reflect this theme? How do the symbols in this poem help convey this theme?
2. What is the tone of the poem?
3. Do you like this poem? Why or why not?

Sir John Suckling and Richard Lovelace

Sir John Suckling(1609—1642) and Richard Lovelace(1618—1657) were two Cavalier poets. Their names were always mentioned together. Some lines chosen below are well-known lines of English poetry. They two were considered by many as twin stereotypes, of the Cavalier ideal though they were sometimes contrasted. Both of them were soldiers in the Cavalier army of Charles I.

Suckling was from an old Norfolk family. He attended Trinity College, Cambridge. He inherited large estates, traveled in Holland, and was knighted on his return in 1630. After 1632 he lived at court in great splendour. When the war broke out, he used his wealth and influence to raise a small company of one hundred men, then fled to France where he, neglected and deprived of the great wealth he had possessed, committed suicide in Paris.

Suckling's works include poems, plays, letters and tracts. Some of his works are very famous. Suckling has enjoyed a steady reputation as one of the most elegant and brilliant of the Cavalier poets.

Lovelace came from an old and wealthy Kentish family. With his good looks and elegant manners, he created quite a stir when he went to study at Oxford University. After graduation he became a favourite courtier under King Charles I and Queen Henrietta Maria. Naturally he was a firm supporter of the King during the Civil War. He was once imprisoned by the Parliamentary army. Then he left England for a time to fight with the French army against the Spanish. When he returned to England he was again put into prison. He lost all his wealth and died in poverty at the age of thirty-nine.

To Althea was supposed to have been written in prison. *Lucasta* was also prepared for print when he was in prison. His brother published his remaining verses, *Lucasta: Posthume Poems*. The poems of Suckling and Lovelace epitomize what we think of as the Cavalier manner: witty, charming, graceful in a way that shows their poetic discipleship to Ben Jonson. Lovelace is more serious than the "natural, easy Suckling", whose poems are sometimes just suave verbal trifles. At its best the poetry of both Suckling and Lovelace is tinged with a slight element of desperation or melancholy which may remind us that behind a facade of gallantry and elegance, their careless, aristocratic lives were crumbling away. Their poems are always concerned, in one way or another, with the passing of time.

The Constant Lover

(Sir John Suckling)

Out upon it! I have loved
Three whole days together!
And am like to love three more,
If it prove fair weather.

Time shall molt away his wings
Ere he shall discover
In the whole wide world again
Such a constant lover.

But the spite on't is, no praise
Is due at all to me.
Love with me had made no stays,
Had it any been but she.

Had it any been but she,
And that very face,
There had been at least ere this
A dozen dozen in her place.

For Study and Discussion

1. Suckling's speaker is bragging about the constancy of his love. Is the speaker serious or consciously ironic?
2. How does the speaker's attitude change in the third stanza, as he begins to compliment his lady?
3. How are the wit and irony of the first two stanzas extended in the last stanza of the poem?

Why So Pale and Wan

(Sir John Suckling)

Why so pale and wan, fond lover?
Prithee, why so pale?
Will, when looking well can't move her,
  Looking ill prevail?
  Prithee, why so pale?

Why so dull and mute, young sinner?
  Prithee, why so mute?
Will, when speaking well can't win her,
  Saying nothing do't?
  Prithee, why so mute?

Quit, quit for shame; this will not move,
  This cannot take her.
If of herself she will not love,
  Nothing can make her:
  The devil take her!

For Study and Discussion

1. The speaker of this poem is attempting to tease an unhappy lover out of his depression. What features of the stanzas give the poem a clever arrangement?
2. What does the surprising ending of the poem suggest about the speaker's attitude?

To Lucasta, Going to the Wars

(Richard Lovelace)

Tell me not, Sweet, I am unkind
That from the nunnery
Of thy chaste breast and quiet mind,
To war and arms I fly.

True, a new mistress now I chase
The first foe in the field;
And with a stronger faith embrace
A sword, a horse, a shield.

Yet this inconstancy is such
As you too shall adore;

I could not love thee, dear, so much,
Loved I not honor more.

For Study and Discussion

1. What is the speaker's attitude toward going to war?
2. What do the last two lines of the poem mean?
3. Do you like this poem? Why or why not?
4. Learn this poem by heart.

Chapter 4 John Milton

John Milton (1608—1674), the most learned poet, is the greatest writer of the 17th century and one of the giants of English literature. He was greatly influenced by the two historical movements: the Renaissance and Reformation. Like Spenser and Shakespeare, he was also one of the Renaissance giants not only in England but also in the whole world. Almost all later poets in English literature respected Milton highly. Milton towers over his age as Shakespeare towers over the Elizabethan Age, and as Chaucer towers over the medieval period.

Milton was born in London in 1608. His education began at St. Paul's School, where he was very hard-working, where he showed prodigious gift as a student of languages mastering Greek, Latin, Hebrew and many modern European languages. He also received very good home education under the influence of his father who, a scrivener, was a Puritan and a lover of music and literature. Milton attended Christ's College, Cambridge University, where he was very popular because of his beauty and talent, where he defined the true aim of knowledge as making the spirit of man "reach out far and wide, until it fill the whole world and the space: far beyond with the expansion of its divine greatness", where he graduated B. A. in 1629 and M. A. in 1632.

After graduation he did not enter the ministry as expected. He retired to his father's country house at Horton in Buckinghamshire where he did further reading for about 6 years (1632—1638). Most critics agree that this period was very important in his whole life. At Horton, he read day and night. He read about everything that was ever written in English, Latin, Greek, Italian and Hebrew, studying literature, science, theology and music. His poetic compositions came only occasionally during this period of intense private study. In

1634, he wrote *Comus*, a masque, at the request of a nearby noble family. In 1637, he contributed a volume to memorialize Edward King, a young minister, who had been a classmate of Milton at college and who got drowned at sea. This contribution is *Lycidas*, the finest pastoral elegy in English. Some critics agree that in nobleness of language and sentiment, *Lycidas* has no matches in the English language. It is guessed that *L'Allegro and Il Penseroso*, the twin lyrical poems describing respectively the cheerful social mood and the meditative solitary mood of the poet, were written during the Horton years. It should not be forgotten that when he was still at Cambridge he wrote his first important work *On the Morning of Christ's Nativity*.

Basically, during the Horton years, Milton was preparing himself for more ambitious undertakings, in religion and politics as well as in poetry.

In 1638, he left England and traveled on the Continent to put the finishing touches on an already splendid education, visiting famous literary figures, artists and leading intellectuals including Galileo whose influence on Milton can be felt in the latter's poems. Late in 1639, hearing the news that the King and the Parliament broke, he returned to England, thinking he should not be traveling for amusement abroad while the fellow citizens were fighting for liberty at home.

Milton's religious ideas influenced his political and literary careers. In his opinion, the core of the Christian religion was the individual's relation to God. Each person should be free to develop his or her own understanding of God's word through careful and dedicated study of the Bible. He thought the Church of England still retained many of those rituals and institutions of authority which were characteristic of Catholicism and which stood between the individual and God. These rituals and institutions were enforced by a hierarchy in both church and state, and ultimately by a king who ruled by divine right. For Milton and most of his fellow Puritans, the only King was God, and the only true voice of authority was God's as he spoke to each individual Christian.

Milton's marriages also influenced his career as a fighter and poet (writing some sonnets to mourn his second wife). His first wife was Mary Powell. They got married in June, 1642. Being the daughter of a royalist family, unable to share Milton's political views, Mary, within six weeks after the wedding, returned to her parents' house. For the next two years Milton saw nothing of her and the law did not allow divorce. Then Mary returned to him and bore him three daughters. Mary died in 1652. In 1656, Milton married Catharine Woodcock, who died in childbirth in 1658, for whom he wrote *Methought I Saw My Late Espoused Saint*. In 1663, Milton married his third wife, Elizabeth Minshull.

Owing to his religious, political and matrimonial ideas, Milton wrote a series of pamphlets on marriage, freedom of press, the defense of English people who executed Charles I. In his pamphlets on marriage and divorce, he was concerned with the husband's problem and showed a high respect for women as intellectual companions and comrades rather than housekeepers and childbearers, stating that incompatibility was cause sufficient to make divorce legal. *Areopagitica*(1644) was a declaration of people's freedom of the press. As spokesman of the Revolution, when the European scholar Salmasius was hired by Charles I to accuse the English people of regicide, Milton, already Latin Secretary to the Council of Foreign Affairs, was entrusted with the task of answering him. In 1651, he published his pamphlet *Defence of the English People* in Latin, stating that by the law of God the people have the right to get rid of a king who turns from a prince to tyrant. Salmasius died in the effort of counterattacking Milton. But other people continued the job. Milton replied to them in his *Second Defence of the English People* (1654). It was while he was engaged in this project that Milton went blind (1652), doubtlessly due to the severe eyestrain brought on by ceaseless reading and Latin composition. He served the Commonwealth until Charles II was restored to throne (1660).

1660 witnessed the collapse of the cause to which Milton was dedicated and the imprisonment of him. Through the intervention of friends who carried some influence with the new royal government, and maybe also thanks to his blindness, Milton was not executed. He was let off with a fine and some loss of property.

Then living in poverty, silence, obscurity and seclusion from all but his family members, Milton began his dream of a poet. With the help of his family members, he completed *Paradise Lost* (1665), and then got it published (1667). This poem of "justifying the ways of God to men" was recognized at once as a supreme epic achievement despite the many difficulties it presented, despite its unfamiliar meter (blank verse was rare outside drama) and despite the unpopularity of its attitudes and Milton's reputation as a dangerous man. Milton thought of himself as "God's English Poet". He felt that his verse originated in and was guided by the Holy Spirit. This long poem in blank verse was written in a style combining the grand sonority and power of the classical epic with scrupulous subtlety and precision.

The stories of *Paradise Lost* (in 12 books) were taken from the *Old Testament*: the creation, the rebellion in Heaven by Satan and his fellow-angels, their defeat and expulsion from Heaven, the creation of the earth and of Adam and Eve, the fallen angels in hell plotting against God, Satan's temptation of Eve, and the departure of Adam and Eve from Eden.

This long epic is obviously the product of Milton's Age. In Satan he praised his challenge and revolt to God. As a Puritan Milton should have praised God but in his epic God was not as good as expected. So people find the hidden meaning: the whole poem is a challenge to the victory of the royal government. The war between God and Satan echoes the Civil War between the Crown and the parliament. Through this poem, Milton expressed his love of freedom.

Although the poem was claimed "to justify the ways of God to man" i. e. to preach submission to the Almighty, the real idea is the heroic revolt against God's authority.

Before his death Milton published two other works on a grand scale: *Paradise*

Regained (1671) and *Samson Agonistes* (1671).

When I Consider How My Light Is Spent[1]

When I consider how my light[2] is spent
Ere half my days[3], in this dark world and wide,
And that one talent[4] which is death to hide[5],
Lodged[6] with me useless, though my soul more bent[7]
To serve therewith[8] my Maker, and present
My true account[9], lest he returning chide;
"Doth God exact day-labor, light denied?"[10]
I fondly[11] ask; but Patience to prevent
That murmur[12], soon replies, "God doth not need
Either man's work or his own gifts; who best
Bear his mild yoke[13], they serve him best. His state
Is kingly. Thousands[14] at his bidding speed
And post o'er land and ocean without rest:
They also serve who only stand and wait."

Notes

1. Milton's sonnet on his blindness is very close in theme to that on his 23rd birthday. But the absolute repose of the latter sonnet's final line is beyond anything in the earlier one. The rhyme scheme of this sonnet is: abba abba cdc cdc.
2. light—the literal meaning is that he has gone blind; the deep meaning is that life is spent.
3. ere half my days—before half my days (the life expectancy is one hundred years according to Plato and the Bible).
4. talent—a pun, meaning both his light and his literary talent.
5. which is death to hide—to hide which is death.
6. lodged—is lodged.
7. though my soul more bent—though my soul be eager.
8. therewith—with which, "which" refers to talent.
9. my true account—what I have done.
10. Doth God exact day-labor, light denied? —Does God want (need) our day—lab or when light is denied?
11. fondly—foolishly.
12. murmur—complaint.
13. mild yoke—the responsibility and duty God asked people to shoulder.
14. thousands—thousands of angles.

For Study and Discussion

1. What is the theme of this sonnet?
2. How is the word "talent "used? Is Milton's talent really useless? Why is it "death" to hide it?
3. How do you understand the word "wait", the last word of the whole sonnet? Can we say Milton was passive and doing nothing?

Paradise Lost[1]

What though the field be lost?[2]
All is not lost: the unconquerable will,
And study[3] of revenge, immortal hate,
And courage never to submit or yield;
And what is else not to be overcome?[4]
That glory never shall his wrath or might[5]
Extort from me.[6] To bow and sue for grace[7]
With suppliant knee, and deify his power[8]
Who, from the terror of this arm[9], so late
Doubted his empire[10]—that were low indeed;
That were an ignominy and shame beneath
This downfall; since, by fate, the strength of gods[11],
And this Empyreal substance[12], cannot fail[13]
Since, through experience of this great event[14],
In arms not worse[15], in foresight much advanced[16],
We may with more successful hope resolve,
To wage by force or guile[17] eternal war,
Irreconcilable to our grand Foe[18],
Who now triumphs, and in th' excess of joy
Sole reigning[19] holds the tyranny of Heaven.

Notes

1. These lines are part of Satan, the hero's speech in Hell. He was encouraging his fellows to fight again God.
2. What though the field be lost? —What does it matter though we lost on the battle field?
3. study—pursuit.
4. what is else not to be overcome? —with unconquerable will, study of revenge and courage, what can not be conquered by us?

5. his wrath or might—God's anger and power.
6. That Glory never shall his wrath or might/Extort from me. —His anger and power shall never extort (spoil) that glory from me. That Glory is the glory of Satan.
7. sue for grace—beg for pardon.
8. deify his power—admire his power.
9. this arm—Satan's forces.
10. doubted his empire—the frightened God's doubt whether he could maintain the rule of Heaven.
11. gods—the defeated angels.
12. this Empyreal substance—the Heavenly force, referring to the force of Satan.
13. fail—cease to exist.
14. experience of this great event—the lessons we got from the failure on the battlefield in heaven.
15. not worse—better.
16. much advanced—much considered and better prepared.
17. by force or guile—by force or wisdom.
18. our grand Foe—God.
19. sole reigning—ruling by himself.

For Study and Discussion

1. What spirit of Satan is shown in this part of speech?
2. Do you think his speech is forceful? How is it forceful? If you were one of the defeated angels, could you be cheered up by this speech?
3. Choose some lines that you like best and explain why you like them?
4. Can you tell what poetic form is used here?

Part Four
The Eighteenth Century

Chapter 1 General View of the 18th-century English Poetry

The Enlightenment. The 18th century England, first ruled by Queen Anne (1702—1714) and then under the reign of three Georges (George I (1714—1727), George II (1727—1760), George III (1760—1820)), saw rapid development of industarial capitalism. Great changes took place in social life. The Enlightenment, as a progressive intellectual movement throughout the Western Europe in the 18th century, greatly influenced the English social life and literature. Generally speaking, the Enlightenment movement was an expression of struggle of the bourgeoisie against feudalism. The enlighteners fought against class inequality, stagnation, prejudices and other survivals of feudalism. They thought that the chief means for improving society was "enlightenment" or "education" of the people. The English enlighteners were different from those of France, for they appeared not before but after the bourgeois revolution. They did not need to carry out any revolution, and what they strove for was to carry the revolution through to the end. Most of the English writers of this century were enlighteners. They were bourgeois democratic thinkers. They fell into two groups: the moderate and the radical. The moderate supported the principles of the existing social order and considered that partial reforms would be sufficient to the improvement of society. This group included such writers as Alexander Pope, Joseph Addison and Richard Steele, Daniel Defoe, Samuel Richardson and Samuel Johnson. These writers thought that the existing social order of the day was essentially fair and just. On this basis they tried to work out a standard of moral conduct which could be more suitable to the existing social conditions. The radical group might include such writers as Jonathan Swift, Henry Fielding, Tobias George Smollett, Oliver Goldsmith and Richard Brinsley Sheridan. They stressed the difference between what they called "the proper moral standards" and the bourgeois-aristocratic society of their age. They struggled for more resolute democratization in the management of the government and defended the interests of the exploited people.

Neo-classical Poetry. The 18th century has been regarded as the age of prose. But English poetry did not stop developing. During the Augustan age (1700—1745), which marks the triumph of neo-classicism, English poets endeavored to imitate the styles of Virgil, Horace, Cicero, and Lucretius, and others of the age of Augustus Caesar in Rome, who in their day had sought to imitate the methods of the classical Greek writers of a few centuries earlier. In poetry the most outstanding feature was the domination of the heroic couplet. During this period certain literary kinds changed much for the worse. The lyric, one of the glories of the Elizabethan age and the first half of the 17th century, had become trivial and empty. On the other hand, satire flourished. The consummate exemplar of English neo-classical poetry was Alexander Pope, who perfected the heroic couplet and displayed masterful skills in didactic and satiric poems. The neo-classical spirit in English poetry was carried on by two later writers after Pope's death. One was Samuel Johnson (1709—1784), who wrote two famous satiric poems by use of the heroic couplet: *London* (1738) and *The Vanity of' Human Wishes* (1749). The other was Oliver Goldsmith (1730—1774), who dealt with the English and Irish social vices in his two popular poems: *The Traveller* (1764) and *The Deserted Village* (1770). The latter has become one of the classics in English poetry.

The Approach to Romanticism. During the later 18th century, many poets, revolting against the set and formal rules of the classical tradition, turned to nature and the simple life and to the past, particularly medieval tales and ballads. Instead of confining themselves to the Town, the anti-Popeans turned away from the metropolitan outlook and spirit to nature and rural life. Their subject-matter became the remote and unfamiliar, or the out-of-door aspects of the world, or human nature in terms of the brotherhood of men. They renewed the sensuous elements of love and adventure characteristic of the old Romans. In place of the precision, symmetry, and regularity of the Augustan school, the poets of the new school substituted a deepening sense of the wonder and mystery of life. In place of the conventional diction and the classic couplet, they revived earlier verse forms, such as the Spenserian stanza and the ode, and endeavored to attain a simplification of diction. It is true that the prevailing standards of the neo-classical forms often cropped up in one way or another in work of these poets of revolt, but the subject-matter manifested a more direct break with rigid tradition. The essential ideas were a belief in the intuitive powers of the imagination, in the value of the individual as opposed to group conformity and external authority, in the exaltation of rural life and external nature over urban life, of content over form, of subjective over the objective, of emotion and imagination over the intellect and judgment.

The new poetic school, which has been called the pre-romantic school, includes such poets as James Thomson, Edward Young, William Collins, Thomas Gray, James Macpherson, Thomas Percy, Thomas Chatterton, William Cowper, George Crabbe, William Blake and Robert Burns. The last two, often regarded as the representatives of the pre-romantic poetry, are the most important among them.

Chapter 2 Alexander Pope

English neo-classical literature found fine expression in poetry first. Alexander Pope (1688 — 1744) was a typical representative. He was born in London in the year of the Glorious Revolution: his father was a merchant of Catholicism. Because of a prejudice against the Catholic in the public schools and universities and his own physical weakness and deformity, he had little formal schooling, but was taught by a family priest, without attending any university. When he was only 16, he wrote his *Pastorals*, and exhibited his talent as a poet. Being a Catholic, he was debarred from many official employments. So he made up his mind to make literature his life work. A few years later his *An Essay on Criticism* was published and brought him fame. The publication of his *The Rape of the Lock* in 1712 made him well-known and much honoured in England. He was called by Voltaire with ecstasy, "the best poet of England and, at present, of all the world."

For the next twelve years he devoted himself to poetry and translating Homer. He translated *The Iliad* and *The Odessey*. His translation was characterized by elegant and artificial language of his day, but Homeric strength and simplicity were lost. Then he wrote his *An Essay on Man* and *The Dunciad*. His fame as a poet was firmly established and his works brought him wealth. In his last years he was fully devoted to poetry, living peacefully in his villa at Twickenham on the Thames, where he was buried after he died in 1744.

An Essay on Criticism was Pope's first famous work. As a comparative study of the criticism on poetry, it summed up the theories of the poetic criticism advanced by Horace, and then by Boileau. Pope eulogized the ancient classics and advocated a careful study and a faithful representation of their rules and standards. His emphatical presentation of classicism has been regarded as a significant manifesto of English neo-classicism.

An Essay on Criticism is Pope's chief contribution to literary criticism, written in heroic couplets. The poem contains 744 lines and is divided into three parts. He first deplores the lack of true taste among the critics of his day and, urging the need to turn to nature for guidance. He highly praises the Ancients, especially Homer and Virgil, and declares that to follow nature is equivalent to follow the Ancients and their rules for literature. Next he warns the critics against various unsound critical standards and touches upon the current literary problems. Then he gives his advice on the laws of criticism to be observed and ends by eulogizing the great critics in history, including Aristotle and others.

The Rape of the Lock is a mock-heroic poem, which exhibits his startling faculty as a satirist. The poem, on the surface, dealt with a story of trivial meaning. Lord Petre, a coxcomb at the court of Queen Anne, snipped a lock of hair from the abundant curls of an attractive maid of honour named Arabella Fermor, and therefore the two families were caught up into a fierce quarrel, which soon became the talk of London. With his penetrating insight, Pope saw through it the idle life of the aristocracy. The first edition was published in 1712, consisting of two cantoes. Its success spurred Pope to lengthen the poem by three more cantoes. Instead of depicting the gods or great heroes of a great epic, Pope related such a trivial story and introduced salamanders, sylphe, sprites and gnomes to make a more perfect burlesque of an epic poem. This sharp contrast between the verse form and its content enhanced the satirical power of the poem.

Among Pope's work *The Dunciad* holds an important position. It is an ostensible controversy concerning the comment on Shakespeare, but turns to be a revengeful satire upon his numerous contemporaries who have aroused his anger or whose works he depreciates. Though his personal spite and petty quarrels devalue the poem to some extent, the satirical poem is significant when the lashing of his witty and bitter satire sweeps the artificial poetry of his day.

Unlike most of his contemporaries who were plunged into the collision of the two political parties, Pope never sided with the Whigs or the Tories. His success as a poet was extraordinarily great.

Pope's mastery of the heroic couplet seemed the perfect expression of the moral and intellectual values of an age that admired clarity and order. Part of Pope's skill was reducing his meaning to unforgettable aphorisms, so that many of his lines have become proverbial. "Fools rush in where angels fear to tread;" "Hope springs eternal in the human breast;" "The proper study of mankind is man." But above all he succeeded in giving infinite variety to the potentially rigid couplet, by subtle alterations of rhythm and vowel sounds.

No authors except Shakespeare and Milton have given to the English language so many quotable lines and phrases as Pope. His neat couplets are easy to remember, and his comments on life learning are usually brief, clever, and exact. For example,

Hope springs eternal in the human breast:
Man never is, but always to be blest.

All nature is but art, unknown to thee;
All chance, direction, which thou canst not see;
All discord, harmony not understood;
All partial evil, universal good;
And spite of pride, in erring reason's spite,
One truth is clear, Whatever is, is right.

A wit's feather, and a chief a rod;
An honest man's the noblest work of God.

'Tis education forms the common mind:
Just as the twig is bent the tree's inclined.

A little learning is a dangerous thing;
Drink deep, or taste not the Pierian spring:
There shallow drafts intoxicate the brain,
And drinking largely sobers us again.
True ease in writing comes from art, not chance,
As those move easiest who have learned to dance.
Tis not enough no harshness gives offense—
The sound must seem an echo to the sense.

To err is human, to forgive divine.

For fools rush in where angels fear to tread.

An Essay on Criticism[1]

Some to conceit[2] alone their taste confine,
And glitt'ring thoughts struck out[3] at ev'ry line;
Pleas'd with a work where nothing's just[4] or fit,
One glaring chaos and wild heap of wit:
Poets, like painters, thus unskill'd to trace
The naked nature and the living grace[5],
With gold and jewels cover ev'ry part,
And hide with ornaments their want of art[6].
　　True wit is Nature to advantage drest[7],
What oft was thought, but ne'er so well expressed;
Something whose truth convic'd at sight we find,
That gives us back the image of our mind[8].
As shades more sweetly recommend the light[9],
So modest plainness sets off sprightly wit;
For works may have more wit than does 'em good,
As bodies perish through excess of blood.
　　Others for language all their care express[10],
And value books as women men, for dress.
Their praise is still[11]—the style is excellent;
The sense they humbly take upon content[12].
Words are like leaves; and where they most abound,

Much fruit of sense beneath is rarely found[13].
False eloquence, like the prismatic glass,
Its gaudy colors spreads on ev'ry place;
The face of Nature we no more survey,
All glares alike, without distinction gay[14].
But true expression, like th' unchanging sun,
Clears and improves whate'er it shines upon;
It gilds all Objects, but it alters none.
Expression is the dress of thought, and still
Appears more decent as more suitable[15].
A vile conceit in pompous words expressed
Is like a clown[16] in regal purple drest:
For diff'rent styles with diff'rent subjects sort[17],
As several garbs with country, town, and court.
Some by old words to fame have made pretense,
Ancients in phrase, mere moderns in their sense[18].
Such labour'd nothings[19], in so strange a style,
Amaze the unlearn'd, and make the learned smile;
Unlucky, as Fungoso[20] in the play,
These sparks[21] with awkward vanity display
What the fine gentleman wore yesterday;
And but so mimic ancient wits at best,
As apes our grandsires in their doublets drest[22].
In words as fashions the same rule will hold,
Alike fantastic if too new or old[23]:
Be not the first by whom the new are try'd,
Nor yet the last to lay the old aside.

Notes

1. The Poem *An Essay on Criticism* is written in heroic couplets (i. e. rimed couplets in iambic pentameter). In accordance with the more standard edition of the poem, some nouns are capitalized and old spellings are kept for certain words (e. g., "Fantastick" for "fantastic", "Music" for "music", "vary'd" for "varied", "expressed", "dressed", etc.)
2. Conceit—fantastic notion.
3. struck out—devised, invented.
4. just—proper.
5. to trace /The naked nature and the living grace—to portray nature in its plainness and

objects of charm derived from real life ("nature" here refers to the objective world of reality).

6. want of art—lack of artistic skill.
7. drest—adorned.
8. Something whose truth convinc'd at sight we find,/That gives us back the image of our mind—Here the normal word order of the first line should be "Something of whose truth we find ourselves convinced at sight." "Image" means "the imperfect notion of a thing". "Something "refers to "True wit", mentioned above. The two lines together mean: True wit, the truth of which is instantly convincing to us, restores to us what we have only an imperfect notion of (in our mind).
9. Shades more sweetly recommend the Light—i. e., the light looks brighter when set in contrast with the shades.
10. Others for language all their care express—other show all their care for the language used.
11. still—ever, always.
12. upon content—on acquiescence.
13. where they most abound,/Much fruit of sense beneath is rarely found—where there are too many words, they rarely express much sense. "they" refers to "words".
14. gay—brilliant in colour.
15. still/Appears more decent as more suitable—The more suitable the expression, the more decent it ever appears.
16. Clown-an ignorant or ill—bred man.
17. diff'rent Styles with diff'rent Subjects sort—Different styles agree with (or are fit for) different subjects. "Sort": agree with.
18. Ancients in phrase, mere moderns in their sense—They are ancients when judged by their phrases, but they are mere moderns when judged by the ideas they express. In other words, they express their modern ideas quaintly in old phrases.
19. labor'd Nothings—much elaborated, meaningless expressions.
20. Fungoso—a character in Ben Jonson's *Everyman out of His Humour*, who is described as one "that follows the fashion far off like a spy". He buys clothes to imitate a spruce courtier, but fails, the fashion changing so fast that his money is thrown away.
21. Sparks—men of fashion.
22. in their doublets drest—dressed in their doublets("their"=our grandsires).
23. Alike fantastic if too new, or old—They are both fantastic whether the words used are too new or too old for the ideas.

For Study and Discussion

1. How much do you know about neo-classicism?

2. What is the peculiar style of Pope's poem?
3. What is heroic couplet?
4. Do you agree with Pope's ideas?
5. How do you understand the last two lines?

Chapter 3 Thomas Gray

Thomas Gray (1716 — 1771) was considered England's foremost poet in his day, but he turned down the position of poet laureate. He is remembered today chiefly for his *Elegy Written in a Country Churchyard*.

Gray was the only surviving child in a family of eight. By keeping shop, his mother earned the money to send him to Eton and Cambridge. Gray had a three-year Continental tour with his former classmate and fellow writer, Horace Walpole. Then he settled down in cloistered bachelor retirement at Cambridge, where he was a scholar of classical literature, and a poet in residence. He enjoyed the quiet life as a Cambridge professor. On one occasion, however, a practical joke so shattered his nerves and disrupted the "noiseless tenor" of his ways that he moved to another of Cambridge's several colleges—a change which for him was a cataclysmic upheaval.

Gray's life was peaceful and quiet, but his poetry was venturesome. Without discarding what he believed was good in the old, neoclassic tradition, he explored new and unfamiliar areas in poetry writing. His use of personification, high-flown allusions, and conventional poetic diction are representative of his ties to the earlier style. But while Pope reflected fashionable city taste, Gray, like the later poets William Wordsworth and other Romantic poets, turned to country life and humble people for inspiration. He dealt in honest and homely emotion and brought back into poetry the use of the first-person singular, considered a barbarism by the 18th century norms, which dictated suppression of the ego and concealment of emotion. Not only Gray's treatment of nature, but his interest in the past, in Celtic and Norse folklore and simple, primitive cultures, has been seen as a fore-shadowing of themes that would find their fullest expression in the Romantic movement of the 19th century. But Gray can be appreciated on his own terms, free from theories about his preparing the way for the Romantic period.

Gray, a painstaking writer, produced only few poems. It took him nine years to complete *Elegy Written in a Country Churchyard*. Samuel Johnson may have thought Gray dull, but most readers agreed with General Wolfe, who before the battle of Quebec in 1759, said of the "Elegy": "I would rather be the author of those lines than take Quebec."

The term "elegy", first used to describe any serious meditative poem, is now used to refer to a poem that laments the death of a particular person. Gray's poem laments the passing of all people, but ends with an epitaph for a particular person, and is thus an elegy in both senses.

Chapter 4 William Collins

William Collins (1721—1759) was the son of a hatter at Chichester and was educated at Winchester and Oxford. He has been known for a series of "Odes": *Ode to Evening*, *Ode on the Poetical Character*, *Ode on the Popular Superstitions of the Highlands of Scotland*. His best known ode is *Ode to Evening*, which shows the poet's great zest for the beauty of nature and protest against the poetic tradition of neo-classicism. Collins shows his gift in both the short lyrical expressions and longer attempts at melodious verse. He pays special attention to the choice of words in his verse, so that there is a generally high level of artistic excellence in his mature work.

With some money he inherited, he traveled for a while, but fits of depression gradually deepened into insanity. He spent his last years in Chichester, forsaken by all but a small circle of loyal friends. As the century progressed he gained in reputation, although the attempt to find signs of incipient madness in his vividly realized imaginary figures is regrettable. The Romantics admired his poems and felt a kin to him as they did to Thomas Chatterton and Robert Burns. *The Ode to Evening*, which combines a chaste and cool classicism with a delicate feeling for landscape and mood, is one of the delightful poems of the century.

Ode to Evening[1]

If aught of oaten stop, or pastoral song,
  May hope, chaste Eve, to soothe thy modest ear,
  Like thy own solemn springs,
  Thy springs and dying gales,
O nymph reserved, while now the bright-haired sun
Sits in yon western tent, whose cloudy skirts,
  With brede[2] ethereal wove,
  O'erhang his wavy bed:
Now air is hushed, save where the weak-eyed bat,

With short shrill shriek flits by on leathern wing,
Or where the beetle winds
His small but sullen horn,
As oft he rises 'midst the twilight path,
Against the pilgrim borne in heedless hum:
Now teach me, maid composed,
To breathe some softened strain,
Whose numbers stealing through darkening vale,
May not unseemly with its stillness suit,
As, musing slow, I hail
Thy genial loved return!
For when thy folding-star[3] arising shows
His paly circlet, at his warning lamp
The fragrant Hours, and elves
Who slept in flowers the day,
And many a nymph who wreathes her brows with sedge,
And sheds the freshening dew, and, lovelier still,
The pensive Pleasures sweet,
Prepare thy shadowy car.
Then lead, calm vot'ress, where some sheety lake
Cheers the lone heath, or some time-hallowed pile,
Or upland fallows gray
Reflect its last cool gleam.
But when chill blustering winds, or driving rain,
Forbid my willing feet, be mine the hut
That from the mountain's side
Views wilds, and swelling floods,
And hamlets brown, and dim-discovered spires,
And hears their simple bell, and marks o'er all
Thy dewy fingers draw
The gradual dusky veil.
While Spring shall pour his showers, as oft he wont,
And bathe thy breathing tresses, meekest Eve;
While Summer loves to sport
Beneath thy lingering light;
While sallow Autumn fills thy lap with leaves;
Or Winter, yelling through the troublous air,
Affrights thy shrinking train,
And rudely rends thy robes;

So long, sure-found beneath the sylvan shed,
Shall Fancy, Friendship, Science, rose-lipped Health,
    Thy gentlest influence own,
    And hymn thy favorite name!

Notes

1. Collins borrowed the metrical structure and the rhymeless lines of this ode from Milton's translation of Horace, Odes I. 5 (1673). The text printed here is based on the revised version, published in Dodsley's Miscellany (1748).
2. brede—embroidery.
3. folding-star—the evening star, which signals the hour for herding the sheep into the sheepfold.

For Study and Discussion

Collins's odes are addressed to personified abstractions which are rendered vividly and pictorially, in the expressive, attitudes and allegorical groups. Take this ode for example, what do you think of Collins' odes?

Chapter 5 Oliver Goldsmith

Oliver Goldsmith (1728—1774) was the most versatile and lovable genius of the 18th century. He is one of the important poets among the romantic school of his age. His poem *The Deserted Village* is one of the most familiar poems in English language. In his manner, especially in his poetry, Goldsmith was much influenced by his friend Dr. Johnson and the classicists. But in his matter, in his sympathy for nature and human life, he belongs to the school of romanticism and sentimentalism.

Goldsmith was born into an Irish family. He studied at Trinity College where he took his B. A. Then he entered Edinburgh University to study medicine. In Edinburgh for a couple of years he became popular as a singer of songs and a teller of tales. Later he wandered like a cheerful beggar across Europe, singing and playing his flute for food and lodging. After a year or more of Vagabondage he returned to London in 1756. In 1759 he published his first original book *An Enquiry into the Present State of Polite Learning in*

Europe, in which he makes a survey of the cultural state of European countries, from ancient times through the middle ages to the 18th century in France, Holland, Italy, Germany and England. From then on, Goldsmith became a busy writer. After he met Samuel Johnson who was a sort of literary dictator of the day, he became one of the members of Johnson's club. In 1766, his novel *The Vicar of Wakefield* appeared, which definitely established his fame as a writer. The publication of his poem *The Deserted Village* and his best comedy *She Stoops to Conquer* greatly enhanced his fame in literature.

But his habitual extravagance and generosity kept him always in debt, no matter how ample his income was. When he was in funds he lived richly; when he was without money, he borrowed. He died with the debt of a prodigious sum(for a man whose only source of income was writing) of £2,000.

His two important poems, *The Traveler* (1764) and *The Deserted Village*, are distinguished for the purity and harmony of their language. The couplets of *The Deserted Village* lack the rhetoric and formality of Pope's or Johnson's couplets and become almost lyrical in sound and movement.

The poem, *The Deserted Village* written in heroic couplets, is Goldsmith's best poem. The poem begins with the poet's happy reminiscences of his home village. Then he expressed his lament that the happy village life is gone. He puts the blame on the enclosure movement. Goldsmith describes how the peasants become homeless and landless, how the poor men become beggars and the poor women become prostitutes.

This poem was a sharp protest against the large-scale enclosures of common land for the rich landlords and capitalists. The poem also reflects the poet's conservative stand, looking backward with nostalgia at the deserted village which merely illustrated the replacement of the feudal countryside by capitalist agriculture.

The Deserted Village

Sweet Auburn! loveliest village of the plain,
Where health and plenty cheer'd the labouring swain,
Where smiling spring its earliest visit paid,
And parting summer's lingering blooms delayed:
Dear lovely bowers of innocence and ease,
Seats of my youth, when every sport could please,
How often have I loitered o'er thy green,
Where humble happiness endeared each scene;
How often have I paused on every charm,
The sheltered cot, the cultivated farm,
The never-failing brook, the busy mill,
The decent church that topped the neighbouring hill,
The hawthorn bush, with seats beneath the shade,

For talking age and whispering lovers made;
How often have I blest the coming day,
When toil remitting lent its turn to play,
And all the village train, from labour free,
Led up their sports beneath the spreading tree,
While many a pastime circled in the shade,
The young contending as the old surveyed;
And many a gambol frolicked o'er the ground,
And sleights of art and feats of strength went round;
And still, as each repeated pleasure tired,
Succeeding sports the mirthful band inspired;
The dancing pair that simply sought renown,
By holding out to tire each other down;
The swain mistrustless of his smutted face,
While secret laughter titlered round the place;
The bashful virgin's sidelong looks of love,
The matron's glance that would those looks reprove:
These were thy charms, sweet village! sports like these,
With sweet succession, taught e'en toil to please;
These round thy bowers their cheerful influence shed,
These were thy charms—but all these charms are fled.

Sweet smiling village, loveliest of the lawn,
Thy sports are fled, and all thy charms withdrawn;
Amidst thy bowers the tyrant's hand is seen,
And desolation saddens all thy green:
One only master grasps the whole domain,
And half a tillage stints thy smiling plain;
No more thy glassy brook reflects the day,
But choked with sedges, works its weedy way;
Along thy glades, a solitary guest,
The hollow-sounding bittern guards its nest;
Amidst thy desert walks the lapwing flies,
And tires their echoes with unvaried cries.
Sunk are thy bowers in shapeless ruin all,
And the long grass o'ertops the moldering wall,
And, trembling, shrinking from the spoiler's hand,
Far, far away, thy children leave the land.

For Study and Discussion

1. What is the theme of the poem?
2. Discuss Goldsmith's couplets.

Chapter 6 William Blake

William Blake (1757—1827) was a major prophet of the Romantic Movement and of the revolt against the mechanical tyranny of the capitalist world. His achievement was a breakthrough in the Romantic Movement.

Blake has little schooling, but his father, a hosier in London, kept him well supplied with books and prints of great paintings. He liked reading Shakespeare, Milton and Chatterton. At 10, he expressed the wish to be a painter. So he was sent to a drawing school and was apprenticed to an engraver.

Some objectors of Blake called him madman. He was not, but as a child, he did often say words of near madness, claiming to have seen a tree filled with angels, the prophet Ezekiel, or God at his window. Maybe this eccentricity helped to shape him into a poet.

In 1782, he got married to Catherine Boucher who, though illiterate, proved to be an excellent wife, sympathizing with and sharing interests in his work which was not well accepted.

His talent for sketching is seen in his illustrations not only of his own poems but also of Milton's *Paradise Lost*, Dante's *Divine Comedy*, Thomas Gray's poems and Edward Young's *Night John*. But he never got rich in this trade and remained poor all his life.

In his early attempts at poetry, in his first collection of poems *Poetical Sketches* (1783), he tried the Spenserian stanza, Shakespearean and Miltonic blank verse, the ballad form and lyric meters. He showed contempt for classicist rule of reason and a strong sympathy for the freshness of Elizabethan poetry.

"Without contrast", wrote Blake, "there is no progression". His *Songs of Innocence* (1789) and *Songs of Experience* (1794) clearly reflect this idea. In these two works, Blake, the great poet of contraries, points out the need for both childhood innocence and the wisdom gained by experience. These two works, which contain some of the most beautiful lyrics in the English language, clearly show the contrast. In the *Songs of Innocence* (1789), Blake depicts the happiness of a child before it knows anything about the pains of existence. The poet expresses his delight in the world of romanticness, the sun, the hills, the streams, the insects and the flowers, the innocence of the child and of the lamb. Blake sings of the mirth of the life and the emotion inseparable from the surroundings.

In the *Songs of Experience*(1794), there is no longer the innocence. The poems are pictures of neediness and distress and show sufferings of the poor. The salvation is through passionate revolt, through revolution. Blake was conscious of "some blind hand" crushing the life of man, as man crushes the fly. Blake's style is symbolic, with which, he shows his progressive democratic ideas.

Comparative studies of the poems in the two works may help to see the contrast which marks a progress in his outlook on life. The bright picture of the happy world full of delight, harmony and love changes into the dark painting of the miserable world. The images change with the change of ideas.

Blake's support of the French Revolution (1789) was life-long. Under the impetus of it, Blake wrote a series of long poems called *Prophecies*, with a symbolism hard to understand. His *The French Revolution* (1791) describes the eve of the attack on the Bastill (14 July, 1789).

He also wrote *The Marriage of Heaven and Hell*(1790) in prose.

He was one of the revolutionary thinkers of that time. And his revolutionary ideas and enthusiasm were in some sense owed to Thomas Paine whom he helped to escape punishment. When old, he gave up poetry and devoted himself to painting and engraving. In 1827, this good, honest, great, "crazy" poet and painter died in obscurity and poverty.

Blake is a forerunner of the Romantic Movement. And this is fully justified. The greatness of Blake lies in his mastery, in art and verse, of an extreme and moving simplicity. William Wordsworth thus commented on Blake: "There is something in the madness of this man which interests me more than the sanity of Lord Byron or Walter Scott." And Blake's lyric poetry displays the characteristics of the romantic spirit. What's more, Blake's revolutionary passion was very much similar to that of Shelly, especially in imagery and symbolism.

The Lamb[1]

Little Lamb, who made thee?
Dost thou[2] know who made thee?
Gave thee life & bid thee feed,
By the stream & o'er the mead;[3]
Gave thee clothing of delight,
Softest clothing woolly bright;
Gave thee such a tender voice,
Making all the vales rejoice!
Little Lamb, who made thee?

Dost thou know who made thee?
Little Lamb, I'll tell thee,
Little Lamb, I'll tell thee!
He is called by thy name,
For he calls himself a Lamb.
He is meek & he is mild,
He became a little child;
I a child & thou a lamb,
We are called by his name.
Little Lamb God bless thee.
Little Lamb God bless thee.

Notes

1. This is taken from *Songs of Innocence*.
2. Dost thou—Do you.
3. mead—meadow.

For Study and Discussion

1. What does the Lamb represent?
2. Can you find evidence that the Lamb represents joy and innocence?

The Tyger[1]

Tyger! Tyger! burning bright[2]
In the forests of the night,
What immortal hand or eye
Could frame thy fearful symmetry[3]?

In what distant deeps[4] or skies
Burnt the fire of thine eyes?
On what wings dare he aspire?
What the hand dare seize the fire?

And what shoulder & what art,
Could twist the sinews of thy heart?
And when thy heart began to beat,
What dread hand? and what dread feet?

What the hammer? what the chain?
In what furnace was thy brain?

What the anvil? what dread grasp
Dare its deadly terrors clasp?

When the stars threw down their spears,
And water'd heaven with their tears,
Did he[5] smile his work to see?
Did he who made the Lamb[6] make thee?

Tyger! Tyger! burning bright
In the forests of the night,
What immortal hand or eye
Dare frame thy fearful symmetry?

Notes

1. This is taken from *Songs of Experience*. Tyger—tiger.
2. burning bright—the eyes shining bright.
3. the fearful symmetry—the body of the tiger is symmetric and frightening as well.
4. deeps—deep seas.
5. he—God.
6. Lamb—Jesus Christ.

For Study and Discussion

1. What is the tiger used as? Is it mainly used as a symbol of the fearful power of worldly experience?
2. What is the symbolic meaning of the tiger? What ideas does the poet want to express?

London[1]

I wander thro'[2] each charter'd[3] street,
Near where the charter'd Thames does flow,
And mark in every face I meet
Marks of weakness, marks of woe.

In every cry of every Man,
In every Infant's cry of fear,
In every voice, in every ban[4],
The mind-forg'd manacles I hear.

How the Chimney-sweeper's cry
Every black'ning Church appalls[5];
And the hapless Soldier's sigh

Runs in blood down Palace walls.
But most thro' midnight streets I hear
How the youthful Harlot's curse
Blasts[6] the new-born Infant's tear,
And blights[7] with plagues the Marriage hearse[8].

Notes

1. This is taken from *Songs of Experience*.
2. thro'—through.
3. charter'd—chartered, pre-empted as private property, and rented out.
4. ban—curse.
5. appalls—frighten greatly, shock.
6. blasts—make...dry.
7. blights—destroys.
8. the Marriage hearse—the poet is comparing marriage to funeral.

For Study and Discussion

1. Why does the poet use "every" many times? What effect can it produce?
2. Why do the youthful Harlots curse?
3. Which image strikes you most? Why?
4. Is this the kind of London you expected? What should London be like?

Chapter 7 Robert Burns

Robert Burns (1759—1796), the greatest poet of Scotland, is often called a peasant poet or farmer poet. He was, indeed, born into a farmer's family. His father was open-minded and knowledgeable. It is from his father that Burns received most of his learning and love for books. Because of his father's early death (1784), he, the oldest of the seven children, took up responsibility of supporting the whole family when he was only 25. Of course, he was already a chief laborer and master hand at the plough at the age of 16.

When he was very young, he had some schooling, but very little. His total schooling added up to only two years and a half. But he liked reading. He was mainly self-taught, though the literati of Edinburgh hailed him in 1786 as "Heaven-taught plowman" whose poems were the spontaneous overflow of his native feelings, which belief he himself sometimes fostered. The fact was that he read vastly and from his early years, partly influenced by his mother, he had a very intimate knowledge of Scottish folk songs and the works of Scottish poets as well as other non-Scottish poets. He always succeeded in squeezing out time for reading. He managed to read and write a little every day after work. Even while working in the fields he would sing to himself, putting new words to old tunes, thus composing his poems.

In 1786, when life was too hard for his family, he resolved to go to Jamaica for a living. To raise money for the voyage, his friends helped him to publish his first volume of poetry entitled *Poems Chiefly in the Scottish Dialect* (1786). This collection took Scotland by storm. All kinds of people, high and low, literary and illiteracy, even plowboys and maid servants who earned little money, bought this book and read it eagerly. The success made Burns change his mind. Instead of going abroad, he hurried to Edinburgh where he was lionized, but where his peasant roughness soon jarred the refined sensibilities of polite society. When his novelty wore off, he left Edinburgh where he did not belong. He then traveled in Scotland and northern England collecting ballads. After that, he returned to his farm and married Jean Armour, in 1788, who inspired him to write some of his finest poems.

In 1789, he was appointed excise man with small salary. He supported the French revolution, and, this endangered the retention of his office.

His great poetic genius was cut short by his long illness. He died in 1796, when he was only 37 years old.

In his poems, Burns propagated the progressive ideas of the French Revolution, the ideas of democracy and freedom, sang praise of the Scottish patriotism (e. g. Scots Wha Hae), expressed his love (e. g. A Red, Red Rose, etc.), found beauty and pleasure in nature.

Most of his poems were written in Scottish dialect and remain excellent. He is loved by the common people. Lu Xun praised him as "a poet of the laboring people." In fact, when he died, the whole country united to honor him and to contribute to the support of his destitute family. Burns was hailed as the national poet of Scotland. He was Scottish to the core. And, he was beloved by the Scottish people because it is he who exalted and gave new dignity to the simple aspects of their lives.

A Red, Red Rose[1]

O[2] my Luve's[3] like a red, red rose,
    That's newly sprung in June;
O my Luve's like the melodie
    That's sweetly play'd in tune.

As fair art thou, my bonie lass[4],

So deep in luve am I;
And I will luve thee still[5], my dear,
Till a' the seas[6] gang dry[7].

Till a' the seas gang dry, my dear,
And the rocks melt wi' the sun:
I will luve thee still my dear,
While the sands o' life shall run[8].

And fare thee weel[9], my only Luve,
And fare the weel, a while[10]!
And I will come again, my Luve,
Tho' it were ten thousand mile!

Notes

1. This lyric is in the metrical form of the ballad stanza. The rhyme falls on the second and fourth lines of each stanza. The first and third lines have four feet while the second and the fourth have three feet.
2. O—Oh.
3. luve—love.
4. bonnie lass—pretty girl.
5. still—always, forever.
6. a' the seas—all the seas.
7. gang dry—go dry.
8. While the sands o'life shall run—As long as I live. "Sands" refers to the sand-glass for measuring the passage of time.
9. fare thee weel—farewell to you.
10. a while—for a short period of time.

For Study and Discussion

1. How does the speaker describe his love?
2. What do you know about the girl's voice?
3. What rhetoric devices does the speaker use to express his love?
4. Is there any poem comparable to this one? Mention it and explain why.
5. Why is this poem so popular with many readers?
6. How is love connected with the outside world?

Auld Lang Syne[1]

Should auld[2] acquaintance be forgot,

And never brought to min'[3]?
Should auld acquaintance be forgot,
And days o'lang syne[4]?

(Chorus)

For auld lang syne, my dear,
For auld lang syne.
We'll tak a cup o' kindness[5] yet,
For auld lang syne.

We twa hae[6] run about the braes[7].
And pu'd[8] the gowans[9] fine.
But we've wandered mony[10] a weary foot,
Sin' auld lang syne.

(Chorus)

We twa hae paidled[11] i' the burn[12],
From morning sun till dine[13];
But seas between us braid[14] hae roared,
Sin auld lang syne.

(Chorus)

And there's a hand, my trusty fiere[15],
And gie's[16] a hand o' thine[17];
And we'll tak[18] a right gude-willie waught[19],
For auld lang syne.

(Chorus)

And surely ye'll be[20] your pint-stowp[21],
And surely I'll be mine;
And we'll tak a cup o'kindness yet,
For auld lang syne.

(Chorus)

Notes

1. Auld Lang Syne—long ago.
2. auld—old.
3. min'—mind.
4. days o'lang syne—days of long ago.
5. cup o'kindness—cup of friendship wine.

6. twa hae—two have.
7. braes—slopes.
8. pu'd—pulled.
9. gowans—daisies.
10. mony—many.
11. paidled—paddled, waded.
12. I'the burn—in the rivulet (stream).
13. dine—dinner, noon.
14. braid—broad.
15. fiere—friend, fellow.
16. gie's—give us.
17. o' thine—of yours.
18. tak—take.
19. gude-willie waught—a cup of kindness. gude-willie—good will, friendly, waught—a deep draught.
20. ye'll be—you'll drink.
21. pint-stowp—a pint-cup. This line means you should surely drink as much as possible and to your content.

For Study and Discussion

1. What is the theme of this poem?
2. Why do people sing this song world-wide?
3. What is meant by "cup o'kindness"?
4. What make you think the people in this poem were childhood friends?
5. What gives you the idea that they are now rather old?

John Anderson, My Jo[1]

John Anderson my jo, John,
    When we were first acquent[2]
Your locks were like the raven[3],
    Your bonie[4] brow was brent[5];
But now your brow is beld[6], John,
    Your locks are like the snaw[7]
But blessings on your frosty[8] pow[9],
    John Anderson my jo!
John Anderson my jo, John,
    We clamb[10] the hill thegither[11],
And monie[12] a cantie[13] day John,

We've had wi'[14] ane anither[15];
Now we maun[16] totter[17] down, John,
And hand in hand we'll go,
And sleep thegither at the foot,
John Anderson my jo!

Notes

1. jo—sweetheart.
2. acquent—acquainted.
3. Your locks were like the raven—Your hair was black.
4. bonie—handsome, beautiful.
5. brent—high and smooth.
6. beld—bald.
7. snaw—snow.
8. frosty—frost-like.
9. pow—head.
10. clamb—climbed.
11. thegither—together.
12. monie—many.
13. cantie—cheerful, delightful, spirited.
14. wi'—with.
15. ane anither—one another.
16. maun—must.
17. totter—walk unsteadily.

For Study and Discussion

1. Many are the poems for young love dedicated to the beauty and strength of men and women. But this is a love lyric written to one who is old. How is it unusual and delightful?
2. This poem shows the sincere contentment and fulfillment of a love. The speaker has a fond memory of the past. What does the speaker compare their whole life to? How do you like this image?
3. Say something about your feeling about this poem. Have you ever read such lyrics for old love? What are the titles of similar poems?
4. Can you find in this poem a secret of the old couple's happiness together?
5. Which image strikes you most?

Part Five
The Nineteenth Century (Ⅰ)

Chapter 1 The English Romantic Movement

The Political Background. The romantic period showed its appearance between the year 1798, in which William Wordsworth and Samuel Taylor Coleridge published their *Lyrical* Ballads showed its appearance, and 1832, when Sir Walter Scott died, when other major writers of the earlier century were either dead or no longer productive, and when the passage of the first *Reform Bill* inaugurated the Victorian era of cautious readjustment of the political power to the economic and social realities of a new industrial age. The Industrial Revolution of the latter part of the 18th century transformed England from a primarily agricultural society, where wealth and power had been largely concentrated in the land holding aristocracy, to a modern industrial nation, in which the balance of economic power was shifted to large-scale employers, who found themselves ranged against an immensely enlarging and increasingly restive working class. Against the unspeakable misery and degradation went up a potent cry for better conditions in factory, poorhouse, and prison, for more humane treatment of children, for improving educational facilities. This change occurred in a context first of the American Revolution and then of the French Revolution, of wars, of economic cycles of inflation and depression, and of the constant threat of the social structure from imported revolutionary ideologies to which the ruling classes responded by heresy-hunts and the repression of traditional liberties. In England this period was one of harsh repressive measures.

Romantic Movement. By the beginning of the 19th century a movement had taken place in intellectual life. It influenced not only literature but also art, music, philosophy; it manifested itself not only in England but also in Germany and France. It displayed the spirit of idealism as opposed to realism. The advocates of the spirit were Rousseau in France, and Schelling, Schlegel, and Lessing in Germany. The literary aims and ideals of the 18th century were swept aside. Great was the development in all fields of literature—in poetry, in fiction, in the essay, and in literary criticism. English letters were characterized by an emotional and imaginative quality and by individuality in style. The so-called Lake School of English poets expressed new theories as to the subject-matter and language of poetry. The later romanticists were poets of revolt who, unlike the Lake School, never recanted their revolutionary principles.

In the early period of the French Revolution all the major poets were in sympathy with it, and Robert Burns, William Blake, William Wordsworth, and Samuel Taylor Coleridge were among its fervent adherents. Later, even after the first boundless expectations had been disappointed by the events in France, the younger poets, including Byron, Shelley, and Keats felt that its example, when purged of its errors, still comprised man's best hope.

Wordsworth undertook to justify the new poetry by a critical manifesto or statement of poetic principles, in the form of an extended *Preface* to the second edition of *Lyrical Ballads* in 1800, which he enlarged still further in the third edition of 1802. In it he set himself in opposition to the neo-classical writers of the preceding century who, to his view, had imposed on poetry artificial conventions which distorted its free and natural development. Wordsworth's *Preface* deserves its reputation as a turning point in English literature. In the *Preface* Wordsworth stated the major poetical principles that the Romantic poets were to follow.

1. Subject. "The principle object... was to choose incidents and situations from common life, and to relate or describe them, throughout, as far as was possible in a selection of language really used by men... " To obtain such situations, "Humble and rustic life was generally chosen, because, in that condition, the essential passions of the heart find a better soil in which they can attain their maturity, are less under restraint, and speak a plainer and more emphatic language; because in that condition of life our elementary feelings coexist in a state of greater simplicity, and, consequently, may be more accurately contemplated, and more forcibly communicated; because the manners of rural life germinate from those elementary feelings, and from the necessary character of rural occupations, are more easily comprehended, and are more durable; and, lastly, because in that condition the passions of men are incorporated with the beautiful and permanent forms of nature."

2. Style. "My purpose was to imitate, and as far as possible, to adopt the very language of men;" and therefore Wordsworth believed in avoiding "personifications of abstract ideas" and "what is usually called poetic diction." To him "poetry is the spontaneous overflow of powerful feelings" and "takes its origin from emotion recollected in tranquility."

Lyrical Ballads was a joint work of Wordsworth and Coleridge. In most of his poems Coleridge, like Wordsworth, dealt with the everyday things of this world. But according to the agreed division of labor in *Lyrical Ballads*, Coleridge's function was to achieve wonder by a frank violation of natural laws and the ordinary course of events, in poems of which "the incidents and agents were to be, in part at least, supernatural." He opened up the realm of mystery and magic, in which ancient folklore, superstition, and demonology are used to impress upon the reader the sense of occult powers and unknown modes of being.

Such poems are usually set in the distant past or in far away places, or both. *The Ancient Mariner*, *Christabel*, and *Kubla Khan*, by Coleridge, and *La Belle Dame sans Merci* and *The Eve of St. Agnes*, by John Keats, are good specimens of such kind of poems.

Romantic Poets. Romanticism found a suitable expression in poetry in the Romantic period. The English poets brought their poetic talents into full play, and produced a body of verse which is comparable to Elizabethan poetry. The major poets of the Romantic period were Wordsworth and his friend Coleridge, Byron, Shelley and Keats. The older poets represented by Wordsworth made an impressive contribution to poetry, and the younger poets represented by Byron and Shelley also did a wonderful work in shaping verses. Keats had his own contribution to the English poetry by presenting to readers a world different from that created by both the older and the younger group of poets just mentioned above. Keats' poetry has its own special beauty.

Chapter 2 William Wordsworth

William Wordsworth (1770—1850), one of the greatest poets of England, was born in a lawyer's family. He became an orphan at the age of 14. He was brought up by relatives who sent him to school at Hawkshead in the beautiful Lake District in Northwestern England. The beauty of nature attracted him greatly. Nature became his best teacher. The flowers, hills, stars, birds and all things of nature were of greater fascination. So he early developed and cherished a love of nature.

He was educated at Cambridge University where he spent four years, beginning from 1787. Influenced by the young republicans there, he was politically enthusiastic about and sympathetic with the French Revolution (1789). He visited France twice, the first time in 1790, the second time in 1792, where he loved a French girl and they had a daughter, but they were not married. For economic reason and relationship with his relatives, he had to leave France, his girl and his daughter. Of course, his poems of this period were more or less full of democratic ideas.

In 1795, Wordsworth and his sister Dorothy settled down at Racedom in Somersetshire, where they enjoyed the nature, where they, in 1797, made friends with Coleridge, with whom Wordsworth collaborated and published *Lyrical Ballads* (1798) which marked the break with classicism and the beginning of the Romantic revival in England.

Wordsworth had his own principle of poetry. He declared that "all good poetry is the spontaneous overflow of powerful feeling." He appealed directly to individual sensations,

i. e. pleasure, excitement and enjoyment as the foundation in the creation and appreciation of poetry. Poetry "takes its origin from emotion recollected in tranquility." A poet's emotion extends from affair to nature, but emotion immediately expressed is as raw as wine newly bottled. Tranquil contemplation of an emotional experience matures the feeling and sensation, and makes possible the creation of good poetry like the mellowing of old wine. The function of poetry lies in its power to give an unexpected splendor to familiar and commonplace things, to "incidents and situations from common life." All kinds of people, ordinary peasants, children, even outcasts, can enter poetry.

As to language used in poetry, he advocated using the language of the common people. Imagination was very important in poetic creation. All these principles were stated in the *Preface* to the *Lyrical Ballads*, which served as the manifesto of the English Romantic Movement in poetry.

With the establishment of the Jacobin dictatorship (May 1793—July 1794) and the rise of Napoleon (November 1799—April 1814) in France, Wordsworth lost his former political fervor and changed his attitude toward the Revolution. He retired to the northern Lake District and later accepted the office of a distributor of stamps and was made poet laureate.

Wordsworth wrote a great many poems, fresh in imagination, simple, plain and vivid in language but profound in meaning. He was especially good at writing about nature and common people. Hence he was called the poet of nature. He was also referred to as one of the Lake Poets because he lived in the lake district. His later major works, to mention a few here, include *Lucy Poems* (1799), *Ode to Duty* (1807), *The Excursion* (1814) and his long poem *The Preclude* (1850). He also wrote a lot of sonnets.

Wordsworth's sister, Dorothy, is worth a brief remark. She, as advisor and commentator of William's poems, helped him a lot in his poetic creation.

My Heart Leaps Up[1]

My heart leaps up when I behold
　　A rainbow in the sky:
So was it when my life began;
So is it now I am a man;
So be it when I shall grow old,
　　Or let me die!
The Child is father of the Man;
And I could wish my days to be
Bound each to each by natural piety.[1]

Note

1. As distinguished from piety based on the Scriptures, in which God makes the rainbow

the token of covenant with Noah and all his descendants. The religious sentiment that binds Wordsworth's mature self to that of his childhood is a continuing responsiveness to the miracle of ordinary things.

For Study and Discussion

1. Think about the first two lines. What conclusion would you draw from the next four lines?
2. Would you say that the quality expressed in these first six lines is indispensable to production of true poetry?
3. What do you understand by line 7?
4. Interpret "natural piety". Now give the central thought of the poem as a whole.

I Wandered Lonely as a Cloud[1]

I wandered lonely as a cloud
That floats on high o'er vales and hills,
When all at once I saw a crowd,
A host, of golden daffodils;
Beside the lake, beneath the trees,
Fluttering and dancing in the breeze.

Continuous as the stars that shine
And twinkle on the milky way,
They stretched in never-ending line
Along the margin of a bay:
Ten thousand saw I at a glance,
Tossing their heads in sprightly dance.

The waves beside them danced; but they
Out did the sparkling waves in glee:
A poet could not but be gay,
In such a jocund company:
I gazed—and gazed—but little thought
What wealth the show to me had brought:

For oft, when on my couch I lie[2]
In vacant or in pensive mood,
They flash upon that inward eye
Which is the bliss of solitude;
And then my heart with pleasure fills,
And dances with the daffodils.

Notes

1. The rhyme scheme of this poem is ababcc. The lines are iambic tetrameter.
2. The last stanza describes the kind of recollection in tranquility from which this poem arose, two years after the original experience, which Dorothy Wordsworth described in her *Grasmere Journals* for April 15, 1802.

For Study and Discussion

1. Some people say this poem is one of Wordsworth's choice bits of photography. Do you agree with this? Why?
2. Can you see the poet wandering along "lonely as a cloud that floats on high o'er vales and hills?" From this point on, notice the careful attention he gave to the picture he was taking—he got color, motion and setting. Describe the scene as you see it through his eyes.
3. What made the daffodils seem to dance?
4. What is the meaning of the last stanza?
5. What is the thought that you get from the poem as a whole?
6. Talk about the image of "loneliness" in this poem.

Chapter 3 Samuel Taylor Coleridge

Samuel Taylor Coleridge (1772—1834) had one of the most fertile and versatile minds in English literature. His poetic output is relatively small although it contains such masterpieces as *The Rime of the Ancient Mariner*, *Kubla Khan*, and *Frost at Midnight*. His work as a literary critic and theorist, however, is massive, and his judgments and ideas are still enormously influential today. The fact that many of Coleridge's most ambitious literary projects were never completed should not obscure the awesome value and scope of what he actually accomplished.

Coleridge was born in rural Devonshire, the youngest of fourteen children. His father was a clergyman. He was ten years old when his father died, and he was sent to live and attend school in London. He was an enthusiastic and extraordinarily brilliant student. When he went on to attend Cambridge University in 1791, he was already a proficient scholar. Yet Coleridge found even less at Cambridge that really interested him than Wordsworth did. He fell into idleness, carelessness, and debt, and in 1793 he left Cambridge to join the army. But he was miserable as a soldier, and with the help of his brothers he was sent back to Cambridge for a second chance. He left again in 1794, however, without taking a degree.

As a young man Coleridge held radical views on politics and religion. He had been fired with wild enthusiasm for the French Revolution. During the summer of 1794 he met Robert Southey. The two friends set about planning a small Utopian community in America. Coleridge named it "Pantisocracy" (equal rule by all). But both of them were dreamers without any means to put their plan into practice.

In 1797 he met William Wordsworth. Thus began the happiest and most productive time of Coleridge's life. The two poets published their *Lyrical Ballads*. The first poem in this collection is Coleridge's masterpiece, *The Rime of the Ancient Mariner*. Coleridge's specific role in *Lyrical Ballads* was "directed to persons and characters supernatural".

In 1798 Coleridge went to Germany with Wordsworth and Dorothy, the latter's sister, at the university of Gottingen, he began his lifelong study of Kant and other German philosophers. Coleridge played an important role in introducing the advances of German philosophy to English poets and thinkers.

Coleridge was also a literary critic good at giving lectures. He was the most eloquent speaker and conversationalist of the Romantic Age. His lecture on Shakespeare and other writers have become classics of literary criticism. During the next few years he also wrote for newspapers and magazines. He created a periodical called *The Friend*, and wrote a successful tragedy called *Remorse*.

His last notable work was *Biographia Literaria*. By then he had abandoned the revolutionary ardor of his youth and turned conservative.

The works of Coleridge naturally divide themselves into three classes—the poetic, the critical and the philosophical, corresponding to the early, the middle, and the later periods of his career. He is famous for his poetry. He produced three main poems.

The poem *The Rime of the Ancient Mariner* is his masterpiece. It was first included in *Lyrical Ballads*. It tells a strange story in the form of ballad. Three guests are on their way to a wedding party, but one of them is detained by an ancient mariner. The mariner tells him of his adventures on the sea. When his ship sails towards the South Pole, an albatross comes through the snow-fog and alights on the rigging. The mariner is thoughtless enough to smooth it. Then a misfortune falls on the ship. The whole crew, with the exception of the mariner, dies of thirst as a punishment for the act of inhospitality. The spell breaks only when the mariner repents his cruelty.

The atmosphere and the beauty of music and imagery make the poem stand alone of its kind. The poem is one of the masterpieces of the Romantic poetry.

Kubla Khan or *A Vision in a Dream* is said to have been composed in the summer of

1797. The poet dropped asleep after taking an anodyne which was prescribed to him for his health. He was reading from an old book of travels entitled *Purchas his Pilgrimage* the following passage: "In Xamdu did Cublai Can build a stately palace, encompassing sixteen miles of plain ground with a wall, where in are fertile meadows, pleasant springs, delightful streams, and all sorts of beasts of chase and game, and in the midst there of a sumptuous house of pleasure." According to Coleridge, he "continued for about three hours in profound sleep" and "during which time…he could not have composed less than from two to three hundred lines." The author went on to say that on awaking he appeared to himself to have a distinct recollection of the whole, and taking his pen, ink, and paper, instantly and eagerly wrote down the lines that are here preserved. At this moment, he was unfortunately called out by a person on business from Porlock, and detained by him above an hour, and on his return to his room, found, to his no small surprise and mortification, that with the exception of eight or ten scattered lines and images, all the rest had passed away like the images on the surface of a stream into which a stone had been cast. So the poem was left a fragment.

Although the greater part of the fragment has to do with *Kubla Khan* and his pleasure-dome, the mention of "an Abyssinian maid" playing "on her dulcimer" and "singing of Mount Abora" seems to be entirely extraneous material. Thus the poem has no coherent meaning and is wrapped up in an atmosphere of the supernatural and the fantastic. However, the poetic imagery and the haunting melody in the poem have attracted many students of English literature.

Coleridge is a great poet. He wrote with excellent techniques. He is a medievalist, fond of the unusual and supernatural things. His imaginative power is intense and his language melodious. His early poetry shows the influence of Gray and Blake, especially of the latter. In his later poems his imagination is bridled by thought and study.

Coleridge was also a literary critic, good at giving lectures. He was the first critic of the Romantic school. Between 1808 and 1815 he delivered a series of lectures on Shakespeare, which were later collected in his *Notes and Lectures on Shakespeare*. His most important prose work is *Biographia Literaria*, or *Sketches of My Literary Life and Opinions*, which afforded the new Romantic poetry a new principle of criticism, whose task was not to judge but to appreciate and interpret. According to Coleridge, the poet was a creator and the critic was an assistant in the work of creation. The poet, as a man endowed with imaginative genius and fine perception, must be allowed to present the truth in his own without regard to rules or models. And the critic must enter into the poet's purpose and art, and interpret ideas and beauty for the benefit of the reader. Just like Wordsworth his ideas became conservative in his later years.

The Rime of the Ancient Mariner

(PART I)

It is an ancient Mariner,
And he stoppeth one of three.
—"By thy long grey beard and glittering eye,
Now wherefore stopp'st thou me?

The Bridegroom's doors are opened wide,
And I am next of kin;
The guests are met, the feast is set:
May'st hear the merry din."

He holds him with his skinny hand,
"There was a ship," quoth he.
"Hold off! unhand me, grey-beard loon!"
Eftsoons[1] his hand dropt he.

He holds him with his glittering eye—
The Wedding-Guest stood still,
And listens like a three years' child:
The Mariner hath his will.

The Wedding-Guest sat on a stone:
He cannot choose but hear;
And thus spake on that ancient man,
The bright-eyed Mariner.

"The ship was cheered, the harbour cleared,
Merrily did we drop
Below the kirk[2], below the hill,
Below the lighthouse top.

The Sun came up upon the left,
Out of the sea came he!
And he shone bright, and on the right
Went down into the sea.

Higher and higher every day,
Till over the mast at noon[3]—"
The Wedding-Guest here beat his breast,
For he heard the loud bassoon.

The bride hath paced into the hall,
Red as a rose is she;

Nodding their heads before her goes
The merry minstrelsy.

The Wedding-Guest he beat his breast,
Yet he cannot choose but hear;
And thus spake on that ancient man,
The bright-eyed Mariner.

"And now the STORM-BLAST came, and he
Was tyrannous and strong:
He struck with his o'ertaking wings,
And chased us south along.

With sloping masts and dipping prow,
As who pursued with yell and blow
Still treads the shadow of his foe,
And forward bends his head,
The ship drove fast, loud roared the blast,
And southward aye we fled.

And now there came both mist and snow,
And it grew wondrous cold:
And ice, mast-high, came floating by,
As green as emerald.

And through the drifts[4] the snowy clifts[5]
Did send a dismal sheen:
Nor shapes of men nor beasts we ken—
The ice was all between.

The ice was here, the ice was there,
The ice was all around:
It cracked and growled, and roared and howled,
Like noises in a swound![6]

At length did cross an Albatross,
Thorough[7] the fog it came;
As if it had been a Christian soul,
We hailed it in God's name.

It ate the food it ne'er had eat[8],
And round and round it flew.
The ice did split with a thunder-fit;
The helmsman steered us through!

And a good south wind sprung up behind;
The Albatross did follow,
And every day, for food or play,
Came to the mariner's hollo!

In mist or cloud, on mast or shroud[9],
It perched for vespers[10] nine;
Whiles all the night, through fog-smoke white,
Glimmered the white Moon-shine."

"God save thee, ancient Mariner!
From the fiends, that plague thee thus! —
Why look'st thou so?"With my cross-bow
I shot the ALBATROSS.

Notes

1. Eftsoons—at once.
2. kirk—church.
3. over...noon—The ship reaches the equator.
4. drifts—mists.
5. clifts—iceberge.
6. swound—swoon.
7. Thorough—through.
8. eat—old form of "eaten".
9. shroud—rope of the rigging.
10. vespers—evenings.

For Study and Discussion

1. Describe the atmosphere of the poem. Cite words, phrases, and vivid images that contribute to the atmosphere.
2. Do you think the Albatross takes on a religious significance?
3. To what extent does the presence of the wedding guest influence your own response to the poem?

Chapter 4 George Gordon Byron

For many of his contemporaries in England, Europe, and America, George Gordon Byron (1788 — 1824) was the embodiment of the Romantic spirit, both in his poetry and in his personal life. Proud, passionate, rebellious, deeply marked by painful and often mysterious experiences in the past, yet fiercely and defiantly committed to following his own individual destiny—this was the image that Byron displayed for his contemporaries and passed on to subsequent ages.

Byron was descended from two aristocratic but violent and undisciplined families. His father, a reckless English sea captain and fortune hunter, was called "Mad Jack" Byron. His mother, Catharine Gordon of Gight, came from a line of fiery tempered, lawless Scottish nobles. Byron was born in London, but at the age of three, shortly after his father died, he was taken by his mother to Aberdeen, where he was brought up in the strict religious environment of Scottish Presbyterianism. Byron's mother was fond of him but very ill-tempered, and she often quarreled with her impetuous, high-spirited son. Although an extremely handsome boy, Byron had been born with a clubfoot. The pain and self-consciousness caused by this deformity was aggravated by a corrective shoe, which Byron's mother, taking the advice of an inept physician, forced him to wear. Byron struggled all his life with the physical and psychological effects of his deformity. He was especially proud of his athletic prowess at swimming, riding, boxing, and cricket, and of his good looks, which he was always fearful of losing.

When Byron was ten years old, his great uncle, known as the "Wicked Lord", died, and Byron inherited his title to become the sixth Lord Byron. Byron was also heir to the ancestral estate, Newstead Abbey. He was sent to Harrow, one of England's most prestigious private schools, and then to Cambridge University. It was at Cambridge that Byron began to write poetry, and to assume a flamboyant, outrageous style of life that would become his trademark. He spent much of the money he inherited on expensive clothes and decorations for his college rooms; he entertained lavishly; he kept horses and a pet bear; and he loved to shock his friends by drinking out of a cup made from a human skull. In 1807 Byron published his lyric poems in a small volume called *Hours of Idleness*. The volume was sharply attacked in the influential *Edinburgh Review*, and Byron responded with his first important poem, a biting satire in the 18th century manner, called *English Bards and Scotch Reviewers*.

In 1809, after graduating from Cambridge, Byron set out with a close friend on an extended tour of countries not immediately involved in the Napoleonic Wars: Spain, Portugal, Albania, Greece, Asia Minor. He used the experiences of this journey as the materials for the first two cantos of a marvelous poetic travelogue entitled *Childe Harold's Pilgrimage*, which he published soon after his return to England in 1812. The work was enormously successful. As Byron himself recalled, "I awoke one morning and found myself famous." He became the greatest literary and social celebrity of Regency London. His reputation grew still further with the publication of a series of Romantic verse narratives with exotic, Near-Eastern settings: *The Giaour*, *The Corsair*, *and Lara*. The appeal of these poems lay only partly in their descriptions of foreign scenes and customs. In them, and in the verse drama a few years later, Byron displayed the figure subsequently known as the "Byronic hero"—a passionate, moody, restless character who has exhausted most of the world's excitements, and who lives under the weight of some mysterious sin committed in the past. His proud, defiant individualism refuses to be limited by the normal institutional and moral strictures of society. He is an "outsider" whose daring life both isolates him and makes him attractive. Most of Byron's readers identified him personally with his heroes. And despite his protests that such connection should never be taken seriously, it seems clear Byron partly enjoyed the identity, at least at the beginning of his career, and sometimes tried to project it in his own behavior.

In 1815, at the height of his popularity, Byron married Annabella Milbanke, who sought to make him into a conventional and respectable husband. But Byron was soon involved in bitter quarrels with his wife over his unconventional behavior and his continuing love affairs. When she left him after only a year of marriage, Byron found himself surrounded by scandal and ostracized by the very society that had made him its favorite. Bitter but defiant as always, Byron left England on April 25, 1816, never returning.

Byron resumed his travels in Europe, living first at Geneva in Switzerland, where he became the close friend of Shelley and where he produced a magnificent third canto of *Childe Harold*. Then he moved to Venice, where he perpetuated his reputation for fast living and began his greatest work, the satirical epic *Don Juan*. Byron's hero is not the adult Don Juan, the notorious lover who would seem to lie closest to Byron's own personality and to that of his earlier "Byronic heroes". He is rather an original version of the boyish and youthful Don Juan, a fresh, energetic, impressionable young man whose curiosity and attractiveness to women enable Byron to expose both the foolishness and cruelty of life and the wonderful richness of earthly experience. Byron himself makes his presence felt in *Don Juan* primarily through the voice of the narrator, who appears to be making up his poem as he goes along and who recounts the adventures of Don Juan (a younger version of himself) with a splendid balance of satire and sympathy.

Byron eventually moved to Pisa where he again joined Shelley, who was living there among a small circle of friends. After Shelley's death and the breakup of the "Pisan

Circle", Byron again grew restless. Always an ardent spokesman for political freedom, he saw Greece, the ancient home of democracy, struggling to win its independence from Turkey. He invested a great deal of money and energy in organizing an expedition, which he himself led, to help the Greek cause. While training troops in the squalid, marshy town of Missolonghi, he was stricken with a severe fever. Byron died on April 19, 1824, shortly after his thirty-sixth birthday. Although his practical contribution to the Greek army was insignificant, his presence and tragic death produced a vital spark of inspiration for the eventual liberation of the country. He is still regarded in Greece as a national hero.

Despite his status as the archetypal Romantic, Byron had stronger ties to the 18th century than any of his contemporaries. He was a great admirer of Dryden and Pope, and he was sharply critical of all his fellow Romantics, except Shelley, for having devoted themselves to "a wrong revolutionary poetical system". His affinities with the 18th century are apparent not only in *English Bards and Scotch Reviewers*, *Don Juan*, and his other satires, but also in many of his shorter lyrics and songs. Some of these extend the Cavalier tradition of elegant, graceful compliment to a lady. Others belong to the gentlemanly 18th century tradition of witty, extemporaneous reflection on a passing occasion. As a man Byron was capable of many moods and many roles, and we can see this reflected in the variety of his poetry. But behind all the different roles and postures we sense that powerful, self-conscious personality that holds as much fascination for us today as it did for Byron's own era.

In 1809, after graduating from Cambridge University, Byron set out with a close friend on an extended tour of countries in Europe. He used the experiences of this journey as the material of the long poem, *Childe Harold's Pilgrimage*.

The poem contains four cantos. It is written in Spenserian stanza. The hero is a young man called Childe Harold, who comes from an English aristocratic family. Harold hates English high society and loves freedom. He leaves his own country and begins to travel in several different countries of Europe. The whole poem deals with his travels and visits in some of the counties. The descriptions of the hero's travels reveal Byron's own philosophical and political ideas.

The first canto deals with the hero's journey in Portugal and Spain. Byron praises Portugal as the "delicious land where fruits of fragrance blush on every tree". Then he draws up pictures of the people's poverty and shows his deep sympathy with the poor there. Then he depicts the Spaniards in their struggle against foreign aggression. He calls on them to fight against their enemy.

The second canto describes Albania and Greece. In Greece he finds the Greek have become slaves of the Turks. Byron laments over their fallen state, He reminds them of their heroic past, and encourages them to rise up to struggle for liberty with their own arms.

The third canto was written six or seven years later than the first two cantos. It was written after Byron was driven out of his motherland. It begins and ends with Byron's touching address to his daughter, Ada, whom he left in England and could never see again. Then he describes Waterloo. He condemns the reaction that set up in Europe after the downfall of Napoleon. He glorifies the French Revolution. He believes that the people will see victory though Revolution fails and the kings are restored to their thrones.

The fourth canto describes Italy. Byron praised Italy and the Italian people who have given the world great writers and thinkers like Petrarch, Dante, Boccaccio and Galileo. He laments over the sorrowful state of the Italian people who are under the control of Austrians. He exposes the reactionary rulers of Europe. He shows his ardent love of freedom and his belief in the people's final triumph. He calls on the Italian people to restore their glorious past.

Don Juan was written in Italy. It consists of sixteen cantos. The poem had been regarded as Byron's masterpiece. The story of the poem took place in the latter part of the 18th century.

Don Juan is a Spanish youth of aristocratic birth. This long poem describes Don Juan's adventures in many countries. The hero is made to participate in different historical events. Thus one can get a panoramaic view of the social life of the time. The poem begins with descriptions of the hero's childhood. Then it describes his love affairs with a married woman. When the love affair is discovered, he is sent abroad. The ship is wrecked. His fellow travelers die, he survives and swims to a Greek island where he is saved by a girl. They fall in love. But their love affair is broken when the girl's father returns to the island. Then Don Juan is sold as a slave. In the capital of Turkey, Constantinople, he is bought by the Sultana (sister of the king) who has taken a fancy to him. Then Don Juan lives with the girl in the guise of a woman. He goes through many adventures there. Then he runs away to the camp of the Russian army that is besieging the Turkish fortress.

Then Don Juan is sent to St. Petersburg. Empress Catherine sends him to England on a political mission. The last canto of the poem gives a satirical description of English ruling classes and social conditions. The hero shows his disgust for the vanity and hypocrisy of English high society.

Byron did not finish the poem. He meant to make the hero take part in the French Revolution and die a heroic death. Byron wrote a lot of short lyrics. All of them are beautifully written. The best-known pieces are *She Walks in Beauty*, *When We Two Parted*, *Hebrew Melodies*, *On This Day I Complete My Thirty-Sixth Year*! He also wrote some poetic dramas such as the philosophical *Manfred*(1817) and the mysterious *Cain*(1821), and some political satirical poems.

Meanwhile he was politically active. Upon his return to England in 1811, Byron took his seat in the House of Lords. Being indignified at the parliamentary measure introduced for the brutal punishment of the Luddites, he made a famous speech in the House of Lords on February 27, 1812, defending the rights of the oppressed workers and opposing the reactionary policy of the English government. The wording of his speech was very fiery and moving. Byron's fierce condemnation on the injustice of his society and his great sympathy for he Luddites as well as for the oppressed people were further exhibited in his poems such as *Ode to the Framers of the Frame Bill* (1812), *Song For The Luddites* (1816), and in his second speech made in the House of Lords on April 21, 1812, on the Irish question. These speeches and poems, together with his other ones, were a series of violent attacks on the government and they greatly enraged the English ruling class.

Byron is the most excellent representative of English Romanticism. He was one of the most influential poets of his time. His literary career was closely linked with the struggle and progressive movements of his age. He opposed oppression and slavery, and had an ardent love for liberty. He praised the people's revolutionary struggles in his works. His poems are favorites of the British workers and the labouring people of other countries. Engels in *The Condition of the Working Class in England* stressed the fact that Byron was widely read among the workers. Byron's influence has shown itself in the works of the Chartist Poets in England and the progressive poets in many other countries.

His poems show energy and vigor, romantic daring and powerful passion. Some of his poems show Byron's individual heroism and pessimism.

She Walks in Beauty[1]

1

She walks in beauty, like the night
　　Of cloudless climes and starry skies;
And all that's best of dark and bright
　　Meet in her aspect[2] and her eyes:
Thus mellowed to that tender light
　　Which heaven to gaudy day denies.

2

One shade the more, one ray the less,
　　Had half impaired the nameless grace
Which waves in every raven tress,
　　Or softly lightens o'er[3] her face;
Where thoughts serenely sweet express
　　How pure, how dear their dwelling place.

3

And on that cheek, and o'er that brow,
　　So soft, so calm, yet eloquent,
The smiles that win, the tints that glow,
　　But tell of days in goodness spent,
A mind at peace with all below,
　　A heart whose love is innocent!

Notes

1. One of the lyrics in *Hebrew Melodies* (1815) written to be set to adaptations of traditional Jewish tunes by the young musician Isaac Nathan. Byron wrote the lines the morning after he had met his beautiful young cousin by marriage, Mrs. Robert John Wilmot, who wore a black mourning gown brightened with spangles.
2. aspect—facial expression.
3. o'er—over.

For Study and Discussion

1. Describe the aesthetical sense of the poem.
2. The lady being praised is compared to the night. What particular aspects of the night are singled out in the comparison?
3. How do we know that the lady's beauty depends on a balance of opposites? How does her appearance express her thoughts and past experience?

Chapter 5 Percy Bysshe Shelley

Percy Bysshe Shelley (1792—1822) is a contradictory and challenging figure. His writing is at once the most passionate and intense of all the Romantic poets, and yet the most intellectual, the fullest of philosophical speculation and technical experiment. And although he was the most committed of the Romantic poets to social action, to improving the lot of all people, his political writing is harder to grasp and less accessible than that of the others. He made brilliant innovations and experiments in poetic language, and he wrote a magnificent essay on the meaning and importance of poetic language, and he wrote a magnificent essay on the meaning and importance of poetry (*The Defence of Poetry*, 1821). Yet it is precisely Shelley's stylistic experiments and his fervent ambition to push language into the realm of the inexpressible that make him at times forbiddingly difficult. In his personal life Shelley was uncommonly generous, responsive, and sympathetic to the sufferings of others—yet his fierce devotion to ideals about what human life could attain sometimes put him out of touch with the immediate feelings and needs of those around him. One thing is certain: the only way for any reader to come to terms with Shelley as a man and a writer is with an open mind and a willingness to envision new possibilities for human experience and expression.

Like Byron, Shelley was born into an upper-class family. His father, Timothy Shelley, was a rather conservative member of parliament from Sussex, a county just south of London. Shelley was sent to Eton. It was at Eton that Shelley first became determined to fight against the forces of injustice and oppression in life. In 1810 he went to Oxford University, where he and a close friend wrote a pamphlet called *The Necessity of Atheism*. Shelley refused to deny that he had written the pamphlet when called before the authorities, and he was expelled after only six months at Oxford.

Shelley then went to London, where he fell in love and eloped with Harriet Westbrook, an attractive, warmhearted girl who Shelley thought was being oppressed by her father. When they were married, Harriet was sixteen, Shelley eighteen. Both families were, of course, unhappy about the marriage. Harriet and Shelley had to live on their own with little money. They went to Ireland for a time to work for Catholic emancipation and improved living conditions for the poor. Returning to London, Shelley joined the circle of the radical social philosopher William Godwin, whose wife, Mary Wollstonecraft, had been one of the earliest and most effective advocates for the rights of women. In 1814 Shelley fell in love with Mary, the brilliant daughter of Godwin and Mary Wollstonecraft. Committed to the idea that human relationships should not be restricted by law or social convention, Shelley went to live with Mary in France for a time.

When Shelley returned with Mary to England, he found himself branded a revolutionary and a social outcast. He was happiest living abroad, and he spent the summer of 1816 on the shores of Lake Geneva, in Switzerland, where he was visited by and became friends with Byron. But a crisis arose later that year—Harriet drowned herself in a fit of despair. Shelley was stricken with grief and remorse, and to make matters worse, the courts denied Shelley custody of the two children born to him and Harriet. Like Byron, Shelley felt himself an alien and an outcast in his own country. In 1818, soon after he and Mary were married, they left England for Italy, where Shelley would live for the rest of his life.

Shelley's four years in Italy, from 1818 until his death in 1822, were a time of poor health, of financial difficulty, of restless moving about from place to place, and of further personal tragedy. Between 1818 and 1819, two of his children by Mary, Clara and William, died. Yet Shelley was able during these years to produce an astonishing amount and range of magnificent poetry. In 1818 he began the philosophical drama that many readers consider his masterpiece, *Prometheus Unbound*. In 1819 he completed *Prometheus Unbound* and wrote his great *Ode to the West Wind*. In 1820 he produced a visionary satire called *The Mask of Anarchy* and a delicate philosophical nature-fable called *The Sensitive Plant*. The year 1821 saw the publication of *Epipsychidion*, a difficult and experimental poem about the transcendent possibilities of human love, and of *Adonais*, Shelley's great elegy on the death of John Keats. In 1822 he completed *hellas*, a lyrical drama about the Greek war of liberation against the Turks. At his death he was at work on The *Triumph of Life*, which some readers think would have been his finest work had he lived to complete it. In addition to these major works, Shelley wrote in each of these years many of the intense, beautifully crafted shorter lyrics for which he is so well known.

The last two years of Shelley's "Italian Period" were happier than the first two. He and Mary finally settled at Pisa, where they were joined by a group of close friends who came to be known as the "Pisan Circle". Shelley's accidental death came suddenly and in a manner almost miraculously predicted in the famous concluding stanza of *Adonais*:

> ...my spirit's bark is driven,
> Far from the shore, far from the trembling throng
> Whose sails were never to the tempest given;
> The massy earth and sphered skies are riven!

Shelley loved boats and frequently used them as images or symbols in his poetry. On July 8, 1822, he and his friend Edward Williams set out in Shelley's small boat, the Don Juan, to sail across the Gulf of Spezzia. A violent storm arose and both Williams and Shelley, who could not swim, were swept overboard. Their bodies were found on the beach several days later. Shelley's ashes were buried in the Protestant cemetery at Rome, near the grave of Keats.

Byron thus commented on Shelley, "he was, without exception, the best and least selfish man I ever knew. I never knew one who was not a beast in comparison". Matthew Arnold thought that Shelley's character was too sensitive for a really great writer and called him a "beautiful and ineffectual angel, beating in the void his luminous wings in vain". But Shelley was not ineffectual, and he was not so cut off from the realities of life as Arnold suggests. Although dedicated to the idea that by perfecting their own nature people could liberate themselves from the pain and injustice of present existence, Shelley had a shrewd and informed comprehension of the complexities of earthly life. And his generous, unselfish personality also contained elements of sophisticated playfulness and good humor—he was not beyond laughing at himself. Intellectually, he was an immensely learned and well-read man capable of more refined and original philosophical thinking than any other English Romantic, including Coleridge. Wordsworth said, "Shelley is one of the best artists of us all: I mean in workmanship of style."

Queen Mab is Shelley's first long poem of importance. It expresses almost all his major political ideas. It is written in the form of a fairy tale dream. The fairy Queen Mab carries off in her celestial chariot a beautiful and pure maiden called Ianthe, and shows her the past, present and future of mankind. Through the mouth of the fairy queen the poet attacks the tyranny of gold, militarism and religious superstition. The poem has nine cantos. The first two cantos deal with a vision of the woeful past, the last two with an ideal view of the happy future, while the five middle cantos are devoted to a fierce attack on the social evils of the day. In the third canto the idle life of the exploiting class is exposed. In the fourth canto the ruling class is attacked and criticized. Shelley points out that plunderous war is used as a weapon by the oppressors to attain their selfish ends, and state apparatus is used as a tool in suppressing the people. In the fifth canto the miserable lives of the poor people and their hatred for tyranny are described. In the last two cantos the fairy queen comforts Ianthe by a glimpse of the happy future when science and love will make a paradise of earth.

Queen Mab is a revolutionary poem condemning tyranny and exploitation and the unjust war waged by the rich to plunder wealth. However, Shelley in this poem was merely a Utopian-Socialist in views, looking forward to a happy future for mankind but rejecting the path of revolution by violence. The poem is loved by the English working class.

The Revolt of Islam is another important long poem. It tells of the insurrection of the people of Islam. The people's fighting spirit is roused by a hero and his sister. Inspired by the brother and sister, the people rise up to revolt against their rulers. The revolt is temporarily successful, but the tyrants win the support of foreign allies and return to suppress the uprising. Finally the revolt fails, and the heroic brother and sister are burnt at the stake.

In this poem, the French Revolution of 1789 is implied. With the overthrow of Napoleon, the restoration of the old order had temporarily triumphed throughout Europe and the working people had been thrown into abject misery. England was confronted with acute social conflicts and widespread discontent. In this poem, Shelley calls on the people to carry on their struggle for liberty, but he does not realize the importance and the necessity of armed struggle for a better society.

Prometheus Unbound, a lyrical drama, is Shelley's masterpiece. The story was taken from Greek mythology. According to Greek myth, Prometheus stole fire from heaven and taught men how to use it. For this he was punished by Zeus, the supreme god, who chained him to a rock on Mt. Caucasus, where during the daytime a vulture fed on his liver, which was restored each succeeding night. So the figure of Prometheus has been symbolic of those noble-hearted revolutionaries, who devote themselves to the just cause of the people and suffer great pains at the hands of tyrants.

The theme of this poetical drama is borrowed from the Greek tragedian Aeschylus' play *Prometheus Bound*. But the two plays are quite different in ending. Aeschylus made Prometheus finally reconcile with Zeus. This ending could not be accepted by Shelley. In order to express his faith in the ultimate victory of the people, Shelley made Prometheus the representative of mankind, who has four noble qualities: shaping intellect, heroic endurance, defiance against tyranny and love of mankind. Though chained to the rock, he has "great allies" in the world. Mother Earth supports him by giving him strength to endure all sufferings and sending the spirits of heroes and martyrs to cheer him. Lovely shapes of Faith and Hope hover around him. His bride Asia awaits him in the distance. With a firm confidence in the final triumph of his just cause, Prometheus is perfectly calm in his sufferings. He knows the reign of Zeus, the symbol of reaction, is but a passing period in the life of the universe, so to the last he refuses to yield to the tyrants in heaven. Finally Zeus is overthrown by Demogorgon, the symbol of change and revolution, and driven into the eternal abyss, Prometheus is set free by Hercules, the most valiant hero in Greek mythology. As Prometheus throws off his fetters, the whole world joins in a chorus to celebrate his liberation. Prometheus' triumph symbolizes the victory of mankind over tyranny and oppression.

The Masque of Anarchy is one of Shelley's political lyrics. It deals with the infamous Peterloo Massacre which happened on August 16, 1819. In that event hundreds of jobless workers were killed or wounded. Shelley uses this poem to expose the essential nature of the so-called "free competition" under capitalism. In the poem, kings, priests, bankers and lawyers all crowd to welcome Anarchy as their "Law and God". So "Anarchy" in this poem means the tyranny of a handful of oppressors and exploiters over the masses. The first part of the poem describes the contemporary rules of England. In the second part the poet sings of the men of England, their strength and future victory, he calls upon them to rise against the oppressors and blood-suckers.

Another of Shelley's well-known political lyrics is the *Song to the Men of England*. In this lyric, the capitalist society is divided into two hostile classes: the bourgeoisie and the proletariat. Shelley calls upon the working class to fight against their rulers and exploiters.

During his stay in Italy from 1818 to 1822, Shelley wrote a great deal of short lyrics, political and personal, on love and nature. Among his lyrics, the political ones include *Sonnet: England* in 1819, *Ode to Naples*, *Ode to Liberty*, *A New National Anthem*, and the greatest political lyric *Song to the Men of England*. As for his lyrics on nature, the two best-known ones are *Ode to the West Wind* (1819) and *To a Skylark* (1820). His other lyrics on nature are mainly *Hymn of Appollo*, *The Cloud* and *To the Moon*. Shelley's love lyrics, numerous and widely known, including mainly *Love's Philosophy*, *I Fear Thy Kisses*, *Gentle Maiden*, *One Word Is Too Often Profaned* and *When the Lamp Is Shattered*. In his love lyrics, Shelley regards love as the noblest thing in the universe, as the thing of extreme purity and as a feeling of devotion and worship. He believes that the noblest love in the human world may lead mankind to a state of harmony, happiness, peace and perfection. He advocates that love should be elevated high above the vulgar, practical attitude toward it.

Shelley's short poems on nature and love form an important part of his literary output. To him nature exists as an unseen life of the universe and his love of nature is almost boundless. Shelley's love is not limited to mankind, but extended to every living creature. Flowers, trees, the sea, mountains and clouds are not only personified but also inspired or spiritualized. Shelley holds passionate communion with the universe. He becomes one with the lark, with the cloud, and with the west wind. This passionate love of nature is but an expression of the poet's eager aspiration for something free from the squalor of real life.

Upon the death of John Keats, Shelley wrote *Adonias*, an elegy lamenting the early death of his friend and fellow-poet Keats. The poem ranks with Milton's *Lycidas* as one of the few great elegies of the language; and considering its poetic quality, the nobility of its sentiment, its genuine personal grief, the interest of its subject, and the poetic friendship which it enshrines, there is no poem of its kind that claims a higher place.

Shelley loved the people and hated their oppressors and exploiters. He called on the people to overthrow the rule of tyranny and injustice and prophesied a happy and free life for mankind. He stood for this social and political ideal all his life. He and Byron are justifiably regarded as the two great poets of revolutionary romanticism in England.

Mrs. Shelley wrote, "Shelley loved the people; and respected them as often more virtuous, as always more suffering, and therefore more deserving of sympathy, than the great. He believed that a clash between the two classes of society was inevitable, and he eagerly ranged himself on the people's side."

With the deep insight of a proletarian revolutionary teacher, Marx pointed out: "The real difference between Byron and Shelley is this: Those who understand them and love them consider it fortunate that Byron died at thirty six, because if he lived longer he would have become a reactionary bourgeois. On the other hand they grieved that Shelley died at twenty-nine, because he was essentially a revolutionist and he would always have belonged to the vanguard of socialism."

In the *Condition of the Working Class in England* Engels wrote: "Shelley, the genius, the prophet, Shelley, and Byron, with his glowing sensuality and his bitter satire upon our existing society, find most of their readers in the proletariat."

Ode to the West Wind[1]

1

O wild West Wind, thou breath of Autumn's being,
Thou, from whose unseen presence the leaves dead
Are driven, like ghosts from and enchanter fleeing,

Yellow, and black, and pale, and hectic red,
Pestilence-stricken multitudes: O Thou,
Who chariotest[2] to their dark wintry bed

The winged seeds, where they lie cold and low,
Each like a corpse within its grave, until
Thine azure sister of the Spring[3] shall blow.

He clarion o'er the dreaming earth, and fill
(Driving sweet buds like flocks to feed in air)
With living hues and odours plain and hill:

Wild Spirit, which art moving everywhere;
Destroyer and Preserver;[4] hear, O hear!

2

Thou on whose stream, 'mid the steep sky commotion,
Loose clouds like Earth's decaying leaves are shed,
Shook[5] from the tangled boughs of Heaven and Ocean[6],

Angels of rain and lightning:[7] there are spread
On the blue surface of thine aery surge,
Like the bright hair uplifted from the head

Of some fierce Maenad[8], even from the dim verge
Of the horizon to the zenith's height,
The locks of the approaching storm.[9] Thou Dirge

Of the dying year[10], to which this closing night
Will be the dome of a vast sepulcher,
Vaulted with all thy congregated might

Of vapours, from whose solid atmosphere[11]
Black rain and fire and hail will burst: O hear!

3

Thou who didst waken from his summer dreams
The blue Mediterranean, where he lay[12],
Lulled by the coil[13] of his crystalline streams,

Beside a pumice isle[14] in Baise's bay[15],
And saw in sleep old palaces and towers
Quivering within the wave's intenser day[16],

All overgrown with azure moss and flowers
So sweet, the sense faints picturing them![17] Thou
For whose path the Atlantic's level powers[18]

Cleave themselves into chasms, while far below
The sea-blooms and the oozy woods which wear
The sapless foliage of the ocean, know

Thy voice, and suddenly grow grey with fear,
And tremble and despoil themselves:[19] O hear!

4

If I were a dead leaf thou mightest bear;
If I were a swift cloud to fly with thee;
A wave to pant beneath thy power, and share

The impulse of thy strength, only less free
Than thou, O Uncontrollable! If even
I were as in my boyhood, and could be

The comrade of thy wanderings over Heaven,
As then, when to outstrip thy skiey speed[20]
Scarce seemed a vision; I would ne'er have striven

As thus with thee in prayer in my sore need[21].
Oh! Lift me as a wave, a leaf, a cloud!
I fall upon the thorns of life! I bleed!

A heavy weight of hours has chained and bowed
One too like thee:[22] tameless, and swift, and proud.

5

Make me thy lyre, even as the forest is:
What if my leaves are falling like its own!
The tumult of thy mighty harmonies

Will take from both a deep, autumnal tone[23],
Sweet though in sadness. Be thou, Spirit fierce,
My spirit! Be thou me, impetuous one!

Drive my dead thoughts over the universe
Like withered leaves to quicken a new birth!
And, by the incantation of this verse,

Scatter, as from an un-extinguished hearth
Ashes and sparks, my words among mankind!
Be through my lips to unawakened Earth

The trumpet of a prophecy! O Wind,
If Winter comes, can Spring be far behind?

Notes

1. The ode is lyric poem of some length, dealing with a lofty them in a dignifies manner and originally intended to be sung. The English odes are generally of three types: (1) the

Pindaric ode, following the pattern originated by the ancient Greek Poet Pindar, (2) the Cowleyan ode, named after Abratian ode, named after the ancient Roman poet Horace. *Shelley's Ode to the West Wind* is of the Horatian type, i. e. , with stanzas of uniform length and arrangement. Here we find a variant of the original Italian pattern: five 14-lined stanzas of iambic pentameter, each of the stanzas containing four tercets and a closing couplet. The rime scheme is aba, bcb, cdc, ded, ee.

2. chariotest—"est" is here added to the verb stem "chariot" to indicate the second person singular, after the subject "thou".
3. thine azure sister of the Spring—referring here to the east wind (as "sister" to the west wind).
4. Destroyer and Preserver—The west wind is considered the "Destroyer", for driving the last signs of life from the trees; it is considered the "Preserver", for scattering the seeds which will come to life in the spring.
5. shook—"Shook" used for "shaken" is an archaism.
6. the tangled boughs of Heaven and Ocean—The line between the sky and stormy sea is indistinguishable, the whole space from the horizon to the zenith being covered with trailing storm cloud.
7. Angels of rain and lighting—The "angels" refer here to the "clouds", the messengers of rain and lightning.
8. Maenad—a very frenzied woman in Greek mythology, a priestess of Bacchus, the God of wine.
9. The locks of the approaching storm—referring here to the "clouds".
10. Thou dirge/of the dying year—referring to the west wind.
11. from whose solid atmosphere—"whose" here refers to "vapours".
12. where he lay—"He" here refers to the Mediterranean.
13. coil—referring here to the noise of the tide.
14. Pumice Isle—the name of an isle near Naples, Italy, which is formed by deposits of lava (熔岩)from Vesuvius, a volcano nearby.
15. Baiae's bay—a favorite resort of the ancient Romans on the coast of Campanis, at the western end of the Bay of Naples.
16. intenser day—The translucency(半透明) of the water is more intense than the dazzling daylight above its surface. "Day" here refers to "daylight".
17. So sweet, the sense faints picturing them—so sweet that one feels faint in describing them.
18. the Atlantics' level powers—the waves of the Atlantic Ocean moving on its flat surface.
19. The sea-blooms and the oozy woods which wear / The sapless foliage of the ocean, know /Thy voice, and suddenly grow gray with fear, / And tremble and despoil themselves—The plants at the bottom of the ocean, the rivers and the lakes also fall under the influence of the west wind which announces the change of the season.

20. thy skiey speed—thy airy and ethereal speed("skiey", poetical, variant of "skyey", meaning: of the sky, ethereal).
21. As thus with thee in prayer in my sore need—praying to you, in my great need, in this way (the two lines below are the poet's prayer to the west wind).
22. One too like thee—referring to Shelley himself.
23. The tumult of thy mighty harmonies / Will take from both a deep, autumnal tone—The tumult of thy mighty harmonies will take a deep autumnal tone from both my depressed feeling and the falling leaves.

For Study and Discussion

1. What are the three dominant images in the first three parts of the poem? How does the effect of the wind on each of these elements in nature bear out Shelly's characterization of the wind as "destroyer and preserver"?
2. The speaker's relation to the wind develops in a dramatic way during the course of the poem, particularly in stanzas 4 and 5. What is the speaker's attitude toward himself and his relation to the wind at the end of stanza 4? How does this change in stanza 5?
3. Line 54 has often been criticized by modern critics as showing too much self-pity. Do you agree with this criticism, or do you think that the feeling of the line is justified by the violent descriptions that precede it? Explain.

Chapter 6 John Keats

John Keats (1795—1821) died when he was only twenty-six, an age at which Wordsworth had still not begun to write the poems for which he is known today. The brevity and intensity of Keats's career are unmatched in English poetry. He achieved so much at such a young age that readers have always marvelled at his potential had he lived to reach artistic maturity.

Keats came from very humble origins. His father, the keeper of a livery stable, was killed in a fall from a horse when Keats was eight. His mother died of tuberculosis when he was fourteen. Keats had been fortunate enough as a boy to attend an excellent private school near London, where his young teacher introduced him to poetry, music, and the theater. But soon after his mother died, his guardian, a hardheaded businessman, took Keats out of school and made him an apprentice to a surgeon and apothecary. In 1815 Keats continued his study of medicine formally at Guy's Hospital in London. He was qualified the next year to practice as an apothecary, but it was at this time that he decided, much to his guardian's displeasure, to devote his life to poetry.

Keats had become friends in London with Leigh Hunt, a well-known literary critic and political radical, who encouraged Keats to become a writer. Hunt also introduced him to other leading literary figures of the day, among whom were Hazlitt, Lamb, and Shelley. Hunt and the circle provided Keats with a friendly and encouraging audience. But Keats had his difficulties at first. Some of his early poems lacked the control and originality of expression that characterize his best verse. A long mythological poem entitled *Endymion*, published in 1818, was severely attacked by the reviewers, and at least some of their criticisms were justified. Keats himself realized that *Endymion* had its faults, that in writing it he was learning and experimenting— "fitting myself for verses fit to live", as he says in the preface. He was already at work on an even more ambitious project, an epic inspired by Milton's *Paradise Lost*, which he was to call *Hyperion*. Keats was driven by an increasingly independent sense of his own artistic potential, and by a burning ambition to measure himself against the greatest English poets: Spenser, Shakespeare, Milton, and Wordsworth.

The year 1818 was harsh for Keats. He was able to take the negative reviews of *Endymion* in his stride, but personal problems began to weigh heavily on him. As the eldest of four children, Keats felt a special responsibility and closeness to his two brothers and his sister. When his brother George, who had immigrated to America, ran into financial difficulties, Keats worked hard to earn extra money to help him. His younger brother Tom contracted tuberculosis, and Keats cared for him constantly, running the risk, of contracting the disease himself. In the autumn of 1818, Keats fell desperately in love with Fanny Brawne, a pretty, lively girl to whom he soon became engaged. But by this time Keats's own poor health, poverty, and relentless devotion to poetry made an immediate marriage impossible. The year came to a dismal end with Tom's death in December.

In January 1819 Keats took a much-needed vacation from London and spent a few days with some very good friends near the southern coast of England. As a relief from his taxing work on *Hyperion*, Keats set about writing a less ambitious, more romantic poem based on the legend of Saint Agnes' Eve (which falls on January 20). The result was one of Keats's greatest poems, *The Eve of St. Agnes*, which marks the beginning of one of the most extraordinarily productive periods in all of English literature. In less than nine months, from January to September, Keats produced an astonishing sequence of masterpieces: *La Belle Dame Sans Merci*, six great odes, a long poem *Lamia*, and a group of magnificent sonnets. During the last few months of 1819 Keats went back to *Hyperion*, this time with a new vision of what his most ambitious understanding could become.

But Keats's career was to be cut tragically short just as he was beginning to realize his full potential. The first clear signs of the tuberculoses he had always feared became apparent in February 1820. He weakened rapidly during the spring and summer. His close friend, the painter Joseph Severn, persuaded him to spend the fall and winter in Italy. But Keats had given up all hope of recovery. He died in Rome on February 23, 1821.

Of Keats's longer poems the more important ones are *Lamia*, *The Eve of St. Agens* and *Isabella*. All these poems deal with the theme of love and the cost of the true lovers in the society of tyranny and oppression. *Lamia* is based upon a Greek legend and the heroine is an enchantress who turns from a serpent into a beautiful woman and who loves and is loved by a young man named Lycius. Their love is discovered on their wedding day by a sage named Appollonius. As a result, the enchantress is turned once again into a serpent and vanishes and the couple is cruelly separated. Beauty was killed. Reason overcame passion. *The Eve of St. Agnes*, with a medieval background, tells a story which is similiar to Shakespeare's *Romeo and Juliet*. The ending is much better than that of *Romeo And Juliet* and *Liangshanbo and Zhuyingtai*. The story in *Isabella* was taken from *Decameron* by Giovanni Boccaccio, a great Italian writer in the period of Renaissance. In the poem, Isabella loves Lorenzo, a young man of a lower social rank than that of Isabella's family. In order to separate Isabella from Lorenzo, Isabella's brothers murder Lorenzo. Isabella loves Lorenzo so much that she digs up his head from under the earth and buries it in a flowerpot, but her cruel brothers take the pot away and Isabella dies of a broken heart. Through the descriptions of the devoted lovers fighting for the realization of their love against their enemies and oppressors, John Keats showed his great sympathy for the unfortunate lovers and his deep hatred of the brutal oppressors.

Among Keats's shorter poems, the most important pieces are his immortal odes, including mainly *To Autumn*, *Ode On Melancholy*, *Ode to a Nightingale* and *Ode on a Grecian Urn*. The last two odes have generally been considered jointly as the height of Keats' poetic achievement. In the two odes full of rich poetic imagery, enchanting lyricism and nearly perfect turns of phrase, Keats shows his immense admiration for lasting beauty in the world of art as well as his intense personal yearning for freedom from human miseries. *Ode to a Nightingale* is generally known to have been written after the poet had an actual experience of listening to the nightingale singing one day. The poem consists of eight stanzas and each stanza has ten lines. In the poem, Keats tells what happens in his mind while he is listening to the song of a nightingale. In the first stanza the poet shows himself in a state of uncomfortable drowsiness under the magic of the nightingale's song. Envying the happiness of the bird, Keats longs for a draught of wine, which takes him out of himself, and allow him to join his existence with that of the bird, and by the power of wine and imagination he could leave the world in which life is full of pain and misery, sorrow and despair, and the world in which the young die and the old suffer. Here the poet shows his deep understanding of the miseries of the lower people in his society and great sympathy for the poor and unfortunate people. And here one can see clearly the poet's inner contradiction between the ugly social reality all round him and his vain attempt to leave it or forget it and through his contrasting the joys of the "immortal bird" with the "hungry generations"are fully highlighted. By saying the word "Forlorn", the poet ends the poem with and acute sense of pain.

Keats learned the art of poetry, mainly from the poets of the English Renaissance, such as Spenser and Shakespeare, from Milton and from Dante, a great Italian poet. He even said that whenever he had difficulty writing his poems, he stopped to read Shakespeare for inspiration. The artistic aim in his poetry was always to create a beautiful world of imagination as opposed to the sordid reality of his day. He sought to express beauty in all of his poems. His leading principle is: " Beauty is truth, truth beauty". He is a voice through which beauty expresses itself. He is part of the nature which he describes. He expresses the delight which comes not only through the eye and the ear but also through the senses of touch, taste and smell. His poetry is distinguished by sensuousness and the perfection of form. So Keats has always been known as a sensuous poet. His ability to appeal to the senses through language is virtually unrivaled.

Some of his poems touch upon the burning political problems of his day. He showed his dissatisfaction with the capitalist society and described the sufferings of the poor people.

On First Looking into Chapman's Homer[1]

Much have I travell'd in the realms of gold,
  And many goodly states and kingdoms seen;
  Round many western islands have I been
Which bards in fealty to Apollo hold.
Oft of one wide expanse had I been told
  That deep-brow'd Homer ruled as his demesne[2];
  Yet did I never breathe its pure serene[3]
Till I heard Chapman speak out loud and bold:
Then felt I like some watcher of the skies
  When a new planet swims into his ken;
Or like stout Cortez when with eagle eyes
  He star'd at the Pacifi—cand all his men
Look'd at each other with a wild surmise—
  Silent, upon a peak in Darien.

Notes

1. Keats's former schoolteacher, Charles Cowden Clarke, introduced him to Homer in the robust translation of the Elizabethan poet George Chapman. They read through the night, and Keats walked home at dawn; this sonnet, his first great poem, reached Clarke by the ten o'clock mail that same morning. That it was Ballboa, not Cortez, who

caught his first sight of the Pacific from the heights of Darien, in Panama, matters to history but not to poetry.

2. demesne—realm, feudal possession.
3. pure serene—clear expanse of air.

For Study and Discussion

1. How does the metaphor of travel is used in this poem?
2. What is the main scheme of the poem?

On the Grasshopper and Cricket

The poetry of earth is never dead:
    When all the birds are faint with the hot sun,
    And hide in cooling trees, a voice[1] will run
From hedge to hedge about the new—mown mead;[2]
    That is the Grasshopper's—he takes the lead
    In summer luxury[3],—he has never done
With his delights;[4] for when tired out with fun
He rests at ease beneath some pleasant weed.
The poetry of earth is ceasing never:
    On a lone winter evening, when the frost
    Has wrought a silence, from the stove there shrills
The Cricket's song, in warmth increasing ever[5],
    And seems to one in drowsiness half lost[6],
    The Grasshopper's among some grassy hills.[7]

Notes

1. a voice—In fact the grasshopper doesn't produce a "voice" in the strict sense of the word. It refers to the sound produced by the vibrations of its wings. The same is true with the cricket.
2. mead— (poetical) meadow, "Dead"(in the first line) and "mead" don't really rhyme with each other. They are only "eye rhymes" or spelling rhymes.
3. he takes the lead in summer luxury—he (or, his music) plays the leading role in the many pleasures that summer has to offer.
4. he has never done with his delights—he has never finished with his delights; his delights never come to an end.
5. in warmth increasing ever—in ever increasing warmth; in warmth that is increasing all the time.

6. to one in drowsiness half-lost—to one half-lost in drowsiness; to one who is half-asleep.
7. And seems... the Grasshopper's...—And (the Cricket's song) seems to be the Grasshopper's song...

For Study and Discussion

1. What is the theme of the poem?
2. Why of all creatures are the grasshopper and the cricket singled out to represent the poetry of earth?

To Autumn[1]

1[2]

Season of mists and mellow fruitfulness,
Close bosom-friend of the maturing[3] sun;
Conspiring with him how to load and bless
With fruit the vines that round the thatch-eves[4] run;
To bend with apples the moss'd cottage-trees,
And fill all fruit with ripeness to the core;
To swell the gourd, and plump the hazel shells
With a sweet kernel; to set budding more,
And still more, later flowers for the bees,
Until they think warm days will never cease,
For Summer has o'er-brimm'd their clammy cells.

2

Who hath not seen thee oft amid thy store?
Sometimes whoever seeks abroad[5] may find
Thee sitting careless[6] on a granary floor,
Thy hair soft-lifted by the winnowing wind;
Or on a half-reap'd furrow sound asleep,
Drows'd with the fume of poppies[7], while thy hook[8]
Spares the next swath and all its twined flowers:
And sometimes like a gleaner thou dost keep
Steady thy laden head[9] across a brook;
Or by a cyder-press[10], with patient look,
Thou watchest the last oozings hours by hours.

3

Where are the songs of Spring? Ay[11], where are they?
Think not of them, thou hast thy music too,—
While barred[12] clouds bloom the soft-dying day,

And touch the stubble-plains with rosy hue;
Then in a wailful choir the small gnats mourn
Among the river sallows, borne aloft
Or sinking as the light wind lives or dies;
And full-grown lambs loud bleat from hilly bourn;[13]
Hedge-crickets sing; and now with treble soft
The red-breast whistles from a garden-croft;
And gathering swallows twitter in the skies.

Notes

1. Two days after this serene and gracious ode was composed, Keats wrote to a friend: " I never liked stubble fields so much as now—Aye, better than the chilly green of the spring. Somehow a stubble plain looks warm in the same way that some pictures look warm—this struck me so much in my Sunday's walk that I composed upon it. "
2. The first stanza has only one sentence. Syntactically it is a sentence with a subject but without a predicate.
3. the maturing sun—the sun which matures fruit and crops.
4. thatch-eves—thatch-eaves.
5. whoever seeks abroad—anyone who goes to the open fields. Note that "seek" is here used in its old sense of "resort to", and "abroad" in its old sense of "out of doors".
6. careless—here, carefree.
7. poppies—which are often seen in wheat fields in England.
8. hook—scythe.
9. the laden head—your head which is laden with gleaning.
10. cyder-press—cider-press.
11. Ay—Yes.
12. barred—having bands of different colors.
13. bourn—domain.

For Study and Discussion

1. The poem consists of three stanzas. What specific aspect of autumn is described in each of them?
2. What stylistic devices are used in this poem?
3. Write an appreciation of the poem.

Part Six
The Nineteenth Century (Ⅱ)

Chapter 1 General View of the English Poetry

Political background. Queen Victorian came to the throne in 1837 and died in 1901. Victorian Age usually refers to the time between 1832 when the First Reform Bill was passed and 1901 when the Queen Victorian died. In this period, England became a typical capitalist country. Its policy of colonial expansion brought England to its highest point of the development as a world power. London had become the center of western civilization. England had controlled most of the markets in the whole world. But at the same time, England was witnessing a sharpening of contradictions, both at home and abroad. The Reform Bill in 1832 did not in the least improve the living conditions of the working class. The great misery of the workers led to an upsurge of labour Movements. In 1836 arose the working class movement known as the Chartist Movement. After 1840, the movement took on a more socialistic and revolutionary character. Demonstrations occurred in industrial centers. On several occasions the general strike was measurably effective. As trade improved and economic conditions became more settled, the movement languished and died. The significance of the Chartist Movement is that for the first time in England the people were class-conscious in their opposition to the bourgeoisie. It was the vanguard of the radical working-class movement.

This period was an age of invention in medicine and natural science. In communication and transportation came the greatest advance in material progress: the building of railroads, communication by telephone, telegraph, and the wire-less, the beginning of the automobile and of transportation by air. Industry was revolutionized by the application of machinery, steam, and electricity. The art of photography was perfected. Despite all aspects of scientific progress, however, very little was accomplished in abolishing the sordid industrial slavery of men, women, and children.

Victorian Poetry (also called Post-romantic Poetry) Victorian literature was written mainly for the people, and reflected the pressing social problems and philosophies of a complex era. The age was prevailingly one of social restraints and taboos, reminiscent in this respect of the Puritan period. The writers, whether poets or novelists or essayists, are didactic and purposeful in writing. In the Victorian Age the dominant literary form was the novel. But in poetry of this period we also find some important figures, such as Alfred Tennyson and Robert Browning. The connection between poetry in the Romantic and Victorian ages is close. Victorian poets derive from their Romantic predecessors. Tennyson is a follower of Shelley, and Arnold is a follower of Wordsworth. Most Victorian writers, both in poems and in essays, dealt with the same religious issues that had been a central concern for Wordsworth, Blake, and Shelley. That is why some literary critics call them post-romantics. So, the energy of Romantic poetry persists, but it is channeled into a strict concern for disciplined forms. It is significant that the most influential poet in the Victorian age was Keats, the most form-conscious of the Romantics. The Victorian poets endeavored to search for appropriate modes. All of them seem driven to experiment in a variety of ways. In versification, although making considerable use of traditional forms, such as the sonnet, most of them preferred new or unusual metrical patterns, as did Swinburne, Gerard Manley Hopkins, and later, Thomas Hardy. In line with their metrical experiments were their experiments in the art of narrative poetry. During an age which witnessed the emergence of the novel as one of the dominant forms of literature, the poets sought new ways of telling stories in verse, as Tennyson's *Maud* or Browning's *The Ring and the Book* will illustrate. Some of them, such as George Meredith, Morris, and Emily Bronte, novelists as well as poets, were especially aware that poetry can offer unusual resource for the writers of narratives, as demonstrated by Morris's early poems or Meredith's *Modern Love*. One of the significant experiments in poetic forms was the dramatic monologue, which was used a lot in Tennyson's and Robert Browning's poems, and actually became Browning's favorite form.

The Victorian writers had an eager and earnest response to the expanding horizons of 19th century English social life. They dealt with some frequently recurring subjects, including a preoccupation with man's relationship to God, and also an acute awareness of time, past, present, and future. One topic that links their writings together is love, for love, despite the reputed strain of puritanism in the age, is as prominent in Victorian poetry as it had been in the time of John Donne and his followers. The Victorian poets explored the timeless equilibrium of lovers pictured by D. G. Rossetti, or the poignant experience of isolation by Matthew Arnold and Christian Rosssetti or the hostility of partners of a shattered marriage in Meredith's *Modern Love*. All these aspects, and more, are present in the poetry of Robert Browning and his comprehensive exploration of such relationships linking him to his contemporaries.

Aestheticism and Pre-Raphaelites. Aestheticism is a term given to a movement in art and poetry of the late 19th century. The origins of this movement are to be found in the work of several German writers of the Romantic period—notably Kant, Schelling, Goethe and Schiller. They all agreed that art must be autonomous and that the artist should not be beholden to anyone. The artist was someone special, different from others. The major implication of the new aesthetics standpoint was that art had no reference to life, and therefore had nothing to do with morality. In the later Victorian period, Swinburne proposed the art for art's sake theory. Walter Peter advocated the view that life itself should be treated in the spirit of art. Their ideas had a deep influence on the poets of the 1890s. Aestheticism seems to have been a kind of reaction against the materialism and capitalism of the later Victorian period, and also against the Philistines who embodied what has been described as the "bourgeois ethos." Aestheticism in poetry is closely identified with the Pre-Raphaelites and shows a tendency towards withdrawal or aversion. Many poets of the period strove for beautiful musical effects in their verses rather than sense. They aspired to sensuousness and to what has become known as "pure poetry". They also revived archaistic modes and archaic language and revived an extensive use of classical mythology as a framework for expressing ideas. Medievalism and the interest in chivalry and romance became important parts of the aesthetic cult. William Morris, D. G. Rossetti and Swiburne are the major writers in this group.

Chartist Poetry. During the Chartist Movement the Chartist writers introduced a new theme into literature, that is, the struggle of the proletariate for their rights. They reflected the working class's living conditions and strove to arouse the workers'class consciousness. They inherited the best traditions of English humanist and democratic literature and highlighted an irreconcilable struggle between the proletariat and the ruling classes. They expressed their firm faith in the ultimate victory of the laboring people. Chartist poetry played an important part during the movement. It was heroic and revolutionary in spirit. The major Chartist poets are Ernest Jones and Thomas Cooper. Thomas Hood should also be mentioned, although he is usually not included into the Chartist poets. Hood described realistically the laboring people's miseries and expressed his deep sympathy for the poor. His *Song of the Shirt* has become one of the famous poems.

Chapter 2 Elizabeth Barrett Browning

The Victorian Age produced a number of women poets. Elizabeth Barrett (1806—1861) is one of them. Before she met Robert Browning and married him in 1846, she was better-known than he was. During their courtship she wrote a series of forty-four sonnets celebrating their love. When she showed the poems to Browning after their marriage, he immediately insisted that they be published. Because of their private nature, they were given the deliberately misleading title of *Sonnets from the*

Portuguese as if Elizabeth had translated the poems from that language. Browning thought them "the finest sonnets in any language since Shakespeare". The judgment is understandably exaggerated, but the best of the sonnets do possess a fervent and arresting eloquence that may remind us of the Elizabethans.

One Word More is addressed by Browning to her and is a kind of counter-tribute to her most perfect work, the *Sonnets from the Portuguese*, which contains the record of their courtship and marriage. Her early life was shadowed by illness and affliction. And her early poetry (*The Seraphim*, 1838, *Poems*, 1844) shows in many places the defects of unreality and of overwrought emotion natural to work produced in the loneliness of a sick-chamber. The best known of these early poems are perhaps *Lady Geraldine's Courtship*, where she works under the influence of Tennyson's idylls, and *The Cry of the Children*, where she voices the humanitarian protest against the practice of employing childlabour in mines and factories. After her marriage and removal to Italy her health improved: she could stand up and even gave birth to some children. Her art also greatly strengthened. She was deeply interested in the struggle of Italy to shake off her bondage from Austria, as is shown by her *Casa Guidi Windows*, published in 1851. In 1857 appeared her most ambitious work, *Aurora Leigh*, a kind of versified novel of modern English life, with a social reformer and humanitarian, of aristocratic lineage, as hero, and a young poetess, in large part a reflection of Mrs. Browning's own personality, as heroine. *Aurora Leigh* shows the influence of a great novel-writing age, when the novel was becoming more and more imbued with social purpose. It attempts unsuccessfully to perform in verse the social function which Dickens, George Eliot, Kingsley, and others, strove to perform in prose. The interest in public questions also appears in Mrs. Browning's *Poems before Congress* (1860), and in her *Last Poems*(1862).

Mrs. Browning's technique is uncertain, and she never freed herself from her characteristic faults of vagueness and unrestraint. But her sympathy for noble causes, the elevation and ardor of her moods of personal emotion, and the distinction of her utterance at its best, tempt the readers to overlook her technical limitations. She shares her husband's strenuousness and optimism, but she speaks always from the feminine vantage-ground. Her characteristic note is that of intimate, personal feeling; even *Casa Guidi Windows* has been aptly called "a woman's love making with a nation."

Sonnets from the Portuguese

21

Say over again, and yet once over again,
That thou dost love me. Though the word repeated
Should seem "a cuckoo song", as thou dost treat it,
Remember, never to the hill or plain,
Valley and wood, without her cuckoo strain
Comes the fresh Spring in all her green completed.

Beloved, I, amid the darkness greeted
By a doubtful spirit voice, in that doubt's pain
Cry, "Speak once more—thou lovest!"Who can fear
Too many stars, though each in heaven shall roll,
Too many flowers, though each shall crown the year?
Say thou dost love me, love me, love me—toll
The silver iterance! —only minding, Dear,
To love me also in silence with thy soul.

For study and Discussion

1. What do you think of the sonnets of Elizabeth Barrett Browning?
2. Study the poetess's handiay of traditional sonnet from. Does she follow the Shakespearean Pattern?

Chapter 3 Alfred Tennyson

For more than fifty years, Alfread Tennyson (1809—1892) was recognized among his contemporaries as the greatest poet of the Victorian England. He was made poet laureate in 1850 when Wordsworth died. Victorian readers looked to him for poetic pronouncements on the major issues affecting their lives. Yet Tennyson's status as a public poet is only part of his identity. As a man he was intensely private and introspective, and some of his greatest work as an artist depends upon the creation of very personal and subjective moods or states of mind. In the largest sense it is this division in Tennyson between his public and private selves, between social and purely artistic commitments, that makes him such a prominant figure for the Victorian Age.

He was born in the village of Somersby, in Lincolnshire, and was the fourth of twelve children. His father, the Reverend George Tennyson, was an intelligent and cultivated but very unhappy man given to periods of severe depression. He educated his children himself in classical and modern languages, but he also disturbed and terrified them with his emotional instability. Thus Tennyson grew up as a sensitive and well-read but often melancholy boy. He enjoyed the companionship of his brothers and sisters, but he also spent long periods of time by himself, roaming the Lincolnshire countryside both day and night. He began writing poetry before he was ten, and in 1827, when he was eighteen, he and his brother Charles published anonymously *Poems by Two Brothers*. More than half of the poems in this volume are by Tennyson himself, and they are strongly influenced by Byron and Scott.

Also in 1827 Tennyson went to study at Cambridge University, and the poems he had published drew him to the attention of a small group of brilliant undergraduates who called themselves the "Apostles". These friends encouraged Tennyson to devote his life to poetry, and their intellectual and artistic interests played a significant role in shaping his early career. Tennyson found his closest friend among this group—Arthur Henry Hallam, a highly gifted and charming young writer who Tennyson later said was "as near perfection as a mortal man could be". Hallam's urbanity and charm offset Tennyson's own shyness and awkwardness. In 1830 the two friends traveled together in Europe, and Hallam became engaged to Tennyson's sister Emily. In the same year Tennyson published *Poems, Chiefly Lyrical*, the first volume of verse to appear under his own name. Though not a success, it was a clear reflection of his development as a poet during the years at Cambridge.

In 1831 Tennyson had to leave Cambridge without a degree because of financial difficulties and family dissension. He published another volume of poems in 1832, but this collection, like that of 1830, was not well received by the reviewers. Already discouraged and uncertain of his future, Tennyson was absolutely shattered in 1833 by the news that his friend Hallam had died suddenly in Vienna. The immediate effect of his grief and of the other setbacks he had suffered was a period in Tennyson's life sometimes referred to as the 'ten years' silence. He published nothing during this time, and most of his friends thought he would never write again. But Tennyson spent these years privately revising his published poems and working on new and more ambitious projects. It was during these years, as he later told his son, that "in silence, obscurity, and solitude he perfected his art."

Tennyson returned to public notice in 1842 with the publication of *Poems*, in two volumes. This collection firmly established his reputation and initiated the fifty-year period in which he was the major figure in Victorian poetry. In 1850 he published *In Memoriam*, a sequence of elegiac and meditative poems to commemorate the experience of Hallam's death. In that same year he was made poet laureate, and he married Emily Sellwood, with whom he had first fallen in love in 1836. In 1883 he was made a peer of the realm and was thus accorded the title of Lord. He died in 1892, with a reputation among all classes of readers that grew until it eventually exceeded Byron's in the early years of the twentieth century.

In his appearance and behavior as well as in his writing, Tennyson fulfilled the Victorian idea of what a poets should be. As a huge man with a great mane and shaggy beard, he was often dressed in a picturesque fashion, and he read his poems in public with a resounding voice and with the rough manners of a man from the countryside. He earned considerable money from his poetry—as much as £10,000 a year—and was able to buy a house on the Isle of Wight, where he lived quietly, as he preferred. He also became the personal friend of Queen Victoria and often read to her privately at Buckingham Palace. His most ambitious project, *Idylls of the King*, is a series of poetic narratives based on the legend of *King Arthur and the Round Table* (an "idyll" is a poetic picture or description). Addressed to Prince Albert, *Idylls of King* uses a medieval context to assess the values and achievements of Victorian England.

Tennyson's poetic output was vast and extremely varied. He wrote lyrics, dramatic monologues, plays, long poetic narratives, elegies, and poems commemorating specific occasions. But three characteristics distinguish all his best verse, from the beginning to the end of his long career. First, there is Tennyson's total mastery of the sounds and rhythms of the English language. The twentieth-century poet W. H. Auden said that Tennyson had "the finest ear, perhaps, of any English poet." Second, Tennyson has a genius for evoking moods and states of mind in his poems. Particularly characteristic is his ability to create a sense of nostalgia, a wistful longing for the past or for remote experiences. And no English poet surpasses Tennyson in linking descriptions of nature or setting a state of mind. The opening of *Mariana*, for example, takes the readers inside the mental world of the title figure without saying a word directly about what she thinks or feels:

With blackest moss the flower-plots
Were thickly crusted, one and all;
The rusted nails fell from the knots
That held the pear to the gable wall.
The broken sheds looked sad and strange:
Unlifted was the clinking latch;
Weeded and worn the ancient thatch
Upon the lonely moated grange.

Third, and in partial contrast to the mainly artistic skills just mentioned, there is Tennyson's engagement with the main political, religious, and scientific issues of his day. Tennyson is not a philosophical or intellectual poet, but his mind brooded honestly and responsively on the problems of Victorian industrialism and material progress, on war and colonial expansion, and on the threats to Christian belief posed by Darwinian theory and other biological and geological discoveries:

Are God and Nature then at strife,
That Nature lends such evil dreams?
So careful of the type she seems
So careless of the single life...
(in Memoriam 55, line 5-8)

Tennyson's willingness to express his worries about such large public issues in his poems shows the importance of his work for Victorian readers and the readers of today.

Break, Break, Break

Break, break, break,
    On thy cold gray stones, O Sea!
And I would[1] that my tongue could utter
    The thoughts that arise in me.
O, well for the fisherman's boy,
    That he shouts with his sister at play!
O, well for the sailor lad,
    That he sings in his boat on the bay!

And the stately ships go on
    To their haven under the hill;
But O for the touch of a vanished hand[2],
    And the sound of a voice that is still![3]

Break, break, break
    At the foot of thy crags, O Sea!
But the tender grace of a day that is dead
    Will never come back to me.

Notes

1. I would—I wish.
2. a vanished hand—referring to the hand of the poet's dead friend Arthur Hallam.
3. a voice that is still—referring to the voice of the poet's dead friend Arthur Hallam

For Study and Discussion

1. What feelings arise in the speaker as he looks out at the sea breaking endlessly against the shore?
2. How does the speaker's mental state compare to that of "the fisherman's boy"(Line 5) and "the sailor lad"(Line 7)?
3. How does the setting intensify the speaker's mood?

The Eagle: A Fragment

He clasps the crag with crooked hands;
Close to the sun in lonely lands,
Ringed with the azure world, he stands.

The wrinkled sea beneath him crawls:
He watches from his mountain walls,
And like a thunderbolt he falls.

For Study and Discussion

1. What qualities of natural power and grandeur does the eagle possess in Tennyson's poem?
2. What is the importance of eagle's situation and of the speaker's perspective on him?
3. What element of contrast or tension can you find between the two stanzas of the poem? Pay attention to Line 3 which ends with the words "he stands", and Line 6 which ends with the words "he falls."
4. What rhetorical device is used strikingly in the first two lines?

Chapter 4 Robert Browning

Robert Browning(1812—1889) is thought today as the most important Victorian poet after Tennyson. During much of his own career, however, he was better appreciated by readers of a younger generation than by his immediate contemporaries.

Browning was an adventurous and experimental poet, and his verse seemed to open new possibilities to younger Victorians who felt that Tennyson had done all that could be done with traditional subjects and forms. Toward the end of his career, Browning came to be revered by a wide range of readers, many of who insisted on making him the voice of wise and reassuring optimism. Browning Societies sprang up in England and America to study the "message" of his writing. But as Browning himself seems to have realized, the meaning of his best poetry was more evasive and complicated than these organized admirers were prepared to allow.

Browning was born in Camberwell, then a comfortable, attractive suburb only three miles from central London. His father, an official of the Bank of England, was a well-read and cultivated man. Browning attended a boarding school, but was also tutored at home in ancient and modern languages, in music, and in horsemanship. He read extensively in his father's excellent library, and he spent hours looking at the Italian Renaissance Paintings in the Dulwich Art Gallery, only half an hour's walk from his house. Browning's mother, to whom he was particularly close, was a gentle, loving woman with strong religious convictions. Browning spent most of his early life in this comfortable, cultivated family environment. It was not until he was married, at age of thirty-four, that he established his own life independent of his parents.

Browning began writing poetry at a very early age. He was barely five years old when he wrote his first poem and hid it under a sofa cushion. His first book of poetry, a highly personal and confessional work entitled *Pauline* appeared when he was twenty-one, and shows the influence of Byron and especially of Shelley, his idol among the Romantic poets *Pauline* was sharply and accurately criticized by the philosopher John Stuart Mill for its "intense and morbid self-consciousness. "In his next two volumes of verse Browning moved away from the subjective immaturity of *Pauline* toward a more objective and analytical approach to experience. For ten years, between 1837 and 1847, Browning devoted himself to writing for the theater. Although he was not successful as a playwright, he discovered during these years that his real ability as a writer lay in adapting the techniques of dramatic writing to poetry. His development is reflected in a remarkable series of poetic pamphlets called *Bells and Pomegranates*, written between 1841 and 1846. Included in these pamphlets is *Pippa Passes*, the most interesting of his early poetic dramas. In 1845, Browning met Elizabeth Barrett who was six years older and much better known than he was. The story of the love and courtship of Browning and Elizabeth Barrett is well known through the letters they exchanged and through Elizabeth's own love sonnets. After sixteen months of frustrated courtship, Browning finally decided that Elizabeths' father would never allow her to marry and that she had to be "rescued "for the sake of her own health and happiness. They were secretly married in the autumn of 1846, and eloped to Italy, where they lived until her death in 1861.

The Brownings seem to have been almost ideally happy in Italy. Browning himself had always been interested in Italian art and history. He delighted in studying the great paintings in Florence, where they lived for most of the time, and in championing the cause of Italian independence. His literary imagination flourished as never before. It was while living in Italy that he published his honest volume of poems, *Men and Women*(1885). This collection reflects Browning's intense interest in the Italian Renaissance, and it displays his complete mastery of the poetic form through which he was to achieve his greatest success, the dramatic monologue. Browning himself described his "poetry always dramatic in principle" as "so many utterances of so many imaginary persons, not mine". This formulation is central to Browning's dramatic monologues, in which imagined speaker rather than Browning himself often based on famous figures from history or art but sometimes entirely Browning's own invention—utter their thoughts to implied listeners. In the process these speakers reveal to us, as readers, aspects of themselves and their feelings of which they are unaware. Browning's models in writing this kind of poem were the soliloquies in Shakespeare's plays and the poems of John Donne. Previous writers of the nineteenth century, Byron and Tennyson, for example, had adopted this form, but it was Browning who explored its possibilities to the full. When Elizabeth Barrett Browning died in 1861, Browning returned to London and began working on *Dramatis Personae* (1864), another collection of the dramatic monologues. He also wrote *The Ring and the Book*(1868—1869), his longest and most ambitious work, on which the principle of the dramatic monologues extended to project a single murder story from ten different points of view. Browning's fame as a poet gradually spreaded beyond the small group of young intellectuals who had admired his earlier work. He enjoyed the life of a literary celebrity, dining out so often at the homes and clubs of friends and admirers that Tennyson sarcastically predicated that Browning would die in his dinner jacket. He spoke out vigorously on most of the main issues of the day, and this helped to make him set up the image as a man of victorian Age. But Browning remained curiously reluctant to comment on the meaning of his own poems, preferring to express himself indirectly through the personages he created in them. Some people have felt that the image of the socially confident literary celebrity Browning adopted in his later years was itself a kind of mask, behind which Browning's true character remains mysterious. In any case, Browning had the satisfaction of enormous public fame during the last part of his career, even if this fame was not always based on an open and accurate understanding of his work. He died at the age of seventy-two, and was buried in Westminster Abbey.

Two aspects of Browning's poetry are particularly significant for understanding his influence on twentieth-century poetry and his appeal to readers today. First, there is Browning's interest in psychology, in the conscious and unconscious workings of the human mind. In his concern with the devious thinking and complex motives of the characters in his dramatic monologues, Browning is closer to later Victorian novelists such as George Eliot and George Meredith than to the poets of his own generation. But Browning goes beyond these novelists in his extraordinary openness to evil, obsessive, and abnormal states of mind. He once commented that "all morbidness of the soul is worth the soul's study". Browning also differs from his contemporaries in the degree of objectivity with which he presents the personalities of the speakers in his dramatic monologues. Browning does not pass judgment on these speakers for us. Instead, he involves the readers fully in the desires and energies, both good and bad, of his speakers, and then leaves us to get our own moral bearings and to sit in judgment on what we have experienced.

Second, Browning's importance derives from his stylistic experimentation. Following the example of Donne and his own desire to break with the traditional decorum of most English poetry, Browning makes deliberate use of rough colloquial diction and word order, of surprising and even grotesque rhymes, and of harsh rhythms and metrical patterns. Browning's general purpose in exploring these uses of language was to bring his poetry more closely in touch with the irregular, unpredictable, and often distorted movements of the minds of his speakers. More conservative readers have sometimes found Browning's style unpleasing in its deliberate awkwardnesses and lack of musicality. But for writers and readers interested in expanding the expressive resources of English poetry, Browning opened up new possibilities and helped prepare the way for some of the best poetry of our own era.

My Last Duchess[1]

That's my last Duchess painted on the wall,
Looking as if she were alive. I call
That piece of a wonder, now: Fra Pandolf's hands[2]
Worked susily a day, and there she stands.
Will't please you sit and look at her? I said
"Fra Pandolf" by design[3], for never read
Strangers like you that pictured countenance[4],
The depth and passion of its earnest glance,
But to myself they turned (since none puts by
The curtain I have drawn for you, but I)[5]
And seemed as they would ask me, if they durst
How such a glance came there;[6] so, not the first
Are you to turn and ask thus. Sir, 'twas not
Her husband's presence only, called that spot
Of joy into the Duchess' cheek:[7] perhaps
Fra Pandolf chanced to say "Her mantle laps
Over my lady's wrist too much,"[8] or "Paint
Must never hope to reproduce the faint
Half-flush that dies along her throat":[9] such stuff
Was courtesy,[10] she thought, and cause enough
For calling up that spot of joy. She had
A heart—how shall I say? —too soon made glad,
Too easily impressed; she liked whate'er
She looked on, and her looks went everywhere.
Sir, 'twas all one![11] My favour at her breast[12],
The dropping of the daylight in the West,
The bough of cherries some officious fool[13]
Broke in the orchard for her, the white mule
She rode with round the terrace—all and each
Would draw from her alike the approving speech,
Or blush, at least. She thanked men—good; but thanked
Somehow—I know not how—as if she ranked
My gift of a nine-hundred-years-old name
With anybody's gift.[14] Who'd stoop to blame
This sort of trifling?[15] Even had you skill
In speech—(which I have not)—to make your will
Quite clear to such a one, and say, "Just this

Or that in you disgusts me; here you miss,
Or there exceed the mark"[16]—and if she let
Herself be lessoned so, nor plainly set
Her wits to yours[17], forsooth[18], and made excuse,
—E'en then would be some stooping;[19] and I choose
Never to stoop. Oh, sir, she smiled, no doubt,
Whene'er I passed her; but who passed without
Much the same smile? This grew; I gave commands;
Then all smiles stopped together.[20] There she stands
As if alive.[21] Will 't please you rise? We'll meet
The company below,[22] then. I repeat,
The Count your Master's known munificence
Is ample warrant that no just pretence
Of mine for dowry will be disallowed[23];
Though his fair daughter's self, as I avowed
At starting,[24] is my object. Nay, we'll go
Together down, sir![25] Notice Neptune, though,
  Taming a sea horse, thought a rarity,
Which Claus of Innsbruck cast in bronze for me![26]

Notes

1. This is one of the best known of Browning's dramatic monologues. The dramatic monologue written by Browning contains simply a speech by some imaginary person on one particular occasion in his life. The speaker in this poem is apparently a certain duke of Ferrare, a northern Italian city near Venice. This feudal ruler who had ruthlessly put to death his first wife (referred to here by him as "my last duchess") is negotiating with an envoy from a certain count for the hand of the count's daughter, and in this monologue the duke is trying to tell the envoy very frankly about his "last duchess" whose portrait they had been looking at in the course of the interview. Here the heartlessness and barbaric cruelty of a despotic ruler of early Renaissance Italy is very vividly pictured, though the poet's censure on the highly refined tyrant seems to be lost in the ample humour throughout the poem. *My Last Duchess* is written in heroic couplets, but most of the lines being "run—on" lines and the riming syllables often getting little or no stress, the metrical effect of the poem almost resembles that of blank verse.
2. Fra Pandolf's hands—Fra Pandolf is obviously an invented name for the friar who painted the portrait of the duchess on the wall. ("Fra" is an Italian word meaning "Brother". A friar in Italy is generally addressed as "Fra" and many painters in medieval and Renaissance Italy were friars).
3. by design—on purpose.
4. that pictured countenance—that face in the picture (or painting).
5. (since none puts by/The curtain I have drawn for you, but I)—This parenthetical

remark by the duke indicates that the latter has drawn the curtain in order to show to his guest the portrait of his"last duchess" behind it.

6. How such a glance came there—How did it happen that there was such a look on the duchess' face in that portrait?
7. called that spot/Of joy into the Duchess's cheek—caused that happy smile(or blush)/to appear on the face of the duchess ("that spot of joy"=that mark which indicates joy).
8. Her mantle laps/over my Lady's wrist too much—Her cloak covers up too much of my lady's wrist. This is an imagined flirtatious remark made by the painter to the duchess, apparently suggesting to her to show more of her wrist as she sits for her portrait.
9. the faint/Half-flush that dies along her throat—the indistinct halfredness on her face that spreads down to her throat(this redness is apparently caused by her blushing).
10. such stuff/ Was courtesy—such nonsensical talk was a compliment paid to her.
11. 't was all one! —it was all the same (i. e. , all the things enumerated below produced the same effect on her).
12. My favour at her breast—a present given by me and worn by her at her breast.
13. some officious fool—some obliging person("fool"is used here sarcastically to refer to some silly person who may be in love with the duchess or may simply try to please her by giving her a bunch of flowers).
14. she ranked/My gift of a nine-hundred-year-old name/With anybody's gift—She considers the title of the Duchess of Ferrara (which I gave her by marrying her)as no better than a simple gift given to her by some one of no importance ("nine-hundred-year-old name"refers to the Duke's family being an ancient family with a long history of 900 years).
15. Who'd stoop to blame/This sort o trifling? —who would lower oneself to find fault with this kind of frivolous behaviour?
16. here you miss, /Or there exceed the mark—In this respect you don't do enough (to please me) and in that respect you go too far.
17. if she let/Herself be lessoned so, nor plainly set/Her wits to yours—if she let herself be admonished in this way, and do not argue with you.
18. forsooth(archaic)—indeed (used here ironically).
19. E'en then would be some stooping—Even in that case it would mean that I should be lowering my dignity;even in that case l should lose my full dignity.
20. This grew; I gave commands;/Then all smiles stopped together—As the duchess began to show more affection to everybody, I ordered that she should be put to death and she died. ("This grew"=this developed and became more serious;"then all smiles stopped together" is a neat but subtle and cold—blooded way of saying, "she died"or "I killed her").
21. There she stands/As if alive—Here the duke is referring to the portrait of his"last duchess"on the wall.
22. We'll meet/The company below—We shall meet the others downstairs. (The speaker of the poem, the duke, is negotiating with the envoy of the count for a second wife.

After showing the picture of his last duchess on the wall upstairs, the duke and the envoy go downstairs to meet the others who are already gathered there).

23. no just pretence/Of mine for dowry will be disallowed—i. e., the count will not refuse to allow his fair claim for a dowry for the count's daughter(if he were to marry her). ("pretence"=claim; "disallow"=refuse to allow).
24. at starting—at the beginning(of four interview).
25. Nay, we'll go/Together down, sir—Here the duke politely suggests that he and the envoy walk downstairs together abreast of each other, obviously after the latter has insisted on the duke's precedence.
26. Notice Neptune, though,/Taming a sea-horse, thought a rarity,/Which Claus of Innsbruck cast in bronze for me—Here the duke is pointing to a bronze statue of Neptune taming a sea-horse(a statue made by a famous sculptor from Innsbruck and considered a rare and precious work of art), as he and the envoy are going down to join the company below. Naptune is the god of the sea, hom Greek mythology. Claus is an imaginary sculptor, who comes from Innsbruck, the capital of Tyrol in Austria. These lines show that the duke is a connoisseur of art, but, at the same time, is a despotic husband, cruel and callous.

For Study and Discussion

1. What passages in the Duke's monologue suggest that he is an intelligent, cultivated Renaissance nobleman? What passages suggest that he is egotistical, tyrannical, and ruthless?
2. According to the Duke, what was his last duchess like? What does he mean when he says, "She had/A heart...too soon made glad" (Lines 21-22)?
3. The critical point in the Duke's monologue comes in Lines 45-46: "This grew; I gave commands;/Then all smiles stopped together." What seems to have been the duchess' fate? Why do you think Browning suggests this fate so indirectly and ambiguously?
4. Although *My Last Duchess* is written in iambic pentameter couplets, we hardly notice this regular form because the language of the Duke's monologue is so colloquial and natural. What examples can you find in the poem where Browning's writing gives the impression of actual speech?
5. At the end of *My Last Duchess*, the Duke asks the envoy to notice another work of art, a bronze sculpture showing "Neptune.../Taming a sea horse..." (Lines 54-55) What does this work of art suggest about the theme of the poem as whole?

Home-Thoughts, from Abroad[1]

1

Oh, to be in England
Now that April's there,

And whoever wakes in England
Sees, some morning, unaware,
That the lowest boughs and the brushwood sheaf
Round the elm-tree bole[2] are in tiny leaf,
While the chaffinch[3] sings on the orchard bough
In England—now!

2

And after April, when May follows,
And the whitethroat[4] builds, and all the swallows!
Hark, where my blossomed peartree in the hedge
Leans to the field and scatters on the clover
Blossoms and dewdrops—at the bent spray's edge—
That's the wise thrush;[5] he sings each song twice over,
Lest you should think he never could recapture
The first fine careless rapture!
And though the fields look rough with hoary [6]dew,
All will be gay when noontide wakes anew
The buttercups, the little children's dower
—Far brighter than this gaudy melonflower[7]!

Notes

1. The poem contains 20 lines of different lengths with irregular rhymes.
2. bole—trunk of a tree.
3. chaffinch—a small song bird.
4. white-throat-a bird having a white spot around the throat.
5. thrush—a song bird.
6. hoary—grey or white.
7. The last two lines mean that the gaudy melon flower, symbolic of the rankness of a thern spring, is dull in comparison with the gay buttercups that little children love.

For Study and Discussion

1. It is often the case that we do not appreciate the beauty of places with which we are very familiar until we are away from them. Does this seem to be true of the speaker in "Home Thoughts, from Abroad"? What is the significance of the word unaware in Line 4?
2. What is the meaning of the final contrast in the poem between the bright "buttercups" and "this gaudy melon flower" (L. 19-20)?

Chapter 5 Matthew Arnold

Readers have long debated whether Matthew Arnold (1822—1888) is more important as a poet than as a critic. Certainly his achievement in both literary forms is impressive. In his poetry, Arnold confronts more directly than either Tennyson or Browning the central Victorian problem of remaining human in the dehumanizing atmosphere of a modern industrial society. In his critical essays, Arnold tries to answer the questions about modern life that he poses but leaves for the most part unanswered in his poems.

Arnold's father, Dr. Thomas Arnold, was an important religious and educational reformer who became headmaster of the Rugby School, one of the most prestigious private schools in England. Arnold was deeply influenced by his father's ideas, but he also showed a certain rebellious defiance of his father's rigorous principles. When Arnold left Rugby to attend Oxford University in 1841, he assumed the style of an aristocratic wit and dandy famous for his elegant, colorful clothes and flippant manner. He did not work particularly hard at Oxford, and only by desperate last-minute cramming did he manage a respectable performance on his final examinations. But underneath the casual manner that Arnold cultivated as a young man was a wide-ranging intellect and a sensitive, brooding imagination. Even before he abandoned his youthful dandyism, Arnold was beginning to write poems that would surprise his closest friends and family with their meditative intensity and power of symbolic suggestion.

In 1851 Arnold became a government inspector of schools, a position he held for over thirty years. The job was a demanding one and left him with less free time for his own writing than other major Victorian writers had. Yet Arnold wrote continually throughout these years. Arnold's career as a writer may be divided roughly into four phases. Most of his poems appeared during the 1850's: a volume entitled *The Strayed Reveller and Other Poems*, published in 1849, was followed by additional volumes in 1852 and 1853. During the 1860's the focus of his writing shifted from poetry to literary and social criticism. In 1865 the first series of his *Essays in Criticism* was published, and in 1869, *Culture and Anarchy*, a fierce attack on middle-class materialism and narrow-mindedness, considered by many to be his finest work. In the 1870s Arnold devoted himself mainly to writing about education and religion. Finally, in the 1880s he returned to literary criticism and wrote the second series of his *Essays in Criticism*, published soon after his death in 1888.

One of the most fascinating questions presented by Arnlod's career is why he virtually gave up writing poetry after 1860. Some have suggested that he was discouraged by the cool public reception of his poems; others have thought that he felt he had exhausted his sources of poetic inspiration. The main reason, however, seems to be that Arnold was uneasy about the kind of poetry he was producing. Many of his best poems convey a melancholy, pessimistic sense of the dilemmas of modern life, without offering any secure source of hope, joy, and permanent value. Arnold described the limitations of this kind of poetry in criticizing one of his own major poems in the preface to his collection of 1853: "... the suffering finds no vent in action;... a continuous state of mental distress is prolonged, unrelieved by incident, hope, or resistance;... there is everything to be endured, nothing to be done." "it was-not enough," Arnold felt, "for poetry to express the pain and difficulty of life-it must also inspirit and rejoice the reader." But if, in being true to his own poetic instincts, Arnold could not provide readers with sufficient spirit and joy, he could still help them find permanent values in other writers—in the Greeks, in Dante, in Shakespeare, and in the best writers of his own century. Arnold's literary criticism became in part a quest for those qualities that he found lacking or imperfectly realized in his own poems.

Whatever Arnold's sense of his own poetic shortcomings may have been, today his poetry seems distinctively expressive of mid-Victorian anxiety precisely because it avoids offering optimistic answers to the doubtful questions it raises. From the more balanced and objective perspective of his later years, Arnold himself came to feel confident that he had after all spoken responsibly to and for his era. Writing to his mother in 1869, Arnold observed: "My poems represent, on the whole, the main movement of mind of the last quarter of a century, and thus they will probably have their day as people become conscious to themselves of what that movement of mind is, and interested in the literary productions which reflect it. It might be fairly urged that I have less poetic sentiment than Tennyson, and less intellectual vigor and abundance than Browning; yet because I have perhaps more of a fusion of the two than either of them, and have more regularly applied that fusion to the main line of modern development, I am likely enough to have my turn, as they have had theirs." Arnold has indeed had his turn in our own century, as readers have responded to the haunting sense of loneliness and isolation in his poems, and to the beauty of his verse.

Chapter 6 Dante Gabriel Rossetti

Dante Gabriel Rossetti (1828—1882), the son of an Italian patriot who had been forced to emigrate to England, was a painter and poet who, when he was just twenty years old, helped found the Pre-Raphaelite Brotherhood. The painters and writers who joined Rossetti in this group wished to revitalize English art by returning to the simple designs and pure colors that prevailed in Italian painting before the time of Raphael, the great Renaissance master. Rossetti himself was particularly obsessed with an imaginary ideal of feminine beauty, an ideal inspired both by Dante and other early Italian poets and by Keats. In 1850 Rossetti found what he thought was a living embodiment of that ideal in Elizabeth Siddall, the favorite model of the Pre-Raphaelite painters. Much of Rossetti's poetry was inspired by his love for her. But their relationship was a troubled one, and in 1862, two years after they were married, Elizabeth committed suicide. Rossetti was stricken with grief and guilt, and in a romantic gesture he buried the manuscripts of his poems with her. Several years later he had second thoughts. The manuscripts were dug up, and in 1870 Rossetti published them as a series of sonnets called *The House of Life*. Rossetti's poetic exploration of the relation of the spirit to the body in human love was violently attacked as immoral in a pamphlet entitled *The Fleshly School of Poetry*. The attack contributed to the mental instability that plagued Rossetti for the rest of his life.

In composing poetry, Rossetti paid great attention to beauty of diction, beauty of rhythm and beauty of imagery. It has been well said that he remained a poet in his painting and a painter in his poetry. But his whole life was passed in a world of imagination. In spite of the fact that he was the son of an Italian patriot, he had no political enthusiasm which for many poets often kindles the highest poetic exuberance.

The Sonnet

(from *The House of Life*)

A Sonnet is a moment's monument
        Me morial from the Soul's eternity
        To one dead deathless hour. Look that it be,
Whether for lustral[1] rite or dire portent,
Of its own arduous fullness reverent;

Carve it in ivory or in ebony,
As Day or Night may rule; and let Time see
Its flowering crest impearled and orient.

Sonnet is a coin; its face reveals
The soul—its converse, to What Power 'tis due—
Whether for tribute to the august appeals
Of life, or dower in Love's high retinue,
It serve; or, 'mid the dark wharf's cavernous breath,
In Charon's[2] palm it pay the toll to Death.

Notes

1. lustral—purification.
2. Charon—the ferryman who, for a fee, rowed the souls of the dead across the river Styz.

For Study and Discussion

1. What is the theme of the poem?
2. How do you understand "the soul's eternity" in Line 2?

Part Seven
The Twentieth Century

Chapter 1 General View of the English Poetry

Political background. Toward the end of the 19th century, England had become the leading imperialist power in world affairs. The Boer War (1899—1901) further showed the true nature of the imperialist policy of the English government. The first decade of the 20th century saw the further rise of the working class movement and the agitation of the petty bourgeoisie against the imperialist policy of the English government. Since the World War I the increasing economic power of the United States has lowered the position of Great Britain in world affairs and influenced every phase of English social life. The October Socialist Revolution which happened in Russia in 1917 was a great encouragement to the English workers and the intellectuals who fought against the big bourgeoisie for a better social system. In 1920 the British Communist Party was formed. In the same year Northern Ireland began to have its own parliament and two years later Southern Ireland became the Irish Free State. England was also threatened by the world economic crisis of 1929—1932 . Since World War Ⅱ , Great Britain, weakened to a great extent, has become subordinate to the United States. All the great changes find their echoes in the literature of the 20th century.

The Poetic Revolution and T. S. Eliot. The early 20th century saw a technical revolution in English poetry. The revolution was started by the Imagists. The Imagist movement, influenced by T. E. Hulme's insistence on hard, clear, precise images and encouraged by Ezra Pound when he lived in London just before World War I, fought against romantic fuzziness and facile emotionalism in poetry. The movement developed simultaneously on both sides of the Atlantic, and its early members included Amy Lowell, Richard Aldington, Hilda Doolittle, John Gould Fletcher, and F. S. Flint. Imagists insisted on direct treatment of the thing, whether subjective or objective, on the avoidance of all words that did not contribute to the presentation, and on a freer metrical movement than a strict adherence to the sequence of a metronome could allow. All this encouraged precision in imagery and freedom of rhythmic movement, but more was required for the production of poetry of any real scope and interest. Imagism went in for the short, sharply etched, descriptive lyric, but it had no technique for the production of longer and more complex poems.

Other new ideas about poetry helped to develop this technique. Sir Herbert Grierson's great edition of the poems of John Donne in 1912 both reflected and encouraged a new enthusiasm for the 17th century metaphysical poetry. The revival of interest in metaphysics brought with it a desire on the part of some pioneering poets to introduce into their poetry a much higher degree of intellectual complexity than had been found among the Victorians or the Georgians. The full subtlety of French Symbolist poetry also now came to be appreciated. At the same time a need was felt to bring poetic language and rhythms closer to those of conversation or at least to spice the formalities of poetic utterance with echoes of the colloquial and even the slangy. Irony and wit with the use of puns, helped to achieve that union of thought and passion which T. S. Eliot saw as characteristic of the metaphysicals and wished to bring back into modern poetry. A new critical and a new creative movement in poetry went hand in hand, with Eliot the high priest of both. It was Eliot who extended the scope of imagism by bringing the English metaphysicals and the French symbolists to the rescue, thus adding new criteria of complexity and allusiveness to the criteria of concreteness and precision stressed by the imagists. It was Eliot, too, who introduced into modern English and American poetry the kind of irony achieved by shifting suddenly from the formal to the colloquial or by oblique allusions to objects or ideas that contrasted sharply with those carried by the surface meaning of the poem. Thus between 1911 (the first year of the Georgian poets) and 1922 (the year of the publication of *The Waste Land*) a major revolution occurred in English poetic theory and practice. This revolution determined the way in which most serious poets and critics now think about their art.

The posthumous publication of the poetry of Gerard Manley Hopkins in 1918 encouraged further experimentation in language and rhythms. Hopkins combined absolute precision of the individual image with a complex ordering of images and a new kind of metrical patterning. The young poets of the early 1930's were much influenced by Hopkins as well as by Eliot.

Other Famous Poets in Early 20th Century. Meanwhile the remarkable career of William Butler Yeats, stretching across the whole modern period, showed how a truly great poet can at the same time reflect the varying developments of his age and maintain an unmistakably individual accent. Beginning among the aesthetes of the 1890s, turning later to a more tough and spare ironic language without losing his characteristic verbal magic, working out his own notions of symbolism and bringing them in different ways into his poetry, developing in his full maturity a rich symbolic and metaphysical poetry with its own curiously haunting cadences and its imagery both shockingly realistic and movingly suggestive, Yeats's work is itself a history of English poetry between 1890 and 1939. Yeats is the greatest English-speaking poet of his age.

Another two resounding names in early 20th-century English poetry are Thomas Hardy and A. E. Housman. Both of them, in some aspects, inherited English poetic traditions. Their poetic scene is usually laid in the countryside. Their major concern is often shown to the life of the unhappy farmers. Both Thomas Hardy and Housman had pessimistic vision of human life.

Poetry of World War I. World War I was a destructive war to Europe. It wiped out a whole generation of young men and shattered so many illusions and ideals. It left throughout Europe a sense that the bases of civilization had been destroyed and that all traditional values had been wiped out. Those English poets who were involved on the front during the war, however romantically they may have felt about the war when they first joined up, soon realized its full horror. This realization affected both their imaginations and their poetic techniques. They had to find a way of expressing the terrible truths they had experienced, and even when they did not express them directly the underlying knowledge affected the way they wrote.

The Georgian poetry was in vogue at the time the war broke out. The Georgian poetry appeared in five anthologies edited by Edward Marsh and published between 1912 and 1922 during the reign of George V. The major poets represented were: A. E. Housman, W. H. Davies. Walter de la Mare, John Masefield, Ralph Hodgson, Edward Thomas, James Stephens, J. C. Flecker, Andrew Young, Siegfried Sassoon, Rupert Brooke, Wilfred Owen, Robert Graves, Edmund Bluden and D. H. Lawrence. Their poetry in the five volumes was marked by a quiet traditionalism and represented an attempt to wall in the garden of English poetry against the disruptive forces of modern civilization. Cultured meditations alternated with self-conscious exercises in the exotic. Sometimes the magical note was authentic and sometimes the meditative strain was original and impressive. At the beginning of the war some of them wrote patriotic poems such as Rupert Brooke's *The Solider*. But as the war went on, with more and more people killed and the survivors increasingly disillusioned, the whole world on which the Georgian imagination rested came to appear unreal. They began to expose the cruelty of the war and condemn the war-makers.

Between The Wars: W. H. Auden and His Generation. The postwar disillusion of the 1920's was a spiritual matter, just as Eliot's *The Waste Land* was a spiritual and not a literal waste-land. Depression and unemployment in the early 1930s, followed by the rise of Hitler and the cruel shadow of Fascism and Nazism over Europe, with its threat of another war, represented another sort of waste land which produced another sort of effect on poets and novelists. The impotence of capitalist governments in the face of Hitlerism combined with economic dislocation to turn the majority of young intellectuals in the 1930s to the political left. The 1930's were the Red decade, because only the Left seemed to offer any solution. The major figure in English poetry of this period was W. H. Auden. The early poetry of Auden and his contemporaries cried out for "the death of the old gang" and a clean sweep politically and economically. The Spanish Civil War, which broke out in the summer of 1936, was regarded as a rehearsal for an inevitable World War Ⅱ and thus further emphasized the inadequacy of politicians. Yet though all this is reflected passionately in the literature of the period, particularly in the poetry, it was not accompanied by any interesting developments in technique; many younger writers were more anxious to express their attitudes than to construct new kinds of works of art. The outbreak of World War II in September, 1939, following very shortly on Hitler's pact with Russia, which shocked and disillusioned so many of the young Left wing writers, marked the sudden end of the Red decade; the concern of writers in Britain now was to maintain their integrity and indeed their existence in what was from the beginning expected to be a long and destructive war. This they did surprisingly well, but nevertheless this second war brought inevitable exhaustion: English literature has never quite recovered the vitality and interest in technical experimentation that marked the twenty years after about 1912.

Poetry after Mid-Century. English poetry after mid-century showed a tendency of revivifying inherited artistic forms and the humanist tradition of Western cultural values. A group of poets known as "the Movement" reject the rigidity of the T. S. Eliot formulations and try to carve out a middle course of their own. Perhaps the most significant critical champion of the Movement is the poet, critic, and scholar Donald Davie, whose entitled book *Purity of Diction in English Verse* (1952), sets out to demonstrate the 18th-century virtues of plainness, clarity, economy of metaphor, and urbanity of statement in which the Augustan poets excelled and the romantic poets were often deficient. His second critical work, *Articulate Energy: An Inquiry into the Syntax of English Poetry* (1955) argues for the advantages of retaining prose syntax in poetry. The Movement poets were popular in the fifties, sixties, and seventies. The major figures among them were: Donald Davie, Philip Larkin, Thom Gunn, Kingsley Amis, Elizabeth Jennings and John Wain.

Some later poets, in one direction or another, break out of the chastened humanism of the Movement. New forces kept coming in during the sixties and seventies. English poetry today is more diverse than before. There are various kinds of pop poetry associated with jazz and intended for performance at large gatherings there is also delicate, sophisticated verse in which the meaning is set off and enhanced by reticence. Between these two extremes are a great variety of poets with a great variety of talents. Since the end of the 1950's a new element of both rhetoric and myth has been coming into English poetry. The recent famous poets are: Ted Hughes and Tony Harrison.

Chapter 2 Thomas Hardy

Thomas Hardy (1840—1928) is better known as a novelist than as a poet. Yet he began his literary career by writing poems, and after the hostile public response to his last novel, *Jude the Obscure* (1896), he devoted his final thirty years of life almost exclusively to poetry. The appeal of Hardy's poetry is not as obvious as that of the other major Victorian poets, but his reputation, having declined somewhat after the first quarter of the twentieth century, has grown steadily in recent years. The main concerns of his poetry are essentially those of his fiction—the forces both inside and outside human life that lead, almost inevitably to sorrow, regret, frustration and loss.

Hardy was born near Dorchester, in the center of the area of southwest England which he referred to in his fiction as the ancient name of Wessex. He was trained as an architect. In 1861 he went to London for further study and to practice his profession. He also began writing poems and short stories. In 1868 he submitted his first novel to a publisher. It was rejected, but Hardy was encouraged to try again, and in 1871 a second novel, *Desperate Remedies*, was published. Another novel appeared the following year, and Hardy gave up his profession as an architect to devote full time to his writing. His career as a novelist extended from 1871 to 1896. After that he returned to poetry. His first collection, *Wessex Poems*, was published in 1898. Between 1903 and 1908 appeared *The Dynasts*, a vast epic-drama based upon the Napoleonic Wars. At his death in 1928, he was widely admired. His ashes were buried in Westminster Abbey, but in accordance with his wishes, his heart was removed and buried in the parish churchyard of his native village in Dorsetshire.

Hardy's best poems usually present situations that illustrate his concern with circumstances or forces beyond human control. Hardy is often described as a gloomy pessimist who believed in the impersonal and generally negative power of fate. But it is important to recognize that while the sadness in Hardy's writing is sometimes attributed to causes remote from human will and consciousness, more often it springs from within, from our own insatiable desires, emotions, and illusions. And while the prevailing mood in Hardy's poetry is somber, there is also a very rich and positive feeling for the ancient landscape and cultural roots of rural England, for patterns of life so old that they come to seem archetypal.

In style Hardy's poems create an impression of plainness or ruggedness, in keeping with his rural background and his lack of extensive formal education. But the colloquial directness of his language is very much a matter of conscious selection and craft. Even Hardy's frequent use of archaic words or of homely diction is part of a deliberate reaction against the ornate, elaborate language of some late-Victorian verse. Hardy's poetry may appear to lack sophisticated complexity and glamour, but its surface simplicity is deceptive. Its deep integrity will consistently reward a reader who is free of presumptions about what fine poetry should be.

The Man He Killed

"Had he and I but met
By some old ancient inn,
We should have sat us down to wet
Right many a nipperkin![1]

"But ranged as infantry,
And staring face to face,
I shot at him as he at me,
And killed him in his place.

"I shot him dead because—
Because he was my foe,
Just so: my foe of course he was;
That's clear enough; although

"He thought he'd 'list[2], perhaps,
Off-hand like—just as I—
Was out of work—had sold his traps—
No other reason why.

"Yes; quaint and curious was is!
You shoot a fellow down
You'd treat if met where any bar is,
Or help to half-a-crown."[3]

Notes

1. nipperkin—a small drink.
2. 'list—enlist.
3. help to half-a-crown—lend a coin worth two and a half Shilling.

For Study and Discussion

1. Who is the speaker in this poem? What experience has he just gone through?

2. How does Hardy create the sense in this poem that human life is subject to circumstances and forces beyond our control? Why does the speaker pause and then repeat the word "because"?

A Broken Appointment

You did not come,
And marching Time drew on, and wore me numb.—
Yet less for loss of your dear presence there
Than that I thus found lacking in your make
That high compassion which can overbear
Reluctance for pure loving-kindness' sake
Grieved I, when, as the hope-hour stroked its sum,
You did not come.

You love not me,
And love alone can lend you loyalty;—
I know and knew it. But, unto the store
Of human deeds divine in all but name,
Was it not worth a little hour or more
To add yet this: Once you, a woman, came
To soothe a time-torn man; even though it be
You love not me?

For Study and Discussion

1. How do you appreciate this poem?
2. Discuss the poetic form of the poem.

Chapter 3 Gerard Manley Hopkins

Gerard Manley Hopkins (1844—1889) is in many respects a deeply characteristic Victorian writer. Although not widely read or appreciated until the 20th century—his poems were not published until 1918. He is surely a remarkable experimenter and innovator in the rhythm, vocabulary, and formal arrangements of English verse. As much as any other Victorian poet, including Browning, Hopkins has influenced the direction of modern English and American poetry. Yet in his expressions of intense spiritual anxiety and in his passionate devotion to the unique particularized beauty of the natural world, he is very much a nineteenth-century poet. To read Hopkins well, one must learn to value the Victorian dimension of his writing as well as its advanced, forward-looking modernity.

Hopkins was born into a large and very religious English Family. He was often unhappy while attending the Highgate School in northwest London, but in 1863 he went to study classics at Oxford University, and there his brilliant intellect and imagination began to flower He was a student of Walter Pater, the eloquent late-Victorian spokesman for artistic experience as the only stable source of value in the modern world. And he was influenced by the Oxford Movement, which sought to revive the ritualistic and dogmatic traditions of the Church of England. The original leader of the Oxford Movement, John Henry Newman, had left the church of England in 1845 to become a Roman Catholic. After a period of deep religious turmoil, Hopkins himself, under Newman's sponsorship, joined the Catholic Church in 1866. In 1868 he entered the Society of Jesus, one of the most intellectually demanding and disciplined orders of the Church. Before becoming a Jesuit, Hopkins burned all the poems he had written up to that time, feeling that his artistic interests were incompatible with strict devotion to his religious obligation. He did not begin writing poetry again until 1875 or 1876, and even then he resisted his friend's suggestion that he publish at least some of his poems. In 1877 he became an ordained priest and served in a number of parishes, including one in a depressing working class district of Liverpool. In 1884 he was appointed Professor of Classics at University College, Dublin. Hopkins died in Dublin of typhoid fever in 1889, when he was only forty-four. His poems were finally published in 1918 by his close friend, the poet Robert Bridges.

Chapter 4 A. E. Housman

A. E. Housman's poetic output was small and concentrated, both in the number of poems he published and in the succinctness of his individual lyrics. Yet he was regarded by many of his contemporaries as the finest lyric poet since Tennyson. By profession he was an eminent classical scholar, and as a poet his chief aim was to follow the lyric poets of classical antiquity in conveying emotional intensity and profundity by the simplest and most efficient poetic means possible.

Alfred Edward Housman (1859 — 1936) was born in Worcestershire, a county in western England, near the Shropshire border. He studied classical literature and philosophy at Oxford University, but in 1881 he amazed his teachers and fellow students by failing his honors examination. He had to take a civil service job, but he continued to pursue classical studies independently, and he gradually built up an excellent reputation through his meticulous scholarly contributions to learned periodicals. His classical scholarship as characterized by an impersonal striving for accuracy that shows almost no trace of the poignant feelings often expressed in his poetry. He was a brilliant and bitter controversialist, capable of delivering the most savage attacks on other scholars with whom he disagreed. In 1892 Housman was made professor of Latin at University College, London, and from 1911 until his death in 1936 he held a similar professorship at Cambridge University.

Housman published only two small volumes of poems during his lifetime—*A Shropshire Lad* (1896) and *Last Poems* (1922). Most of the poems have a rural or pastoral setting, and many of them focus on the experiences of the "Shropshire lad", whom Housman himself described as an imaginary figure, with something of "my own temper and view of life".

Housman's favorite subject is the ill-fated "lad" enacting his tragic and brief life against a background of the passing beauties and eternal patterns of the natural world. Housman is as aware as Hardy of the grimness and pain of life, but his awareness takes the form of a more subdued irony and a more poignant melancholy. In contrast to the often harsh, rugged qualities of Hardy's verse, Housman's writing has a smooth, carefully wrought cadence. In 1933 Housman gave a lecture entitled *The Name and Nature of Poetry*, in which he argued that poetry had an almost physical effect on the reader, so intimate that it was impossible to analyze and explain it. For many readers Housman's finest poems create just this sort of direct intimacy.

When I Was One-and-Twenty

When I was one-and-twenty
I heard a wise man say,
Give crowns and pounds and guimeas
But not your heart away;
Give pearls awky and rubies
But keep your fancy free.
But I was one-and-twenty,
No use to talk to me.

When I was one-and-twenty
I heard a wise man say again,
"The heart out of the bosom
Was never given in vain;
'Tis paid with sighs a plenty
And sold for endless rue."
And I am two-and-twenty,
And oh, 'tis true,' tis true.

For Study and Discussion

1. What was the speaker's first reaction to the advice he was given? How does he feel about the advice now that he is a year older? What must have happened to him to make him change his mind?
2. Houseman is often praised for the succinctness with which he expresses emotion in his poems. What evidence can you find in "When I Was One-and-Twenty" to support this view? Look particularly at the last two lines of each stanza.

With Rue My Heart Is Laden

With rue my heart is laden
For golden friends I had,
For many a rose-lipped maiden
And many a lightfoot lad.

By brooks too broad for leaping
The lightfoot boys are laid;
The rose-lip girls are sleeping
In fields where rose fade.

For Study and Discussion

What does Houseman convey the speaker's sadness through the two contrasting images of nature in the last stanza—the " brooks too broad for leaping" and the" fields where roses fade"? How do these natural images relate to the repeated epithets applied to the speaker's friends, " lightfoot" and" rose-lipped" (Lines 3 and 7)".

Chapter 5 William Butler Yeats

William Butler Yeats (1865 — 1939), early in his life, resolved to become a great literary artist, and at the end of his life he was judged by many to be among the greatest poets who had ever lived. The British poet Edwin Muir has defined the source of Yeats' poetry as " a magnificent temperament associated with a magnificent style".

Yeats was an Irishman of Anglo-Norman descent. He spent part of his childhood in Sligo, on the northwest coast of Ireland. There he became acquainted with traditional Irish legends and lore. His father, a painter, moved the family between Dublin and London, where Yeats attended school and spent much time reading, pursuing his interests in Irish legend and Romantic idealism and occult philosophies. Mixed into his thought were the mysticism of Blake, the Romantic idealism of Shelley, and the aesthetic ideas of the Pre-Raphaelites.

By the time he moved to London in 1887, his goals as an artist were fixed. He was particularly interested in making the Irish people conscious of their past and in resurrecting a heroic ideal by which they could live. His first book of poetry, published in 1889, and *The Celtic Twilight*, published in 1893, drew on ancient Irish legend. The beautiful Maud Gonne, whom Yeats met in 1889, drew him into the Irish National movement, about which Yeats had strong doubts. Lady Gregory, who shared his interest in Irish legend, joined with him in founding an Irish National Theater. After returning to Ireland in 1896, Yeats gave less attention to poetry and devoted himself largely to drama and forming the Abbey Theater.

Maud Gonne's marriage to John MacBride, in 1903, marked an important change in Yeats' life. Disappointed in love, he was resolved to make great poetry out of his experience, seeking perfection "of the work" instead of "perfection of the life", as he called it in a late poem. Yeats was working to toughen his poetry and to bring it more into touch with the language and preoccupations of the modern world. He was working to simplify his style, to rid it of Romantic vagueness, and to bring it close to the rhythms of everyday speech. His aim was to write poems "as cold and passionate as the dawn". In his aims and practice, and rejection of late Victorian poetic modes, Yeats gave impetus to the Modernist movement in poetry, which in Ezra Pound, T. S. Eliot, Edith Sitwell and others sought a fresh language, new rhythms, and an extension of poetic subjects.

Throughout his poetic career, Yeats sought to unify his experience of the world and gain for his poems a central illuminating vision comparable to that of Dante and Shelley, one that would pull together the thousand separate fragments of everyday life. He sought that vision in the mysticism of Blake and occult philosophies, drawing these various ideas together in his philosophical and historical book, *A Vision*, published in 1925. He saturated his poetry with these ideas, constructing in various volumes of poetry a composite portrait of a complex modern being. No single poem revealed Yeats' personality completely: each poem provided some insight into a moment of thought or feeling. At the same time, these poems took the pulse of current thought and feeling.

In 1917 Yeats married the English woman Georgie HydeLecs, and his two children were born in 1919 and 1921. He became a senator in the Irish Free State founded in 1921. In 1923, he was awarded the Nobel Prize for literature. By the time of his death in 1939, Yeats had become the leading poet of his age, who had taught "the free man how to praise". W. H. Auden wrote of him in his great elegiac poem, *In Memory of W. B. Yeats* (D. Jan, 1939).

When You Are Old

When you are old and gray and full of sleep,
And nodding by the fire, take down this book,
And slowly read, and dream of the soft look
Your eyes had once, and of their shadows deep;

How many loved your moments of glad grace,
And loved your beauty with love false or true,
But one man loved the pilgrim soul in you,
And loved the sorrows of your changing face;

And bending down beside the glowing bars
Murmur, a little sadly, how Love fled
And paced upon the mountains overhead
And hid his face amid a crowd of stars.

For Study and Discussion

1. What book do you think the speaker is asking the woman to read?
2. What does the phrase "pilgrim soul" tell you about the woman? How does the speaker

contrast his love for her with the love of others?

3. What evidence can you find to show that the speaker's love was not reciprocated and was finally withdrawn?

The Lake Isle of Innisfree[1]

I will arise and go now, and go to Innisfree,
And a small cabin build there, of clay and wattles made:
Nine bean-rows will I have there, a hive for the honeybee,
And live alone in the bee-loud glade[2].

And I shall have some peace there, for peace comes dropping slow,
Dropping from the veils of the morning to where the cricket sings;
There midnight's all a glimmer, and noon a purple glow,
And evening full of the linnet's wings[3].

I will arise and go now, for always night and day
I hear lake water lapping with low sounds by the shore[4];
While I stand on the roadway, or on the pavements gray,
I heard it in the deep heart's core[5].

Notes

1. The poem is one of Yeats' best known lyrics. Written in 1893, it is one of the poet's early work under the influence of the Pre-Raphaelites in late 19th-century England. Tired of the life of his day, Yeats sought to escape into an ideal "fairy land" where he could live calmly as a hermit and enjoy the beauty of nature. In his opinion, the best remedy for the emptiness of his age seemed to lie in a return to the simplicity of the past. The poem is closely-woven, easy, subtle and musical. The poem consists of three quatrains of iambic pentametre, with each stanza rimed abab. Innisfree is an inlet in the lake in Irish legends. Here the author is referring to a place for hermitage.
2. the bee-loud glade—an open place in the wood where bees buzz loudly.
3. full of the linnet's wings—here referring to the fact that lots of linnets(红雀) fly here and there.
4. lapping...by the shore—flowing against the shore.
5. in the deep heart's core—at the bottom of my heart.

For Study and Discussion

1. What is the poet's attitude toward life in this poem?
2. Discuss the images used in this poem.

Chapter 6 Thomas Stearns Eliot

Thomas Stearns Eliot (1888—1965) is the pivotal leader among English writers during the first half of the 20th century. He was not only a great poet, a great critic, a fine playwright, but also he sought to become the conscience of his generation, deliberately fitting himself for this role, which he summed up in a celebrated phrase when he defined his beliefs as "classicist in literature, royalist in politics, and Anglo-Catholic in religion".

When Eliot began to publish verse at the age of twenty-six, his first few readers were generally shocked by what they took to be a dry, over clever, revolutionary use of language and syntax. Fifty years later, when his name was surrounded by an air of majesty unique in his time, that same verse still had a contemporary ring to it. Today he seems to have been a representative of an age in which many people, feeling themselves barren because of their doubt, searched for an experience of faith.

Eliot was born in St. Louis, Missouri. He attended Harvard University, and subsequently the Sorbonne in Paris and Oxford University in England. World War I caught him in England, where he worked for a time in Lloyd's Bank, married, and finally settled for good. In the 1920s he joined the London publishing house that later became Faber and Faber, and in 1927 he became a British subject. In the following years, he avoided publicity and deliberately cultivated a shy aloofness, lightened by an almost youthful sense of humor.

What Eliot achieved was an exact expression for the spiritual disease of the twentieth century.

After the unquenchable optimism of the Victorian Age had burned itself out in World War I, a period of intense questioning began. One by one, what had seemed established certainties were questioned. A society that had appeared both stable and progressive for over a century broke into fragments. Eliot's classic expression of the temper of his age is *The Waste Land*, a poem which, despite its extreme difficulty, brought him immediate fame. *The Hallow Men* published two years after *The Waste land*, is almost as powerful an expression of an age of doubt that longs in despair for belief. In the early 1920's Eliot's attitude toward the world was negative. He watched it carefully and hated what he saw. He cultivated an ironic, detached, corrosive manner in his poetry, and when he wrote prose, it was with the didactic purpose of turning his readers away from what he considered the self-indulgence of the Romantics and toward the sterner splendors of Elizabethan drama and seventeenth-century metaphysical poetry. He wished to discourage the easy acceptance of popular favorites like Milton or Shelley in order to make room for neglected masters like John Donne.

Little by little Eliot's negative attitude toward society changed. Close study of Dante brought him to consider traditional Christianity as the one chance of finding a still center in the midst of chaos. His poem *Ash Wednesday*, written following his confirmation in 1927 in the church of England was a significant step in this direction. But the final expression of a long process of thought took place nine years later when he wrote the first *Four Quartets*. These poems were published in 1943 and conclude his major work as a poet with a new serenity of outlook.

In the latter part of his life, Eliot turned more and more to playwriting and to the writing of essays and books discussing social and religious themes, notably *Notes Toward a Definition of Culture* and *The Aims of Education*. It was his aim to revitalize poetic drama, to write plays that would seem perfectly natural to audiences although the characters were speaking poetry. One of his modern plays, *The Cocktail Party*, had a long run in both London and New York, but his earlier play, *Murder in the Cathedral*, is closest to traditional poetic drama.

As a poet, Eliot is above all an intellectual, one who has put much hard thinking into his verse and who demands an equal amount of thought from the reader. He can encompass poignant feeling when he chooses, but his habitual choice is to establish an exact equation between feeling and thought. Some of his poems are difficult because the links between the ideas have been suppressed. Consequently, the reader must study these poems carefully to piece together into a logical sequence the seemingly isolated statements.

It can be said that Eliot has changed the direction of modern writing more sharply than did any of his contemporaries. He changed it in the direction of precision and complexity, and of wide-ranging reference, so that all of history is brought into his poetry. And he moved it toward deep but highly controlled emotion—emotion, as some of his poems imply, that is much too serious to be stated in consciously "poetic" language. In 1948 he was awarded the Nobel Prize in literature.

One of the earliest poems to earn fame for T. S. Eliot, *The Love Song of J. Alfred Prufrock* was written in 1910 when the poet was still a student at Harvard University. It was finished in 1911 when he was in Munich in Germany. It first appeared in the magazine *Poetry* in Chicago in 1915 and was the titular poem of Eliot's first book of poetry published in England in 1917, *Prufrock And Other Observations*, which was followed by an American edition under the title of poems in 1920. The poem is a sort of dramatic monologue in lines of varying lengths and occasional rimes. It falls under the influence of the French symbolists of late 19th century and of the Imagists of early 20th-century American poetry. Here Eliot was partly following the aim of the Imagists to restore to poetry the precise use of visual images and to avoid all looseness of expression and sentiment, and was partly trying to convey the spontaneity of the ideas and feelings welling up his mind, by resorting to the psychological principle of the association of ideas, and to the use more or less of the "stream-of-consciousness" technique. So in the poem there is no sequence of events, nor passage of time. There are random transitions from certain thoughts and feelings of the speaker of the monologue to certain others, interrupted by descriptive passages of the external elements of the fog, the women in the room, etc.

In spite of its title, the poem is not a love song in the strict sense of the term. It contains references to the speaker Prufrock's love affairs, it is true, but the theme of the poem is a much broader one: "it deals with the thoughts of the central figure Prufrock intermixed with random descriptions of his environment. If one takes into consideration the quotation from Dante's *Inferno* that immediately follows the title of the poem and that prefixes the confession of a speaker in the Italian epic, *The Love Song of J. Alfred Profrock* is actually no other than the confession of Prufrock, a middle-aged man and a romantic aesthete who is bored with his ineffectual life and is faced with despair because he wishes but is unable to break away from his meaningless existence or to find the right answers to "the overwhelming question" always occurring to him. In this sense, the poem is a mild satire on the decadence and futility of life in the upper classes in bourgeois society.

Published in 1922 in *The Criterion* and dedicated to Ezra Pound, T. S. Eliot's poem *The Waste Land* is 433 lines long. *The Waste Land* itself is a desolate and sterile country ruled by an impotent king. The whole poem is divided into five parts: I. "The Burial of the Dead," representing the stirring life in the land after the barren winter; II. "The Game of Chess," contrasting the splendors of the past represented by Cleopatra with uneasiness and despair of modern life; III. "The Fire Sermon," making an imaginative silhouette sketch of the ugliness of cities and the mechanization of modern life and emotion; IV. "Death by Water," presumptively proving by the vision of a drowned Phoenician sailor that water is not only the constructive source of life but also the destructive source of death because of drowning and also its absence as well, which causes drought; and V. "What the Thunder Said," presenting a picture through symbols of the Grail legend, of the drought, the decay and emptiness of modern life.

The theme of the poem is modern spiritual barrenness, the despair and depression that followed World War I, the sterility and turbulence of the modern world, and the decline and break-down of Western culture. The poem's noticeable characteristics are varied length and rhythm to harmonize with the changing subject matter, the unrhymed lines, lots of borrowings from some 35 different writers, the employment of materials such as the legends of the Holly Grail, Frazer's anthropological work *The Golden Bough*, several popular songs, and passages in six foreign languages, including *Sanskrit*. The poem, therefore, is obscure and hard to understand, needless to say its absence of logical continuity. The poem *The Waste Land* by T. S. Eliot, nevertheless, is broadly acknowledged as one of the most recognizable landmarks of Modernism.

The Love Song of J. Alfred Prufrock[1]

S'io credesse che mia risposta fosse
A persona che mai tornasse al mondo,
Questa fiamma staria senza piu scosse.
Ma percioche giammai di questo fondo
Non torno viva alcun, s'iodo il vero,
Senza tema d'infamia ti rispondo[2].

Let us go then, you and I,
When the evening is spread out against the sky
Like a patient etherized[3] upon a table;
Let us go, through certain half-deserted streets,
The muttering retreats
Of restless nights in one-night cheap hotels
And sawdust restaurants with oyster-shells:
Streets that follow like a tedious argument
Of insidious intent[4]
To lead you to an overwhelming question...
Oh, do not ask, "What is it?"
Let us go and make our visit.

In the room the women come and go
Talking of Michelangelo[5].

The yellow fog that rubs its back upon the window-panes,
The yellow smoke that rubs its muzzle on the window-panes,
Licked its tongue into the corners of the evening,
Lingered upon the pools that stand in drains,
Let fall upon its back the soot that falls from chimneys,
Slipped by the terrace, made a sudden leap,
And seeing that it was a soft October night,
Curled once about the house, and fell asleep.

And indeed there will be time[6]
For the yellow smoke that slides along the street,
Rubbing its back upon the window-panes;
There will be time, there will be time
To prepare a face[7] to meet the faces that you meet;
There will be time to murder and create,

And time for all the works and days of hands[8]
That lift and drop a question on your plate;
Time for you and time for me,
And time yet for a hundred indecisions,
And for a hundred visions and revisions,
Before the taking of a toast and tea[9].

In the room the women come and go
Talking of Michelangelo.

And indeed there will be time
To wonder, "Do I dare?" and, "Do I dare?"
Time to turn back and descend the stair,
With a bald spot in the middle of my hair [10]—
(They will say: "How his hair is growing thin!")[11]
My morning coat, my collar mounting firmly to the chin,
My necktie rich and modest, but asserted by a simple pin —
(They will say: "But how his arms and legs are thin!")
Do I dare
Disturb the universe[12]?
In a minute there is time
For decisions and revisions which a minute will reverse.

For I have known them all already, known them all—
Have known the evenings, mornings, afternoons,
I have measured out my life with coffee spoons;
I know the voices dying with a dying fall[13]
Beneath the music from a farther room.
        So how should I presume?

And I have known the eyes already, known them all—
The eyes that fix you in a formulated phrase[14],
And when I am formulated[15], sprawling on a pin,
When I am pinned and wriggling on the wall,
Then how should I begin
To spit out all the butt-ends of my days and ways[16]?
        And how should I presume?

And I have known the arms already, known them all—
Arms that are braceleted and white and bare
(But in the lamplight, downed with light brown hair!)
Is it perfume from a dress
That makes me so digress?

Arms that lie along a table, or wrap about a shawl.
    And should I then presume?
    And how should I begin?

* * * * * * * * * *

Shall I say, I have gone at dusk through narrow streets
And watched the smoke that rises from the pipes
Of lonely men in shirt-sleeves, leaning out of windows?...

I should have been a pair of ragged claws[17]
Scuttling across the floors of silent seas.

* * * * * * * * * *

And the afternoon, the evening, sleeps so peacefully!
Smoothed by long fingers,
Asleep ... tired ... or it malingers[18],
Stretched on the floor, here beside you and me.
Should I, after tea and cakes and ices,
Have the strength to force the moment to its crisis?
But though I have wept and fasted, wept and prayed,
Though I have seen my head (grown slightly bald) brought in upon a platter,
I am no prophet[19]—and here's no great matter;
I have seen the moment of my greatness flicker,
And I have seen the eternal Footman hold my coat, and snicker[20],
And in short, I was afraid.

And would it have been worth it, after all,
After the cups, the marmalade, the tea,
Among the porcelain, among some talk of you and me,
Would it have been worth while,
To have bitten off the matter with a smile[21],
To have squeezed the universe into a ball
To roll it towards some overwhelming question[22],
To say: "I am Lazarus[23], come from the dead,
Come back to tell you all, I shall tell you all" —
If one, settling a pillow by her head
    Should say: "That is not what I meant at all.
    That is not it, at all."

And would it have been worth it, after all,
Would it have been worth while,
After the sunsets and the dooryards and the sprinkled streets,
After the novels, after the teacups, after the skirts that trail along the floor —
And this, and so much more? —

It is impossible to say just what I mean!
But as if a magic lantern threw the nerves in patterns on a screen[24]:
Would it have been worth while
If one, setting a pillow or throwing off a shawl,
And turning toward the window, should say:
 "That is not it at all,
 That is not what I meant, at all."
* * * * * * *
No! I am not Prince Hamlet, nor was meant to be[25];
Am an attendant lord, one that will do
To swell a progress[26], start a scene or two,
Advise the prince; no doubt, an easy tool,
Deferential, glad to be of use,
Politic, cautious, and meticulous;
Full of high sentence[27], but a bit obtuse;
At times, indeed, almost ridiculous—
Almost, at times, the Fool[28].

I grow old ... I grow old...
I shall wear the bottoms of my trousers rolled[29].

Shall I part my hair behind?[30] Do I dare to eat a peach?
I shall wear white flannel trousers, and walk upon the beach.
I have heard the mermaids singing[31], each to each.

I do not think that they will sing to me.

I have seen them riding seaward on the waves
Combing the white hair of the waves blown back
When the wind blows the water white and black.

We have lingered in the chambers of the sea
By sea-girls wreathed with seaweed red and brown
Till human voices wake us, and we drown[32].

Notes

1. Alfred Prufrock—obviously a fictitious name whose confession of his life and love, thoughts and feelings makes up the poem.
2. S'io credesi che mia risposta fosse...senza tema d'infamia ti rispondo—a quotation from Dante's *Inferno*, *Canto* XXXVII. Lines 61-66. The passage may be rendered into English as follows: " If I thought that my answer were being made to someone who would ever return to earth, this flame would remain without further movement; but since no one

has ever returned alive from this depth, if what I hear is true, I answer you without fear of infamy." The speaker of these lines is Guidode Montefeltro who is placed in the eighth circle of hell for giving evil counsel to a pope and, wrapped in a flame, is speaking from its trembling tip. This quotation suggests that the poem that follows is likewise a confession and that the speaker assumes the reader to be in the same hell he himself is in.

3. etherized—anesthetized, with the application of ether on a patient, for a major surgical operation. The simile of an etherized patient conveys the stillness of the evening.
4. Streets that follow like a tedious argument/ Of insidious intent—Note the curious comparison of "streets" to "a tedious argument of insidious intent...".
5. Michelangelo—Buonarroti Michelangelo (1475—1564), a great Italian sculptor, painter and poet of the Renaissance.
6. there will be time—Here and in the subsequent uses of the word "time", the author is making an allusion to a passage in "Ecclesiastes": "To everything there is a season, and a time to every purpose under heaven. A time to be born, a time to die; a time to plant, and a time to pluck that which is planted, a time to kill, and a time to heal,...a time to weep, and a time to laugh, a time to mourn, and a time to dance;...a time to keep silence and a time to speak."
7. to prepare a face—to do one's facial make-up before going to meet friends.
8. all the works and days of hands—Here is an allusion to "Works and Days", the title of a didactic poem concerning rural labour, written by the early Greek poet Hesiod (8th century B. C.)
9. Before the taking of a toast and tea—Here "the taking of a toast and tea" brings the speaker back from his wandering thoughts given above to his trivial realities of life.
10. Time to turn back and descend the stair/With a bald spot in the middle of my hair —Here again the speaker comes down to earth, so to speak.
11. (They will say: "How his hair is growing thin!")—"They" refers to the women the speaker is familiar with; "his" refers to the speaker.
12. Do I dare/Disturb the universe—"Disturb the universe" is obviously an ironical overstatement.
13. a dying fall—See Shakespeare's play Twelfth Night, I, 4: "That strain again! It had a dying fall." There the lovesick Duke is commending the music he hears: here the author uses the expression to refer to affected upper-class speech accents, meaning: a sinking of tone.
14. The eyes that fix you in a formulated phrase—the eyes that reduce you to a formula, the eyes that make an estimate of you with a phrase or a formula.
15. And when I am formulated—when I am estimated with a specific phrase or formula.
16. To spit out all the butt-ends of my days and ways—to utter vehemently all the deeply-embedded thoughts reflecting my life and ways of living.

17. a pair of ragged claws—a crab. Here the poet means that it would be a relief to lead a merely instinctual life (such as that of a crab) that involves no moral decisions and revisions.
18. malingers—pretends to be sick.
19. Though l have seen my head (grown slightly bald) brought in upon a platter/I am no prophet—an allusion taken from the Bible. Salome asked for the head of John the Baptist to be brought in on a platter as a reward for her dance before Herod (See St. Mark, 6, or St. Matthew, 14, in the New Testament). The speaker here suggests that he has visualized himself to be a great man ready for the sacrifice of his life (like John the Baptist), but then he realizes that he is not a prophet, so he needs not be afraid of having to make the sacrifice of a prophet like John the Baptist (see the words following: "and here's no great-matter").
20. I have seen the eternal Footman hold my coat, and snicker—The speaker here visualizes himself in his customary social environment in which a footman (a man-servant who admits visitors and takes their coats) usually takes his coat. "Footman" is capitalized because it is used here as a symbol of death.
21. To have bitten off the matter with a smile—to break off his old way of life and to do or say something of importance ("with a smile" indicates doing or saying the thing in a light, off-handed manner).
22. To have squeezed the universe into a ball/To roll it towards some overwhelming question—See the English poet Andrew Marvell's (1621—1678) *To His Coy Mistress*: "Let us roll all our strength and all/Our Sweetness up into one ball." ("some overwhelming question"= some question of great importance).
23. Lazarus—the sick and poor beggar in Jesus' parable of the rich man and the beggar. (See St. Luke, 16: 19-31, in the New Testament) Lazarus returns from the dead, according to the Bible. Here the speaker refers to himself making a confession, like Guido de Montefeltro in Dant's Inferno.
24. But as if a magic lantern threw the nerves in patterns on a screen—an image equivalent to"telling you all"in the 10th line above.
25. I am not Prince Hamlet, nor was meant to be—Here the speaker suggests that he is not and cannot hope to be a great man.
26. To swell a progress—(跑龙套) A progress was a ceremonial royal journey, here he thinks of himself as an "extra" or an actor of no importance, a minor actor participating in a progress in a play.
27. Full of high sentence—expressing worthy sentiments. (See Chaucer's *The Canterbury Tales*, *the General Prologue*, Line 306.)
28. the Fool—referring to the fool as a character in Elizabethan drama, who is given the permission not only to do the clowning but also to quibble with his superiors.
29. I shall wear the bottoms of my trousers rolled—Presumably here the speaker is

referring to the adoption of the new fashion of trouser cuffs.

30. Shall I part my hair behind—Here the speaker is referring to a daring new hair style. He seems to contemplate a series of faintly daring gestures in defiance of advanced age.
31. I have heard the mermaids singing—See John Donne's poem, *Go and Catch a Falling Star*: "Teach me to hear mermaids singing." "Mermaids singing" is something that is considered to be an impossibility. Here the speaker is visualizing something impossible in his life experience.
32. Till human voices wake us, and we drown—Here the speaker suggests that he is brought back to reality from his wandering thoughts and visions. So he ends his monologue.

For Study and Discussion

1. Is the poem a love song in the strict sense of the term?
2. What is the function of the quotation from Dante's *Inferno* that immediately follows the title of the poem?
3. Do you think the poem is a mild satire?
4. Quote two lines which present the most vivid image.

Chapter 7 Rupert Brooke

Though Rupert Brooke (1887—1915) was early identified with the Georgian poets, much of his verse reflected his interest in John Donne and the early 17th century dramatist John Webster, on whom he wrote a dissertation at Cambridge University. In the years before World War I, Brooke suffered an unhappy love affair that brought him close to mental collapse. He broke with friends and turned back to traditional Victorian attitudes that he had repudiated in his college days. In 1913 he traveled in the United States, Canada, and the Pacific, spending several months in Tahiti, where he wrote some of his most famous poems. Following his enlistment in the navy and brief service in Belgium, he wrote his war sonnets, among them *The Soldier*. Traditional not only in form, these poems were the last of that period to express idealistic patriotism in the face of war. Unlike Siegfried Sassoon and, Wilfred Owen, Brooke did not live to witness the horror of trench warfare, for he died of blood poisoning en route to the Dardanelles with the British Mediterranean Expeditionary Force.

The Soldier

If I should die, think only this of me,
　　That there's some corner of a foreign field
That is forever England. There shall be
　　In that rich earth a richer dust concealed,
A dust whom England bore, shaped, made aware,
　　Gave, once, her flowers to love, her ways to roam,
A body of England's, breathing English air,
　　Washed by the rivers, blest by suns of home.
And think, this heart, all evil shed away,
　　A pulse in the Eternal mind, no less
　　Gives somewhere back the thoughts by England given;
Her sights and sounds; dreams happy as her day;
　　And laughter, learnt of friends; and gentleness,
　　In hearts at peace, under an English heaven.

For Study and Discussion

1. What are the poet's feelings toward England and the cause for which he may die? What traditional English qualities does he stress?
2. Brooke expresses an ideal of happiness, not the acute reality of his life. What statements in the poem show his awareness of the courage and hope needed to achieve that ideal?
3. T. S. Eliot characterized Georgian poetry in these words: "...the Georgian poets insist upon the English countryside, and are even positively patriotic..." To what extent does *The Soldier* fit this characterization?

Chapter 8 Robert Graves

Robert Graves(1895—1985)was enlisted in 1914 and served with Siegfried Sassoon in a regiment of the Royal Welsh Fusiliers. He was wounded and later suffered shell shock. Graves, like Sassoon, refused to glorify war.

In the years following the war, Graves became a prolific poet, experimenting with a wide variety of verse forms, including folksongs, ballads and poems in the metaphysical vein-employing highly subtle and complex metaphors. In *A Survey of Modernist Poetry* in 1927, Graves, along with the co-author Laura Riding, defined what he felt poetry was now to be engaged in: "The ideal modernist poem is its own clearest, fullest, and most accurate meaning... the poem does not give a rendering of a poetical picture or idea existing outside the poem, but... the poem has the character of a creature by itself." "His poems," declared Richard Wilbur, "... have the air of being spontaneous answers to actual experience."

Graves has also written distinguished fiction, much of which retelling historical and mythological stories. His most controversial book, *The White Goddess*, is a study of the poetic imagination, which Graves claims has its origins in ancient fertility.

In successive editions of his poems Graves has ruthlessly pruned away what he has come to dislike or believes to represent a phase of his poetic career that he has outgrown. He has published over 15 volumes of poetry, of which *Collected Poems* (1959) represents most of what he wants to preserve. He has continued to publish slim volumes of new poetry (*New Poems* 1961; *New Poems* 1962), but the 1959 volume well represents the range and quality of his genius. Its publication was the sign for clear critical affirmation, on both sides of the Atlantic, that Graves is a major English poet of our time. He won the Russell Loines Award for Poetry in 1958 and the Gold Medal of the National Poetry Society of America in 1960.

She Tells Her Love While Half Asleep

She tells her love while half asleep
In the dark hours,
With half-words whispered low:
As Earth stirs in her winter sleep
And puts out grass and flowers
Despite the snow,
Despite the falling snow.

For Study and Discussion

1. What is the central metaphor of this poem?
2. How is a poem about new birth?

Chapter 9 Wystan Hugh Auden

Wystan Hugh Auden (1907—1973) was born, raised, and educated in England. His first poems were published in 1928, and early in his career he became a friend of T. S. Eliot, whose ideas on poetry influenced his work. He was also a friend and colleague of Stephen Spender, Louis MacNeice, and C. Day Lewis, who shared with Auden an interest in politics and who saw themselves bringing new techniques and attitudes to the United States. He became an American citizen in 1946 and made his living though teaching and writing poetry. In 1956, once again back in England, he was elected Professor of Poetry at Oxford University, a post he held until 1961.

Auden's early poems were concerned with revealing the evils of his native country and were intended to shock their readers. He often combined deliberate irreverence with verbal craftsmanship to awaken what he saw as the complacent middle class to the hollowness of their society and the need for reform. It was his impatience with the limits imposed by English society that prompted Auden to move to the United States. To some extent, Auden must have felt that Europe was slowly dying and that his residence in a young nation would bring with it new life. Like Eliot, Auden later in his life returned to the formal practice of Christianity, having grown disenchanted with the socialism he had professed in his youth. His later poetry, though often as satirical as the early poems had been, became increasingly filled with religious themes.

Auden wrote three ambitious long poems: *For the Time Being*, a Christmas oratorio in which he explores the modern significance of the Nativity; *The Sea and the Mirror*, a discourse in poetic form on the relationship between life and art, which takes the form of a commentary on Shakespeare's *The Tempest*; *and The Age of Anxiety*, a work that presents four individuals attempting to find a way out of their spiritual dilemmas. Toward the end of his life, Auden's poetry tended to become mellower, reflecting a spirit that was less urgent in its denunciation of evil. His poetry never lost its moral quality. However, nor did it abandon its concern with the troubles of the modern world.

Auden's poetry has been praised for its vitality, variety, and originality. He imposes new and unexpected patterns on a wide range of forms—from archaic ballads to street-corner blues. Perhaps Auden's most important contribution to 20th century poetry is his experimentation in many verse forms and meters, combining an off-hand informality with remarkable technical skills.

Petition

Sir, no man's enemy, forgiving all
But will its negative inversion, be prodigal:
Send to us power and light, a sovereign touch[1]
Curing the intolerable neural itch,
The exhaustion of weaning, the liar's quinsy[2],
And the distortions of ingrown virginity.
Prohibit sharply the rehearsed response
And gradually correct the coward's stance;
Cover in time with beams those in retreat
That, spotted, they turn though the reveres were great;
Publish each healer that in city lives
Or country house at the end of drives;
Harrow the house of the dead; look shining at
New styles of architecture, a change of heart.

Notes

1. The "king's touch" was often regarded as a miraculous cure for disease (cf. "sovereign" as an adjective, meaning "the best").
2. quinsy—Tonsillitis.

For Study and Discussion

1. How do you appreciate this poem?
2. What is the theme of this poem?

Ballad

O what is that sound which so thrills the ear
Down in the valley drumming, drumming?
Only the scarlet soldiers, dear,
The soldiers coming.
O what is that light I see flashing so clear
Over the distance brightly, brightly?
Only the sun on their weapons, dear,
As they step lightly.

O what are they doing with all that gear;
What are they doing this morning, this morning?
Only the usual maneuvers, dear,
Or perhaps a warning.

O why have they left the road down there;
Why are they suddenly wheeling, wheeling?
Perhaps a change in the orders, dear;
Why are you kneeling?

O haven't they stopped for the doctor's care;
Haven't they reined their horses, their horses?
Why, they are none of them wounded, dear.
None of these forces.

O is it the parson they want, with white hair;
Is it the parson, is it, is it?
No, they are passing his gateway, dear,
Without a visit.

O it must be the farmer who lives so near,
It must be the farmer, so cunning, cunning;
They have passed the farm already, dear,
And now they are running.

O where are you going? stay with me here.
Were the vows you swore me deceiving, deceiving?
No, I promised to love you, my dear,
But I must be leaving.

O it's broken the lock and splintered the door,
O it's the gate where they're turning, turning;
Their feet are heavy on the floor,
And their eyes are burning.

For Study and Discussion

1. Auden uses the traditional ballad form to describe the terror of the modern world. What narrative technique is used to increase gradually the poem's mood of terror?
2. Although the speakers are not identified, what can you infer about their relationship?
3. The word "dear" is repeated in every stanza but the last. In what way is the use of this word ironic?
4. What evidence do you find in the poem to suggest that one of the speakers has betrayed the other? Cite specific lines.

Chapter 10 Philip Larkin

Philip Larkin (1922 — 1985) was born in Coventry. He attended Oxford University.

World War II produced a series of poets like Dylan Thomas whose response to the catastrophe was emotionally intense and often highly rhetorical. This group of poets is sometimes referred to as the "New Apocalypse". In contrast to this group is "The Movement"—a group of poets educated at Oxford University and strongly influenced by W. H. Auden. They are concerned with creating a less intense and colloquial experience and the changes in everyday English life. Larkin has proved to be one of the best poets of this group. He began his career as a novelist. His best poems continue the tradition associated with Thomas Hardy. He has the rare gift of clarity and of casually suggesting the importance of the ordinary.

Going

There is an evening coming in
Across the fields, one never seen before,
That lights so lamps.

Silken it seems at a distance, yet
When it is drawn up over the knees and breast
It brings no comfort.

Where has the tree gone, that locked
Earth to the sky? What is under my hands,
That I cannot feel?

What loads my hands down?

For Study and Discussion

1. Evening is presented as a metaphor for oncoming death. What details develop the metaphor?
2. Why does death seem "silken" at a distance? Why does Larkin stress the experience of hands?

Chapter 11 Dylan Thomas

Dylan Thomas (1914—1953) was a Welsh poet, short-story writer, and playwright, renowned for the unique brilliance of his verbal imagery and for his celebration of natural beauty.

He was born in Swansea, Wales, on October 27, 1914. He attended a grammar school and after that he went to London where, in 1934, his first book of poetry, *Eighteen Poems*, was published. At his early age, he revealed unusual power in using poetic diction and imagery. The volume won him immediate critical acclaim. Thematically, these poems and virtually all that followed seem obscure because they contain elements of surrealism and personal fantasy. But the freshness and vitality of Thomas's language draw the reader into the poems and reveal the universality of the experiences with which they are concerned. This introspective tendency is less apparent in *Deaths and Entrances* (1946) and *In Country Sleep* (1951), which are generally regarded as containing his finest writing. Thomas's other works include *Twenty-five Poems* (1936) and *The Map of Love* (1939), containing both poetry and prose. *A Portrait of the Artist as a Young Dog* (1940) is a group of autobiographical sketches, and *Adventures in the Skin Trade* (published posthumously, 1954) contains an unfinished novel and other prose pieces. During World War II (1939—1945) Thomas wrote scripts for documentary motion pictures.

After the war Thomas was a literary commentator for BBC radio. *Under Milk Wood* (published posthumously, 1954), a play for voices, was originally written for radiobroadcast. When Thomas read it for its first public performance in Cambridge, Massachusetts, in 1953, it was still unfinished. The work became his most famous piece, evoking the lives of the inhabitants of Llareggub, a small, Welsh seaside town. Noted for his readings of his own verse, Thomas became legendary in the United States, where he gave many lecture tours and gained a large audience. Nevertheless, his last years were shadowed by an increasingly tragic view of his own tempestuous life. His death in New York City on November 9, 1953, was brought on by alcoholism.

A Process in the Weather of the Heart

A process in the weather of the heart
Turns damp to dry; the golden shot
Storms in the freezing tomb.

A weather in the quarter of the veins
Turns night to day; blood in their suns
Lights up the living worm.
A process in the eye forwarns
The bones of blindness; and the womb
Drives in a death as life leaks out.

A darkness in the weather of the eye
Is half its light; the fathomed sea
Breaks on unangled land.
The seed that makes a forest of the loin
Forks half its fruit; and half drops down,
Slow in a sleeping wind.

A weather in the flesh and bone
Is damp and dry; the quick and dead
Move like two ghosts before the eye.

A process in the weather of the world
Turns ghost to ghost; each mothered child
Sits in their double shade.
A process blows the moon into the sun,
Pulls down the shabby curtains of the skin;
And the heart gives up its dead.

For Study and Discussion

1. What is this poem about?
2. What images strike you most? Why?

Do Not Go Gentle into That Good Night

Do not go gentle into that good night,
Old age should burn and rave at close of day;
Rage, rage against the dying of the light.

Though wise men at their end know dark is right,
Because their words had forked no lightning they
Do not go gentle into that good night.

Good men, the last wave by, crying how bright
Their frail deeds might have danced in a green bay,
Rage, rage against the dying of the light.

Wild men who caught and sang the sun in flight,
And learn, too late, they grieved it on its way,
Do not go gentle into that good night.

Grave men, near death, who see with blinding sight
Blind eyes could blaze like meteors and be gay,
Rage, rage against the dying of the light.

And you, my father, there on the sad height,
Curse, bless me now with your fierce tears, I pray.
Do not go gentle into that good night.
Rage, rage against the dying of the light.

For Study and Discussion

1. What is the rhyme scheme of this poem?
2. Why does the speaker repeat the line "Rage, rage against the dying of the light"?
3. The sentence "Do not go gentle into that good night" was repeated three times. Why? What is a good night?

Chapter 12 Ted Hughes

Ted Hughes (1930—1998) was versatile. He was a poet, dramatist, critic, and short story writer, standing apart from the poets who came to maturity in the 1950s.

He was born in Mytholmroyd, but he grew up in Mexborough, a coal-mining town in Yorkshire. The harsh landscape of the northern England moors had a strong influence on Hughes's poetry. He was educated at Cambridge University. He has made his living mainly as a teacher and writer. He got married to the American poet Sylvia Plath, who committed suicide in London in 1963. In 1957 they moved to the US where Hughes taught English and creative writing at the University of Massachusetts, Amherst. They returned to England in 1959. He received all the major literary awards in Europe, but no Nobel Prize. He also received the Order of Merit. Hughes died of cancer on October 28, 1998.

He has been named a "survivor-poet" by the critic Alvarez because he parallels human beings with lower animals, creatures that will do anything to ensure survival. Hughes stated that poems, like animals, are each one "an assembly of living parts, moved by a single spirit."

In his early works Hughes questioned man's function in the universal scheme. Looking at the dark aspects of nature, he has stressed the ferocious and demonic rather than the idyllic and beautiful. Within the cruelty and violence of nature, Hughes looks for an understanding of human life and its mysterious bonds with nature.

About his preference of poetic form, Hughes stated in *Poetry in the Making* (1970), that there is no ideal form of poetry or writing. He wrote free verse as well as highly structured forms and rhyme schemes. He gradually abandoned traditional forms and stated that the "very sound of metre calls up the ghosts of the past and it is difficult to sing one's own tune against the choir." Although he wrote for young adults a wide variety of finely illustrated poems, plays and prose, he did not soften his themes of life and death with sentimentality.

Hawk Roosting[1]

I sit in the top of the wood, my eyes closed.
Inaction, no falsifying dream
Between my hooked head and hooked feet:
Or in sleep rehearse perfect kills and eat.

The convenience of the high trees!
The air's buoyancy and the sun's ray
Are of advantage to me;
And the earth's face upward for my inspection.

My feet are locked upon the rough bark.
It took the whole of Creation.
To produce my foot, my each feather;
Now I hold Creation in my foot

Or fly up, and revolve it all slowly —
I kill where I please because it is all mine.
There is no sophistry[1] in my body;
My manners are tearing off heads —

The allotment of death
For the one path of my flight is direct
Through the bones of the living.
No arguments assert my right:

The sun is behind me.
Nothing has changed since I began.
My eye has permitted no change.
I am going to keep things like this.

Note

1. sophistry—he use of clever but misleading arguments.

For Study and Discussion

1. Who is the speaker of this poem?
2. The poem is a soliloquy of the hawk. What is it talking about?
3. In the eyes of the hawk, what is the human world like?
4. Why does the hawk say "There is no sophistry in my body"? Where is sophistry?
5. Paraphrase the last stanza. Recite this stanza.

Snowdrop[1]

Now is the globe shrunk tight
Round the mouse's dulled wintering heart
Weasel and crow, as if moulded in brass,
Move through an outer darkness
Not in their right minds,
With the other deaths. She, too, pursues her ends,
Brutal as the stars of this month,
Her pale head heavy as metal.

Note

1. Seriously interested in shamanism, hermeticism, astrology, and the Ouija board, Hughes examined in several of his later animal poems the themes of survival and the mystery and destructiveness of the cosmos.

For Study and Discussion

1. In what way is the theme of death presented?
2. Why is the earth shrunk tight?
3. What does "dulled wintering heart"refer to?
4. Who is "She" in Line 6?
5. Learn the poem by heart.

Chapter 13 Seamus Heaney

Seamus Heaney (1939—) was born in on April 13, 1939 in Mossbawn, about 30 miles northwest of Belfast in Northern Ireland. He was the first-born of the nine children in the family. He was educated at a local primary school and then at Queen's College (1957—1962) in Belfast where he took a position as a lecturer in English in 1963. He held the chair of Professor of Poetry at Oxford from 1989 to 1994. Since 1976, he spends some time each year teaching at Harvard University.

He is a pride of poetry in the world of English, enjoying his popularity incomparable since William Butler Yeats. He won many different kinds of awards. In 1995, he was awarded the Nobel Prize in Literature.

In the development of his career as a poet, he was influenced by numerous poets such as Robert Frost, Ted Hughes, William Wordsworth, Thomas Hardy, Gerard Manley Hopkins and even Dante.

His first book, *Eleven Poems*, was published in 1965 for The Queen's University Festival. In 1966, Faber published a full collection called *Death of a Naturalist*. This collection met with much critical acclaim. In 1965 he met and married Marie Devlin, with whom he had three children.

In 1969, his second volume, *Door into the Dark*, was published and became the Poetry Book Society Choice for the year. In 1970 and 1971 he was a guest lecturer at the University of California at Berkeley. He returned to Northern Ireland in 1971, and in 1972 he resigned his lectureship at Queen's College, moved his family to Glanmore, in County Wicklow, and published *Wintering Out*.

In his early works, such as *Death of a Naturalist* (1966) and *Door into the Dark* (1969), Heaney is a lyrical nature poet, writing with limpid simplicity about the disappearing world of unspoiled rural Ireland. He moved from Belfast to the Irish Republic in 1972, ultimately settling down in Dublin.

Extremely evocative yet clear and direct, balanced between the personal and the topical, Heaney's carefully crafted poetry has been praised for its powerful imagery, meaningful content, musical phrasing, and compelling rhythms.

In 1975 Heaney began teaching at Carysfort College in Dublin. In 1976 he moved his family to Sandymount, in Dublin. He became Department Head at Carysfort. In 1979 he published *Field Work*, and in 1980, *Selected Poems* and *Preoccupations: Selected Prose*. In

1981 he gave up his post at Carysfort to become a visiting professor at Harvard. In 1982 he won the Bennett Award, and Queen's University in Belfast conferred on him an honorary Doctor of Letters degree. He cofounded Field Day Publishing with Brian Friel and others in 1983. *Station Island*, his first collection in five years, was published in 1984. During that year he was elected the Boylston Professor of Rhetoric and Oratory at Harvard, and Open University awarded him an honorary degree. Also in 1984 his mother, Margaret Kathleen, died. *The Haw Lantern*, published in 1987, contains a brilliant sonnet sequence memorializing her. Heaney's father, Patrick, died after this, and Heaney's latest collection, *Seeing Things*, published in 1991, contains many poems for his father.

Heaney also wrote three volumes of criticism.

He is also a skillful translator. His works in this genre including the medieval Irish *Sweeney Astray* (1984), Sophocles's *Philoctetes* (tr. as *The Cure at Troy*, 1990) and *Antigone*(tr. as *The Burial at Thebes*, 2004), the highly acclaimed *Beowulf* (2000), and the libretto of Jan′ ĉ ek's song cycle *Diary of One Who Vanished* (2001).

His work often deals with "the local"—that is, his surroundings and everything inclusive of them. Particularly this means Ireland, and particularly Northern Ireland. Hints of sectarian violence, which began just as his writing career did, can be found in many of his poems, even works that on the surface appear to deal with something else. Despite his many travels much of his work appears to be set in rural Derry, the county of his childhood. Like the troubles themselves, Heaney's work is deeply associated with the lessons of history, sometimes even prehistory. Many of his works concern his own family history and focus on characters in his own family, which can be read as elegies for those family members. He has acknowledged this trend.

Today, he is undoubtedly the most popular poet writing in English . His books sell by the tens of thousands, and hundreds of "Heaneyboppers" attend his readings.

Exposure

It is December in Wicklow:
Alders dripping, birches
Inheriting the last light,
The ash tree cold to look at.

A comet that was lost
Should be visible at sunset,
Those million tons of light
Like a glimmer of haws and rose-hips,

And I sometimes see a falling star.
If I could come on meteorite!
Instead I walk through damp leaves,
Husks, the spent flukes of autumn,

Imagining a hero
On some muddy compound,
His gift like a slingstone
Whirled for the desperate.

How did I end up like this?
I often think of my friends'
Beautiful prismatic counselling
And the anvil brains of some who hate me

As I sit weighing and weighing
My responsible tristia.
For what? For the ear? For the people?
For what is said behind-backs?

Rain comes down through the alders,
Its low conductive voices
Mutter about let-downs and erosions
And yet each drop recalls

The diamond absolutes.
I am neither internee nor informer;
An inner émigré, grown long-haired
And thoughtful; a wood-kerne

Escaped from the massacre,
Taking protective colouring
From bole and bark, feeling
Every wind that blows;

Who, blowing up these sparks
For their meagre heat, have missed
The once-in-a-lifetime portent,
The comet's pulsing rose.

For Study and Discussion

1. What is the setting of this poem?
2. What does the title "Exposure" mean? What is exposed?
3. What rhetorical devices are used in this poem? Pick some out and comment on how they are used in serving the theme.
4. Which image do you like best? Why?

Digging[1]

Between my finger and my thumb
The squat pen rests; as snug as a gun.

Under my window a clean rasping sound
When the spade sink into gravelly ground:
My father, digging. I look down

Till his straining rump among the flowerbeds
Bends low. Comes up twenty years away
Stooping in rhythm through potato drills
Where he was digging.

The coarse boot nestled on the lug, the shaft
Against the inside knee was levered firmly.
He rooted out tall tops, buried the bright edge deep
To scatter new potatoes that we picked
Loving their cool hardness in our hands.

By God, the old man could handle a spade,
Just like his old man.

My grandfather could cut more turf in a day
Than any other man on toner's bog.
Once I carried him milk in a bottle
Corked sloppily with paper. He straightened up
To drink it, then fell to fight away
Nicking and slicing neatly, heaving sods
Over his shoulder, digging down and down
For the good turf. Digging.

The cold smell of potato mold, the squelch and slap
Of soggy peat, the curt cuts of an edge
Through living roots awaken in my head.
But I've no spade to follow men like them.

Between my finger and thumb
The squat pen rests.
I'll dig with it.

Note

1. This is the first poem in the collection "Death of a Naturalist".

For Study and Discussion

1. To what is the speaker's pen compared? Why is it so compared?
2. What sound image can you find from the digging of the speaker's father? Which words contribute to the construction of the musical effect of the father's digging?
3. Why does the speaker mention his grandfather's digging? How do you understand the use of "Digging" in Line 24?
4. Apparently, the speaker compares his writing to digging, though with different tools from those used by his father and grandfather. Which stanza can support this comparison? What function are the descriptions of the digging of the father and the grandfather?
5. Make your comment on the last line of the poem.

Novel

Part Eight
Evolution of the English Novel

Chapter 1 The Rise of the English Novel

The word "novel" derived from the Italian word "novella", which means "tale, piece of news". Now it is commonly thought that a novel is a form of story or prose narrative containing characters, action and incident, and, perhaps, a plot. The novel is a mixed genre. Several different literary forms contributed to its development: mythology, epic poetry, essay, romance, history, biography, comic and sentimental drama, and so on. Though the novel has changed much to have evolved into its modern sophisticated state, there are still no generally accepted definitions, terminologies for it; nor standard ways of differentiating a novel from other narrative prose. It is much easier to define what is not a novel than to say what a novel is. However, the novel has several distinctive characteristics.

Firstly, unlike mythology or epic poetry, which talks about god or gods, and romance, which tells of stories of heroes who are strong and wise, the novel deals with common men and women and their happiness and laughter; their pain and sorrow.

Secondly, the novel is made up an action, with beginning, middle part and end. They are characterized by coherence, progression, and wholeness. As Philip Stevick puts it in *The Theory of the Novel*, "a novel is a novel insofar as it is an action and as it ceases to be an action it becomes not a novel but something else."

Thirdly, the novel probes into human nature and deals with human relationships and his relationship with the world. Dorothy Van Ghent begins *The English Novel: Form and Function* by writing, "the subject matter of novels is human relationships in which are shown the directions of men's souls". The protagonist of a novel is likely to be an "anti-hero," an "unheroic hero".

Finally, the novel can be a means to express, criticize, or minister to the different aspects of culture. It can deal with the reformation of society, the transformations of consciousness as well as the great events of social and intellectual history.

It took many years for the novel to develop into the present shape. In Italy, in the 14th century, there was a vogue for collections of short tales, of which the most famous is Boccaccio's *Decameron* (1348 — 1358), which had much influence on Chaucer. It is a collection of 100 novellas best known for the bawdy tales of love, appearing in all its possibilities from the erotic to the tragic. These short stories are extremely important in the history and development of the novel because in their method of narration and in their creation and development of characters they are forerunners of the modern novel.

Spain was ahead of the rest of Europe in the development of novel form. At the very beginning of the 14th century, it began to produce novels. The greatest of all Spanish novels is Cervantes's *Don Quixote*, which was written in the early 17th century. It is a humorous novel in the picaresque style. Alonso Quixano, a retired country gentleman in his fifties, lives in an unnamed section of La Mancha with his niece and a housekeeper. He has become obsessed with books of chivalry, and believes their every word to be true, despite the fact that many of the events in them are clearly impossible. Quixano eventually appears to other people to have lost his mind from little sleep and food and because of so much reading. He decides to go out as a knight-errant for adventure. He wears an old suit of armor, renames himself "Don Quixote de la Mancha." His adventures brought him nothing but ridicules and laughs from people. The world of ordinary people, from shepherds to tavern-owners and inn-keepers, as depicted in *Don Quixote*, was groundbreaking. *Don Quixote* stands in a unique position between medieval chivalric romance and a modern novel. The former consist of disconnected stories with little exploration of the inner life of even the main character. The latter are usually focused on the psychological evolution of their characters. *Don Quixote* has exerted a rich and varied influence over later writers, from Cervantes' own lifetime to the present-day.

In England, the novel as a genre, appeared approximately at the same period of time, if not later, than that in Italy and Spain. Numerous works have each been claimed as the first novel in English, such as Thomas Malory's *Le Morte d'Arthur* (published 1485), William Baldwin's *Beware the Cat*, (published 1570, 1584), John Lyly's *Euphues: The Anatomy of Wit* (1578) and *Euphues and his England* (1580), Philip Sidney's *The Countess of Pembroke's Arcadia* (1581), John Bunyan's *The Pilgrim's Progress* (1678), Daniel Defoe's *Robinson Crusoe* (1719) and *Moll Flanders* (1722) and Samuel Richardson's *Pamela* (1740), etc. It is difficult to decide which one should indisputably be entitled the first novel in English partly because of ignorance of earlier works, but largely because the term novel can be defined so as to exclude earlier candidates. Some critics require a novel to be wholly original. Some critics distinguish between the romance (which has fantastic elements) and the novel (which is wholly realistic) and so exclude *Le Morte d'Arthur*. Other critics distinguish between the allegory (in which characters and events have political, religious or other meanings) and the novel (in which characters and events stand only for themselves) and so exclude *The Pilgrim's Progress*. Still other critics require a novel to have a certain length, and so exclude *Oroonoko*, defining it instead as a novella. Ian Watt, in his *The Rise of the Novel: Studies in Defoe, Richardson and Fielding* (1957), strongly contended that Daniel Defoe's *Robinson Crusoe* (1719) should be given the credit. But with the rise of feminist criticism in the 1970s and 1980s and its concomitant rediscovery of forgotten writings by women, it is now often argued that Aphra Behn's *Oroonoko* (1688) is the "first English novel." However, the claims are difficult to sustain. In addition to the usual problems of defining the novel as a genre, Aphra Behn had written at least one epistolary novel prior to *Oroonoko*. The *Love-Letters Between a Nobleman and His Sister predates Oroonoko* by more than five years. However, *Oroonoko* is one of the very early novels in English of the particular sort that possesses a linear plot and follows a biographical model. It is a mixture of theatrical drama, reportage, and biography that is easy to recognize as a novel. It is also the first English novel to show Black Africans in a sympathetic manner.

Whatever the case, two works that appeared at the end of the 16th century are important in the evolution of the extended prose narrative in England. They are John Lily's *Euphues*(in two parts, 1578 and 1580), and Sir Philip Sidney's pastoral romance *Arcadia* (1575). *Euphues, the Anatomy of Wit* and *Euphues and his England*, the second part together form an extensive moral treatise. Euphues, a young man of Athens, arrives at Naples, where he forms a friendship with young Philautus. He falls in love with Lucilla, the betrothed of Philautus, and is duly jilted by that fickle mistress. This is all the action of *The Anatomy of Wit*: but the moralising element is something more considerable. It is about the follies of youth and deals with the subject of friendship. The complications brought about by the action of Lucilla lead to much bitter moralising upon fickleness in general. In *Euphues and his England*, the scene changes from Italy to England. The two friends, now reconciled, proceed to Canterbury, where they are entertained by one Fidus, a pastoral figure of considerable attractiveness; Philautus soon becomes involved in the toils of love, while Euphues plays the part of a philosophical spectator. The former lays siege to the heart of one whose affections are already bestowed, and so, with philosophy for his comfort, he enters upon the wooing of another, with more auspicious result. This brings the action to a close, and Euphues leaves England, eulogising the country and the women it contains, and returns forthwith to nurse his melancholy within his cell at Silexedra. In projecting a moral treatise, Lyly stumbled on the novel, and, considered as such, the work, though with many defects, has, also, abundant merit. It foretells the day of the novel of manners, of the novel involving a detailed analysis of love. It moves away from the fanciful idealism of the medieval romance and suggests an interest in contemporary life.

Sidney wrote his *Arcadia* for the entertainment of his sister, countess of Pembroke. The scene of his story is laid in a beautiful place in Greece named Arcadia, where the retired king brings up his two beautiful daughters. They live a happy and peaceful life. Later two shipwrecked princes come upon the land, and then fall in love with the two princesses. The story mainly deals with their happy love affair. This romance presents an ideal world dreamed by an aristocratic writer in the 16th century. It was popular until the

18th century.

Other interesting attempts at prose narrative from the 16th century are Robert Greene's *Pandosto* (1585), the story of which, later, was used by Shakespeare in *The Winter's Tale*, Thomas Lodge's *Rosalynde* (1590), which was modelled upon Sidney's *Acadia* and the story of which was used by Shakespeare in *As You Like It*, and Thomas Deloney's *Jack of Newbury* and *The Gentle Craft*, in which the cloth-maker's and the shoe-maker's life is presented.

Thomas Deloney appears to have worked as a silk-weaver in Norwich, but lived in London by 1586, and in the course of the next ten years is known to have written about fifty ballads. It is until recently that his more important work as a novelist, in which he ranks with Greene and Nash, has received attention. Less under the influence of John Lyly and other preceding writers than Greene, he is more natural, simple, and direct, and writes of middle-class citizens and tradesmen with light humour. Of his novels, *Thomas of Reading* is in honour of clothiers, *Jack of Newbury* celebrates weaving, and *The Gentle Craft* is dedicated to the praise of shoemakers.

Besides, Thomas Nashe (1567—1601) also made contributions to the development of novel writing in his prose narratives, such as *The Unfortunate Traveller* (1594) and *Jack Wilton*. He was an English pamphleteer, poet and satirist. Thomas Nashe was born in Lowestoft in 1561, and educated at St John's College, Cambridge. After graduating in 1586, he became one of the "University Wits", a circle of writers who came to London in the reign of Queen Elizabeth I, and wrote for the stage and the press. In 1589 his preface to Robert Greene's *Menaphon* was published. The preface attacked contemporary writers who plagiarized from classical authors, and praised Spenser and Greene. *The Anatomie of Absurditie*, also published in 1589, satirized contemporary literature, especially romances. Nashe took part in the Martin Marprelate controversy, answering attacks made on the Church of England by a Puritan group of writers known as Martin Marprelate. Using the pen name 'Pasquil', Nashe may have written several satiric pamphlets, of which *An Almond for a Parrat* (1590) is the only one attributed to him with conviction.

Nashe's best-known work, the novel *The Unfortunate Traveller, or The Life of Jack Wilton* (1594) is now thought to have been the first picaresque novel in English. It is a loosely connected account of adventures real and fictional on the Continent.

The details about Nashe's death are uncertain. He died in 1601, aged 34, and various causes ranging from the plague to food poisoning to a stroke have been suggested. An anonymous contemporary tribute to Nashe said:

Let all his faults sleep with his mournful chest,
And there for ever with his ashes rest.
His style was witty, though it had some gall,
Some things he might have mended, so may all.
Yet this I say, that for a mother wit,
Few men have ever seen the like of it.

Elizabethan Writers made a beginning in novel writing. But the writers of the 17th century did not make big progress in it because of the political and religious controversies which finally dragged England into a civil war. Yet the evolution of novel writing continued, especially in the latter part of the century.

Chapter 2 Aphra Behn

Aphra Behn(July 10, 1640—April 16, 1689) was a prolific writer in the Restoration Period. She wrote numerous plays and hundreds of amorous poems, songs, ballads and novels. She is credited to be one of the first English women to earn their livelihood by authorship. Little is known of her personal history. However, she was said to be firmly dedicated to the restored King Charles Ⅱ. As political parties first emerged during this time, Behn was a Tory supporter. Tories believed in absolute allegiance to the king, who governed by divine right (246). Behn often used her writings to attack the parliamentary Whigs. Like most Tories, Behn was distrustful of the Parliament and Whigs since the Revolution and wrote propaganda in support of the restored monarchy.

Behn wrote several novels of which *Oroonoko* is the most famous. The novel is based on her experience from a visit she made in 1663 to an English sugar colony on the Suriname River, on the coast east to Venezuela(a region later known as Suriname). During this trip she is supposed to have met an African slave leader, whose story formed the basis for the novel.

She was reportedly bisexual, and held a larger attraction to women than to men, a trait that, coupled with her writings and references of this nature, would eventually make her popular in the writing and artistic communities of the 20th century and present day. Aphra Behn died on April 16, 1689, and was buried in Westminster Abbey. Virginia Woolf spoke highly of her, marking her as the forerunner in fighting for women's "right to speak their minds" . Much early criticism emphasized her unusual status as a female writer in a male-dominated literary world; more recent criticism has offered more thorough discussions of her works. Behn's work had eminent influence on the Romantic writers.

Aphra Behn's writing is unique for its time because of her use of the narrator's voice. She takes on a narrative voice that is characteristically her own by using a removed but somehow still involved narrator in *Oroonoko*.

Aphra Behn's Representative Work : *Oroonoko*

Oroonoko, published in 1688, is a short novel whose full title is *Oroonoko*: *or*, *the*

Royal Slave. The protagonist of the novel is Oroonoko, the grandson of an African king, who falls in love with Imoinda, the daughter of the king's top general. The king, too, falls in love with Imoinda and commanded that she become one of his wives. Imoinda and Oroonoko plan a tryst with the help of their friends. However, their secret plan is discovered, and the king seus Imoinda as a slave. Oroonoko is then tricked and captured by an evil English slaver captain. Both Imoinda and Oroonoko are carried to Surinam, at that time an English colony in the West Indies. The two lovers are reunited there, under the new Christian names of Caesar and Clemene, even though Imoinda's beauty has attracted the attention of the English deputy-governor, Byam.

Oroonoko organizes a slave revolt. The slaves are hunted down by the military forces and compelled to surrender on Byam's promise of amnesty. However, when the slaves surrender, Oroonoko is whipped. To avenge his honor, and to express his natural worth, Oroonoko decides to kill Byam. But to protect Imoinda from violation and subjugation after his death, he decides to kill her. The two lovers discuss the plan, and Imoinda willingly agrees. When he stabs her, she dies with a smile on her face. Oroonoko is found mourning by her body and is kept from killing himself, only to be publicly executed. During his death by dismemberment, Oroonoko calmly smokes a pipe and stoically withstands all the pain without crying out.

The novel is written in a mixture of first and third person, as the narrator relates actions in Africa and portrays herself as a witness of the actions that take place in Surinam. At the conclusion of the love story, the narrator leaves Surinam for London.

Aphra Behn did not set out to protest slavery, but however tepid her feelings about slavery, there is no doubt about her feelings on the subject of natural kingship. The final words of the novel are a slight expiation of the narrator's guilt, but it is for the individual man she mourns and for the individual that she writes a tribute, and she lodges no protest over slavery itself.

One potential motive for the novel, or at least one political inspiration, was Behn's view that Surinam was a fruitful and potentially wealthy settlement that needed only a true noble to lead it. Like others sent to investigate the colony, she felt that Charles was not properly informed of the place's potential.

Behn was a political writer of fiction and for the stage, and though not didactic in purpose, most of her works have distinct political content. *Oroonoko* is one of the very early novels in English of the particular sort that possesses a linear plot and follows a biographical model. It is a mixture of theatrical drama, reportage, and biography that is easy to recognize as a novel.

Oroonoko: or, the Royal Slave(excerpt)

The King of Coramantien was himself a man of an hundred and odd years old, and had no son, though he had many beautiful black wives; for most certainly there are beauties that can charm of that color. In his younger years he had had many gallant men to his sons, thirteen of whom died in battle, conquering when they fell; and he had only left him for his successor one grandchild, son to one of these dead victors, who, as soon as he could bear a bow in his hand and a quiver[1] at his back, was sent into the field to be trained up by one of the oldest generals to war; where, from his natural inclination to arms, and the occasions given him, with the good conduct of the old general, he became, at the age of seventeen, one of the most expert captains and bravest soldiers that ever saw the field of Mars[2]: so that he was adored as the wonder of all that world, and the darling of the soldiers. Besides, he was adorned with a native beauty, so transcending all those of his gloomy race that he struck an awe and reverence even into those that knew not his quality; as he did into me, who beheld him with surprise and wonder, when afterwards he arrived in our world.

He had scarce arrived at his seventeenth year, when, fighting by his side, the general was killed with an arrow in his eye, which the Prince Oroonoko (for so was this gallant Moor[3] called) very narrowly avoided; nor had he, if the general who saw the arrow shot, and perceiving it aimed at the prince, had not bowed his head between, on purpose to receive it in his own body, rather than it should touch that of the prince, and so saved him.

'Twas then, afflicted as Oroonoko was, that he was proclaimed general in the old man's place: and then it was, at the finishing of that war, which had continued for two years, that the prince came to court, where he had hardly been a month together, from the time of his fifth year to that of seventeen; and 'twas amazing to imagine where it was he learned so much humanity: or, to give his accomplishments a juster name, where 'twas he got that real greatness of soul, those refined notions of true honor, that absolute generosity, and that softness that was capable of the highest passions of love and gallantry, whose objects were almost continually fighting men, or those mangled or dead, who heard no sounds but those of war and groans. Some part of it we may attribute to the care of a Frenchman of wit and learning, who, finding it turn to very good account to be a sort of royal tutor to this young black, and perceiving him very ready, apt, and quick of apprehension, took a great pleasure to teach him morals, language, and science; and was for it extremely beloved and valued by him. Another reason was, he loved when he came from war, to see all the English gentlemen that traded thither, and did not only learn their language, but that of the Spaniard also, with whom he traded afterwards for slaves.

I have often seen and conversed with this great man, and been a witness to many of his mighty actions; and do assure my reader, the most illustrious courts could not have produced a braver man, both for greatness of courage and mind, a judgment more solid, a wit more quick, and a conversation more sweet and diverting. He knew almost as much as if he had read much. he had heard of and admired the Romans; he had heard of the late Civil Wars in England, and the deplorable death of our great monarch; and would discourse of it with all the sense and abhorrence of the injustice imaginable. He had an extreme good and graceful mien, and all the civility of a well-bred great man. He had nothing of barbarity in his nature, but in all points addressed himself as if his education had been in some European court.

This great and just character of Oroonoko gave me an extreme curiosity to see him, especially when I knew he spoke French and English, and that I could talk with him. But though I had heard so much of him, I was as greatly surprised when I saw him as if I had heard nothing of him; so beyond all report I found him. He came into the room, and addressed himself to me and some other women with the best grace in the world. He was pretty tall, but of a shape the most exact that can be fancied. The most famous statuary could not form the figure of a man more admirably turned from head to foot. His face was not of that brown rusty black which most of that nation are, but of perfect ebony, or polished jet. His eyes were the most awful that could be seen, and very piercing; the white of 'em being like snow, as were his teeth. His nose was rising and Roman, instead of African and flat. His mouth the finest shaped that could be seen; far from those great turned lips which are so natural to the rest of the negroes. The whole proportion and air of his face was so nobly and exactly formed that, bating his color, there could be nothing in nature more beautiful, agreeable, and handsome. There was no one grace wanting that bears the standard of true beauty. His hair came down to his shoulders, by the aids of art, which was by pulling it out with a quill, and keeping it combed; of which he took particular care. Nor did the perfections of his mind come short of those of his person; for his discourse was admirable upon almost any subject: and whoever had heard him speak would have been convinced of their errors, that all fine wit is confined to the white men, especially to those of Christendom; and would have confessed that Oroonoko was as capable even of reigning well, and of governing as wisely, had as great a soul, as politic maxims, and was as sensible of power, as any prince civilized in the most refined schools of humanity and learning, or the most illustrious courts.

This prince, such as I have described him, whose soul and body were so admirably adorned, was (while yet he was in the court of his grandfather, as I said) as capable of love as 'twas possible for a brave and gallant man to be; and in saying that, I have named the highest degree of love: for sure great souls are most capable of that passion.

I have already said, the old general was killed by the shot of an arrow by the side of this prince in battle; and that Oroonoko was made general. This old dead hero had one only daughter left of his race, a beauty, that to describe her truly, one need say only, she was female to the noble male; the beautiful black Venus[4] to our young Mars; as charming in her person as he, and of delicate virtues. I have seen a hundred white men sighing after her, and making a thousand vows at her feet, all in vain, and unsuccessful. And she was indeed too great for any but a prince of her own nation to adore.

Oroonoko coming from the wars (which were now ended), after he had made his court to his grandfather he thought in honor he ought to make a visit to Imoinda, the daughter of his foster-father, the dead general; and to make some excuses to her, because his preservation was the occasion of her father's death; and to present her with those slaves that had been taken in this last battle, as the trophies of her father's victories. When he came, attended by all the young soldiers of any merit, he was infinitely surprised at the beauty of this fair queen of night, whose face and person was so exceeding all he had ever beheld, that lovely modesty with which she received him, that softness in her look and sighs, upon the melancholy occasion of this honor that was done by so great a man as Oroonoko, and a prince of whom she had heard such admirable things; the awfulness wherewith she received him, and the sweetness of her words and behavior while he staid, gained a perfect conquest over his fierce heart, and made him feel the victor could be subdued. So that having made his first compliments, and presented her an hundred and fifty slaves in fetters, he told her with his eyes that he was not insensible of her charms; while Imoinda, who wished for nothing more than so glorious a conquest, was pleased to believe she understood that silent language of new-born love; and, from that moment, put on all her additions to beauty.

The prince returned to court with quite another humor[5] than before; and though he did not speak much of the fair Imoinda, he had the pleasure to hear all his followers speak of nothing but the charms of that maid, insomuch that, even in the presence of the old king, they were extolling her, and heightening, if possible, the beauties they had found in her: so that nothing else was talked of, no other sound was heard in every corner where there were whisperers, but "Imoinda! Imoinda!"

'Twill be imagined Oroonoko staid not long before he made his second visit; nor, considering his quality, not much longer before he told her he adored her. I have often heard him say that he admired by what strange inspiration he came to talk things so soft, and so passionate, who never knew love, nor was used to the conversation of women; but (to use his own words) he said, most happily, some new and, till then, unknown power instructed his heart and tongue in the language of love, and at the same time, in favor of him, inspired Imoinda with a sense of his passion. She was touched with what he said, and returned it all in such answers as went to his very heart, with a pleasure unknown before. Nor did he use those obligations ill, that love had done him, but turned all his happy moments to the best advantage; and as he knew no vice, his flame aimed at nothing but honor, if such a distinction may be made in love; and especially in that country, where men take to themselves as many as they can maintain; and where the only crime and sin with woman is to turn her off, to abandon her to want, shame, and misery: such ill morals are only practised in Christian countries, where they prefer the bare name of religion; and, without virtue or morality, think that sufficient. But Oroonoko was none of those professors[6]; but as he had right notions of honor, so he made her such propositions as were not only and barely such; but, contrary to the custom of his country, he made her vows she should be the only woman he would possess while he lived; that no age or wrinkles should incline him to change; for her soul would be always fine, and always young; and he should have an eternal idea in his mind of the charms she now bore; and should look into his heart for that idea, when he could find it no longer in her face.

After a thousand assurances of his lasting flame, and her eternal empire over him, she condescended to receive him for her husband; or rather, received him as the greatest honor the gods could do her.

There is a certain ceremony in these cases to be observed, which I forgot to ask how 'twas performed; but 'twas concluded on both sides that, in obedience to him, the grandfather was to be first made acquainted with the design: for they pay a most absolute resignation to the monarch, especially when he is a parent also.

On the other side, the old king, who had many wives and many concubines, wanted not court-flatterers to insinuate into his heart a thousand tender thoughts for this young beauty; and who represented her to his fancy as the most charming he had ever possessed in all the long race of his numerous years. At this character, his old heart, like an extinguished brand[7], most apt to take fire, felt new sparks of love, and began to kindle; and now grown to his second childhood, longed with impatience to behold this gay thing, with whom, alas! he could but innocently play. But how he should be confirmed she was this wonder, before he used his power to call her to court (where maidens never came, unless for the king's private use) he was next to consider; and while he was so doing, he had intelligence brought him that Imoinda was most certainly mistress to the Prince Oroonoko. This gave him some chagrin[8]; however, it gave him also an opportunity, one day, when the prince was a-hunting, to wait on a man of quality, as his slave and attendant, who should go and make a present to Imoinda, as from the prince; he should then, unknown, see this fair maid, and have an opportunity to hear what message she would return the prince for his present, and from thence gather the state of her heart, and degree of her inclination. This was put in execution, and the old monarch saw, and burned: he found her all he had heard, and would not delay his happiness, but found he should have some obstacle to overcome her heart; for she expressed her sense of the present the prince had sent her, in terms so sweet, so soft and pretty, with an air of love and joy that could not be dissembled, insomuch that 'twas past doubt whether she loved Oroonoko entirely. This gave the old king some affliction; but he salved it with this, that the obedience the people pay their king was not at all inferior to what they paid their gods; and what love would not oblige Imoinda to do, duty would compel her to.

He was therefore no sooner got to his apartment but he sent the royal veil to Imoinda; that is the ceremony of invitation: he sends the lady he has a mind to honor with his bed, a veil, with which she is covered, and secured for the king's use; and 'tis death to disobey; besides, held a most impious disobedience.

'Tis not to be imagined the surprise and grief that seized the lovely maid at this news and sight. However, as delays in these cases are dangerous, and pleading worse than treason; trembling, and almost fainting, she was obliged to suffer herself to be covered and led away.

They brought her thus to court; and the king, who had caused a very rich bath to be prepared, was led into it, where he sat under a canopy, in state, to receive this longed-for virgin; whom he having commanded should be brought to him, they (after disrobing her) led her to the bath, and making fast the doors, left her to descend. The king, without more courtship, bade her throw off her mantle, and come to his arms. But Imoinda, all in tears, threw herself on the marble, on the brink of the bath, and besought him to hear her. She told him, as she was a maid, how proud of the divine glory she should have been, of having it in her power to oblige her king; but as by the laws he could not, and from his royal goodness would not, take from any man his wedded wife; so she believed she should be the occasion of making him commit a great sin if she did not reveal her state and condition, and tell him she was another's, and could not be so happy to be his.

The king, enraged at this delay, hastily demanded the name of the bold man that had married a woman of her degree without his consent. Imoinda, seeing his eyes fierce, and his hands tremble (whether with age or anger, I know not, but she fancied the last), almost repented she had said so much, for now she feared the storm would fall on the prince; she therefore said a thousand things to appease the raging of his flame, and to prepare him to hear who it was with calmness: but before she spoke, he imagined who she meant, but would not seem to do so, but commanded her to lay aside her mantle, and suffer herself to receive his caresses, or, by his gods he swore, that happy man whom she was going to name should die, though it were even Oroonoko himself. "Therefore," said he, "deny this marriage, and swear thyself a maid." "That," replied Imoinda, "by all our powers I do; for I am not yet known to my husband." "'Tis enough," said the king, "'tis enough both to satisfy my conscience and my heart." And rising from his seat, he went and led her into the bath; it being in vain for her to resist.

Notes

1. quiver—a long case for carrying arrows.
2. the field of Mars—the battle field. In Roman mythology, Mars is the god of war.
3. Moor—a native of Morocco of mixed Arabic and Berber origin.
4. Venus—In Roman mythology, Venus is the goddess of beauty and love.
5. humour—a mood, frame of mind.
6. professor—someone who declares or confesses views.
7. brand—a piece of burning or charred wood.
8. chagrin—disappointment, mortification.

For Study and Discussion

1. Prince Oroonoko is said to have "got that real greatness of soul", and "those refined notions of true honor", whom does the authoress attribute these qualities to? What can we know about the authoress's attitude toward the Moroccans?
2. How does the narrator ensure the reader that the story is a true story? What is the effect of this kind of narration?
3. What kind of woman is Imoinda? How do you know?

Part Nine
The Eighteenth Century English Novel

Chapter 1 The Rapid Growth of the English Novel

Although novel as a genre started late in England, it developed rapidly in the eighteenth century and influenced writers of many countries. Two factors had contributed to this growth. The first factor is that by this time the novel began to be viewed as a form of art, to be evaluated critically in terms of the history of literature. In the middle ages, fictions were considered "lies" and therefore hardly justifiable at all. But now fashion had changed in favour of the novel. Another factor is that the invention of printing created a new market of comparatively cheap entertainment and knowledge. Fiction was no longer a predominantly aristocratic entertainment. The increased public desire for reading and thus, the demand for books helped to create the boom of novels.

The most significant development in the 18th century English literature is the rise and growth of the realistic novel. Fiction writers turned away from the conventions and structures of the heroic romance. They began to portray events and characters drawn from the everyday life of people and emphasize ordinary experience and the development and assertion of the individual personality. Realist writers think they should concern themselves with the here and now, with their own environment and with the political and social movements. They experimented with the techniques and forms that moved the novel closer to maturity, including the epistolary novel, characters drawn from all social levels, and depictions of contemporary life. Some of these novels are didactic in nature. They blend entertainment with ethical instruction; others present detailed portrait of the characters with paramount attention to emotional life. The realistic novels produced by Daniel Defoe, Jonathan Swift, Henry Fielding and Tobias Smollett are the best expressive forms of realism.

Another kind of novel that is prevailing in the 18th century is the sentimental novel or the novel of sensibility. It celebrates the emotional and intellectual concepts of sentiment, sentimentalism, and sensibility. Sentimental novel concentrated on the distresses of the virtuous and attempted to show that a sense of honour and moral behaviors were justly rewarded. It also attempted to show that effusive emotion was evidence of kindness and goodness. Along with a new vision of love, sentimentalism presented a new view of human nature which valued feeling over thinking, passion over reason, and personal instincts of "pity, tenderness, and benevolence" over social duties . Writers who followed this tradition regarded sentiment as a sort of relief for the griefs and heart-aches felt toward the world's wrongs, and as a kind of mild protest against the social injustice. In poetry Edward Young's *Night Thoughts* and Thomas Gray's *Elegy Written in a Country Churchyard* are the examples of sentimental poetry. The classic examples of sentimental novel are Richardson's *Pamela, or Virtue Rewarded* and *Clarissa Harlowe, or the History of a Young Lady*; Goldsmith's *The Vicar of the Wakefield*; and Laurence Sterne's *The Life and Opinions of Tristram Shandy*.

Another genre of fiction was also prominent in the late 18th century, the Gothic Novel, which had been inaugurated in 1764 by Horace Walpole's *Castle of Otranto, A Gothic Story* and developed by Clara Reeve in *The Champion of Virtue, A Gothic Story* (1777). Most Gothic novels were tales of mystery and horror which happened in a gloomy castle of the Middle Ages. They were set in sullen, craggy landscapes and decaying mansions with dark dungeons, secret passages, and stealthy ghosts. They dealt with chilling supernatural phenomena, and often persecution of a beautiful maiden by an obsessed and haggard villain. As in other Gothic novels, the notion of the sublime is central. Eighteenth-century aesthetic theory held that the sublime and the beautiful were juxtaposed. The sublime was awful (awe-inspiring) and terrifying while the beautiful was calm and reassuring. The characters and landscapes of the Gothic rest almost entirely within the sublime, with the heroine the great exception.

Ann Radcliffe was the most gifted writer of Gothic tales. In her *Mysteries of Udolpho* (1794), and better still in *The Italian* (1797), Ann Radcliffe, developed the figure of the mysterious and solitary homme fatal torturing others because himself tortured by unspeakable guilt, who though a villain, usurps the place of the hero in the reader's interest. Matthew Gregory Lewis in *The Monk* (1797), which he wrote at the age of 20, has a similar protagonist, and brings to the fore the elements of diabolism, sensuality, and sadistic perversion which are pungent but submerged components in Mrs. Radcliffe's Gothic formula. Gothicism is apparent also in Romantic poetry: in Coleridge's medieval terror poem *Christabel*, in Byron's recurrent hero-villain, and in Shelley's inclinations toward the fantastic the macabre, and the exploration of the realm of the unconscious mind and of aberrations such as incest.

Chapter 2 Daniel Defoe

Daniel Defoe (1660 — 1731) has been called one of the greatest journalists and the father of journalism.

Defoe was born to a family of Dissenters in London and his father was a butcher; his exact birth date is unknown, maybe it is in 1659 or 1660. Very little is known of Daniel's childhood. Defoe's education began in the Rev. James Fisher's school in Dorking. When he was fourteen, he was enrolled in the Dissenting academy in Newington Green. Morton is seen as a major influence on Defoe's writing style, because he gave his students a thorough grounding in English as well as the customary Greek and Latin; the other influence was the Bible.

At the very beginning, he was a commission agent by trade. He wrote countless essays and pamphlets on economic theory which was advanced for his time. He wrote numerous treatises family matters. But his own marriage to Mary Tuffley turns out to be an unhappy one, despite its length of forty-seven years and fecundity of eight children. Defoe's unstable fortunes, his absence while a fugitive from enemies, his extended visits abroad and creditors make him keep aloof from his family. Defoe faced bankruptcy in 1692. Although he was spared the humiliation, he had to repay what he owned in ten years. Fortunately, he was able to win King William's favor, and was appointed Commissioner of the Glass Duty. Because of his sense of justice, he irritated many high officials and was put into prison and was sentenced to three days in the pillory for "seditious libel against the Church."

He was saved by a pardon some months later from Queen Anne. Later the Earl of Oxford offered him a grant of 1000 pounds to let Defoe climb out of debt and start his own newspaper, the *Review*. After another arrest in 1715 for libel, Defoe spent his time covertly editing other newspapers as he worked on novels such as *Robinson Crusoe* and *Moll Flanders*. He died in 1731, poor and fighting.

Robinson Crusoe is Defoe's masterpiece. It describes an eighteen years old young man living in England. He longs for going on sea voyages, although his father wants him to be a lawyer. He ignored what his father said and goes to the sea with his friend, who finds the reason why Crusoe leaves home and warns him angrily. Crusoe was able to stant another voyage headed to Guiana rather than going home. On the way, the ship is attacked by Turkish pirates, who make Robinson into a slave. Later, Robinson seizes the chance to escape successfully and happens to meet a Portuguese ship whose captain is so kind that he takes them aboard for free and bring them to Brazil, where he decides to buy a plantation, because he learns that it is a good way to make money. Although he becomes a wealthy man, he resolves to go on a business trip for slave dealing. His ship is wrecked in a big storm, and he was left on a deserted island. Robinson has been there for 27 years, during which he makes everything by himself, such as raising crops and goats, building shelter and getting and cooking food. At the very beginning, he leads a hard life, but later he takes all advantages to make it better. After 15 years, he observes cannibalistic savages eating prisoners. Robinson plucks up and saves a prisoner with his gun from the hand of cannibalistic savages.

The prisoner is named Friday by Robinson and turns out to be a good servant. The two live together happily. One day, they save two prisoners. One is a Spaniard; the other is Friday's father, who go back to bring back the rest of the Spaniard's men. Before the two coming back, Crusoe comes across a European boat. One is the captain of a ship whose crew mutinied. Crusoe promises to help them get the ship back on two terms: one is the authority of the island in his hands and another is Friday and Crusoe should be taken to England without payment.

After retaking the captain's ship, Friday and Robinson are taken to England. Even though Crusoe has been gone thirty-five years, he still owned his plantations and is very rich. He gives money to the Portuguese captain and the widow who do him good. He returns to the English, settling in the countryside, marrying and having three children. After his wife dies, he goes to the sea again.

Moll Flanders is another novel by Defoe. It talks about the life story of a woman named Moll Flanders. The full title of the novel is "The Fortunes and Misfortunes of the Famous Moll Flanders, Etc. Who was born in Newgate, and during a life of continu'd Variety for Threescore Years, besides her Childhood, was Twelve Year a Whore, five times a Wife (whereof once to her own brother), Twelve Year a Thief, Eight Year a Transported Felon in Virginia, at last grew Rich, liv'd Honest and died a Penitent". Written from her own Memorandums. It is an apt summary of the whole novel. Moll Flanders is born to a mother who has been convicted of a felony and who is transported to America soon after her birth. When she was three, she ran away from the gypsies with whom she lives together and was taken care of by a parish. At eight, she did odd jobs, such as spinning and sewing with her nurse, who died six years later. Then Moll served as a maid in the Mayor's house and was treated as the daughter of the house, where she was seduced by one of the sons of the family. Abandoned by her first lover, she is compelled to marry his younger brother. Moll gave birth to two children who were taken charge by their grandparents after their father's death a few year later. Then Moll remarried to a tradesman who ran away from the jail and left Moll free to marry illegally after spending her money and went bankrupt.

Moll married a so-called rich gentleman who turned out to be her half brother and gave birth to several children. After returning to her brother husband's hometown Virginia, she met her mother who was transported from Newgate prison, she moved to Bath alone.

She lived with a gentleman whose wife was mad until he was regretful for his sinful way of living. Then parted, leaving the son taken by him. Moll longed for going to north to find a man to get married and left her money taken care of by a sober gentleman who decided to divorce his unfaithful wife to marry Moll after she returned from the north.

Moll met a handsome man and agreeable man and married him for the sake of his money. However, the man married her for the same purpose. Finally, they announced that the marriage was nonexistent. Going back to London, Moll gives birth to a baby whose father was her latest husband and was adopted by a family, she married the man who had taken charge of her money and knew nothing about her life in north living together happily for five years until the man's death.

Moll was too old to attract a new husband and began to steal things, she was careful and was not caught until the time she was stealing some silk. In Newgate prison, she saw her Lancashire husband being brought in for highway robbery. The death sentence was reduced to a lesser sentence, that of transportation to Virginia. So she was transported to Virginia with her Lancashire husband. They ran a tobacco plantation far from the house where her husband/brother and her son lived. Moll told her Lancashire husband the incest marriage after her husband/brother's death. They became rich and returned England to enjoy their lives.

Defoe's reputation did not rise up until a series of biographies and editions of his works were published from 1780 to 1830. He is one of the greatest writers in the eighteenth century, who received widespread and consistent serious critical attention in the twentieth century.

How to Marry Rich When You're Poor: Moll's Third Husband

(an excerpt)

The following excerpt is taken from Part Three of "Moll Flanders". Returning the favor Moll had done for her, the newly married captain's lady invited Moll to stay with her and her husband, and told her husband that Moll was wealthy. This gained Moll many admirers, and she picked out her man: he, believing that she was rich, courted her, saying that he did not care if she were poor. Thus he married her, Then Moll seriously reduced his expectations of her wealth so that he was happy to get anything at all. They then got on their way to his plantations in Virginia. In this part, through the careful manipulation of her new husband, Moll shows us that she has learned a great deal in her first two marriages, relating to us her careful observations of human mores. She no longer depends on luck, or the benevolence of the powerful, but rather on her own wits.

My dear and faithful friend, the captain's wife, was so sensible of the service I had done her in the affair above, that she was not only a steady friend to me, but, knowing my circumstances, she frequently made me presents as money came into her hands, such as fully amounted to a maintenance, so that I spent none of my own; and at last she made this unhappy proposal to me, viz. that as we had observed, as above, how the men made no scruple to set themselves out as persons meriting a woman of fortune, when they had really no fortune of their own, it was but just to deal with them in their own way and, if it was possible, to deceive the deceiver.

The captain's lady, in short, put this project into my head, and told me if I would be ruled by her I should certainly get a husband of fortune, without leaving him any room to reproach me with want of my own. I told her, as I had reason to do, that I would give up myself wholly to her directions, and that I would have neither tongue to speak nor feet to step in that affair but as she should direct me, depending that she would extricate me out of every difficulty she brought me into, which she said she would answer for.

The first step she put me upon was to call her cousin, and to a relation's house of hers in the country, where she directed me, and where she brought her husband to visit me; and calling me cousin, she worked matters so about, that her husband and she together invited me most passionately to come to town and be with them, for they now live in a quite different place from where they were before. In the next place, she tells her husband that I had at least £1,500 fortune, and that after some of my relations I was like to have a great deal more. It was enough to tell her husband this; there needed nothing on my side. I was but to sit still and wait the event, for it presently went all over the neighbourhood that the young widow at Captain—'s was a fortune, that she had at least £1,500, and perhaps a great deal more, and that the captain said so; and if the captain was asked at any time about me, he made no scruple to affirm it, though he knew not one word of the matter, other than that his wife had told him so; and in this he thought no harm, for he really believed it to be so, because he had it from his wife: so slender a foundation will those fellows build upon, if they do but think there is a fortune in the game. With the reputation of this fortune, I presently found myself blessed with admirers enough, and that I had my choice of men, as scarce as they said they were, which, by the way, confirms what I was saying before. This being my case, I, who had a subtle game to play, had nothing now to do but to single out from them all the properest man that might be for my purpose; that is to say, the man who was most likely to depend upon the hearsay[1] of a fortune, and not inquire too far into the particulars; and unless I did this I did nothing, for my case would not bear much inquiry.

I picked out my man without much difficulty, by the judgment I made of his way of courting me. I had let him run on with his protestations and oaths that he loved me above all the world; that if I would make him happy, that was enough; all which I knew was upon supposition, nay, it was upon a full satisfaction, that I was very rich, though I never told him a word of it myself.

This was my man; but I was to try him to the bottom[2], and indeed in that consisted my safety; for if he baulked, I knew I was undone, as surely as he was undone if he took me; and if I did not make some scruple about his fortune, it was the way to lead him to raise some about mine; and first, therefore, I pretended on all occasions to doubt his sincerity, and told him, perhaps he only courted me for my fortune. He stopped my mouth in that part[3] with the thunder of his protestations, as above, but still I pretended to doubt.

One morning he pulls off his diamond ring, and writes upon the glass of the sash in my chamber this line—

'You I love, and you alone.'

I read it, and asked him to lend me his ring, with which I wrote under it, thus—

'And so in love says every one.'

He takes his ring again, and writes another line thus—

'Virtue alone is an estate.'

I borrowed it again, and I wrote under it —

'But money's virtue, gold is fate.'

He coloured as red as fire to see me turn so quick upon him, and in a kind of a rage told me he would conquer me, and writes again thus—

'I scorn your gold, and yet I love.'

I ventured all upon the last cast of poetry, as you'll see, for I wrote boldly under his last—

'I'm poor: let's see how kind you'll prove.'

This was a sad truth to me; whether he believed me or no, I could not tell; I supposed then that he did not. However, he flew to me, took me in his arms, and, kissing me very eagerly, and with the greatest passion imaginable, he held me fast till he called for a pen and ink, and then told me he could not wait the tedious writing on the glass, but, pulling out a piece of paper, he began and wrote again—

'Be mine, with all your poverty.'

I took his pen, and followed him immediately, thus—

'Yet secretly you hope I lie.'

He told me that was unkind, because it was not just, and that I put him upon contradicting me, which did not consist with good manners, any more than with his affection; and therefore, since I had insensibly drawn him into this poetical scribble, he begged I would not oblige him to break it off; so he writes again—

'Let love alone be our debate.'

I wrote again—

'She loves enough that does not hate.'

This he took for a favour, and so laid down the cudgels, that is to say, the pen; I say, he took if for a favour, and a mighty one it was, if he had known all. However, he took it as I meant it, that is, to let him think I was inclined to go on with him, as indeed I had all the reason in the world to do, for he was the best-humoured, merry sort of a fellow that I ever met with, and I often reflected on myself how doubly criminal it was to deceive such a man; but that necessity, which pressed me to a settlement suitable to my condition, was my authority for it; and certainly his affection to me, and the goodness of his temper, however they might argue against using him ill, yet they strongly argued to me that he would better take the disappointment than some fiery-tempered wretch, who might have nothing to recommend him but those passions which would serve only to make a woman miserable all her days.

Besides, though I jested with him (as he supposed it) so often about my poverty, yet, when he found it to be true, he had foreclosed all manner of objection, seeing, whether he was in jest or in earnest, he had declared he took me without any regard to my portion, and, whether I was in jest or in earnest, I had declared myself to be very poor; so that, in a word, I had him fast both ways; and though he might say afterwards he was cheated, yet he could never say that I had cheated him.

He pursued me close after this, and as I saw there was no need to fear losing him, I played the indifferent part with him longer than prudence might otherwise have dictated to me. But I considered how much this caution and indifference would give me the advantage over him, when I should come to be under the necessity of owning my own circumstances to him; and I managed it the more warily, because I found he inferred from thence, as indeed he ought to do, that I either had the more money or the more judgment, and would not venture at all.

I took the freedom one day, after we had talked pretty close to the subject, to tell him that it was true I had received the compliment of a lover from him, namely, that he would take me without inquiring into my fortune, and I would make him a suitable return in this, viz. that I would make as little inquiry into his as consisted with reason, but I hoped he would allow me to ask a few questions, which he would answer or not as he thought fit; and that I would not be offended if he did not answer me at all; one of these questions related to our manner of living, and the place where, because I had heard he had a great plantation in Virginia, and that he had talked of going to live there, and I told him I did not care to be transported.

He began from this discourse to let me voluntarily into all his affairs, and to tell me in a frank, open way all his circumstances, by which I found he was very well to pass in the world; but that great part of his estate consisted of three plantations, which he had in Virginia, which brought him in a very good income, generally speaking, to the tune of £300, a year, but that if he was to live upon them, would bring him in four times as much. 'Very well,' thought I; 'you shall carry me thither as soon as you please, though I won't tell you so beforehand.'

I jested with him extremely about the figure he would make in Virginia; but I found he would do anything I desired, though he did not seem glad to have me undervalue his plantations, so I turned my tale. I told him I had good reason not to go there to live, because if his plantations were worth so much there, I had not a fortune suitable to a gentleman of £1,200 a year, as he said his estate would be. He replied generously, he did not ask what my fortune was; he had told me from the beginning he would not, and he would be as good as his word; but whatever it was, he assured me he would never desire me to go to Virginia with him, or go thither himself without me, unless I was perfectly willing, and made it my choice.

All this, you may be sure, was as I wished, and indeed nothing could have happened more perfectly agreeable. I carried it on as far as this with a sort of indifferency that he often wondered at, more than at first, but which was the only support of his courtship; and I mention it the rather to intimate again to the ladies that nothing but want of courage for such an indifferency makes our sex so cheap, and prepares them to be ill-used as they are; would they venture the loss of a pretending fop now and then, who carries it high upon the point of his own merit, they would certainly be less slighted, and courted more. Had I discovered really and truly what my great fortune was, and that in all I had not full £500 when he expected £1,500, yet I had hooked him so fast, and played him so long, that I was satisfied he would have had me in my worst circumstances; and indeed it was less a surprise to him when he learned the truth than it would have been, because having not the least blame to lay on me, who had carried it with an air of indifference to the last, he would not say one word, except that indeed he thought it had been more, but that if it had been less he did not repent his bargain; only that he should not be able to maintain me so well as he intended.

In short, we were married, and very happily married on my side, I assure you, as to the man; for he was the best-humoured man that every woman had, but his circumstances were not so good as I imagined, as, on the other hand, he had not bettered himself by marrying so much as he expected.

When we were married, I was shrewdly put to it to bring him that little stock I had, and to let him see it was no more; but there was a necessity for it, so I took my opportunity one day when we were alone, to enter into a short dialogue with him about it. 'My dear,' said I, 'We have been married a fortnight; is it not time to let you know whether you have got a wife with something or with nothing?' 'Your own time for that, my dear,' says he; 'I am satisfied that I have got the wife I love; I have not troubled you much,' says he, 'with my inquiry after it..' 'That's true,' says I, 'but I have a great difficulty upon me about it, which I scarce know how to manage.'

'What's that, m dear?' says he.

'Why,' says I, ''tis a little hard upon me, and'tis harder upon you. I am told that Captain—(meaning my friend's husband) 'has told you I had a great deal more money than I ever pretended to have, and I am sure I never employed him to do so.'

'Well,' says he, 'Captain—may have told me so, but what then? If you have not so much, that may lie at his door, but you never told me what you had, so I have no reason to blame you if you have nothing at all.'

'That's is so just,' said I, 'and so generous, that it makes my having but a little a double affliction to me.'

'The less you have, my dear,' says he, 'the worse for us both; but I hope your affliction you speak of is not caused for fear I should be unkind to you, for want of a portion. No, no, if you have nothing, tell me plainly, and at once; I may perhaps tell the captain he has cheated me, but I can never say you have cheated me, for did you not give it under your hand that you were poor? and so I ought to expect you to be.'

'Well,' said I, 'my dear, I am glad I have not been concerned in deceiving you before marriage. If I deceive you since, 'tis ne'er the worse; that I am poor is too true, but not so poor as to have nothing neither'; so I pulled out some bank bills, and gave him about £160. 'There's something, my dear,' said I, 'and not quite all neither.'

I had brought him so near to expecting nothing, by what I had said before, that the money, though the sum was small in itself, was doubly welcome to him; he owned it was more than he looked for, and that he did not question by my discourse to him, but that my fine clothes, gold watch, and a diamond ring or two, had been all my fortune. I let him please himself with that £160 two or three days, and then, having been abroad that day, and as if I had been to fetch it, I brought him £100 more home in gold, and told him there was a little more portion for him; and, in short, in about a week more I brought him £180 more, and about £60 in linen, which I made him believe I had been obliged to take with the £100 which I gave him in gold, as a composition for a debt of £600, being little more than five shillings in the pound, and overvalued too.

'And now, my dear,' says I to him, 'I am very sorry to tell you, that there is all, and that I have given you my whole fortune.' I added, that if the person who had my £600 had not abused me, I had been worth £1000 to him, but that as it was, I had been faithful to him, and reserved nothing to myself, but if it had been more he should have had it.

He was so obliged by the manner, and so pleased with the sum, for he had been in a terrible fright lest it had been nothing at all, that he accepted it very thankfully. And thus I got over the fraud of passing for a fortune without money, and cheating a man into marrying me on pretence of a fortune; which, by the way, I take to be one of the most dangerous steps a woman can take, and in which she runs the most hazard of being ill-used afterwards.

My husband, to give him his due, was a man of infinite good nature, but he was no fool; and finding his income not suited to the manner of living which he had intended, if I had brought him what he expected, and being under a disappointment in his return of his plantations in Virginia, he discovered many times his inclination of going over to Virginia, to live upon his own; and often would be magnifying the way of living there, how cheap, how plentiful, how pleasant, and the like.

I began presently to understand this meaning, and I took him up very plainly one morning, and told him that I did so; that I found his estate turned to no account at this distance, compared to what it would do if he lived upon the spot, and that I found he had a mind to go and live there; and I added, that I was sensible he had been disappointed in a wife, and that finding his expectations not answered that way, I could do no less, to make him amends, than tell him that I was very willing to go over to Virginia with him and live there.

He said a thousand kind things to me upon the subject of my making such a proposal to him. He told me, that however he was disappointed in his expectations of a fortune, he was not disappointed in a wife, and that I was all to him that a wife could be, and he was more than satisfied on the whole when the particulars were put together, but that this offer was so kind, that it was more than he could express.

To bring the story short, we agreed to go. He told me that he had a very good house there, that it was well furnished, that his mother was alive and lived in it, and one sister, which was all the relations he had; that as soon as he came there, his mother would remove to another house, which was her own for life, and his after her decease[4]; so that I should have all the house to myself; and I found all this to be exactly as he had said.

To make this part of the story short, we put on board the ship which we went in, a large quantity of good furniture for our house, with stores of linen and other necessaries, and a good cargo for sale, and away we went.

Notes

1. hearsay—something that you have heard about from other people but do not know to be definitely true or correct.
2. try him to the bottom—to test him thoroughly.
3. He stopped my mouth in that part—he stopped my talking when I talked of that.
4. decease—death.

For Study and Discussion

1. How did Moll make the man believe that she is extremely rich? Why ?
2. Why did Moll say to the man that she is poor?
3. What can we know about Moll's attitude toward men and marriage from this excerpt?
4. The man and Moll conversed on a pane of glass by writing with a diamond ring. They make up a short poem. Study it and tell its main idea.

Chapter 3 Jonathan Swift

Jonathan Swift (1667—1745) was Britain's greatest satirist in the 18th century in the history of English literature.

Jonathan Swift was born in Dublin, Ireland, on November 30, 1667. His parents were English, and his father died before he was born. When he was fourteen, he attended Trinity College. After graduating in 1688, he became the secretary of Sir William Temple. In 1694, he had been a country parson for one year. Before returning to Ireland to become the chaplain of the earl of Berkeley, he was still in the service of Temple. At the same time, he had begun to write satires on the political and religious corruption in his time, such as *A Tale of a Tub* and *The Battle of the Books*. He also wrote a number of political pamphlets in favor of the Whig party. In 1709, he campaigned for the Irish church in London but failed. In 1710, he joined the more conservative Tory party due to his allegiance to the church.

In 1714, although he was famous for his writings, Swift fell out of favor. The Tory government was out of power. Returning to Dublin, he became the dean of St. Patrick's. Swift had become friends with writers such as Alexander Pope in England. After his return to Ireland, Swift became a staunch supporter of the Irish against English attempts to weaken their economic and political power, writing pamphlets such as the satirical *A Modest Proposal*. During his last years, he got a brain disease. He died in 1745. In his will, he left all his property to found St. Patrick's Asylum for lunatics and the incurable.

Swift's chief works are: *The Draper's Letters*, *Gulliver's Travels*, *A Tale of a Tub*. *A Tale of a Tub* supports the position of the Anglican Church against its critics on the left and the right. *The Battle of the Books*, which argues for the supremacy of the classics against modern thought and literature. *A Modest Proposal*, in which the Irish problems of famine and overpopulation could be easily solved by having the babies of poor Irish subjects sold as delicacies to feed the rich.

Swift is a realist writer. The plot of his satires is from imagination. The feature of his satire is outward gravity and an apparent earnestness, which make his satire all the more powerful. The democratic ideas are shown in his works, which sets a good example for the later writers, such as Fielding, Sheridan, Byron and even Bernard Shaw. His language is simple, clear and vigorous. Just as what he says, "proper words in proper place, makes the true definition of a style". There are few ornaments in his writing, but it comes home to the reader. He seems to have no difficulty in finding words to express exactly the impression he wishes to convey. In simple, direct and precise prose, Swift is almost unsurpassed in English literature.

The Battle of the Books is Swift's first notable works, written in 1697 but published in 1704. It is a keen satire upon the two political parties in the controversy and on pedantry in the literary world of the time. It is also a parody of the hero epic. This novel, in some way, only shows some basic ideas and styles of Swift's ironical allegory, therefore it's not a mature works.

Another satirical masterpiece, *A Tale of a Tub*, published in the same year of 1704, is written in a form of a parable satirizing on the various churches of the day. And it is more mature and serious in his writing skills and thoughts revealed in it. Through the title, Thomas Hobbes (British political theorist in the 17th century) and those who take the advantage of the weaknesses of the government and church are obviously attacked by satire. Swift compares them to the whale that is ready to attack he ship, and himself the tub to lure the whale away to protect the church. Holistically, Swift supports the middle course in religion, so his views in this novel don't seem very invasive. However, once having a thorough look through it, lots of strict criticism on the behavior of the church, pungent satire on the three brothers' sophism and sharp ridicule on some theological viewpoints are hiding among he words and sentences. This proves that Swift's religious stand is not steady, or he casts some doubts to the religion.

However, the importance of *A Tale of a Tub* doesn't lie in Swift's attitude toward religion, but the capacity of the tale itself and the typical Swiftian style. Samuel Johnson thought it one of Swift's most strange works. The application of such satirical techniques, inflation, irony, allusion and mockery and so on proves Swift's gift in satire. The two novels—*The Battle of the Books* and *A Tale of a Tub* make Swift well-known as a satirist.

Jonathan's best fictional work is *Gulliver's Travels*. The book consists of four parts, which describes particular voyages of the hero and his adventures .

In the first part, to be a surgeon of a ship. The ship is damaged in a heavy storm and he is left on the shore of the island of Lilliput. When he wakes up, he finds that he is captured and bound by thousands of the inhabitants who are only six-inch tall. Everything on the island is ten times as small as that in the human society. In Lilliput, the two parties are distinguished by wearing high and low heels. (The Tories and the Whigs are satirized). Civil strife and war between Lilliput and the neighboring country often happens just because an argument, for example, "Should eggs be broken at the big end or the little end?" (It reflects the religious controversies between the Catholics and the Protestants in England). On this island, the high official posts are given according to whether the high official can dance on a rope or not (the corruption of the English ruling class was criticized).

In the second part, Gulliver goes to sea again and his ship is destroyed in a big storm.

He is abandoned on the land named Brobdingnagians where all the inhabitants are sixty-foot tall and everything is much taller and bigger than that in the human world. The Brobdingnagians are much better than those in Gulliver's society in wisdom, humanity and stature.

The least interesting is the third part, in which the hero adventures into several places.

The best part of the book is the fourth part, in which Gulliver sails to the country of the Houyhnhnms. Being a captain, he goes to sea, but is deserted on the shore of an island by his crew. The island is governed by the wise horses who are the ruling class. Yahoo, a group of wild animals who are mean, despicable live on the island too, which form sharp contrast with the noble and wise horses. After going back home, Gulliver cannot bear life there any more. In his options, his fellowmen are no better than Yahoos. It means that Swift has a deep love for the ordinary people and hates the ruling class who oppresses the common people.

Chapter 4 Samuel Richardson

Samuel Richardson (19 August 1689—4 July 1761) was an 18th-century English writer. He was born in Mackworth, Derbyshire, and the son of a London carpenter and received not much formal education. Although his parents hoped he would be a priest, financial problems forced him to find a job in the printing business. Thirteen years later he opened his own shop as a stationer and printer and became a famous businessman in the London trade.

Richardson married in 1721 and unfortunately, ten years later, his wife died following the deaths of five children. In 1733, he remarried and had four surviving children. As a printer Richardson published some political writing, such as the Tory periodical *The True Britain*, the newspapers *Daily Journal* (1736-7) and *Daily Gazeteer* (1738), and twenty-six volumes of the *Journals* of the House of Commons.

When Richardson was in his fifties, his literary career began and almost by accident, he wrote his first novel. As a printer, Richardson was asked to help country people write to their families. Some of these letters were from a servant girl, asking her parents what she should do when faced with her master's sexual advances. Richardson's friends and readers liked this kind of plot and asked for more of it, so in 1740, he published *Pamela, or, Virtue Rewarded*. *Pamela* was a huge success. By May 1741 it finished its fourth edition and was adapted as a drama by Goldoni and put it into performance in Italy, as well as in England. Its moral precepts formed the themes of church sermons as well as newspaper debates, while its plot and characters inspired musical adaptations, continuations, operas, and even waxworks. According to Richardson, *Pamela* was a new form of writing as a fiction, an instruction through entertainment.

Richardson's other most popular work, is *Clarissa or, the History of a Young Lady*, also regarded as one of his best works published in 1747-8. This novel is a tragic story about a girl who eloped with her seducer, but is later abandoned.

In 1742, Richardson had begun his work *Clarissa* which became his masterpiece. *Clarissa Harlowe* was published in 1747-1748 in seven volumes. The novel won much admiration, but Richardson was disappointed with some aspects of its reception. Although he had finished the first version of the novel by 1744, he continued to revise it, to ask the opinions of his friends about the plot (though disregard most of their advice), and to worry about its excessive length. The massive work, which concludes more than a million words is regarded as one of the longest novels in the English language.

It tells the story about Clarissa's struggle with her family to avoid marriage to the villian Mr. Soames, her desperate flight from her unbending and despicable family into the arms of Lovelace, her drugged rape, her attempts to escape from Lovelace by soliciting the aid of her unforgiving family, and her dramatic death.

Clarissa Harlowe, the tragic heroine of *Clarissa*, is the extremely beautiful and virtuous young lady. Her family has become wealthy only in recent years.

Her family, is now eager to become the aristocracy by acquiring estates and titles through marriage, forcing her to marry a rich but highly uncultured and unrefined man Roger Solmes against her will and her own sense of virtue.

In order to escape the marriage, she is tricked by a young gentleman of her acquaintance, Lovelace, into escaping with him. Unfortunately, Clarissa remains Lovelace's prisoner for many months. She is kept at many lodgings, and even a brothel. However, she refuses to marry him on many occasions. She eventually runs away but is discovered by Lovelace and is tricked into going back to the brothel.

Lovelace wants to possess Clarissa's body as well as her mind. He believes that if she does not have her virtue anymore, she will be forced to marry him on any terms. The growing passion for Clarissa drives Lovelace to extremes and he rapes her at last by drugging her. Through this action, Clarissa must accept and marry Lovelace. However, Clarissa is even more adamant on not marrying a vile and corrupt individual like Lovelace. Eventually, Clarissa manages to escape from the brothel, but becomes dangerously ill due to the mental duress she has been under for so many months at the hands of Lovelace.

Eventually, Clarissa dies in the full consciousness of her own virtue, and trusting in a better life after death. Lovelace dies from a duel afterwards. Clarissa's relatives finally realize their fault but it is too late.

Around Samuel Richardson, there were many leading figures in 18th century England, such as Samuel Johnson and Sarah Fielding. While he was rivaled with Henry Fielding, and they two have their different literary styles in their own novels.

Richardson's novels were very popular in his time. His last novel, *The History of Sir Charles Grandison*, appeared in 1753-4. His works, along with those of Defoe and Fielding, are widely considered to be the best works in English literature. Although he has been accused of being sentimental in novel writing, his emphasis on detail, his psychological insights into women, and his dramatic technique have earned him a prominent place among English novelists. Richardson received great fame for his novel writing and had many admirers and followers. He died in 1761 in his early seventies, and was buried in St. Bride's Church, London.

Clarissa or, the History of a Young Lady (an excerpt)

As is mentioned above, Clarissa is an epistolary novel (a novel in the form of letters). The following excerpt is Letter 22. It includes a letter written by Clarissa to Miss Howe. She informs her friend of the substance of a letter from Lovelace. She desires leave to go to church. Is referred to her brother, and insultingly refused by him. Her letter to him. His answer.

MISS CLARISSA HARLOWE, TO MISS HOWE SUNDAY MORNING, MARCH 5.

Hannah[1] has just brought me from the private place in the garden-wall, a letter from Mr. Lovelace, deposited last night, signed also by Lord M.

He tells me in it, 'That Mr. Solmes makes it his boast, that he is to be married in a few days to one of the shyest women in England: that my brother explains his meaning: This shy creature, he says, is me; and he assures every one, that his younger sister is very soon to be Mr. Solmes's wife. He tells me of the patterns bespoken which my mother mentioned to me.'

Not one thing escapes him that is done or said in this house.

'My sister, he says, reports the same things; and that with such particular aggravations of insult upon him, that he cannot but be extremely piqued, as well at the manner, as from the occasion; and expresses himself with great violence upon it.

'He knows not, he says, what my relations' inducements can be to prefer such a man as Solmes to him. If advantageous settlements be the motive, Solmes shall not offer what he will refuse to comply with.

'As to his estate and family; the first cannot be excepted against[2]: and for the second, he will not disgrace himself by a comparison so odious[3]. He appeals to Lord M. for the regularity of his life and manners ever since he has made his addresses to me, or had hope of my favour.'

I suppose he would have his Lordship's signing to this letter to be taken as a voucher[4] for him.

'He desires my leave (in company with my Lord), in a pacific manner, to attend my father and uncles, in order to make proposals that must be accepted, if they will see him, and hear what they are: and tells me, that he will submit to any measures that I shall prescribe, in order to bring about a reconciliation.'

He presumes to be very earnest with me, 'to give him a private meeting[5] some night, in my father's garden, attended by whom I please.'

Really, my dear, were you to see his letter, you would think I had given him great encouragement, and that I am in direct treaty with him; or that he is sure that my friends will drive me into a foreign protection; for he has the boldness to offer, in my Lord's name, an asylum[6] to me, should I be tyrannically treated in Solmes's behalf.

I suppose it is the way of this sex to endeavour to entangle the thoughtless of ours by bold supposals and offers, in hopes that we shall be too complaisant or bashful to quarrel with them; and, if not checked, to reckon upon our silence, as assents voluntarily given, or concessions made in their favour.

There are other particulars in this letter which I ought to mention to you: but I will take an opportunity to send you the letter itself, or a copy of it.

For my own part, I am very uneasy to think how I have been drawn on one hand, and driven on the other, into a clandestine[7], in short, into a mere loverlike correspondence, which my heart condemns.

It is easy to see, if I do not break it off, that Mr. Lovelace's advantages, by reason of my unhappy situation, will every day increase, and I shall be more and more entangled. Yet if I do put an end to it, without making it a condition of being freed from Mr. Solmes's address—May I, my dear, is it best to continue it a little longer, in order to extricate myself out of the other difficulty, by giving up all thoughts of Mr. Lovelace? —Whose advice can I now ask but yours.

All my relations are met. They are at breakfast together. Mr. Solmes is expected. I am excessively uneasy. I must lay down my pen.

* * *

They are all going to church together. Grievously disordered they appear to be, as Hannah tells me. She believes something is resolved upon.

SUNDAY NOON.

What a cruel thing is suspense! —I will ask leave to go to church this afternoon. I expect to be denied. But, if I do not ask, they may allege, that my not going is owing to myself.

* * *

I desired to speak with Shorey. Shorey came. I directed her to carry to my mother my request for permission to go to church this afternoon.

What think you was the return? Tell her, that she must direct herself to her brother for any favour she has to ask. —So, my dear, I am to be delivered up to my brother!

I was resolved, however, to ask of him this favour. Accordingly, when they sent me up my solitary dinner, I gave the messenger a billet, in which I made it my humble request through him to my father, to be permitted to go to church this afternoon.

This was the contemptuous answer: 'Tell her, that her request will be taken into consideration to-morrow.'

Patience will be the fittest return I can make to such an insult. But this method will not do with me; indeed it will not! And yet it is but the beginning, I suppose, of what I am to expect from my brother, now I am delivered up to him.

On recollection[8], I thought it best to renew my request. I did. The following is a copy of what I wrote, and what follows that, of the answer sent me.

SIR,

I know not what to make of the answer brought to my request of being permitted to go to church this afternoon. If you designed to shew your pleasantry by it, I hope that will continue; and then my request will be granted.

You know, that I never absented myself, when well, and at home, till the two last Sundays; when I was advised not to go. My present situation is such, that I never more wanted the benefit of the public prayers.

I will solemnly engage only to go thither, and back again.

I hope it cannot be thought that I would do otherwise.

My dejection of spirits will give a too just excuse on the score of indisposition for avoiding visits. Nor will I, but by distant civilities, return the compliments of any of my acquaintances. My disgraces, if they are to have an end, need not be proclaimed to the whole world. I ask this favour, therefore, for my reputation's sake, that I may be able to hold up my head[9] in the neighbourhood, if I live to see an end of the unmerited severities which seem to be designed for

Your unhappy sister, CL. HARLOWE.

TO MISS CLARISSA HARLOWE

For a girl to lay so much stress upon going to church, and yet resolve to defy her parents, in an article of the greatest consequence to them, and to the whole family, is an absurdity. You are recommended, Miss, to the practice of your private devotions. May they be efficacious upon the mind of one of the most pervicacious young creatures that ever was heard of! The intention is, I tell you plainly, to mortify you into a sense of your duty. The neighbours you are so solicitous to appear well with, already know, that you defy that. So, Miss, if you have a real value for your reputation, shew it as you ought. It is yet in your own power to establish or impair it.

JA. HARLOWE.

Thus, my dear Miss Howe, has my brother got me into his snares; and I, like a poor silly bird, the more I struggle, am the more entangled.

Notes

1. Hannah—Servants of the Harlowes, he is faithful to Clarissa.
2. be excepted against—object to; be opposed to.
3. odious—*adj*. Arousing or meriting strong dislike, aversion, or intense displeasure.
4. voucher—*n*. A piece of substantiating evidence; a proof.

5. give him a private meeting—talk with him informally and privately.
6. asylum—*n.* A place offering protection and safety; a shelter.
7. clandestine—*adj.* Kept or done in secret, often in order to conceal an illicit or improper purpose.
8. recollection—*n.* the ability to recall past occurrences the process of remembering (especially the process of recovering information by mental effort).
9. hold up my head—Pull yourself together; feel proud of oneself.

For Study and Discussion

1. In an epistolary novel, the reader has the advantage of knowing the thoughts of the characters or the writer of letters. Take some examples from the excerpt and explain how the character's thoughts are revealed.
2. *Clarissa* is often associated with the beginnings of realism in literature. To what extent is the novel realistic?
3. How are gender divisions marked in *Clarissa*? Is Clarissa an example for all human beings, or just women?
4. Is Clarissa Harlowe a tragic hero? Why or why not?

Chapter 5 Henry Fielding

Henry Fielding, the eldest of seven children, was born on April 22, 1707, at Sharpham Park, in Somerset, England. He was the most outstanding novelist and the founder of English Realistic Novel of the 18th century. His education commenced at home, under the care of Mr. Oliver. Fielding was a versatile man. He was not only a novelist, but also a dramatist, an essayist, a political pamphleteer, a learned authority on law and an able and efficient magistrate and a political economist. He was known for his rich earthy humor and satirical prowess.

As opposed to the middle-class Richardson, Fielding came of a genteel family and enjoyed an excellent education. He spent several years at the famous Eton school and took a degree in letters at the University of Leyden in Holland. Henry's mother died in April, 1718 and his father, Colonel Edmund Fielding, went away to London, leaving the children to his in-laws, the Gould family. A year later, Colonel Fielding remarried an Italian widow and attempted to regain custody of his children from his mother-in-law, Lady Gould. This led to a lengthy law-suit finally settled in 1722. The court granted Lady Gould the custody of her grandchildren and secured their mother's estate. From his own varied and sometimes riotous experiences, he gained a deeper knowledge of life.

Today Fielding is mainly known for his novels. Almost by accident, Fielding *started* writing novels in 1741 and his first major success was *Shamela*, an anonymous parody of Samuel Richardson's sentimental novel *Pamela*. The he produced *Joseph Andrews*(1742), an original work supposedly talking about Pamela's brother, Joseph. Although also begun as a parody, this work developed into an accomplished novel in its own style and is considered to mark Fielding's beginning as a serious novelist.

Joseph Andrews, or *The History of the Adventures of Joseph Andrews and of his Friend Mr. Abraham Adams*, was the first published full-length novel of Henry Fielding, and it considered to be one of the best novels in the English language.

Joseph, the virtuous and true footman, is forced to leave his service of mistress, Lady Booby, because he is no longer able to ward off her amorous advances. He goes out to reunite with his sweetheart, Fanny. While along his journey, misfortunes continually waylay him and his companion Parson Adams. They encounter both kindness and villainy, generosity and selfishness, on their journey. All ends well when Joseph and Fanny are finally wed and the secrets of their parentage is revealed. The novel represents the unit of the two main aesthetics of eighteenth-century literature: the mock-heroic and neoclassical approach of Augustans such as Alexander Pope and Jonathan Swift; and the popular, domestic prose fiction of novelists such as Daniel Defoe and Samuel Richardson.

The novel draws on a variety of inspirations. The work owes much of its humour to the techniques of Cervantes, and its picaresque subject-matter seemingly looses arrangement of events, digressions and lower-class characters. However, it had bawdy humour, an impending marriage and a mystery surrounding unknown parentage, while it is rich in philosophical digressions, classical erudition and social purpose.

Henry Fielding's third novel, *The History of Tom Jones, a Foundling*, was published in England in 1749 and was regarded as his masterpiece. It is a huge work consisting of eighteen books. The book tells the story of Tom Jones from infancy through his marriage to the beautiful and virtuous Sophia Western. It is a comedy and is amusing and all ends well.

In *Tom Jones* the author gives us a vivid panoramic picture of the 18th century England. It describes all kinds of people and social problems, and shows the author's great sympathy for the poor and also his dislike for the wicked and deceitful people.

Through the story, Fielding satirizes the hypocrisy and vanity of his supporting cast. He shows a lusty rascal figure Tom, in fact, an infinitely better human being than the vicious pretenders who surround him and scheme against him while pretended to be those of virtuous men. The hero overcomes not only all external obstacles but, most importantly, his own weaknesses of character, to win both love and fortune in the end.

Mr. Allworthy, a rich and kind-hearted country squire, finds a newborn baby in his bed. Since he can't find the baby's parents, he adopts him and names him Tom. Not long after that, his sister, a prudish spinster before, gets married and gives birth to a boy named Blifil. Blifil is made the lawful heir to his uncle's fortune. After his sister's death, Mr. Allworthy takes Blifil home and brings him up.

Tom and Blifil have different characters and personalities, though they grow in the same house. They fall in love with Sophia at the same time, daughter of a landlord in the vicinity. However, Sophia prefers Tom. In order to gain the fortune of Mr. Allworthy after his death and also the love of Sophia, Blifil plays dirty tricks and speaks ill of Tom. Thereafter, Mr. Allworthy drives Tom out of his house for being deceived by Blifil,.

Then Tom goes to London. After Tom goes away, Sophia's father forces her to marry Blifil. But the girl is strongly against her father's decision and runs away from home to find Tom. Then they encounter many exciting incidents and adventures, which constitute the main parts of the novel.

After their encounter in London, Tom is finally discovered to be Mr. Allworthy's real nephew and Blifil's half brother. Tom and Sophia return to the Mr. Allworthy's house, and Blifil is punished for his misbehaviors.

Fielding died on October 8, 1754 in Lisbon. His travel book, *The Journal of a Voyage to Lisbon*, appeared posthumously in 1755.

In Fielding's works, the central characters are common men with earthly interests, needs and passion. As a great and truthful artist, he showed human nature faithfully and accurately. His characters were not from his imagination, or from models in literature; but from the human nature. The readers could find a great many of living characters in his novels. But Fielding did not simply produce a series of literally portraits of the people whom he had observed and known. Most of his characters are created from both experience and invention, from both observation and imagination.

Fielding insisted on the crucial importance of personal experience. His profound knowledge of human nature was mainly acquired by his deep examination of the inner heart of human beings.

Fielding holds an important position in English literature as a realist novelist, and Fielding is the founder of English realistic novels, so he is also called "The father of English novel". He set up the theory of realism in literary creation which was used by some of followers. His work was based on the exact observation and study of the real life. He made a close and constant study of real men and women in the real world of his own age.

Chapter 6 Oliver Goldsmith

Oliver Goldsmith (1730—1774) was an Anglo-Irish writer, poet, and physician.

His birthplace is not known. It is said that he was born either in the townland of Pallas, or at the Smith Hill House in the diocese of Elphin, County Roscommon. In 1744 Goldsmith went to Trinty College, Dublin. In 1749 he graduated as a Bachelor of Arts; his education seemed to have given him mainly a taste for fine clothes, playing cards, singing Irish airs and playing the flute. He studied medicine desultorily at the University of Edingburgh and the University of Leiden, and set out on a walking tour of Flanders, France, Switzerland and northern Italy, living by his wits (busking with his flute). In 1756 he settled in London, where he took various jobs including apothecary's assistant and usher of a school.

Being in debt and addicted to gambling for many years, Goldsmith worked as a hackwriter and produced a massive output for the publishers of London, but his few painstaking works earned him the company of Samuel Johnson. Because of the combination of his literary work and his dissolute lifestyle, he was given the epithet *inspired idiot* by Horace Walpole . During this period he used the pseudonym "James Willington"(the name of a fellow student at Trinity) to publish his 1758 translation of the autobiography of the Huguenot Jean Marteilhe. Goldsmith made distinguished contributions in several literary forms and was known for his novel *The Vicar of Wakefield* (1766), his pastoral poem *The Deserted Village* (1770) (written in memory of his brother), another poem *The Traveller* , and his plays *The Good-Natur'd Man* (1768) and *She Stoops to Conquer* (1771, first performed in 1773). He is also thought to have written the classic chidren's tale, *The History of Little Goody Two-Shoes*, giving the world that familiar phrase, and a series of essays *The Citizen of the World*. He also wrote a romantic ballad *The Hermit* in 1765.

The Vicar of Wakefield, is Goldsmith's only novel, his masterpiece, on which his fame mainly rests. This novel has been translated into many languages and read throughout the world. The story is about Dr. Primrose, a kind-hearted vicar in a small country village and is told by him in the first person singular. Primrose, together with his wife, two daughters and four sons, lives a happy life prosperously and contentedly. But unfortunately a misfortune befalls them. They lose their fortune and are forced to move to another village where they live under the patronage of a Squire called Thornhill, who turns out to be a wicked ruffian. Thornhill seduces the vicar's elder daughter Olivia and then deserts her. With great sorrow and misery, Olivia leaves home. The vicar goes to look for her and brings her back. Then another misfortune falls upon them. Their house is burnt down in a fire and the vicar is thrown into prison for debt at the lawsuit of Squire Thornhill. In order to avenge his sister the vicar's eldest son George challenges the Squire to a duel, but he is overpowered by ruffians and thrown into prison. Meanwhile, the vicar's younger daughter Sophia is mysteriously carried away by force in a post chaise by an unknown villain. The vicar bears all these misfortunes with fortitude and resignation and even tries to teach and preach to his fellow prisoners in the jail. Luckily, Sophia is rescued by a strange gentleman Mr. Burchell, who turns out to be Sir William Thornhill, the Squire's uncle. Then the squire's villainy is fully exposed. Everything turns out well. Sir William Thornhill marries Sophia; Olivia is married to the squire; George is set free from prison and marries the girl he loves; the vicar gets his release from the jail and restores his lost fortune.

By describing the joys and sorrows of this simple, poor family, Goldsmith shows his sympathy to the family, who represents the oppressed people and condemns Squire Thornhill, who stands for the cruelty, hypocrisy and moral degradation of the wicked feudal landlord and of the city bourgeoisie. But the solution to righting the social wrongs is not satisfactory, for the happy ending of the novel hints the existence of a good and benevolent landlord in the person of Sir William Thornhill whose righteous intervention alone can check the villainy of Squire Thornhill and restore the vicar's family to happiness.

In literary history books the *Vicar of Wakefield* is often described as a sentimental novel, which displays the belief in the innate goodness of human beings. But it can also be read as a satire on the sentimental novel and its values, as the vicar's values are apparently not compatible with the real "sinful" world. It is only with Sir William Thornhill's help that he can get out of his calamities.

Vicar of Wakefield(an excerpt)

Chapter 22

Offences are Easily Pardoned Where There is Love at Bottom.

THE next morning I took my daughter[1] behind me, and set out on my return home. As we travelled along, I strove by every persuasion to calm her sorrows and fears, and to arm[2] her with resolution to bear the presence of her offended mother. I took every opportunity, from the prospect of a fine country, through which we passed, to observe how much kinder Heaven was to us, than we to each other, and that the misfortunes of nature's making were very few. I assured her that she should never perceive any change in my affections, and that during my life, which yet might be long, she might depend upon a guardian and an instructor. I armed her against the censures of the world; showed her that books were sweet, unreproaching[3] companions to the miserable, and that if they could not bring us to enjoy life, they would at least teach us to endure it.

The hired horse that we rode was to be put up that night at[4] an inn by the way, within about five miles from my house; and as I was willing to prepare my family for my daughter's reception, I determined to leave her that night at the inn, and I to return for her, accompanied by my daughter Sophia, early the next morning. It was night before we reached our appointed stage; however, after seeing her provided with a decent apartment, and having ordered the hostess to prepare proper refreshments, I kissed[5] her, and proceeded towards home. And now my heart caught new sensations of pleasure the nearer I approached that peaceful mansion. As a bird that had been frightened from its nest, my affections outwent my haste[6], and hovered round my little fireside with all the rapture of expectation. I called up the many fond things I had to say, and anticipated the welcome I was to receive. I already felt my wife's tender embrace, and smiled at the joy of my little ones. As I walked but slowly, the night waned apace. The laborers of the day were all retired to rest; the lights were out in every cottage; no sounds were heard but of the shrilling cock, and the deep-mouthed watch-dog at hollow distance. I approached my little abode[7] of pleasure, and before I was within a furlong[8] of the place, our honest mastiff[9] came running to welcome me.

It was now near midnight that I came to knock at my door; all was still and silent; my heart dilated with unutterable happiness; when, to my amazement, I saw the house bursting out in a blaze of fire, and every aperture red with conflagration! I gave a loud convulsive outcry, and fell upon the pavement insensible. This alarmed my son, who had till this been asleep, and he perceiving the flames instantly waked my wife and daughter, and all running out naked and wild with apprehension, recalled me to life with their anguish. But it was only to objects of new terror; for the flames had by this time caught the roof of our dwelling, part after part continuing to fall in, while the family stood with silent agony looking on as if they enjoyed the blaze. I gazed upon them and upon it by turns, and then looked round me for my two little ones; but they were not to be seen. 0 misery! "Where," cried I, "where are my little ones?"—"They are burnt to death in the flames," says my wife, calmly, "and I will die with them." That moment I heard the cry of the babes within, who were just awaked by the fire, and nothing could have stopped me. "Where, where are my children?" cried I, rushing through the flames, and bursting the door of the chamber in which they were confined. "Where are my little ones?"—"Here, dear papa, here we are," cried they, together, while the flames were just catching the bed where they lay. I caught them both in my arms. and snatching them ran through the fire as fast as possible, while just as I was got out, the roof sunk in. "—Now," cried I, holding up my children, "now let the flames burn on, and all my possessions perish. Here they are; I have saved my treasure[10]. Here, my dearest, here are our treasures, and we shall yet be happy." We kissed our little darlings a thousand times, they clasped us round the neck, and seemed to share our transports, while their mother laughed and wept by turns.

I now stood a calm spectator of the flames, and after some time began to perceive that my arm to the shoulder was scorched in a terrible manner. It was, therefore, out of my power to give my son any assistance, either in attempting to save our goods, or preventing the flames spreading to our corn. By this time the neighbors were alarmed, and came running to our assistance; but all they could do was to stand, like us, spectators of the calamity. My goods, among which were the notes I had reserved for my daughters' fortunes, were entirely consumed, except a box with some papers that stood in the kitchen, and two or three things more of little consequence, which my son brought away in the beginning. The neighbors contributed, however, what they could to lighten our distress. They brought us clothes, and furnished one of our outhouses with kitchen utensils; so that by daylight we had another, though a wretched dwelling, to retire to. My honest next neighbor and his children were not the least assiduous[11] in providing us with everything necessary, and offering whatever consolation untutored benevolence could suggest.

When the fears of my family had subsided, curiosity to know the cause of my long stay began to take place; having, therefore, informed them of every particular, I proceeded to prepare them for the reception of our lost one, and though we had nothing but wretchedness now to impart, I was willing to procure her a welcome to what we had. This task would have been more difficult but for our recent calamity, which had humbled my wife's pride and blunted it by more poignant afflictions. Being unable to go for my poor child myself, as my arm grew very painful, I sent my son and daughter, who soon returned, supporting the wretched delinquent, who had not the courage to look up at her mother, whom no instructions of mine could persuade to a perfect reconciliation; for women have a much stronger sense of female error than men. "Ah, madam," cried her mother, "this is but a poor place you have come to after so much finery. My daughter Sophy and I can afford but little entertainment to persons who have kept company only with people of distinction. Yes, Miss Livy, your poor father and I have suffered very much of late; but I hope Heaven will forgive you." During this reception the unhappy victim stood pale and trembling, unable to weep or to reply; but I could not continue a silent spectator of her distress; wherefore assuming a degree of severity in my voice and manner, which was ever followed with instant submission: "I entreat, woman, that my words may be now marked once for all; I have here brought you back a poor deluded wanderer: her return to duty demands the revival of our tenderness. The real hardships of life are now coming fast upon us; let us not, therefore, increase them by dissension among each other. If we live harmoniously together, we may yet be contented, as there are enough of us to shut out the censuring world and keep each other in countenance. The kindness of Heaven is promised to the penitent, and let ours be directed by the example. Heaven, we are assured, is much more pleased to view a repentant sinner, than ninety-nine persons who have supported a course of undeviating rectitude. And this is right; for that single effort by which we stop short in the downhill path to perdition, is itself a greater exertion of virtue than a hundred acts of justice. "[12]

Notes

1. daughter—the vicar's eldest daughter Olivia.
2. arm—support and encourage.
3. unreproaching—shouldn't be blamed or punished.
4. put up at—obtain food and lodging at (a place), stay.
5. kissed—it shows father's deep love towards daughter.
6. my affections outwent my haste—this sentence shows the theme of this chapter.
7. abode—formal word which indicates your home or the place where you live.
8. furlong—a unit for measuring length, equal to 220 yards or 201 metres, used mainly in horseracing.
9. mastiff—a large powerful guard dog.
10. treasure—not the vicar's possessions or money, but his children.
11. assiduous—working hard or paying great attention to detail.
12. "is itself a greater exertion of virtue than a hundred acts of justice. "—this sentence also shows the theme of this chapter *Offences are Easily Pardoned Where There is Love at Bottom*.

For Study and Discussion

1. What misfortunes happened to Vicar's family in this chapter?
2. Who give the vicar's family help after the fire broke out?
3. How many persons are there in the vicar's family?
4. What is the theme of this chapter ?
5. What do you think of Dr. Primrose, the vicar?

Part Ten
The Nineteenth Century

Chapter 1 The Prosperous Period in Novel Writing

The 19th century saw prosperity in English novel writing. Two important novelists whose works came at the beginning of this period are Jane Austen (1775—1817) and Sir Walter Scott (1771 — 1832). Jane Austen, with her very acute and exquisite sense of character and scene, has probably never been matched within her deliberately limited range. Her novels are classics of the art of fiction, and once enjoyed they are our friends for life. Scott is a curious case, for in his own time, when he had stupendous success and very wide influence as author of medieval romance such as *Ivanhoe* (1819), he was thought to be not so much a novelist as a historical romancer. In fact, however, he has many weaknesses as a historical romancer and much enduring strength and appeal as a novelist. His finest stories are those with an eighteenth-century background.

The years between 1840 to 1890 represent a peak in English novel writing. The 1840—1890 group begins with Charles Dickens (1812—1870), one of the acknowledged world masters of fiction. Dickens began to write in a slap dash, improvising way, mixing glorious fun with unreal melodrama; then he gradually planned his work carefuly and, while keeping his inimitable humor, filled his writings with a searching criticism of mid-Victorian society. William Makepeace Thackeray (1811—1863) had no such genius, but he had great qualities of his own: a wide scope of knowledge of social life, a wonderful eye and ear for character and scene, a talent for satire and irony, and an easy narrative style that could give rise to passages of great force and beauty. These qualities are perhaps found at their best in *Vanity Fair*, although many critics consider his historical novel, *Henry Esmond*, his masterpiece.

The chief women in this group are Charlotte Brontë(1816—1855), who brought an intense realism into fictions; her sister, Emily Brontë(1818—1848), whose *Wuthering Heights* (1847) is hardly a novel at all in the ordinary sense but rather an impassioned and symbolic prose poem; Elizabeth Gaskell, Charlotte Bronte's biographer, who drew realistic pictures of the working class struggle and life in her masterpiece *Mary Barton*; and Mary Ann Evans (1819—1880), who wrote under the name of George Eliot. The latter was a deeply serious woman with a good intellect as well as a sound knowledge of English provincial life; her very solid virtues are found at their best in *The Mill on the Floss* and *Adam Bede*.

George Meredith (1828—1909), Samuel Butler (1835—1902), and Thomas Hardy (1840—1928) were critical realists in the late 19th century. They showed great concern about the social life, making their fiction reflect social reality and expose social vices. Meredith inherited Thackeray's tradition, and used much satire in his novels, such as *Beauchamp's Career* and *The Egoist*. He satirically described the upper class of England. In his masterpiece *The Egoist*, he describes the harmful influence of bourgeois individualism and egoism on human soul. Samuel Butler wrote three major novels to criticize English bourgeois society. In *Erewhon and Erewhon Revisited Twenty Years Later*, he directs his satire to the religion, philosophy and morality. In his masterpiece *The Way of All Flesh*, he points out the corrupting role of money on human soul, and expresses his bitter hatred for the hypocritical social morality. Hardy is broodingly pessimistic, at his best when his characters are rustic types surrounded by the heaths and vales of the author's native "Wessex". In one-way or another, he reflected the poor farmer's miserable condition under capitalist social system.

Critical realism became the major literary trend in English literature of the period, and the novel became its major form of expression. The critical realists, most of whom were novelists, described with much vividness and artistic skill the chief traits of the English society and criticized the capitalist system from a democratic viewpoint. They not only gave a satirical portrayal of the bourgeoisie and the ruling class, but also showed profound sympathy for the common people. In their best work, the greed and hypocrisy of the upper class are contrasted with the honesty and goodheartedness of the lower class. Hence humour and satire abound in the English realistic novels of this century. Humorous scenes set off the actions of the positive characters, and the humour is often tinged with a lyricism, which serves to stress the fine qualities of such characters. Meanwhile, bitter satire and grotesque are used to expose the seamy side of the bourgeois society. The critical realists showed their strong dislike to the corrupting influence of the rule of cash upon human nature.

Critical realism, which flourished in the forties and the early fifties of the century, was greatly influenced by the working class movement known as the Chartist Movement. It is a progressive trend in English literature. But the critical realists were unable to find a way to eradicate the social evils they knew so well. They did not realize the necessity of changing the bourgeois society through conscious human effort. They were unable to find a good solution to the social contradictions. They usually start with a powerful exposure of the ugliness of the bourgeois world in their novels, but often place happy endings or impotent compromise at the end. So evolution or reformism is what they approved of in dealing with the social problems.

The greatest critical realist of the time was Charles Dickens. William Makepeace Thackeray, Charlotte and Emily Bronte, Elizabeth Gaskell, George Eliot, and Thomas Hardy were other famous critical realists.

Toward the end of the 19th century, English prose fiction suddenly began to travel to very distant places far away from the English social scene. Some novelists represented by Robert Louis Stevenson refused to deal with the social reality, and concentrated their attention on imaginary adventures in novel writing. His *Treasure Island* and *The Strange Case of Dr. Jekyll* and *Mr. Hyde* can be regarded as the examples of new romance; Stevenson has retained his hold on successive generations of readers by the romantic zest of his narrative and a curious charm of style. William Morris (1834—1896), the first English writer who voiced the revolutionary ideal of socialism in his poetry and prose, wrote two prose romances: *A Dream of John Ball* and *News from Nowhere*. In *A Dream of John Ball*, through describing the peasant rising of 1381 led by John Ball, he highly praises the struggle of the English people against their oppressors. In *News from Nowhere*, he pictures the future classless society, and encourages the English working class to fight for the realization of such a society in England.

The nation-wide depression in the late nineteenth century provided the background for the appearance of the decadent literature. Oscar Wilde is the representative among the writers of aestheticism and decadence. Decadence in English literature reflects the crisis of bourgeois culture. It opposes the democratic and progressive tendency in English literature. The group of writers represented by Wilde uphold bourgeois individualism, and their slogan is "art for art's sake". They think that the existing evils in the English society are like incurable diseases impossible to remove. Their writings are like groans of desperate patients. Oscar Wilde's novel *The Picture of Dorian Gray* is a typical decadent novel reflecting the author's aesthetical ideas and immoralism.

Chapter 2 Jane Austen

Jane Austen (16 December 1775—18 July 1817) was one of the nineteenth century British women novelists. And she was also one of the most widely read and most beloved writers in English literature.

Jane Austen was born in a village called Steventon in Hampshire, a small town in southwest England. She was the youngest daughter of the parish's rector and had six brothers and one sister. Like most women of the era, Austen did not receive much formal education. She was educated at home mainly by her father and elder brothers. And she did a fair amount of reading at the same time. In her lifetime, Jane Austen never married and led an uneventful life. She was especially opposed to publicity and popularity. She died quietly as she had lived, at Winchester in 1817, and was buried in the Winchester cathedral. Austen was a bright, attractive little woman. Her sunny qualities are unconsciously reflected in all her books.

Austen began to write at an early age. Her fictions were seldom influenced by the current fashions or by the revolutionary ideas. She never touched upon the class conflicts of her time, and there weren't extremes of wealth and poverty in her works. Her novels are simply stories of the lives and thoughts of the commonplace people of the upper middle class. She restricted her subject matter to a narrow range of society and events: a quiet, prosperous, middle-class circle in provincial surroundings. However, she treated this material with such subtlety of observation, depth of psychological penetration and delicacy of touch that she is ranked among the best of English novelists. Austen's artistic apprenticeship lasted from her teenage years until she was about thirty-five years old. During this period, she tried to write in various literary forms. And the epistolary novel is one of them, which she tried and then abandoned. In total, Jane Austen published four novels anonymously during her lifetime: *Sense and Sensibility* (1811), *Pride and Prejudice* (1813), *Mansfield Park* (1814) and *Emma* (1816), she achieved success as a published writer. The two novels *Northanger Abbey* (1818) and *Persuasion* (1818) were published posthumously. And Austen also left us two unfinished works: *The Watsons* and *Sanditon*. Among her novels, *Pride and Prejudice* and *Emma* have generally been regarded as the most important ones. And *Pride and Prejudice* has been regarded as Jane Austen's masterpiece. Its plot is carefully constructed and it is written in an elegant style. The theme of marriage centers on the conflict between the "prejudice" of Elizabeth and the "pride" of Mr. Darcy. *Emma* is a novel about a young woman's discovery of her own selfishness, and how she learns to cope with it. *Sense and Sensibility* tells us a story of two sisters. One is able to control her emotion with reason, and shows a less enthusiastic attitude to her lover, but finally she wins his heart and happiness. The other possesses sensibility and is of the sentimental and romantic school. She openly expresses her love to her lover. But she is at last deceived by him and suffers a lot. Her other novels, *Mansfield Park* and *Persuasion* are of essentially the same type.

In her novels, the plots are simple and grow naturally out of the characters and their ordinary relations. But incidents and characters are dealt with perfect sureness of touch and with the perfect mastery of assured knowledge. She is good at handling of conversation in her novels. And it is the fine point of her art. The characters are made to reveal themselves through their own words, and Jane Austen seems always able to find the precise expression that accurately fits the character and the occasion. She has a neat humour and a satirical touch. Her style is an almost perfect instrument for her purpose—simple, clear, quiet, precise, keen, suggestive and mildly ironical.

Pride and Prejudice deals with the everyday life of the big and small landowners and their families in the English countryside, particularly with the scene of love and marriage of the younger members of these families. There are five Bennet sisters in all: Jane, Elizabeth, Mary, Kitty and Lydia. They, along with their mother, will be forced off their father's small estate in the event of his death. Lacking a male heir, Mr. Bennet's property has been willed, or entailed, to his nearest male relative, Reverend William Collins. This arrangement has made Mrs. Bennet increasingly anxious to marry off her daughters. When Mr. Bingley, a wealthy young man also from as ungenteel background, rents a nearby manor and arrives with his sister and a friend, Mrs. Bennet's notion that well-managed intrigue will get her daughters husbands seems to have a promise.

Bingley immediately falls in love with Jane because of her beauty and sweetness. His noble friend Mr. Darcy offends Elizabeth by pronouncing her "tolerable" looking and refusing to ask her to dance. From then on, Elizabeth holds a rooted prejudice against Darcy. The younger sisters, Lydia and Kitty, are delighted with the prospects offered by some young military officers stationed in Meryton. One of them, Wickham appeals to Meryton girls due to his handsome appearance. He expresses a special interest in Elizabeth and tells her Darcy's wrongdoing to him. Elizabeth is disposed to return and therefore confirms her prejudice against Darcy.

Attempting to make amends for the conditions of the entail, Reverend Mr. Collins visits the Mr. Bennets with the view of marrying one of the Bennet girls. When Mr. Collins learns Jane is already in love, he proposes immediately to Elizabeth, who refuses his offer because she cannot love him. Shortly thereafter he is accepted by Elizabeth's friend Charlotte Lucas, whom Elizabeth knows to have too much sense not to see that Collins is a fool. When Bingley and his party leave suddenly for London, Elizabeth concludes that Darcy has talked Bingley out of proposing to Jane. Jane visits the Gardiners in London, where she is treated with mere formal politeness by Miss Bingley, who suggests that her brother is to marry Darcy's sister. Learning that Wickham is courting an heiress merely for money, Elizabeth is completely disillusioned: she can only congratulate herself on not being taken in.

Elizabeth meets Darcy by accident while visiting Charlotte and Mr. Collins, who has a living on the estate of Lady Catherine de Bourgh, a haughty snob and Darcy's aunt. Elizabeth is dumbfounded when Darcy suddenly proposes to her, and angrily rejects him, accusing him of separating Bingley and Jane and of being unfair to Wickham and of humiliating her and her relatives. The next day he gives her a letter explaining and justifying his conduct; at first Elizabeth believes it must be false, but gradually she comes to accept the truth of everything Darcy says. She feels ashamed and admits that until this moment she never knew herself. Since then she sees all the characters and incidents in a new light.

Against Elizabeth's advice, Mr. Bennet allows Lydia to visit the family of one of the offices at the fashionable and somewhat notorious resort of Brighton, at that time. Elizabeth herself goes on a tour with the Gardines through scenic Derbyshire. The Gardiners visit Darcy's estate of Pemberly in his absence. The house-keeper gives them a glowing report of her master's character and conduct. Elizabeth has more reason than ever to regret prejudice against the man. When Darcy returns unexpectedly, he is all hospitality and a new understanding is opening. But these possibilities seem dashed by her sister Lydia's elopement with Wickham, who has no intention to marry her. By the social convention of the time the "ruin" of Lydia will affect the marriage ability of all her sisters. Distressed at this news, Elizabeth blurs it out to Darcy. Darcy finds the couple and pressures Wickham into honoring his commitment so that the Bennet family's good name is preserved.

When Bingley and Darcy return to the neighborhood, Bingley and Jane quickly resume their love for one another and become engaged. To Elizabeth's surprise, Lady Catherine de Bourgh arrives and haughtily tries to extract a promise from Elizabeth that she will not marry Darcy. As happens to such domineering intriguers, her aim is undermined by her own actions: Darcy learns of Elizabeth's standing up to his aunt and comes to propose again. This time he is accepted. In a characteristic final comic touch, Mrs. Bennet is ecstatic at the accomplishment of more than she could have imagined in her plans to marry off her daughters.

As the above main plots represents, there is a conservative tendency in this novel from two aspects, the delineation of an ideal feudal society and traditional moralization of women.

Emma, another poplar novel of Austen's, is a maturer work and contains sharper and more direct social criticism. *Emma* is a comedy of complicated plots. The heroine, Emma Woodhouse, was the younger of the two daughters of a wealthy family in the village of Highbury. Her mother died long ago and her governess, Miss Taylor, was her friend more than her teacher. With Miss Taylor's marriage with Mr. Weston, a gentleman nearby in Randalls, Emma felt a melancholy change in her life. Soon Emma got acquainted with a pretty homeless girl at a boarding school, Harriet Smith. She was determined to take Harriet as her protégée and decided to improve her and find a gentleman husband for her. Consequently, Emma, with her overwhelming influence, induced simple-minded Harriet to refuse the proposal by Robert Martin, a young farmer in love with Harriet, who, in Emma's opinion, was inferior to Harriet. Regardless of her brother-in-law Mr. Knightley's repeated warnings, Emma insisted on the prospect of a possible marriage between Harriet and Mr. Elton, a clergyman. To Emma's indignation, Mr. Elton asked for her own hand, mistaking Emma's encouragement of his courtship with Harriet for a sign of her own love for him. In extreme disappointment and humiliation, Mr. Elton soon married a rich but vulgar woman, and both were hostile to Emma and Harriet.

In the meantime, two young people entered Highbury. One is Frank Churchill, the son of Mr. Weston, but now adopted by his mother's family, who eventually came to visit his father and his stepmother after so many delays. The other is Jane Fairfax, an accomplished young lady brought up by Captain Campbell after her parents' early death, who came to live with her aunt Miss Bates for a while. Although Emma wanted to remain single, she always thought that Frank was the only potential candidate if she chose to marry. In others' eyes, apparently Emma and Frank shared an intimate relationship. However, after finding herself unable to love Frank, she attempted to make a match between Harriet and Frank. To her greatest shock, Harriet confessed to Emma her love for Mr. Knightley and her belief in his ardent love for her. Not until then did Emma realize her own deep love for Mr. Knightley.

With the news of Mrs. Churchill's death, the secret engagement between Frank and Jane was finally disclosed, which in part accounted for Jane's consistent coldness to Emma. Emma matured after so many frustrations, and Mr. Knightley declared his love for Emma. Harriet finally married Robert Martin. And the novel ended with three marriages.

Austen's novels, focusing on courtship and marriage, remain well-known for their satiric depictions of English society and the manners of the era. Her insights into the lives of women during the late eighteenth century and the early nineteenth century Regency period-in addition to her ability to handle form, satire, and irony—have made her one of the most studied and influential novelists of her time. As with many great authors, however, her death preceded her renown.

Chapter 3 Walter Scott

Walter Scott (1771—1832) was a Scottish historical novelist and poet popular throughout Europe during his time.

Walter Scott was born in Edinburgh. His father was a barrister. His mother was a well-educated woman and full of strong imagination, who told young Scott a lot of wonderful stories of the past. As a child, Scott suffered from a disease which made him lame. Therefore he was sent away from the city to be with his grandmother who was a perfect treasure house of legends concerning the old Border feuds. Under the influence of her wonderful tales, Scott developed the intense love of Scottish history and tradition, which characterized all his works.

In some ways Scott was regarded as the first English-language author to have a truly international career in his lifetime, because he had many contemporary readers all over

Europe, Australia, and North America. His novels and poetry are still read, and many of his works remain classics of both English-language literature and of Scottish literature. Famous titles include *Ivanhoe*, *Rob Roy*, *The Lady of The Lake*, *Waverley*, *The Heart of Midlothian* and *The Bride of Lammermoor*.

Scott's literary career began with the translation from the German dramatists and poets, such as Goethe and Burger. He then published a three-volume set of collected Scottish ballads, *The Minstrelsy of the Scottish Border*, which firstly showed his interest in Scottish history from a literary standpoint.

In 1805, he published his first original work, *The Lay of the Last Minstrel*, which brought him immediate success. Then he followed with two other long poems, *Marmion* and *The Lady of the Lake*, which aroused Scotland and England to intense enthusiasm and brought the author unexpected fame.

Mainly for his historical novels, Walter Scott is remembered by people. He has been universally considered to be the creator and the great master of historical novel. His novels may be divided into three groups according to their subject matter: the group on the history of Scotland, the group on English history and the group on the history of European countries.

The group on the history of Scotland is the earliest and largest group of Scott's historical novels. The famous novels in this group include *Waverley*, *Old Morality*, *Rob Roy*, and *The Heart of Midlothian*. The central idea of these novels focuses on the Scottish people's brave fight against English government. Walter Scott praises the Scottish people's love for liberty and independence.

Waverley, his first novel, was published in 1814, which was a great success after its publication. It was a tale of the "Forty-Five" Tacobite rising in the Kingdom of Great Britain in 1745 with its English protagonist Edward Waverley. The rebellion against England became the theme of the novel.

Old Morality describes a stirring tale, happening between 1670 and 1671, in which the peasants, armed with scythes and axes, rout a regiment of the royal army. The central idea of the story that the resistance of the Covenanters against the attempts of Charles II to impose episcopacy is clearly presented. Scott shows his deep sympathy to the peasants.

The Heart of Midlothian, whose background is the riot of 1736, tells a story about a peasant girl who manages to procure a pardon for her sister who has been sentenced to death on a charge of child-murder.

Rob Roy, the best known of this group, describes the 1715 uprising of the Scottish Highlanders against the English yoke. The novel tells a story of Francis, to whom some misfortune happens. He is the son of a rich London merchant and meets a bitter enemy in the sixth son of his uncle, who attempts to kill Francis and rob his father. With the help and support of Rob Roy, who is the leader of the Scottish Highlanders in revolt against the English rule, Francis's enemy is killed. Thus Francis becomes an eyewitness to the struggle between the Scottish people and the English troops.

Novels on English history were written to represent different stages of English history, covering the days after the Norman Conquest, the life during the Tudor Dynasty and the Stuart rule—the English Revolution and the Restoration Period. In this group the best known is *Ivanhoe*.

Set in England in the last years of the 12th century, *Ivanhoe* tells the story of a noble knight involved with King Richard I and his return to England from the Crusades, during which the forces of Christian Europe sought to conquer the Holy Land of Jerusalem from its Muslim occupants. The focus of the book is on the conflict between the Saxons and the Normans. In this novel, as in Scott's other novels, there are descriptions of various strata of people. There are vivid pictures of the swineherd Gurth, the poor fool Wamba and the peasant hero Robin Hood, the outlaw. Beside these lively images of people, Ivanhoe, the hero of the novel, is a rather pale figure who acts only as a link between the various characters and events in the novel.

There are some novels on the history of other countries, among which the best-known one is *Quentin Durward*. It deals with the historical events under the reign of King Louis XI in France.

Scott is the first novelist to recreate the past. He relied upon careful studies and investigations into the details of historical life and he is also a romantic. By combining historical fact with romantic imagination, he gives a picturesque representation of many historical personages and events in his novels.

Scott always combines historical events closely with the fates of individuals. The interaction between historical life and individual life always helps unfold the plot of his novel. *Ivanhoe* is a good illustration. Its plot develops through the interaction of the national struggle between the Saxons and Normans on the one hand, and Ivanhoe's personal adventures on the other. Scott usually makes young man of noble birth his nominal heroes, who are usually pale figures, and are often thrown into close companionship with ordinary people and go through a series of hardships and adventures. The function of these heroes is to hold together the numerous incidents of the plot and introduce other characters far more interesting than themselves.

Scott always gives thought and attention to the role and fates of the ordinary people. People from different social strata characterize Scott's works.

Scott is conservative. He opposes "extremes" in the people's struggles, and regards compromise as the best means in solving social contradictions. He sometimes approaches the truth of history and shows the decay of the old and the victory of the new social forms.

Scott's novels paved the way for the development of the realistic novel of the 19th century. In a sense, Scott's literary career marks the transition from romanticism to realism in English literature of the 19th century.

Ivanhoe (an excerpt)

The following excerpt is taken from Chapter 28 of "Ivanhoe". After the tournament, the gravely wounded Ivanhoe was tended by Isaac and Rebecca. When Ivanhoe weakly regained consciousness, Rebecca promised him that she was a mistress of the healing arts and would restore his health in eight days.

Chapter 28

Our history must needs retrograde[1] for the space of a few pages, to inform the reader of certain passages material to his understanding the rest of this important narrative. His own intelligence may indeed have easily anticipated that, when Ivanhoe sunk down, and seemed abandoned by all the world, it was the importunity[2] of Rebecca which prevailed on her father to have the gallant[3] young warrior transported from the lists to the house which for the time the Jews inhabited in the suburbs of Ashby.

It would not have been difficult to have persuaded Isaac to this step in any other circumstances, for his disposition was kind and grateful. But he had also the prejudices and scrupulous timidity of his persecuted people, and those were to be conquered.

"Holy Abraham!" he exclaimed, "he is a good youth, and my heart bleeds to see the gore trickle down his rich embroidered hacqueton, and his corslet of goodly price—but to carry him to our house!

—Damsel[4], hast thou well considered?[5]—he is a Christian, and by our law we may not deal with the stranger and Gentile[6], save for the advantage of our commerce."

"Speak not so, my dear father," replied Rebecca; "we may not indeed mix with them in banquet and in jollity; but in wounds and in misery, the Gentile becometh the Jew's brother."

"I would I knew what the Rabbi Jacob Ben Tudela would opine[7] on it," replied Isaac;—"nevertheless, the good youth must not bleed to death. Let Seth and Reuben bear him to Ashby."

"Nay, let them place him in my litter," said Rebecca; "I will mount one of the palfreys[8]."

"That were to expose thee to the gaze of those dogs of Ishmael and of Edom," whispered Isaac, with a suspicious glance towards the crowd of knights and squires. But Rebecca was already busied in carrying her charitable purpose into effect, and listed not what he said, until Isaac, seizing the sleeve of her mantle, again exclaimed, in a hurried voice—"Beard of Aaron! —what if the youth perish!

—if he die in our custody, shall we not be held guilty of his blood, and be torn to pieces by the multitude[9]?"

"He will not die, my father," said Rebecca, gently extricating herself from the grasp of Isaac"he will not die unless we abandon him; and if so, we are indeed answerable for his blood to God and to man."

"Nay," said Isaac, releasing his hold, "it grieveth[10] me as much to see the drops of his blood, as if they were so many golden byzants from mine own purse; and I well know, that the lessons of Miriam, daughter of the Rabbi Manasses of Byzantium whose soul is in Paradise, have made thee skilful in the art of healing, and that thou knowest the craft of herbs, and the force of elixirs. Therefore, do as thy mind giveth thee—thou art a good damsel, a blessing, and a crown, and a song of rejoicing unto me and unto my house, and unto the people of my fathers."

The apprehensions of Isaac, however, were not ill founded; and the generous and grateful benevolence of his daughter exposed her, on her return to Ashby, to the unhallowed gaze of Brian de Bois-Guilbert.

he Templar twice passed and repassed them on the road, fixing his bold and ardent look on the beautiful Jewess; and we have already seen the consequences of the admiration which her charms excited when accident threw her into the power of that unprincipled voluptuary[11].

Rebecca lost no time in causing the patient to be transported to their temporary dwelling, and proceeded with her own hands to examine and to bind up his wounds. The youngest reader of romances and romantic ballads, must recollect how often the females, during the dark ages, as they are called, were initiated into the mysteries of surgery, and how frequently the gallant knight submitted the wounds of his person to her cure, whose eyes had yet more deeply penetrated his heart.

But the Jews, both male and female, possessed and practised the medical science in all its branches, and the monarchs and powerful barons of the time frequently committed themselves to the charge of some experienced sage among this despised people, when wounded or in sickness. The aid of the Jewish physicians was not the less eagerly sought after, though a general belief prevailed among the Christians, that the Jewish Rabbins were deeply acquainted with the occult sciences, and particularly with the cabalistical art, which had its name and origin in the studies of the sages of Israel.

Neither did the Rabbins disown such acquaintance with supernatural arts, which added nothing (for what could add aught?) to the hatred with which their nation was regarded, while it diminished the contempt with which that malevolence[12] was mingled.

A Jewish magician might be the subject of equal abhorrence with a Jewish usurer, but he could not be equally despised. It is besides probable, considering the wonderful cures they are said to have performed, that the Jews possessed some secrets of the healing art peculiar to themselves, and which, with the exclusive spirit arising out of their condition, they took great care to conceal from the Christians amongst whom they dwelt.

The beautiful Rebecca had been heedfully brought up in all the knowledge proper to her nation, which her apt and powerful mind had retained, arranged, and enlarged, in the course of a progress beyond her years, her sex, and even the age in which she lived. Her knowledge of medicine and of the healing art had been acquired under an aged Jewess, the daughter of one of their most celebrated doctors, who loved Rebecca as her own child, and was believed to have communicated to her secrets, which had been left to herself by her sage father at the same time, and under the same circumstances. The fate of Miriam had indeed been to fall a sacrifice to the fanaticism[13] of the times; but her secrets had survived in her apt pupil.

Rebecca, thus endowed with knowledge as with beauty, was universally revered and admired by her own tribe, who almost regarded her as one of those gifted women mentioned in the sacred history. Her father himself, out of reverence for her talents, which involuntarily mingled itself with his unbounded affection, permitted the maiden a greater liberty than was usually indulged to those of her sex by the habits of her people, and was, as we have just seen, frequently guided by her opinion, even in preference to his own.

When Ivanhoe reached the habitation of Isaac, he was still in a state of unconsciousness, owing to the profuse loss of blood which had taken place during his exertions in the lists. Rebecca examined the wound, and having applied to it such vulnerary remedies as her art prescribed, informed her father that if fever could be averted, of which the great bleeding rendered her little apprehensive, and if the healing balsam of Miriam retained its virtue, there was nothing to fear for his guest's life, and that he might with safety travel to York with them on the ensuing day. Isaac looked a little blank at this annunciation. His charity would willingly have stopped short at Ashby, or at most would have left the wounded Christian to be tended in the house where he was residing at present, with an assurance to the Hebrew to whom it belonged, that all expenses should be duly discharged. To this, however, Rebecca opposed many reasons, of which we shall only mention two that had peculiar weight with Isaac. The one was, that she would on no account put the phial of precious balsam into the hands of another physician even of her own tribe, lest that valuable mystery should be discovered; the other, that this wounded knight, Wilfred of Ivanhoe, was an intimate favourite of Richard Coeur-de-Lion[14], and that, in case the monarch should return, Isaac, who had supplied his brother John with treasure to prosecute his rebellious purposes, would stand in no small need of a powerful protector who enjoyed Richard's favour.

"Thou art speaking but sooth[15], Rebecca," said Isaac, giving way to these weighty arguments—"it were an offending of Heaven to betray the secrets of the blessed Miriam; for the good which Heaven giveth, is not rashly to be squandered upon others, whether it be talents of gold and shekels of silver, or whether it be the secret mysteries of a wise physician—assuredly they should be preserved to those to whom Providence hath vouchsafed them. And him whom the Nazarenes of England call the Lion's Heart, assuredly it were better for me to fall into the hands of a strong lion of Idumea than into his, if he shall have got assurance of my dealing with his brother. Wherefore I will lend ear to thy counsel, and this youth shall journey with us unto York, and our house shall be as a home to him until his wounds shall be healed. And if he of the Lion Heart shall return to the land, as is now noised abroad, then shall this Wilfred of Ivanhoe be unto me as a wall of defence, when the king's displeasure shall burn high against thy father. And if he doth not return, this Wilfred may natheless[16] repay us our charges when he shall gain treasure by the strength of his spear and of his sword, even as he did yesterday and this day also. For the youth is a good youth, and keepeth the day which he appointeth, and restoreth that which he borroweth, and succoureth the Israelite, even the child of my father's house, when he is encompassed by strong thieves and sons of Belial."

It was not until evening was nearly closed that Ivanhoe was restored to consciousness of his situation. He awoke from a broken slumber, under the confused impressions which are naturally attendant on the recovery from a state of insensibility. He was unable for some time to recall exactly to memory the circumstances which had preceded his fall in the lists, or to make out any connected chain of the events in which he had been engaged upon the yesterday. A sense of wounds and injury, joined to great weakness and exhaustion, was mingled with the recollection of blows dealt and received, of steeds rushing upon each other, overthrowing and overthrown—of shouts and clashing of arms, and all the heady tumult of a confused fight. An effort to draw aside the curtain of his conch was in some degree successful, although rendered difficult by the pain of his wound.

To his great surprise he found himself in a room magnificently furnished, but having cushions instead of chairs to rest upon, and in other respects partaking so much of Oriental costume, that he began to doubt whether he had not, during his sleep, been transported back again to the land of Palestine. The impression was increased, when, the tapestry being drawn aside, a female form, dressed in a rich habit, which partook more of the Eastern taste than that of Europe, glided through the door which it concealed, and was followed by a swarthy[17] domestic.

As the wounded knight was about to address this fair apparition, she imposed silence by placing her slender finger upon her ruby lips, while the attendant, approaching him, proceeded to uncover Ivanhoe's side, and the lovely Jewess satisfied herself that the bandage was in its place, and the wound doing well. She performed her task with a graceful and dignified simplicity and modesty, which might, even in more civilized days, have served to redeem it from whatever might seem repugnant to female delicacy. The idea of so young and beautiful a person engaged in attendance on a sick-bed, or in dressing the wound of one of a different sex, was melted away and lost in that of a beneficent being contributing her effectual aid to relieve pain, and to avert the stroke of death. Rebecca's few and brief directions were given in the Hebrew language to the old domestic; and he, who had been frequently her assistant in similar cases, obeyed them without reply.

Notes

1. retrograde—direct backwards.
2. importunity—repeated requests.
3. gallant—(old use) brave.
4. damsel—(old use) girl, young unmarried woman.
5. hast thou well considered—have you well considered
6. Gentile—person who is not Jewish.
7. opine—(formal) have or express the opinion.
8. palfreys—horses, especially for woman to ride.
9. multitude—the common people.
10. grieveth—grieves, causes to feel grief.
11. voluptuary—person who gives himself up to luxury and sensual pleasures.
12. malevolence—ill will.
13. fanaticism—violent, unreasoning enthusiasm.
14. Richard Coeur-de-Lion—The King of England and the head of the Norman royal line, the Plantagenets. He is known as "Richard the Lion-Hearted" for his valor and courage in battle, and for his love of adventure.
15. Thou art speaking but sooth—You are saying the truth.
16. natheless—neverthless.
17. swarthy—having a dark complexion.

For Study and Discussion

1. Why does Rebecca insist on tending Ivanhoe? What do you think of what she does?
2. What's the attitude of Isaac towards Rebecca's determination to transport Ivanhoe from the lists to the house?
3. How does Rebecca persuade Ivanhoe to stay for recovery?
4. Rebecca plays an important role in this chapter, make a comment on her.
5. What quality can you see from Ivanhoe? Give your opinion.

Chapter 4 Charles Dickens

Charles Dickens, pen-named "Boz", was the most popular English novelist of the Victorian era, as well as the outstanding representative of English critical realism. He published extensively and was considered a literary celebrity throughout England for the rest of his life.

Charles Dickens (1812—1870) was born at Landport, Hampshire, on February 7, 1812, the second of eight children. His mother served to Lord Crew, and His father, John Dickens, was a clerk in the Navy Pay Office. He could earn much money, but failed to manage it successfully. When Dickens was twelve, his father was taken to debtors' prison. Then the boy was taken out of school and had to earn his living in a blacking factory where the unregulated, stiff and cruel work conditions left a deep impression on Dickens. His experiences exerted great impact on his fiction. He later expressed these experiences in the semi-autobiographical novel *David Copperfield*. As a young boy, Charles Dickens was greatly influenced by the stories his nursemaid told him. In addition, Dickens loved to read, with a special fondness for the picaresque novels, such as *Tom Jones* by Henry Fielding, and *Arabian Nights*. It was no doubt that such education played a part in Dickens' future career.

At the age of nineteen, he became a political journalist. His connections to various magazines and newspapers gave him the opportunity to publish his own fiction. In 1836 he published his first collection of realistic sketches and stories under the title of *Sketches by Boz*. In the same year he married Catherine Hogarth, the daughter of a fellow co-worker at his newspaper. But after twenty years of marriage and ten children, he fell in love with Ellen Ternan, an actress many years his junior. Soon after, Dickens and his wife separated, ending a long series of marital difficulties. At the age of twenty-five, he published his first novel *The Pickwick Papers*. Dickens's keen perceptiveness, intimate knowledge and understanding of the people helped him quickly gain world fame. The success of *The Pickwick Papers* made him give up reporting and begin writing novels. In the following years between 1837 and 1841, Charles Dickens published frutifully, *Oliver Twist* (1837), *Nicholas Nickleby* (1838), *Barnaby Rudge* (1841) and *The Old Curiosity Shop* (1841).

In 1842 Dickens made a trip to America, which marked the beginning of a new stage in Dickens' life. During this period, Dickens published Christmas stories, with more serious themes including *A Christmas Carol* (1843), *The Chimes* (1844) and *The Crickets on the Hearth* (1844). In *A Christmas Carol*, he blames society's vices on people's obsession with earning money and acquiring status based on money. The years between 1846 and 1860 was Dickens's golden period of novel productions in which his critical realism themes best expressed. During this period, Dickens spent much of his time travelling on the European continent, especially in France and Italy. The great social movements on the European continent and in England urged him to write novels of sharp social criticism. After living briefly abroad in Italy (1844) and Switzerland (1846), Dickens continued publishing his works, *Dombey and Son* (1848); *David Copperfield* (1849—50); *Bleak House* (1852—53); *Hard Times* (1854); *Little Dorrit* (1857); *A Tale of Two Cities* (1859); and *Great Expectations* (1861). In 1864 Dickens published his last complete novel *Our Mutual Friend*. In these novels, Dickens ruthlessly exposes the social evils and social injustice of his time in the capitalist society and of the English parliamentary system. He often revealed the exploitation and repression of the poor and condemned the public officials and institutions. Besides his exposures, he invented comic characters and demonstrated great sympathy for the oppressed, all of which made him more popular. His fiction, with often vivid descriptions of life in the nineteenth century England, has come to symbolise on a global level Victorian society (1837—1901) as uniformly "Dickensian".

A Tale of Two Cities is a novel with the French Revolution of 1789—1794 as the background and with the two cities London and Paris as the scenes. The novel evolves round the fate of Dr. Manette and his family. In the novel Dickens points out the injustice of oppression and the justification of revolution, and shows his intense hatred for the tyranny of the ruling class. *David Copperfield*, set in early Victorian England against a backdrop of great social change, is often regarded as the semi-autobiography of the author. In this novel, the early life of the hero David is mainly based on the author's unhappy experiences in his childhood. Like Dickens, David works as a child, pasting labels onto bottles. Mr. Micawber is a satirical version of Dickens's father, who can not scrape together the money. But the significance of the novel is far greater than that of its autobiographical element. Through the description of the growth and development of the hero, David Copperfield, from a posthumous boy badly mistreated by his step father and other tyrants to a famous writer by his own efforts, Dickens shows the miseries of child-labor and condemns all kinds of tyranny.

Dickens' health began to deteriorate in the 1860s. On June 9, 1870, Charles Dickens died in Kent at the age of fifty-eight and was buried in Poet's Corner of Westminster Abbey.

Oliver Twist was Dickens's second novel and his first real social novel. The novel tells the story of Oliver, a young orphan raised in a workhouse, who was later sent to an infant farm, run by Mrs. Mann, until he is nine years old. Later he returned to the workhouse again, where he is starved and abused. Young and physically weak as he is, Oliver is mentally powerful and brave enough to advance to the master and "ask for more gruel" on behalf of the group. With the development of the plot, he runs away to London alone to seek for new life. His story demonstrates the hypocrisy of the petty middle-class bureaucrats, who treat a small child cruelly under the mask of the Christian virtue—giving charity to the less fortunate. In this novel, Dickens created a lively picture of low life under the capitalistic system, setting against the seamy underside of the London criminal world. *Oliver Twist* opens with a bitter attack on the nineteenth-century English Poor Laws. These laws were a distorted demonstration of the Victorian middle class's emphasis on the virtues of hard work, so it was written partially in reaction to the Poor Law Amendment Act of 1834. In *Oliver Twist*, Dickens gives a truthful presentation of the sufferances of the poor and oppressed, and bitterly exposes the terrible conditions in the English workhouse and the corruption of the oppressors under the mask of philanthropy. Dickens's *Oliver Twist* (1839) made deep impression on readers with its images of poverty and crime. In addition, with the character of the tragic prostitute, Nancy, Dickens "humanised" such women who were regarded as "unfortunates," inherently immoral casualties of the Victorian economic system.

Great Expectations is the story of Pip, an orphan boy adopted by a blacksmith's family, who ever has good luck and great expectations, and finally loses both his luck and his expectations. In this novel, Pip's sudden rise from country laborer to city gentleman forces him to move from one social extreme to another. Through ups and downs in his life, however, Pip learns how to find happiness. Dickens presented readers the influence of social changes on the middle-class and lower-class people, the corruption of money to human beings as well as the hardships and misery of common people throughout the novel. The major theme in *Great Expectations* is that one must search beyond material wealth and social status, and look for happiness within himself. *Great Expectations* is based on the conditions of early Victorian England: gentlemen and ladies were expected to get thorough classical education and to behave appropriately in social situations; the manners and behaviors of the upper class were very strict and conservative, all of which can be felt in every facet of *Great Expectations*. The greatest difference between *Great Expectations* and other earlier novels is the introduction of dramatic psychological transformations of the main characters, as opposed to characters that are changed only through their circumstances and surroundings. In form, *Great Expectations* belongs to a pattern: the bildungsroman—a story that centers on the education or development of the protagonist. And we can follow closely Pip's development. The genre was popularized and became prevalent in England with such books as Daniel Defoe's *Robinson Crusoe*, and Charlotte Brontë's *Jane Eyre*.

We can say Dickens's writing style is florid and poetic, with a strong comic touch. Dickens is such a great one who is characterized by his perfect combination of realism with romanticism in writing. Thus , it is not hard to understand that Dickens's story is full of legends and melodramas. With the set scenes of London, Dickens is often described as using 'idealised' characters to contrast with the ugly social truths. Creating coincidences is one of Dickens's unique artistic styles, (e. g. , Oliver Twist turns out to be the lost nephew of the upper class family that randomly rescues him from the dangers of the pickpocket group). In a sense, his artistic style—creating coincidences was also characterized by exaggeration. As Dickens himself said, he used romantic realism "largely to express his own moral concepts rather than pursue perfect truth". Such coincidences are major features of the eighteenth century picaresque novels such as Henry Fielding's *Tom Jones*. But, to Dickens, these were not just plot devices, but a sign of the humanism which made him believe that the good wins out in the end and often in unexpected ways. With a good memory and great power of astonishing imagination, Dickens can always make original portrait of characters, and his characters were often memorized by readers. Many of his characters' names provide the reader with a hint in advancing the storyline, such as Mr. Murdstone in the novel *David Copperfield*, which is clearly a combination of "murder" and stony coldness. Dickensian characters, especially their typically whimsical names, are among the most memorable in English literature. Furthermore, Charles Dickens is also a great storyteller. With his large, varied and complicated plots, Dickens displays flexible skills in the handling of the construction, in endowing his characters exactly the actions and words, and in successfully using irony or obvious exaggeration to achieve the penetrating effect of satire. With all his novels and fictional arts, Charles Dickens is one of the great masters in the development of English literature.

Dickens used his unique humor, fierce satire and penetrating insight to expose the dark sides of the society. Meanwhile he showed his great sympathy for the miseries and hardships suffered by the working people. Through his books, we come to understand the virtues of a loving heart and the pleasures of home in a cruelly indifferent world. His writings inspired others, in particular journalists and political figures, to address such problems of class oppression. The exceptional popularity of his novels underscored not only his ability to create compelling storylines and unforgettable characters, but also pointed out that the Victorian public confronted issues of social justice. Among English writers, in terms of his fame and of the public's recognition, he is second only to William Shakespeare. Dickens clearly influenced later Victorian novelists such as Thomas Hardy and George Gissing.

Chapter 5 William Makepeace Thackeray

William Makepeace Thackeray (1811—1863) is one of the outstanding representatives of English critical realism in the 19th century England. Besides a realistic novelist, he is an editor, satirist and moralist.

Thackeray was born in the family of an English official on July 18, 1811. When the boy was five years old his father died, and the mother returned with her child to England. Thackeray was sent first to school at Chiswick, then to Charterhouse in 1822. Charterhouse school was a famous one, but Thackeray detested it for its rude manners, and occasionally referred to it as the "Slaughterhouse". In 1829 he went up to Trinity College, Cambridge. While at the university, he displayed a talent for cartoon drawing, wrote some satirical verses, and edited a student newspaper. In order to be an artist, he left the University in 1830 without taking a degree. After leaving college he traveled through Germany, Italy and France, going in for self-education and art studies. There after he settled down to study law. In 1832, he came into an inheritance of a comfortable fortune and returned to England. Soon he lost his fortune by gambling and bad investments, and had to earn his own living. Disappointed by his failure as an illustrator, he made a bid for literature. In this he was more fortunate. After the publication of *Vanity Fair* in 1848 he began to be recognized as one of the great novelists of his day. In 1860 he took charge of the Cornhill Magazine, which prospered greatly in his hands. For some years he had been suffering from heart trouble, but he worked on steadily. He had just started on his new novel when he died suddenly in December 1863.

While Dickens conveyed a panorama of the lower half of society, Thackeray described that of the upper half. Thackeray was a prolific writer. Of his works the better known are: *The Book of Snobs* (1848), *Vanity Fair* (1847—1848), *Pendennis* (1848—1850), *The Newcomes* (1853—1855) and *The History of Henry Esmond* (1852). In the early 1840s, Thackeray had some success with two travel books, *The Paris Sketch Book* and *The Irish Sketch Book*. His first literary success came with a series of satirical sketches entitled *The Snobs of England*, and these sketches were later collected under the title *The Books of Snobs*, which is also significant in terms of the social values. It is a collection of forty-four sketches, in which the aim of the author's satire and attack is directed to the snobs who are pervasive in every corner of the English society. Thackeray held the belief that all kinds of snobs are the production of the social-political system of England, and thus he not only satirized snobs but made it clear that the complete elimination of snobbery comes after the elimination of all privileged classes, of all suppressions, and all exploitations. Later in the decade, Thackeray had already become a good realistic writer, but the work that really established his fame was the novel *Vanity Fair* in 1847, in which Thackeray drew a broad panorama of social life, ruthlessly criticizing money worship, cruelty and unscrupulousness. After the peak of his literary career, He produced several long novels, notably *Pendennis*, *The Newcomes*, and *The History of Henry Esmond*, but his later works showed a sign of weakness in ideological depth and artistic power.

Vanity Fair, *or A Novel Without A Hero* is unquestionably Thackeray's masterpiece. The title of the novel is suggestive of that Vanity Fair in Bunyan's *The Pilgrim's Progress*, where "all sorts of vanities" are on sale. Thus the title reveals the dark side of social life. Different from Bunyan who gives an allegorical picture of the social realities he dislikes, Thackeray draws a truthful picture, like a realistic painter, of the fortunes and characters of the middle-class people in the middle-nineteenth century. With scathing irony Thackeray exposes the vices of this society: hypocrisy, money-worship, and moral degradation. As the subtitle of the novel suggests, the story is neither with a plot nor a hero; its whole action revolves around two women, Amelia Sedley and Rebecca Sharp. Becky is a clever, unscrupulous and scheming girl. Amelia, a pretty, gentle and simple-minded creature whose father is a rich merchant. After the two girls' graduation, Becky is invited for a short stay at the Sedleys', where she fails to capture Amelia's brother Joseph for husband. Then she comes to the house of Sir Pitt Crawley as a governess, when the secret marriage of Becky and Captain Rawdon, Sir Pitt's second son, comes to light, the wealthy aunt disinherits Rawdon. Meanwhile Amelia, whose father is now bankrupt, marries George Osborne, her childhood sweetheart. Soon George Osborne and Rawdon Crawley, accompanied by their wives, go to the Continent with the British army to fight against Napoleon. At a ball in Brussels George invites Becky to elope with him, but very soon he is killed in the Battle of Waterloo. The widowed Amelia gives birth to a posthumous son, and lives on in dire poverty. After the war is over, Becky and Rawdon stay for some time in Paris, making a living mainly on his cheating in gambling. After their return to London Becky wins her way into the highest society. Due to her flirtations with the vicious old lord Steyne, Rawdon breaks with Becky and goes to the West Indies, where he dies of fever. Becky leaves England to wander alone on the Continent. After many years Becky meets Amelia again, and she tells Amelia of George's infidelity, therefore making it possible for Amelia to marry William Dobbin, her lifelong admirer. Becky also meets Joseph, whom she now captures and controls. After Joseph's death she gets his life insurance money and lives in retirement, spending her time working for the church. The novel is a caustic satire upon the aristocratic-bourgeois society of the time. The characters in the novel are portrayed with great vivacity in a lifelike manner, and Becky Sharp, a talented and resourceful woman, but also an adventuress embodying the many vices of a mammonist society, has become a proverbial figure in English literature.

Just like Charles Dickens, Thackeray is one of the greatest critical realists of the 19th century Europe. He paints life as he has seen it. With his precise and thorough observation, rich knowledge of social life and of the human heart, the pictures in his novels are accurate and true to life.

Besides being a realist and satirist, Thackeray is a moralist. His aim is to produce a moral impression in all his novels.

In terms of techniques Thackeray is obviously influenced by Henry Fielding. To illustrate, Fielding often makes his own comments, in the process of the narration, on certain details or results of the story directly as if he as the novelist were one of the major characters in the story. In *Vanity Fair* Thackeray also makes use of this device to blend his own remarks with the narration of the story and those of the characters.

Besides, Thackeray distinguishes himself to be a master of pure and simple style. His style is characterized by its ease, refinement, and an exquisite naturalness, with which he is able to express his thoughts, emotions, and movement of consciousness perfectly.

Vanity Fair (an excerpt)

The following excerpt is taken from the first part of Chapter 22 of "Vanity Fair". It describes how George felt before the wedding and the ceremonies of the wedding of George Osborne and Amelia Sedley. At the end of this section, the bride and bridegroom depart on their honeymoon.

Chapter 22. A Marriage and Part of a Honeymoon

Enemies the most obstinate and courageous can't hold out against starvation; so the elder Osborne[1] felt himself pretty easy about his adversary in the encounter we have just described; and as soon as George's[2] supplies fell short, confidently expected his unconditional submission. It was unlucky, to be sure, that the lad should have secured a stock of provisions on the very day when the first encounter took place; but this relief was only temporary, old Osborne thought, and would but delay George's surrender. No communication passed between father and son for some days. The former was sulky at this silence, but not disquieted; for, as he said, he knew where he could put the screw upon George, and only waited the result of that operation. He told the sisters the upshot of the dispute between them, but ordered them to take no notice of the matter, and welcome George on his return as if nothing had happened. His cover was laid as usual every day, and perhaps the old gentleman rather anxiously expected him; but he never came. Some one inquired at the Slaughters' regarding him, where it was said that he and his friend Captain Dobbin[3] had left town.

One gusty, raw day at the end of April the rain whipping the pavement of that ancient street where the old Slaughters' Coffeehouse was once situated, George Osborne came into the coffee room, looking very haggard[4] and pale; although dressed rather smartly in a blue coat and brass buttons, and a neat buff waistcoat of the fashion of those days. Here was his friend Captain Dobbin, in blue and brass too, having abandoned the military frock and French. grey trousers, which were the usual coverings of his lanky person.

Dobbin had been in the coffee room for an hour or more. He had tried all the papers, but could not read them. He had looked at the clock many scores of times; and at the street, where the rain was pattering down, and the people as they clinked by in patterns, left long reflections on the shining stone. He tattooed at the table: he bit his nails most completely, and nearly to the quick (he was accustomed to ornament his great big hands in this way): he balanced the tea spoon dexterously[5] on the milk jug: upset it, and in fact showed those signs of disquietude, and practised those desperate attempts at amusement, which men are accustomed to employ when very anxious, and expectant, and perturbed in mind. Some of his comrades, gentlemen who used the room, joked him about the splendour of his costume and his agitation of manner. One asked him if he was going to be married? Dobbin laughed, and said he would send his acquaintance (Major Wagstaff of the Engineers) a piece of cake when that event took place. At length Captain Osborne made his appearance, very smartly dressed, but very pale and agitated as we have said. He wiped his pale face with a large yellow bandanna pocket. handkerchief that was prodigiously scented. He shook hands with Dobbin, looked at the clock, and told John, the waiter, to bring him some curacao. Of this cordial he swallowed off a couple of glasses with nervous eagerness. His friend asked with some interest about his health.

"Couldn't get a wink of sleep till daylight, Dob," said he. "Infernal headache and fever. Got up at nine, and went down to the Hummums for a bath. I say, Dob, I feel just as I did on the morning I went out with Rocket at Quebec."

"So do I," William responded. "I was a deuced deal more nervous than you were that morning. You made a famous breakfast, I remember. Eat something now."

"You're a good old fellow, Will. I'll drink your health, old boy, and farewell to..."

"No, no; two glasses are enough," Dobbin interrupted him. "Here, take away the liqueurs, John. Have some cayenne pepper with your fowl. Make haste though, for it is time we were there."

It was about half an hour from twelve when this brief meeting and colloquy took place between the two captains. A coach, into which Captain Osborne's servant put his master's desk and dressing case, had been in waiting for some time; and into this the two gentlemen hurried under an umbrella, and the valet mounted on the box, cursing the rain and the dampness of the coachman who was steaming beside him. "We shall find a better trap than this at the church door," says he; "that's a comfort." And the carriage drove on, taking the road down Piccadilly, where Apsley House and St. George's Hospital wore red jackets still; where there were oil lamps; where Achilles was not yet born; nor the Pimlico arch raised; nor the hideous equestrian monster which pervades it and the neighbourhood; and so they drove down by Brompton to a certain chapel near the Fulham Road there.

A chariot was in waiting with four horses; likewise a coach of the kind called glass coaches. Only a very few idlers were collected on account of the dismal rain.

"Hang it!" said George, "I said only a pair."

"My master would have four," said Mr. Joseph Sedley's servant, who was in waiting; and he and Mr. Osborne's man agreed as they followed George and William into the church, that it was a "reg'lar shabby turn hout; and with scarce so much as a breakfast or a wedding faviour."

"Here you are," said our old friend, Jos Sedley[6], coming forward. "You're five minutes late, George, my boy.

What a day, eh? Demmy, it's like the commencement of the rainy season in Bengal. But you'll find my carriage is watertight. Come along, my mother and Emmy are in the vestry."

Jos Sedley was splendid. He was fatter than ever. His shirt collars were higher; his face was redder; his shirt frill flaunted gorgeously out of his variegated waistcoat. Varnished boots were not invented as yet; but the Hessians on his beautiful legs shone so, that they must have been the identical pair in which the gentleman in the old picture used to shave himself; and on his light green coat there bloomed a fine wedding favour, like a great white spreading magnolia.

In a word, George had thrown the great cast. He was going to be married. Hence his pallor and nervousness, his sleepless night and agitation in the morning. I have heard people who have gone through the same thing own to the same emotion. After three or four ceremonies, you get accustomed to it, no doubt; but the first dip, everybody allows, is awful.

The bride was dressed in a brown silk pelisse (as Captain Dobbin has since informed me), and wore a straw bonnet with a pink ribbon; over the bonnet she had a veil of white Chantilly lace, a gift from Mr. Joseph Sedley, her brother. Captain Dobbin himself had asked leave to present her with a gold chain and watch, which she sported on this occasion; and her mother gave her her diamond brooch almost the only trinket which was left to the old lady. As the service went on, Mrs. Sedley sat and whimpered a great deal in a pew, consoled by the Irish maid servant and Mrs. Clapp from the lodgings. Old Sedley would not be present. Jos acted for his father, giving away the bride, whilst Captain Dobbin stepped up as groomsman to his friend George.

There was nobody in the church besides the officiating persons and the small marriage party and their attendants. The two valets sat aloof superciliously. The rain came rattling down on the windows. In the intervals of the service you heard it, and the sobbing of old Mrs. Sedley in the pew. The parson's tones echoed sadly through the empty walls. Osborne's "I will" was sounded in very deep bass. Emmy's response came fluttering up to her lips from her heart, but was scarcely heard by anybody except Captain Dobbin.

When the service was completed, Jos Sedley came forward and kissed his sister, the bride, for the first time for many months, George's look of gloom had gone, and he seemed quite proud and radiant. "It's your turn, William," says he, putting his hand fondly upon Dobbin's shoulder; and Dobbin went up and touched Amelia on the cheek.

Then they went into the vestry and signed the register. "God bless you, Old Dobbin," George said, grasping him by the hand, with something very like moisture glistening in his eyes. William replied only by nodding his head. His heart was too full to say much.

"Write directly, and come down as soon as you can, you know," Osborne said. After Mrs. Sedley had taken a hysterical adieu of her daughter, the pair went off to the carriage. "Get out of the way, you little devils."

George cried to a small crowd of damp urchins, that were hanging about the chapel door. The rain drove into the bride and bridegroom's faces as they passed to the chariot. The postilions' favours draggled on their dripping jackets. The few children made a dismal cheer, as the carriage, splashing mud, drove away. William Dobbin stood in the church. porch, looking at it, a queer figure. The small crew of spectators jeered him. He was not thinking about them or their laughter.

"Come home and have some tiffin, Dobbin," a voice cried behind him; as a pudgy hand was laid on his shoulder, and the honest fellow's reverie was interrupted. But the Captain had no heart to go afeasting with Jos Sedley. He put the weeping old lady and her attendants into the carriage along with Jos, and left them without any farther words passing. This carriage, too, drove away, and the urchins gave another sarcastical cheer.

"Here, you little beggars," Dobbin said, giving some sixpences amongst them, and then went off by himself through the rain. It was all over. They were married, and happy, he prayed God. Never since he was a boy had he felt so miserable and so lonely. He longed with a heart sick yearning for the first few days to be over, that he might see her again.

Notes

1. John Osborne—The father of George, he is a successful businessman, and a stern and stubborn patriarch.
2. George Osborne—He is a smart, pampered and flirtatious character, who is very sure of his charms and good looks. He makes an infidel husband. Though a spendthrift, he is also a brave and honorable soldier in His Majesty's -Th Regiment of Foot.
3. Captain Dobbin—Dobbin is the only consistently good character of the story. He is a devoted friend and a true lover. Though his appearance and manners are rather clumsy, his form bamboo like and feet excessively large, he has a heart of gold.
4. haggard—wild in appearance; having a worn or emaciated appearance.
5. dexterously—skillful and competent with the hands.

6. Joseph Sedley—He is Amelia's elder brother, employed in the East India Company in India. He is a fat, pompous and very vain man. He is a coward and an escapist who always flees from difficult situations.

For Study and Discussion

1. What are your growing impressions of Amelia Sedley, on the one hand, and Captain Dobbin, on the other? Do you find yourself beginning either to like or understand these characters more or less as you observe their development?
2. Show how Thackeray's definition of gentleman among the male characters .
3. Compare and contrast George Osborne and William Dobbin.

Chapter 6 Charlotte Brontë

Charlotte Brontë (1816—1855) is a British novelist, a critical realist, whose novels are characterized by a truthful representation of the social realities in the first half of the nineteenth century.

Charlotte Brontë is the eldest of the Brontë sisters. In 1816, Charlotte Brontë was born in a small village in northern England. Her childhood was not so happy. Her father was a poor clergyman. Her mother died in 1812, leaving five daughters and one son in the care of their somewhat severe father. Charlotte and her four sisters had miserable experiences in the charity school where they were ill-treated, and her two sisters Maria and Elizabeth died in the school. Then Charlotte, Emily, and Anne were withdrawn from the school and brought home, and the children's aunt, Elizabeth Branwell, became their new instructor. At the age of nineteen she began to earn her living as a governess. In 1835, Charlotte herself was teaching at Roe Head and helped pay for Emily's schooling there. She stayed for three years then resigned, again returning to Haworth. In 1839 Charlotte obtained a position as governess but disliked it and soon she and her sisters Emily and Anne travelled to Brussels, Belgium to study at the Pensionnat Heger under the instruction of Constantin Heger. They learned French and German and studied literature with the aim to start their own school someday. Unfortunately, the school was a complete failure: the advertisements for the school did not result in a single public response. The year 1842 saw that she went to Brussels, where she studied languages and at the same time worked as a teacher. In 1852, the Reverend Arthur Bell Nicholls, proposed marriage to Charlotte. Unfortunately, Charlotte's father was violently opposed to the match, and Charlotte refused to accept the proposal. The following year, the Reverend Nicholls renewed his proposal to Charlotte and this time Charlotte married him in 1854. Shortly after becoming pregnant, she was diagnosed with pneumonia and died of the disease in 1855. She was, then, only thirty-nine years old.

Charlotte's early experience sowed the seeds of her antipathy and rebellion against the social realities, and of her literary career. As the eldest of the Brontë authors, Charlotte approached her writing career as a means to financial independence and to help support her siblings. Though the remaining children were deeply affected by the death of their two sisters, they filled their spare time with imaginative fantasies and fictitious worlds. Their aunt tried to make sure the girls knew how to run a household, but their minds were more inclined to literature. Their father's well-stocked library was a main source of knowledge. They read the Bible, Homer, Virgil, Shakespeare, Milton, Byron, Scott, and many others, and examined articles from Blackwood's Edinburgh Magazine, Fraser's Magazine, and The Edinburgh Review. In addition, they read history, geography and biographies. As sisters and authors, Charlotte, Emily and Anne gave each other moral support, shared creative ideas and proof-read one another's work. Having discovered some of Emily's poems, Charlotte decided to publish selected poems of all three sisters. In 1846, a collection of their poems was published under the pseudonyms of Currer, Ellis, and Acton Bell. The publication of *Poems by Currer, Ellis and Acton Bell* in 1846 marks the beginning of the literary career of the Brontë sisters. Charlotte's first novel *The Professor*, was also written during this time, though it was initially rejected for publication and was met with very little enthusiasm. However, Charlotte's second novel *Jane Eyre*, was published the following year and was a resounding success, after which Charlotte revealed her identity to her publisher and went on to write several other novels, most notably *Shirley* in 1849 and *Emma*, unfinished. Charlotte Brontë wrote only 20 pages of the manuscript. Charlotte produced four well-known novels in all.

Jane Eyre is Charlotte's most successful and popular novel, and it is, by general consent, a powerful and fascinating story, in which Charlotte puts much of her own experiences, such as the life at Lowood School and the life as a governess. In this novel Jane Eyre is characterized as a simple, kind-hearted, noble-minded woman who pursues a genuine kind of love. Jane Eyre is an orphan girl. She loses her parents shortly after her birth. Her uncle becomes her guardian. After his death her aunt, Mrs. Reed, a harsh unsympathetic woman, becomes rude and unjust to her. Mrs. Reed's own children also find pleasure in teasing and mocking her. One day, unable to bear the ill treatment any longer, Jane tells straight to her aunt's face what she thinks of her. Mrs. Reed is furious and sends Jane to a charity school for poor girls in Lowood, where she lives an intolerable life and stays for 8 years. Then Jane becomes a governess to a little girl in the family of a squire Mr. Rochester. The squire falls in love with her. But while they are about to hold their wedding ceremony in the church, Jane learns that Rochester has got a wife who is mad and locked in a private room. Shocked by the finding, Jane flees from the house. She goes through many hardships. Finally helped by a parson, she gets the job of a teacher in a village school. Meanwhile, a great misfortune befalls Mr. Rochester. His house is destroyed in a fire set by his mad wife who dies a tragic death by jumping off the roof, and he becomes blind. Hearing that Mr. Rochester has become penniless and disabled, Jane Eyre hurries back to him and becomes his wife. One of the central themes of the book is the criticism of the bourgeois system of education. Another problem raised by Charlotte in the novel is the position of women in society. Jane Eyre, the heroine of the novel, maintains that women should have equal rights with men.

In the past 40 years Charlotte Brontë's reputation has risen rapidly, and feminist criticism has done much to show that she was speaking up for oppressed women of every age. Her book had sparked a movement in regards to feminism in literature. The main character, Jane Eyre, was a parallel to herself, a woman who was strong. Another apparent feature of her novels is that she always shows her profound sympathy for the poor and the oppressed, and simultaneously expresses her criticism of the injustices in every corner of the society.

Chapter 7 Emily Brontë

Emily Brontë (1818—1848) is a talented poet and novelist. She wrote only one novel, but one of the best novels in English literature. Many critics take Emily to be the most gifted of the three Bronte sisters.

Emily Brontë was born on July 30th, 1818, the 5th child of the Reverend Patrick Brontë. Just like her sister Charlotte, she had a miserable childhood experience such as the loss of her mother and the unbearable life at charity school. Following the death of her two sisters at the charity school, Emily was taken home, but she would never forget the terrors and the hardships of their lives at school. After that, she very rarely spent any time away from home. In 1835, at the age of seventeen she went to school at Roe Head where Charlotte was teaching, but became so pale and thin that her sister was convinced she would die unless she returned home. The life of Emily Brontë was extremely uneventful, living at a boarding-school, teaching as a governess, losing her health because of illness. Her health, like her sisters', had been weakened by the harsh local climate at home and at school. In September, 1848 she caught a cold during the funeral of her brother in which led to tuberculosis. Refusing medical help, she died on 19 December that year at about two in the afternoon. Emily never made any close friends outside of her family circle and remained single all her life. She was unhappy a great deal about the time, but she pursued all her life for an independence, which never came. Emily seems to have been more liberty-loving than her sisters, as Charlotte wrote, "Liberty was the breath of Emily's nostrils: without it she perished".

Emily lived almost all her life at home, Haworth Parsonage, near the Yorkshire Moors in northern England. She loved this bleak and stormy landscape and much of her writing was inspired by her home. It was the discovery of Emily's poetic talent by Charlotte that led her and her sisters to publish a joint collection of their poetry in 1846, *Poems by Currer, Ellis, and Acton Bell*. In her verses there was not only good technique but a sturdy, vigorous note that was characterized of the lover of freedom who had written the verses. But Emily's literary fame now chiefly rests upon *Wuthering Heights*, the only novel she wrote. The novel was published in 1847 as two volumes of a three volume set (the last volume being *Agnes Grey* by her sister Anne). Its innovative structure somewhat puzzled critics. Although it received mixed reviews when it first came out, the book subsequently became an English literary classic. In 1850, Charlotte edited and published *Wuthering Heights* under Emily's real name.

Wuthering Heights is a novel with a non-linear structure, involving several flashbacks, and two narrators—Mr. Lockwood and Ellen "Nelly" Dean. It is a somber story of love and sorrow and revenge. It tells the tale of the passionate and thwarted love between Heathcliff and Catherine Earnshaw, and how this unresolved passion eventually destroys them and many around them. Mr. Earnshaw brings a child who has been living the life of a waif in the slums of Liverpool. He is of unknown parentage, and Mr. Earnshaw gives him the name of Heathcliff and brings him up as one of his own children. But this arouses the fierce resentment of his son Hindley, and it is only with the daughter Catherine (Cathy) that Heathcliff has, in secret, a warm and human relationship. After Mr. Earnshaw's death, Heathcliff is maltreated by Hindley, now master of the house, and lives like a despised animal. Meanwhile the friendship between Heathcliff and Cathy, however, develops into passionate love. But Cathy is unable to marry Heathcliff because of his low birth. She marries Edgar Linton from the "civilized" household of Thrushcross Grange in the valley, though she doesn't love him. Heathcliff runs away, and is not heard of for three years. When he returns he has become a rich man. The fact that Catherine has married Linton drives Heathcliff to revenge, at first by resuming love with Catherine who soon dies of grief and remorse, secondly by marrying Linton's sister whom he never loves but treats inhumanly for the sake of her brother's marriage to Catherine, finally by forcing Catherine's daughter Cathy to marry his sickly son in order to get the Linton estate into his own possession, before all these he has possessed through powerful means all the property of Hindley and his son Hareton and treats them as cruelly as Hindley treated him before his leaving the place. After his son's death, affection springs up between Cathy and Hareton, and Cathy sets about the latter's education. Heathcliff, now an old man, becomes detached from external reality and longs for the death that will reunite him with Catherine. At his death Hareton and Cathy are left to be happy together. On the last page of the novel a weeping little shepherd boy declares that he has seen the ghosts of the dead Heathcliff and Catherine walking together on the moor. *Wuthering Heights* is based partly on the Gothic tradition of the late eighteenth century. The novel has been studied, analyzed, and discussed from every imaginable critical perspective, yet it remains a mystery to readers.

Today, *Wuthering Heights* has a secure position in the canon of world literature, and Emily Brontë is revered as one of the finest writers of the nineteenth century. Through *Wuthering Heights* she was able to speak her own mind, make clear the power of her voice, and reveal her entire vision of humankind to the world. It has been more than one hundred years since *Wuthering Heights* was first published, yet it is still a widely-read book and is studied in many schools, and almost everyone who has read this novel has been deeply affected by it. Emily died at the age of thirty, only a year after *Wuthering Heights* was published. As a shattering presentation of the doomed love affair between the fiercely passionate Catherine and Heathcliff, it remains one of the most haunting love stories in all of literature.

Chapter 8 George Eliot

George Eliot (1819—1880) was the pseudonym of Mary Ann Evans. She was one of the major critical realists of the mid-19th century.

George Eliot was born on a farm. Her father was a land agent. She studied at a private school. Her mother died when she was 16, and for the next 14 years she kept house for her father. She did a great deal of reading and learned music and the German, French and Italian languages. She had been brought up under strict religious influences, but she early abandoned religious beliefs, became a free thinker, and showed a great interest in social and philosophical problems. She went to London and started to translate two philosophical works from German into English. In 1850 she become the assistant editor of a progressive magazine, *The Westminster Review*. This brought her into personal relation with some well-known writers. One of them was George Henry Lewes, and beginning from 1854 to his death in 1878, he formed an extra-martial union with her because he could not divorce his wife, and his influence upon her was great. George encouraged her to write novels. She was also under the influence of English philosophers known as positives who advocated, in the place of Christian religion, the religion of humanity and sociological ethics. She became a novelist when she was nearly forty years old. She produced three remarkable novels, which made her famous, including *Adam Bede*(1860), *The Mill on the Floss* (1860) and *Silas Marner*(1861). All three novels deal chiefly with rural life, drawn from her own experience and observations in her earlier years in the country, and in these works moral problems are discussed and psychological analyses of character are emphasized. In 1860—61 she visited Florence in Italy, and in 1863 she published *Romola*, a historical novel of the Renaissance in Italy, centering round the famous figure of a religious fanatic, Savonarola and *Felix Holt*, *The Radical* (1866), which depicted the political controversy surrounding the Reform Bill of 1832. Three years later Eliot published *The Spanish Gypsy* (1869), a long narrative poem set in the Spanish Inquisition.

The hero Adam Bede is a village carpenter, an honest young man, who is always ready to help the weak and the suffering. Adam Bede falls in love with a village girl called Hetty Sorrel. But the girl does not love him. She wishes that her husband would be rich and have high social position. Then she gives her heart to a selfish young squire, who has no intention to marry her but just flirts with her. She is seduced and deserted by the squire. Broken-hearted, the girl consents to marry Adam. But before the marriage, she finds that she is pregnant. She goes to look for the squire. As she can't find him she leaves the baby in a wood and later returns to find it dead. So the girl is arrested and put into prison for murdering the child. In prison she is visited and preached to by a young woman preacher called Dinah. The preacher makes Hetty repent. Her sentence is commuted to transportation and a few years later she dies on her way home. Then Adam and the woman preacher fall in love with each other. At the end of the novel they are united. In this novel, George Eliot portrays two pairs: Arthur and Hetty on the one hand, and Adam and the preacher on the other. The first couple are described to be always thinking of their own interest without any consideration of the other, while the second couple are praised for their high moral principles which guide their conduct for the good of others and of themselves. George Eliot was influenced by bourgeois positivism. This novel shows this influence. There is a good deal of psychological analysis of the characters in this novel, and in George Eliot's other novels. The village life on the patriarchal pattern is depicted here and the novelist seems to think highly of it because it produces persons of high moral calibre, although actually the way the characters behave themselves and the problems they face belong essentially to the author's age, although actually the way the characters behave themselves and the problems they face belong essentially to the author's age. The social inequality, especially shown in the different attitude of the publics towards Hetty and Arthur, is touched upon with definite disapproval chiefly on moral grounds, and the author's satisfaction is clearly visible in the scene in which Adam, defying such inequality, challenges and beats up Arthur in their quarrel over Hetty. *Adam Bede* is a powerful novel and a finely written one, with its exaltation of simple people, its psychological analysis of the characters, and its truthful pictures of village life, although it is marred by the pervading and predominant moral tone.

The central characters of the book *The Mill on the Floss* are Tom and Maggie. They are children of a well-to-do miller. Maggie is lively, bright, and full of aspirations and ideals, but the people around her are silly and narrow-minded. They do not understand Maggie's noble ideals. Even her brother Tom can not understand her. Several years later, Maggie grows into a beautiful girl and falls in love with a young man called Philip. Tom learns of their secret meetings, interferes and makes Maggie promise not to see Philip any more. This is the first deep dissension between brother and sister. Then one day, Maggie is going to visit her cousin Lucy. On her way, she meets Lucy's suitor Stephen. When they go boating on the Floss, the young man, attracted by Maggie's beauty, asks her to marry him. Maggie rejects him. Then Tom learns of the matter. He suspects that his sister has been making love with Lucy's lover, Stephen. So he drives his sister out of the house. In spite of that, Maggie still loves her brother. Then there is a flood in their hometown. The girl comes back to save her brother in a boat. The boat is overturned. The brother and sister get reconciled before they are drowned in the flood. In the heroine Maggie, we can see the author's moral principle, but her tragedy shows the irreconcilability of a gifted and noble-minded personality with bourgeois reality represented by these dull and narrow-minded persons.

The novel *Silas Marner* tells a story of a weaver, who has been forced to leave his native town by a false charge of theft and settles in another village. Then he works very hard and earns a lot of gold. But his gold is stolen by the Squire's second son. For this he suffers a mental stupor. One cold winter evening, a baby girl crawls into his hut. Silas Marner adopts her. This gives a new meaning to his life. Sixteen years later, his adopted daughter is grown up into a very beautiful girl, and is about to be married. The draining of a pond near his hut reveals the body of the Squire's second son with the stolen gold. The Squire's elder son now acknowledges himself to be the father of the girl by a secret marriage, but the girl refuses to leave Silas Marner. They live happily together.

Middlemarch, a Study of Provincial Life is one of George Eliot's last novels and a work of maturity. In spite of looseness of construction, *Middlemarch* is George Eliot's great novel because many characters of different types are vividly portrayed and many social problems are discussed in the course of the portrayals of these characters, and one gets a broad realistic picture of the society in a provincial town of 19th-century England.

Eliot's novels, for the most part, describe rural life, deal with moral problems and contain psychological studies of the characters. She has rich humor and keen observation, and her characters are real men and women of her time. She writes very faithfully about the rural artisans, farmers, the country clergy, and other native people, and she fully realizes that the working people like Adam Bede and Silas Marner are much better than the landed aristocracy. Her novels are very philosophical. The philosophy she preaches is idealistic. She believes that all contradictions of social life can be solved by converting mankind to the religion of humanity. With her the transition from critical realism to naturalism began in English literature.

Middlemarch (an excerpt)

The following selection is Chapter **28** *of "Middlemarch". In this episode, Dorothea arrives at Lowick with her husband in January, after their honeymoon. Dorothea, who had been so dejected during their honeymoon, feels revived by being home, in familiar surroundings. However, she is still haunted by the knowledge that her vision of marriage is yet unfulfilled, and the depressing atmosphere of Lowick. Her sister Celia finally arrives, brightening up the place with her presence; Celia tells Dorothea of her engagement to Sir James, and Dorothea is very happy for her sister. Casaubon first noticed Dorothea for her intelligence and assertiveness. However, these very qualities make him unhappy after his marriage. Casaubon isn't the "great soul" that Dorothea wants him to be, and she isn't the docile, submissive woman he wants her to be.*

CHAPTER XXVIII

1st Gent. All times are good to seek your wedded home
Bringing a mutual delight.
2d Gent. Why, true.
The calendar hath not an evil day
For souls made one by love, and even death
Were sweetness, if it came like rolling waves
While they two clasped each other, and foresaw
No life apart.[1]

Mr. and Mrs. Casaubon, returning from their wedding journey, arrived at Lowick Manor[2] in the middle of January. A light snow was falling as they descended at the door, and in the morning, when Dorothea passed from her dressing-room avenue the blue-green boudoir[3] that we know of, she saw the long avenue of limes lifting their trunks from a white earth, and spreading white branches against the dun and motionless sky. The distant flat shrank in uniform whiteness and low-hanging uniformity of cloud. The very furniture in the room seemed to have shrunk since she saw it before: the slag in the tapestry looked more like a ghost in his ghostly blue-green world; the volumes of polite literature[4] in the bookcase looked morn like immovable imitations of books[5]. The bright fire of dry oak-boughs burning on the dogs seemed an incongruous renewal of life and glow—like the figure of Dorothea herself as she entered carrying the red-leather cases containing the cameos for Celia.

She was glowing from her morning toilet as only healthful youth can glow: there was gem-like brightness on her coiled hair and in her hazel eyes; there was warm red life in her lips; her throat had a breathing whiteness above the differing white of the fur which itself seemed to wind about her neck and cling down her blue-gray pelisse with a tenderness gathered from her own, a sentient commingled innocence which kept its loveliness against the crystalline purity of the outdoor snow. As she laid the cameo-cases on the table in the bow-window, she unconsciously kept her hands on them, immediately absorbed in looking out on the still, white enclosure which made her visible world.[6]

Mr. Casaubon, who had risen early complaining of palpitation, was in the library giving audience to his curate Mr. Tucker. By-and-by Celia would come in her quality of bridesmaid as well as sister, and through the next weeks there would be wedding visits received and given; all in continuance of that transitional life understood to correspond with the excitement of bridal felicity[7], and keeping up the sense of busy ineffectiveness, as of a dream which the dreamer begins to suspect. The duties of her married life, contemplated as so great beforehand, seemed to be shrinking with the furniture and the white vapor-walled landscape[8]. The clear heights where she expected to walk in full communion[9] had become difficult to see even in her imagination; the delicious repose of the soul on a complete superior had been shaken into uneasy effort and alarmed with dim presentiment. When would the days begin of that active wifely devotion which was to strengthen her husband's life and exalt her own? Never perhaps, as she had preconceived them; but somehow—still somehow. In this solemnly pledged union of her life, duty would present itself in some new form of inspiration and give a new meaning to wifely love.

Meanwhile there was the snow and the low arch of dun vapor[11]—there was the stifling oppression of that gentlewoman's world, where everything was done for her and none asked for her aid—where the sense of connection with a manifold pregnant existence had to be kept up painfully as an inward vision, instead of coming from without in claims that would have shaped her energies[12]. —"What shall I do?" "Whatever you please, my dear." that had been her brief history since she had left off learning morning lessons and practising silly rhythms on the hated piano. Marriage, which was to bring guidance into worthy and imperative occupation, had not yet freed her from the gentlewoman's oppressive liberty: it had not even filled her leisure with the ruminant joy of unchecked tenderness. Her blooming full-pulsed youth stood there in a moral imprisonment which made itself one with the chill, colorless, narrowed landscape, with the shrunken furniture, the never-read books, and the ghostly stag in a pale fantastic world that seemed to be vanishing from the daylight.

In the first minutes when Dorothea looked out she felt nothing but the dreary oppression; then came a keen remembrance, and turning away from the window she walked round the room. The ideas and hopes which were living in her mind when she first saw this room nearly three months before were present now only as memories: she judged them as we judge transient and departed things. All existence seemed to beat with a lower pulse than her own, and her religious faith was a solitary cry, the struggle out of a nightmare in which every object was withering and shrinking away from her. Each remembered thing in the room was disenchanted, was deadened as an unlit transparency, till her wandering gaze came to the group of miniatures, and there at last she saw something which had gathered new breath and meaning: it was the miniature of Mr. Casaubon's aunt Julia, who had made the unfortunate marriage—of Will Ladislaw's grandmother. Dorothea could fancy that it was alive now—the delicate woman's face which yet had a headstrong look, a peculiarity difficult to interpret. Was it only her friends who thought her marriage unfortunate? or did she herself find it out to be a mistake, and taste the salt bitterness of her tears in the merciful silence of the night? What breadths of experience Dorothea seemed to have passed over since she first looked at this miniature! She felt a new companionship with it, as if it had an ear for her and could see how she was looking at it. Here was a woman who had known some difficulty about marriage. Nay, the colors deepened, the lips and chin seemed to get larger, the hair and eyes seemed to be sending out light, the face was masculine and beamed on her with that full gaze which tells her on whom it falls that she is too interesting for the slightest movement of her eyelid to pass unnoticed and uninterpreted. The vivid presentation came like a pleasant glow to Dorothea: she felt herself smiling, and turning from the miniature sat down and looked up as if she were again talking to a figure in front of her. But the smile disappeared as she went on meditating, and at last she said aloud—

"Oh, it was cruel to speak so! How sad—how dreadful!"

She rose quickly and went out of the room, hurrying along the corridor, with the irresistible impulse to go and see her husband and inquire if she could do anything for him. Perhaps Mr. Tucker was gone and Mr. Casaubon was alone in the library. She felt as if all her morning's gloom would vanish if she could see her husband glad because of her presence.

But when she reached the head of the dark oak there was Celia coming up, and below there was Mr. Brooke, exchanging welcomes and congratulations with Mr. Casaubon.

"Dodo!" said Celia, in her quiet staccato; then kissed her sister, whose arms encircled her, and said no more. I think they both cried a little in a furtive manner, while Dorothea ran down-stairs

to greet her uncle.

"I need not ask how you are, my dear," said Mr. Brooke, after kissing her forehead. "Rome has agreed with you, I see—happiness, frescos, the antique—that sort of thing. Well, it's very pleasant to have you back again, and you understand all about art now, eh? But Casaubon is a little pale, I tell him—a little pale, you know. Studying hard in his holidays is carrying it rather too far. I overdid it at one time"—Mr. Brooke still held Dorothea's hand, but had turned his face to Mr. Casaubon—"about topography, ruins, temples—I thought I had a clew, but I saw it would carry me too far, and nothing might come of it. You may go any length in that sort of thing, and nothing may come of it, you know."

Dorothea's eyes also were turned up to her husband's face with some anxiety at the idea that those who saw him afresh after absence might be aware of signs which she had not noticed.

"Nothing to alarm you, my dear," said Mr. Brooke, observing her expression. "A little English beef and mutton will soon make a difference. It was all very well to look pale, sitting for the portrait of Aquinas, you know—we got your letter just in time. But Aquinas, now—he was a little too subtle, wasn't he? Does anybody read Aquinas?"

"He is not indeed an author adapted to superficial minds,"

said Mr. Casaubon, meeting these timely questions with dignified patience.

"You would like coffee in your own room, uncle?" said Dorothea,

coming to the rescue.

"Yes; and you must go to Celia: she has great news to tell you,

you know. I leave it all to her."

The blue-green boudoir looked much more cheerful when Celia was seated there in a pelisse exactly like her sister's, surveying the cameos with a placid satisfaction, while the conversation passed on to other topics.

"Do you think it nice to go to Rome on a wedding journey?" said Celia, with her ready delicate blush which Dorothea was used to on the smallest occasions.

"It would not suit all—not you, dear, for example," said Dorothea, quietly. No one would ever know what she thought of a wedding journey to Rome.

"Mrs. Cadwallader says it is nonsense, people going a long journey when they are married. She says they get tired to death of each other, and can't quarrel comfortably, as they would at home.

And Lady Chettam says she went to Bath." Celia's color changed again and again-seemed

To come and go with tidings from the heart, As it a running messenger had been.

It must mean more than Celia's blushing usually did.

"Celia! Has something happened?" said Dorothea, in a tone full of sisterly feeling. "Have you really any great news to tell me?"

"It was because you went away, Dodo. Then there was nobody but me for Sir James to talk to," said Celia, with a certain roguishness in her eyes.

"I understand. It is as I used to hope and believe," said Dorothea, taking her sister's face between her hands, and looking at her half anxiously. Celia's marriage seemed more serious than it used to do.

"It was only three days ago," said Celia. "And Lady Chettam is very kind."

"And you are very happy?"

"Yes. We are not going to be married yet. Because every thing is to be got ready. And I don't want to be married so very soon, because I think it is nice to be engaged. And we shall be married

all our lives after."

"I do believe you could not marry better, Kitty. Sir James is a good, honorable man," said Dorothea, warmly.

"He has gone on with the cottages, Dodo. He will tell you about them when he comes. Shall you be glad to see him?"

"Of course I shall. How can you ask me?"

"Only I was afraid you would be getting so learned," said Celia, regarding Mr. Casaubon's learning as a kind of damp which might in due time saturate a neighboring body.

Notes

1. The epigram is supposed to be written by George Eliot herself.
2. Lowick Manor—the house of Mr. Casaubon.
3. the blue-green boudoir—the bow-windowed room with portraits of old Casaubon members on the wall. In Chapter IX Dorothea has chosen it as her bedroom.
4. polite literature—classic works of ancient Greece and Rome.
5. immovable imitations of books—not real books or only having the appearance of books.
6. Here a sharp contrast is set between the cold, lifeless, dull house and Dorothea who is full of youthful life and vigor.
7. bridal felicity—the happiness of marriage.
8. the white vapour-walled landscape—the landscape covered with white snow.
9. in full communion—share completely or communicate perfectly.
10. the delicious repose of the soul on a complete superior— referring to Dorothea's dream of fulfilling something great by marrying somebody superior, somebody who can guide her.
11. the low arch of dun vapour—the grey sky which seems low because of the dull weather.
12. where the sense of connection... her energy—the desire to live a colourful and meaningful life was only a dream and there was hardly anything she could spend her energies on.

For Study and Discussion

1. Where is this chapter set?
2. How did Dorothea feel about her marriage when she returned from her honeymoon?
3. How does the description of environment signify the feeling of characters, esp. that of Dorothea?

Chapter 9 Thomas Hardy

Thomas Hardy (1840—1928) was a novelist, short story writer, and a poet. He was one of the representatives of the English critical realism at the turn of the 20th century.

Thomas Hardy was born on June 2, 1840, in Higher Bockhampton in Dorset, a rural region of southwestern England which he called Wessex in his books. His father was a stone mason and a violinist. His mother enjoyed reading and relating all the folk songs and legends of the region. Influenced by his parents, Hardy gained all the interests that would appear in his novels and his own life: his love for architecture and music, his interest in the lifestyles of the country folk, and his passion for all sorts of literature. His father wanted him to become a builder. So he studied and practiced architecture until 1867. Hardy showed great interest in literature and philosophy. After he gave up architecture, he made literature as his profession, and at first he wrote poetry. But his verses could find no market in the literary circle, so on the advice of George Meredith, he tried his hands in novel.

His first novel was published in 1871 under the title of *Desperate Remedies*. It was the author's first critical and financial success. It also paved the way for his lifelong efforts in the field of novel writing. And then his important novels were published one after another, which made him one of the greatest of English novelists. Hardy also produced a number of minor tales.

Although he wrote a great deal of poetry, Hardy is best remembered for the novels and short stories he wrote between 1871 and 1895. He had a deep emotional bond with the rural way of life which he had experienced as a child, but he was also aware of the changes which were in progress and the current social problems from the innovations in agriculture, just before the Industrial Revolution he captured the epoch that changed the English countryside—the unfairness and hypocrisy of Victorian sexual behavior.

But as a novelist, his greatest achievements lie in the novels of character and environment, this group of novels are characterized by sharp social criticism and pessimistic belief in mystic fate or chance. Among his famous novels the best-known are *Tess of the D'Urbervilles* and *Jude the Obscure*. *Tess of the D'Urbervilles* shows the misfortune of his characters from the viewpoint of the cruel fate, his characterization and truthful representation of the lives of his characters such as Tess, reveal that the misfortune is evidently determined by the social problems. The other remarkable but perhaps the most pessimistic of Hardy's novels *Jude the Obscure*, is an account of an ambitious rustic trapped between his intellect and his sensuality, as a result it led to destruction.

In these novels, Hardy truthfully depicts the impoverishment and decay of the small farmers. These laborers are mercilessly exploited by the rich land owners. Hardy is sad to see the decline of the patriarchal mode of life in rural England. This is one of the reasons for the growing pessimism in his novels. His pessimistic philosophy seems to show that mankind is subjected to the rule of some hostile and mysterious fate, which brings misfortune to human life. Most of Hardy's novels are tragic, though *Under the Greenwood Tree* has an ideal character possessed by no other of the novels. But even here the happy ending refuses to go further, it is only achieved by ending the story with the marriage of the hero and heroine; for all its moment of joy and charm, the texture of the narrative has already suggested the bitter ironies of which life is capable. In order to emphasize the disparity between human desire and ambition, his later work explores those ironies with an almost malicious staging of coincidence; on the one hand he doesn't know what fate has in store for the characters, on the other hand Hardy cannot understand that it is not fate, but the system of capitalist exploitation that is responsible for the tragic lives of the people whom he describes in his novels. Aside from this, strong elements of naturalism and symbolisms are defects that spoil the mainly realistic effect of his art at times.

In many respects, Hardy was trapped in the middle age between the nineteenth and twentieth centuries, between Victorian sensibilities and more modern ones, and between tradition and innovation. As some families of the ancient aristocracy, or "old money", faded into obscurity, businessmen and entrepreneurs, or "new money", joined the ranks of the social elite. Tess's family in *Tess of the d'Urbervilles* illustrates this change, as Tess's parents, the Durbeyfields, lose themselves in the fantasy of entering an ancient and aristocratic family, the d'Urbervilles. Hardy's novel strongly suggests that such a family history is not only meaningless but also utterly undesirable. Hardy's views on the subject were shocking to the conservative and status-conscious British readers, and *Tess of the d'Urbervilles* was full of widespread controversy in England.

Hardy was frustrated by the controversy caused by his work, and in the end he gave up novel-writing altogether following *Jude the Obscure*. He spent the rest of his career writing poetry. Though today he is remembered somewhat more for his novels, he was an acclaimed poet in his time, so he was buried in the prestigious Poet's Corner of Westminster Abbey following his death in 1928.

Tess of the d'Urbervilles is about a peasant girl whose father is in the hope of changing the poor and miserable condition of the family. He sends Tess to claim kin with a distant relative noble D'Urberville family. The young master Alec seduces her, and the following pregnancy forces her to return home in disgrace. After the unexpected death of her baby Tess goes to work as a dairymaid on a farm, where she and Angel Clare—a son of a wealthy clergyman, fall in love and get married. Owing to her sincere love for Clare, Tess confesses on the wedding night of her earlier misfortune in the hands of Alec, but her husband is unable to understand and forgive her. Clare deserts her and goes to Brazil. Later, Tess returns to Alec to be his mistress in order to support the life of her family after the untimely death of her father. To her surprise, Clare returns from abroad because he regrets for his ruthless treatment of her whom he still loves. In this situation, Tess kills Alec in a fit of anger and despair, for she thinks he has ruined all her life, then she escapes with Clare. Before they are discovered, Tess and Clare spend a couple of days of real love and happiness in a distant forest, which she has been pursuing all her life. Then Tess is arrested and sentenced to death. Though the life of Tess involves a number of accidental events which seem to contribute to her tragedy, such as her father's discovery of their kindred with the noble D'Urberville family, yet as is seen in the story, the real causes of her tragedy lie in the wicked nature and hypocritical morality of the bourgeois society.

The tragedy of Tess is an exposure of the wicked oppressors represented by Alec and it also criticizes the hypocritical moral of the society. The author expresses his hypocritical moral of the society and his sympathy for the poor people such as Tess and her family. Among the English novels of critical realism, the novel stands out for its deep sympathy for the simple rural folk, and for its searching exposition and condemnation of the social injustice and bourgeois morality.

Part Eleven
The Twentieth Century

Chapter 1 The Development of the English Novel

The Novel in the Pre-War Period. At the beginning of the 20th century, critical realism continued to be the major literary tradition in novel writing. Three writers came to prominence who inherited their 19th century predecessors, tradition in writing. Their chief concern is with society itself—its organization, outlook, values, and tone. H. G. Wells (1866—1946), Arnold Bennett (1867—1931), and John Galsworthy (1867—1933), the three writers in question, are far from being alike either as men or as writers, but in their fiction they all have a sociological foundation in common.

Wells, the most brilliant, never thought of himself as a literary artist, and made no secret of the fact that he made use of the novel as a critic of society. He was one of the last representatives of English critical realism. He was much concerned about the crying contradictions of bourgeois civilization and made protests against imperialism and fascism. But being a bourgeois intellectual himself, he was unable to find a proper solution to social problems. He wanted to substitute the decaying capitalist social order with a system called "technocracy", that is, a society ruled by engineers and scientists, and he believed that it was possible to improve the capitalist society. Many of his novels are science romances in which he drew satirical picture of the English or European society of his time, exposing the ugly feature of the oppressors. His well-known novels are *The Time Machine*, *The Invisible Man*, *The War in the Air and The Shape of Things to Come*.

Arnold Bennett's fiction is varied and uneven, but the best of it is a solidly realistic record of the society he knew as a boy in that provincial region known, because it was the center of the pottery industry, as "The Potteries". There is an easy, unforced charm as well as a solid realism in his writings, which he learned from French novelists during the years he lived in France. Bennett's masterpiece is *The Old Wive's Tale* (1908).

John Galsworthy (1867—1933) made his reputation in Britain before World War I, not only through his novels, which were sharply critical of the property-owning class to which he himself belonged; but also through his realistic and well-constructed plays. It was, however, with the publication of *The Forsyte Saga* (1906—1921) that he achieved during the 1920's a world-wide body of admiring readers who felt that his wide social range, his honest criticism of his own class, his deep compassion, his essential Englishness, made him the representative English novelist of his time. He was awarded the Nobel Prize in 1932, the first English writer of fiction after Kipling to be so honored.

Rudyard Kipling (1856—1936) and Joseph Conrad (1857—1924) are two writers of this period who are different from the three writers mentioned above. Rudyard Kipling was born in India and educated in England. He did newspaper work in India from 1882 to 1889. During the Boer War(1899—902) he worked for a newspaper for the British aggressors in South Africa. Kipling was both a poet and a story-writer. His reputation rests on his poems and short stories, which deal with the daily life of the ordinary British officials and military men in India or in other colonial and semi-colonial countries. His stories are fascinating, but glorify the colonial expansion of the British imperialism. His best stories are found in *The Jungle Book*, *Plain Tales From the Hills* and *Action and Reaction*. In his novel *Kim*, he describes how an Irish orphan in India learns obedience and endurance from a lama and serves a British colonel as a secret agent.

Joseph Conrad, a Pole by birth who became a captain in the British merchant marine, is one of the important novelists at the beginning of the 20th century. Conrad is often thought to be simply a romantic storyteller just because he shows us so many sailors and ships in far-off places. However, he is a novelist who is deeply concerned with character, with behavior of individuals in moments of great stress and with the fundamental nature of human life and destiny. These themes he often treats in a symbolical way, so that in reading Conrad we must always try to be aware of the depths of meaning below the surface of the narrative. His famous novel is *Heart of Darkness* in which he draws on his Congo River experience to create an atmosphere of darkness and horror in the midst of which the hero recognizes a deep inner kinship with the corrupt villain, the Belgian trader who has lost all his earlier ideals and succumbed to the worst elements in the native life he had hoped to improve. In *Lord Jim* (1890), another famous novel by Conrad, by using the device of an intermediate narrator, he probes the meaning of a gross failure of duty on the part of a romantic and idealistic young sailor, and by presenting the hero's life from a series of different points of view, he keeps the moral questioning continuing to the end. The use of intermediate narrators and multiple points of view is common in Conrad; it is his favorite way of suggesting the complexity of experience and the difficulty of judging human actions.

The Novel between the Two World Wars. World War I removed the interest of the more literary critics of fiction from the sociological novels of Wells, Bennett, and Galsworthy and fixed that interest on novels and novelists of a very different kind. Instead of looking outward toward society itself, these new novelists tended to look inward and describe what was happening in the minds of their characters. So Virginia Woolf (1882—1941), one of these new novelists and a very brilliant woman, would attack Bennett because he did not seem to her to bring any illusion of life into the novel. (But this was true only from her own point of view, and if a Bennett novel is weak in its inward life, a Virginia Woolf novel is weak in its outward life—in the relation of its characters to society.) Literary fashion in England, following a general European movement, now insisted that fiction to be of any significance, should explore the depths and recesses of personality, revealing an unending stream of impressions, feelings, and thoughts, and showing us fewer people if necessary, but telling us everything about them. This new method in fiction is known as stream of consciousness.

A master of this method was James Joyce(1882—1941). His genius, especially in *Ulysses*(1922), cannot be questioned, and his stature and influence as a novelist has been great. He has an astonishing passion for and knowledge of language. He is a master of words.

E. M. Forster (1879—1970) published most of his novels well before World War I, but his finest novel, *A Passage to India* (1924), did not appear until the twenties, and he stands quite apart from the older sociological novelists. His work is easier to enjoy than to describe. He cares nothing for a broad picture of people and society. His own point of view shapes and colors all his novels, and he tries to give the reader certain supremely important, all-revealing moments in the lives of his characters.

Virginia Woolf believed that the significant modern novel should reflect the inner life of its characters, and with this aim in mind, she made several difficult, subtle, and not always successful experiments. But in novels like *To the Lighthouse*(1927) and *Between the Acts* (1941), she succeeds triumphantly creating fiction of deep human interest and strange beauty.

D. H. Lawrence(1885—1930) was another important figure in English fiction of this period. He too looks inward, not to show us a stream of impressions as Virginia Woolf does, but to explore those mysterious areas of feeling of which we are hardly conscious but which can strongly influence our lives. Lawrence was certainly a man of genius, and his writing reveals a marvelously sensitive feeling for nature and a gift for description.

The Novel since World War Ⅱ. Since World War Ⅱ, much new fiction has been published. The craftsmanship, the writing, are on a high level. But this contemporary fiction lacks size and weight, profound originality, and the kind of urgency that makes the novel seem important. These shortcomings may be due to a change of attitude in the reading public itself, for it will be found that it is precisely at those times when people are passionately eager to read fiction-as they were, for example, during the middle years of the nineteenth century, that the novel develops toward greatness.

Chapter 2 John Galsworthy

John Galsworthy (1867 — 1933) was an English realistic novelist, playwright and the winner of the Nobel Prize for Literature in 1932.

Galsworthy was born in an established wealthy bourgeois family. Although he studied law at Oxford, he traveled a lot after graduation and began his literary life at the age of twenty-eight. He published his first book under the pseudonym John Sinjohn. It was a collection of short stories, which was followed by two novels. However, they got little literary attention. *The Island Pharisees* was the first book which came out under his real name, and it was his first significant social novel, giving a critical portrayal of bourgeois life.

The Man of Property, a novel with harsh criticism of the upper-middle class, was a milestone in the development of Galsworthy's literary career, showing his maturity and consummate craftsmanship and establishing his literary status as a representative of bourgeois realism in the 20th century English novel. While writing his next novel, *In Chancery*, Galsworthy began to have the idea of creating a series of novels to portray the history of English bourgeois life. He carried out this project in his masterpiece *The Forsyte Saga*. It took him twenty-two years to accomplish this monumental work. *The Forsyte Saga* contains a series of novels chronicling three generations of the Forsytes, a large upper-middle-class family with wealth and success in the business world. It is a chronicle about forty years, from the eighties of the nineteenth century to the twenties of the twentieth century. It profoundly and vividly presents a true-to-life picture of the English bourgeois society and reflects his main theme, that is, the possessive instinct of the propertied class. His first trilogy *The Forsyte Saga* consists of *The Man of Property*, *The Indian Summer of a Forsyte* (interlude), *In Chancery*, *Awakening* (interlude) and *To Let*, and it was continued by the second trilogy *A Modern Comedy* which consists of *The White Monkey*, *A Silent Wooing* (interlude), *The Silver Spoon*, *Passer-By* (interlude) and *Swan Song*. During the last years of his life Galsworthy wrote three minor significant novels which make up his third trilogy *The End of the Chapter*.

Galsworthy was also a playwright. He wrote twenty-eight plays. His plays touched on and examined the burning social problems of his time and took up special social grievance.

In his late years Galsworthy had a high international reputation. He co-founded the international writers' organization pen club in 1924 and was the president. He was conferred the degree of Doctor of Literature by Oxford University in 1931, and then he received the Nobel Prize for Literature in 1932 "for his distinguished art of narration which takes its highest form in *The Forsyte Saga*". He died on January 31, 1933.

The Forsyte Saga is generally applied to the Forsyte family in two trilogies: *The Forsyte Saga* and *A Modern Comedy*. In his great work, Galsworthy tells the story about the propertied Forsyte family living between 1886 to 1926, and through this work, he presents the gradual decay and the decline of the bourgeois class.

In the first and the most important trilogy *The Forsyte Saga*, Galsworthy describes the three generations' love and hostility of the large upper-middle-class Forsyte family. It includes *The Man of Property*, *The Indian Summer of a Forsyte* (interlude), *In Chancery*, *Awakening* (interlude) and *To Let*, and the main character is Soames Forsyte, a prosperous lawyer, who is portrayed as a typical "man of property".

The Man of Property is the first volume of this trilogy and regarded as the summit of Galsworthy's critical realism works. In *The Man of Property*, Soames Forsyte marries Irene, the daughter of a poor professor. Irene is young and beautiful, she loves art and has her noble ideas of life. But Soames only sees her just as a valuable piece of property and neglects her feeling and desires, so Irene is very unhappy. Later, Soams employs an architect named Bosinney to build a country house for his wife named Robin Hill. In the process of the designing and the building, Irene and Bosinney attract each other because of their common interest in art. Then Soames finds that they have fallen in love, he revenges Bosinney by suing him at the court for spending more money than stipulated. Bossinney happens to have a car accident in a London fog and has a tragic death. Thus, the triangular relationship of Soames, Irene and Bosinney ends. Irene returns to Soames's house but refuses to have anything to do with Soames, so Soames wins only an empty triumph. In this story, Galsworthy definitely takes the side of Irene and Bosinney, shows great sympathy for them, and describes them as people rebels and struggles against the stifling atmosphere of the practical money-making bourgeois world of the Forsytes, and have a common belief in art and beautiful noble life.

The second novel *In Chancery* is about the marriage between Soames and Annette Lamotte, a pretty French girl. According to Galsworthy, this marriage is a compromise between money and beauty, in other words, it is a triumph of money's power by which Soames buys himself a pretty wife. Later, they have a daughter named Fleur, who inherits the possessive instincts of the father. Therefore, Soames loves his daughter very much. After twelve years lonely life and getting divorced from Soames, Irene is married to young Jolyon, Soames's cousin, who has shown a growing love for her. Their marriage is a real unity of feelings and aspirations. Later, this happy couple has a son called Jon.

To Let is the third novel with the setting of twenty years after the events of *In Chancery*. In this novel, Fleur and Jon fall in love. Fleur takes the initiative in this love.

With Forsyte's determination and instinct, she has great eagerness and hope for her marriage, even after she knows the former relationship of their parents. But Jon is in anguish when Jolyon, his father, is forced to reveal to him Irene's past relationship with Soames. Finally, Jon leaves Fleur with fortitude and makes a voyage to America, and he is joined by Irene after Jolyon's death. Fleur, compelled by his father, marries Michael Mont, heir to a barony. At the end of this story, the desolate Soames gets to know that his French wife betrays him and has a lover outside of marriage, and he finds that Robin Hill, Irene's house, is empty and to let. Thus the era of Forsyte has passed.

Galsworthy's art crafts were greatly influenced by the French and Russian novelists, particularly Turgenev. His works give a panorama of contemporary England and are accepted as faithful patterns of English life for a time. His satire and critics were directed particularly at the propertied bourgeois class. He exposed the wealthy class, diagnosed the social disease, penetrated into the most sensitive innermost feelings of the human heart and drew human passions with psychological depth. However, his criticism of the bourgeoisie was still only limited to the ethic and aesthetic aspects. Because he was conservative at heart, he suggested no remedies to the social disease, but aimed to improve his class, and wished it could retain its ruling position in society. His works have a sense of fatalism and show a growing compassion for the class from which he sprang. Facing the crisis of British imperialism and the growing forces of socialism, Galsworthy began to idealize the decadent bourgeoisie. His works, particular those written after World War I and the October Revolution, evidently reflect his bourgeois conservatism.

Galsworthy was also a great stylist, writing in a naturalistic way. His language is clear, simple, concise, direct and exact. His style was exceptional for its strength and elasticity, its brilliant illustrations and deep psychological analysis. He is good at reflecting the feelings of the heroes, and his power of depicting their fiercest passion such as avarice, hate, fear, revenge, remorse is notable.

In Chancery (an excerpt)

The following is the seventh chapter of "In Chancery", the second novel of "The Forsyte Saga". It is titled "Birth of a Forsyte", telling the birth of Soames's daughter, Fleur. Because of the danger of his wife's premature childbirth, Soames had to choose between his wife and the baby. This chapter vividly shows Soames's thought about his dilemma, and his final decision fully reflects his possessive instinct.

Chapter Ⅻ Birth of a Forsyte

Soames walked out of the garden door[1] crossed the lawn, stood on the path above the river, turned round and walked back to the garden door, without having realised that he had moved. The sound of wheels crunching the drive convinced him that time had passed, and the doctor gone. What, exactly, had he said?

"This is the position, Mr. Forsyte. I can make pretty certain of her life if I operate, but the baby will be born dead. If I don't operate, the baby will most probably be born alive, but it's a great risk for the mother—a great risk. In either case I don't think she[2] can ever have another child. In her state she obviously can't decide for herself, and we can't wait for her mother. It's for you to make the decision, while I'm getting what's necessary. I shall be back within the hour."

The decision! What a decision! No time to get a specialist down![3] No time for anything!

The sound of wheels died away, but Soames still stood intent; then, suddenly covering his ears, he walked back to the river. To come before its time like this[4], with no chance to foresee anything, not even to get her mother[5] here! It was for her mother to make that decision, and she couldn't arrive from Paris till to-night! If only he could have understood the doctor's jargon, the medical niceties, so as to be sure he was weighing the chances properly; but they were Greek to him[6]—like a legal problem to a layman. And yet he must decide! He brought his hand away from his brow wet, though the air was chilly. These sounds which came from her room! To go back there would only make it more difficult. He must be calm, clear. On the one hand life, nearly certain, of his young wife, death quite certain, of his child; and—no more children afterwards! On the other, death perhaps of his wife, nearly certain life for the child; and—no more children afterwards! Which to choose?... It had rained this last fortnight—the river was very full, and in the water, collected round the little house-boat moored by his landing-stage, were many leaves from the woods above, brought off by a frost. Leaves fell, lives drifted down—Death! To decide about death! And no one to give him a hand. Life lost was lost for good[7]. Let nothing go that you could keep; for, if it went, you couldn't get it back. It left you bare, like those trees when they lost their leaves; barer and barer until you, too, withered and came down. And, by a queer somersault of thought, he seemed to see not Annette lying up there behind that window-pane on which the sun was shining, but Irene[8] lying in their bedroom in Montpellier Square, as it might conceivably have been her fate to lie, sixteen years ago. Would he have hesitated then? Not a moment! Operate, operate! Make certain of her life! No decision—a mere instinctive cry for help, in spite of his know—ledge, even then, that she did not love him! But this! Ah! There was nothing overmastering in his feeling for Annette! Many times these last months, especially since she had been growing fright- ened, he had wondered. She had a will of her own, was selfish in her French way. And yet—so pretty! What would she wish—to take the risk. 'I know she wants the child,' he thought. 'If it's born dead, and no more chance afterwards—it'll upset her terribly. No more chance! All for nothing! Married life with her for years and years without a child. Nothing to steady her! She's too young. Nothing to look forward to, for her—for me! For me!' He struck his hands against his chest! Why couldn't he think without bringing himself in—get out of himself[9] and see what he ought to do? The thought hurt him, then lost edge[10], as if it had come in contact with a breastplate. Out of oneself! Impossible! Out into soundless, scentless, touchless, sightless space! The very idea was ghastly, futile! And touching there the bedrock of reality, the bottom of his Forsyte spirit, Soames rested for a moment. When one ceased, all ceased; it might go on, but there'd be nothing in it![11]

He looked at his watch. In half an hour the doctor would be back. He must decide! If against the operation and she died, how face her mother and the doctor afterwards? How face his own conscience? It was his child that she was having. If for the operation—then he condemned them both to childlessness. And for what else had he married her but to have a lawful heir? And his father—at death's door, waiting for the news! 'It's cruel!' he thought; 'I ought never to have such a thing to settle! It's cruel!' He turned towards the house. Some deep, simple way of deciding! He took out a coin, and put it back. If he spun it, he knew he would not abide by what came up! He went into the dining-room, furthest away from that room whence[12] the sounds issued. The doctor had said there was a chance. In here that chance seemed greater; the river did not flow, nor the leaves fall. A fire was burning. Soames unlocked the tantalus. He hardly ever touched spirits, but now—he poured himself out some whisky and drank it neat[13] craving a faster flow of blood. 'That fellow Jolyon[14],' he thought; 'he had children already. He has the woman I really loved; and now a son by her! And I—I'm asked to destroy my only child! Annette can't die; it's not possible. She's strong!'

He was still standing sullenly at the sideboard when he heard the doctor's carriage, and went out to him. He had to wait for him to come downstairs.

"Well, doctor?"

"The situation's the same. Have you decided?"

"Yes," said Soames; "don't operate!"

"Not? You understand—the risk's great?"

In Soames' set face nothing moved but the lips.

"You said there was a chance?"

"A chance, yes; not much of one."

"You say the baby must be born dead if you do?"

"Yes."

"Do you still think that in any case she can't have another?"

"One can't be absolutely sure, but it's most unlikely."

"She's strong," said Soames; "we'll take the risk."

The doctor looked at him very gravely. "It's on your shoulders,"[15] he said; "with my own wife, I couldn't."

Soames' chin jerked up as if someone had hit him.

"Am I of any use up there?" he asked.

"No; keep away."

"I shall be in my picture-gallery, then; you know where."

The doctor nodded, and went upstairs.

Soames continued to stand, listening. 'By this time to-morrow,' he thought, 'I may have her death on my hands.' No! it was unfair—monstrous, to put it that way! Sullenness dropped on him again, and he went up to the gallery. He stood at the window. The wind was in the north; it was cold, clear; very blue sky, heavy ragged white clouds chasing across; the river blue, too, through the screen of goldening trees; the woods all rich with colour, glowing, burnished-an early autumn. If it were his own life, would he be taking that risk? 'But she'd take the risk of losing me,' he thought, 'sooner than lose her child! She doesn't really love me!' What could one expect—a girl and French? The one thing really vital to them both, vital to their marriage and their futures, was a child! 'I've been through a lot for this,'[16] he thought, 'I'll hold on—hold on. There's a chance of keeping both—a chance!' One kept till things were taken—one naturally kept! He began walking round the gallery. He had made one purchase lately which he knew was a fortune in itself, and he halted before it—a girl with dull gold hair which looked like filaments of metal gazing at a little golden monster she was holding in her hand. Even at this tortured moment he could just feel the extraordinary nature of the bargain he had made—admire the quality of the table, the floor, the chair, the girl's figure, the absorbed expression on her face, the dull gold filaments of her hair, the bright gold of the little monster. Collecting pictures; growing richer, richer! What use, if...![17] He turned his back abruptly on the picture, and went to the window. Some of his doves had flown up from their perches round the dovecot, and were stretching their wings in the wind. In the clear sharp sunlight their whiteness almost flashed. They flew far, making a flung-up hieroglyphic against the sky. Annette fed the doves; it was pretty to see her. They took it out of her hand; they knew she was matter-of-fact. A choking sensation came into his throat. She would not—could nod die! She was too—too sensible; and she was strong, really strong, like her mother, in spite of her fair prettiness

It was already growing dark when at last he opened the door, and stood listening. Not a sound! A milky twilight crept about the stairway and the landings below. He had turned back when a sound caught his ear. Peering down, he saw a black shape moving, and his heart stood still. What was it? Death? The shape of Death coming from her door? No! only a maid without cap or apron. She came to the foot of his flight of stairs and said breathlessly:

"The doctor wants to see you, sir."

He ran down. She stood flat against the wall to let him pass, and said:

"Oh, Sir! it's over."

"Over?" said Soames, with a sort of menace; "what d'you mean?"

"It's born, sir."

He dashed up the four steps in front of him, and came suddenly on the doctor in the dim passage. The man was wiping his brow.

"Well?" he said; "quick!"

"Both living; it's all right, I think."

Soames stood quite still, covering his eyes.

"I congratulate you," he heard the doctor say; "it was touch and go."[18]

Soames let fall the hand which was covering his face.

"Thanks," he said; "thanks very much. What is it?"

"Daughter—luckily; a son would have killed her—the head."

A daughter!

"The utmost care of both," he hearts the doctor say, "and we shall do. When does the mother come?"

"To-night, between nine and ten, I hope."

"I'll stay till then. Do you want to see them?"

"Not now," said Soames; "before you go. I'll have dinner sent up to you." And he went downstairs.

Relief unspeakable, and yet—a daughter! It seemed to him unfair. To have taken that risk—to have been through this agony—and what agony! —for a daughter! He stood before the blazing fire of wood logs in the hall, touching it with his toe and trying to readjust himself. 'My father!' he thought. A bitter disappointment, no disguising it! One never got all one wanted in this life! And there was no other—at least, if there was, it was no use!

While he was standing there, a telegram was brought him.

"Come up at once, your father sinking fast. [19]

—MOTHER."

He read it with a choking sensation. One would have thought he couldn't feel anything after these last hours, but he felt this. Half-past seven, a train from Reading[20] at nine, and madame's train, if she had caught it, came in at eight-forty—he would meet that, and go on. He ordered the carriage, ate some dinner mechanically, and went upstairs. The doctor came out to him.

"They're sleeping."

"I won't go in," said Soames with relief. "My father's dying; I have to—go up. Is it all right?"

The doctor's face expressed a kind of doubting admiration. 'If they were all as unemotional' he might have been saying.

"Yes, I think you may go with an easy mind. You'll be down soon?"[21]

"To-morrow," said Soames. "Here's the address."

The doctor seemed to hover on the verge of sympathy.

"Good-night!" said Soames abruptly, and turned away. He put on his fur coat.

Death! It was a chilly business. He smoked a cigarette in the carriage—one of his rare cigarettes. The night was windy and flew on black wings; the carriage lights had to search out the way. His father! That old, old man! A comfortless night—to die!

The London train came in just as he reached the station, and Madame Lamotte, substantial, dark-clothed, very yellow in the lamplight, came towards the exit with a dressing-bag.

"This all you have?" asked Soames.

"But yes; I had not the time. How is my little one?"

"Doing well—both. A girl!"

"A girl! What joy! I had a frightful crossing!"[22]

Her black bulk, solid, unreduced by the frightful crossing, climbed into the brougham.

"And you, mon cher[23]?"

"My father's dying," said Soames between his teeth. "I'm going up. Give my love to Annette."

"Tiens!"[24] murmured Madame Lamotte; "quel malheur[25]!"

Soames took his hat off, and moved towards his train. 'The French!' he thought.

Notes

1. the garden door—the door of a building which opens toward the garden.
2. she—Annette, Soames's second wife.
3. No time to get a specialist down—No time to get an obstetrician from the city of London to his house in the suburb.
4. To come before its time like this—To have a premature childbirth like his wife, Annette's case.
5. her mother—Madame Lamotte.
6. they were Greek to him—It's difficult for him to understand them; they were beyond his understanding.
7. for good—forever.
8. Irene—Soammes's first wife, the pretty daughter of a poor professor.
9. get out of himself—get out of his limitation.
10. lost edge—lost sharpness.
11. When one ceased, all ceased; it might go on, but there'd be nothing in it! —When one ceased to exist, the world ceased to exist; the world might go on, but there would be nothing in it, if he had no heir.
12. Whence—from where.
13. drank it neat—drank it without adding in soda water to dilute it.
14. Jolyon—Jolyon Forsyte, Soames's cousin, who married Irene after her divorce from

Soames.

15. It's on your shoulders—You are responsible for it.
16. I've been through a lot for this—I have gone through a lot for this; I have suffered a lot from this.
17. What use, if...! —what use is it, if he would have no heir!
18. it was touch and go! —it was a great risk; it was a very narrow escape.
19. your father sinking fast—your father is dying.
20. Reading— a town to the west of London.
21. You'll be down soon? —You will be back here soon?
22. I had a frightful crossing! —I had a terrible time when I was crossing the English Channel.
23. mon cher—French, my dear.
24. Tiens! —French, "Oh!"
25. quel Malheur! —French, what misfortune!

For Study and Discussion

1. How does Soames show his possessive instinct?
2. Why Soames chose to give her wife an operation when learning the risk?
3. What was Soames feeling when he was informed that his newly-born baby was a girl?

Chapter 3 Joseph Conrad

Joseph Conrad (1857 — 1924) was a Polish-born English novelist and short story writer.

Conrad was born in Ukraine in Poland in 1857 and had a harsh childhood. His family was exiled to Russia because of his father's political activity. Conrad's mother died of tuberculosis when he was 7, and his father a short time afterwards. Conrad was brought up by his uncle, who loved him very much. In 1874 he began his career as a sailor which supplied much material for his writing. Then he spent 4 years in the French merchant navy, mastering the fundamentals of seamanship and French as his second language. He made acquaintances with many people who introduced him to drama, opera and theater. Meanwhile, he was strengthening his maritime contacts, and soon became an observer on pilot boats. The workers he met on the ship and all the experiences they told to him laid the groundwork for much of the vivid detail in his novels.

By 1878, Joseph had made his way to serve on British cargo ships and eventually qualified as First Mate and Master. He learned English with astonishing rapidity until he could write it with eloquence and even with masterly economy. He became a British subject in 1886. Later he settled in England and spent his time writing. His voyages to East and the travel to the Congo supplied his many novels in which the sea plays a dominant role. In the summer of 1889, Conrad began the crucial transition from sailor to writer by starting his first novel, *Almayer's Folly*. He chose to write in English which is his third language. He often presented his characters amid violence and danger, and used rich and vivid words to capture and reveal their elusive moods. The major creative and prolific phase of Conrad's writing career spanned from 1897 to 1911, during which time he created *Lord Jim*, *The Nigger of the Narcissus*, *Youth*, *Heart of Darkness*, *Nostromo*, *The Secret Agent*, and *Under Western Eyes*, and other works. "*Lord Jim*" (1900) and "*Nosromo*" (1904) are generally regarded as his finest novels, but *Heart of Darkness*, one of his most famous short novels, is widely regarded as a significant work of English literature and part of the Western canon. Conrad died of a heart attack on August 3, 1924 and was buried in Canterbury.

Heart of the Darkness was partly based on Conrad's four-month journey to the Belgian Congo in 1890. It is a novel that presents human behaviour in all complexities, explores the unconscious mind of human beings and questions the European colonial undertaking. The story centers around Marlow, an introspective sailor, and his journey up the Congo River to meet Kurtz, who was reputed to be an idealistic man of great abilities, but degenerated to be a greedy and savage colonist.

Heart of the Darkness uses the story-within-a story device which is also called framed narrative in literary terms, and Marlow is the narrator who tells about his journey in Africa. He takes a job as a captain and works for a company whose only interest is ivory. When he does the job, he encounters many people he dislikes and witnesses the suffering of the native workers. He often hears of and becomes curious about a man named Kurtz who has a high reputation in many areas of expertise. Then he learns that he is to travel up the Congo River to reach Kurtz. After a suspiciously deliberate delay for repairing the ship, Marlow finally set off with five other white men. His steamer is attacked by the natives, but they are saved because of Marlow's intelligence. They finally arrive at the inner station of the company, and Marlow meets an unnamed Russian, who is the assistant of Kurtz and idolizes him. From the Russian, Marlow knows that Kurtz is no more the idealistic man having great expectation to civilize the natives. He used his gun and personal charisma to take over the native tribes and made them worship him as god. He forced them to fight against the other tribes to get their ivory, and obtained a great deal of wealth. But now, the Russian informs Marlow that Kurtz is seriously ill and nearly to die, and he worries that Kurtz's reputation will be destroyed. Thus, Marlow promises to the Russian that he will maintain Kurtz's reputation as a great man and tries to get the seriously inn Kurtz away. Near death, Kurtz has an enigmatic desire to remain part of the native culture such as the tribal fire, dance and the darkness. Marlow begins to see the great Kurtz that the others has described and admired. Kurtz gives Marlow a photograph of a beautiful girl who Marlow assumes is Kurtz's fiancée. Before his death, Kurtz seems to experience a moment of clarity and utters his last words "The horror! The horror!" which Marlow believes is Kurtz's reflection on his life. Marlow doesn't inform the manager of the death of Kurtz and reveal his degeneration to anyone. When Marlow goes back to Europe, the news about the death of Kurtz is revealed by the manager's child-servant. He finally meets Kurtz's fiancée who is still in mourning. Marlow tells her that Kurtz's last words were her name instead of "The horror! The horror!"

Heart of Darkness is regarded as Conrad's masterpiece and a classic work in English literature. It bridges the Victorian values and the ideals of modernism. The story obviously centers on the motif of imperialism. It is one of the first literary works to give a vivid description and show a critical view of European imperial activities. Conrad's earlier novels are primarily objective, descriptive and thematically clear, but in this novel, Conrad uses a lot of symbols and tends to be interior, suggestively analytic and highly psychological, to some extent, it introduces a new mode into his fiction. Some critics thinks *Heart of Darkness* is Conrad's first but also the only symbolic work. What's more, this fiction shows an occupation with psychology and unconscious mind. It is full of alienation, confusion and profound doubt about imperialism. Therefore, *Heart of Darkness* is a work with the Conrad's literary language precise and consistent. Because of the influence of his former two languages, Conrad's English seems unusual. While writing his novel, Conrad used precision language with consistency, and he was fond of using triple parallelism, and rhetorical abstraction.

Heart of Darknes' (an excerpt)

The following is taking from Conrad's "Heart of Darkness". In this excerpt, Marlow took over the post of a captain who had been killed by one of the African natives, and traveled up the river to the company's station. On his way to the journey, he witnessed the miserable black men's life under the inhuman exploitation of the whites. He was disguised by the greed of the European and their brutal exploitation of the natives. At the station, Marlow heard of the remarkable man, Mr. Kurtze, a successful agent of the company, taking a charge of a trading post.

"I had my passage on a little sea-going steamer. Her captain was a Swede, and knowing me for a seaman, invited me on the bridge. He was a young man, lean, fair, and morose, with lanky hair and a shuffling gait. As we left the miserable little wharf, he tossed his head contemptuously at the shore. 'Been living there?' he asked. I said, 'Yes.' Fine lot these government chaps —are they not? ' he went on, speaking English with great precision and considerable bitterness. ''It is funny what some people will do for a few francs a month. I wonder what becomes of that kind when it goes upcountry?' I said to him I expected to see that soon. 'So-o-o! ' he exclaimed. He shuffled athwart, keeping one eye ahead vigilantly. 'Don't be too sure,' he continued. 'The other day I took up a man who hanged himself on the road. He was a Swede, too. ''Hanged himself! Why, in God's name?' I cried. He kept on looking out watchfully. 'Who knows? The sun too much for him, or the country perhaps. '

"At last we opened a reach.[1] A rocky cliff appeared, mounds of turned-up earth by the shore, houses on a hill, others with iron roofs, amongst a waste of excavations, or hanging to the declivity. A continuous noise of the rapids above hovered over this scene of inhabited devastation. A lot of people, mostly black and naked, moved about like ants. A jetty projected into the river. A blinding sunlight drowned all this at times in a sudden recrudescence of glare. 'There's your Company's station,' said the Swede, pointing to three wooden barrack-like structures on the rocky slope. 'I will send your things up. Four boxes did you say? So. Farewell. '

"I came upon a boiler wallowing in the grass, then found a path leading up the hill. It turned aside for the boulders, and also for an undersized railway-truck lying there on its back with its wheels in the air. One was off. The thing looked as dead as the carcass of some animal. I came upon more pieces of decaying machinery, a stack of rusty rails. To the left a clump of trees made a shady spot, where dark things seemed to stir feebly. I blinked, the path was steep. A horn tooted to the right, and I saw the black people run. A heavy and dull detonation[2] shook the ground, a puff of smoke came out of the cliff, and that was all. No change appeared on the face of the rock. They were building a railway. The cliff was not in the way or anything; but this objectless blasting was all the work going on.

"A slight clinking behind me made me turn my head. Six black men advanced in a file[3], toiling up the path. They walked erect and slow, balancing small baskets full of earth on their heads, and the clink kept time with their footsteps. Black rags were wound round their loins, and the short ends behind waggled to and fro like tails. I could see every rib, the joints of their limbs were like knots in a rope; each had an iron collar on his neck, and all were connected together with a chain whose bights swung between them, rhythmically clinking. Another report from the cliff made me think suddenly of that ship of war I had seen firing into a continent. It was the same kind of ominous voice; but these men could by no stretch of imagination[4] be called enemies. They were called criminals, and the outraged law, like the bursting shells, had come to them, an insoluble mystery from the sea. All their meagre breasts panted together, the violently dilated nostrils quivered, the eyes stared stonily uphill. They passed me within six inches, without a glance, with that complete, deathlike indifference of unhappy savages. Behind this raw matter one of the reclaimed, the product of the new forces at work, strolled despondently, carrying a rifle by its middle. He had a uniform jacket with one button off, and seeing a white man on the path, hoisted his weapon to his shoulder with alacrity. This was simple prudence, white men being so much alike at a distance that he could not tell who I might be. He was speedily reassured, and with a large, white, rascally grin, and a glance at his charge, seemed to take me into partnership in his exalted trust. After all, I also was a part of the great cause of these high and just proceedings.

"Instead of going up, I turned and descended to the left. My idea was to let that chain-gang get out of sight before I climbed the hill. You know I am not particularly tender; I've had to strike and to fend off. I've had to resist and to attack sometimes—that's only one way of resisting—without counting the exact cost, according to the demands of such sort of life as I had blundered into. I've seen the devil of violence, and the devil of greed, and the devil of hot desire; but, by all the stars! these were strong, lusty, red-eyed devils, that swayed and drove men—men, I tell you. But as I stood on this hillside, I foresaw that in the blinding sunshine of that land I would become acquainted with a flabby, pretending, weak-eyed devil of a rapacious and pitiless folly. How insidious he could be, too, I was only to find out several months later and a thousand miles farther. For a moment I stood appalled, as though by a warning. Finally I descended the hill, obliquely, towards the trees I had seen.

"I avoided a vast artificial hole somebody had been digging on the slope, the purpose of which I found it impossible to divine. It wasn't a quarry or a sandpit, anyhow. It was just a hole. It might have been connected with the philanthropic desire of giving the criminals something to do. I don't know. Then I nearly fell into a very narrow ravine, almost no more than a scar in the hillside. I discovered that a lot of imported drainage-pipes for the settlement had been tumbled in there. There wasn't one that was not broken. It was a wanton smash-up. At last I got under the trees. My purpose was to stroll into the shade for a moment; but no sooner within than it seemed to me I had stepped into the gloomy circle of some Inferno.[5] The rapids[6] were near, and an uninterrupted, uniform, headlong, rushing noise filled the mournful stillness of the grove, where not a breath stirred, not a leaf moved, with a mysterious sound—as though the tearing pace of the launched earth had suddenly become audible.

"Black shapes crouched, lay, sat between the trees leaning against the trunks, clinging to the earth, half coming out, half effaced within the dim light, in all the attitudes of pain, abandonment, and despair. Another mine on the cliff went off,[7] followed by a slight shudder of the soil under my feet. The work was going on. The work! And this was the place where some of the helpers had withdrawn to die.

"They were dying slowly—it was very clear. They were not enemies, they were not criminals, they were nothing earthly now—nothing but black shadows of disease and starvation, lying confusedly in the greenish gloom. Brought from all the recesses of the coast in all the legality of time contracts, lost in uncongenial surroundings, fed on unfamiliar food, they sickened, became inefficient, and were then allowed to crawl away and rest. These moribund shapes were free as air—and nearly as thin. I began to distinguish the gleam of the eyes under the trees. Then, glancing down, I saw a face near my hand. The black bones reclined at full length with one shoulder against the tree, and slowly the eyelids rose and the sunken eyes looked up at me, enormous and vacant, a kind of blind, white flicker in the depths of the orbs, which died out slowly. The man seemed young—almost a boy—but you know with them it's hard to tell. I found nothing else to do but to offer him one of my good Swede's ship's biscuits I had in my pocket. The fingers closed slowly on it and held—there was no other movement and no other glance. He had tied a bit of white worsted round his neck—Why? Where did he get it? Was it a badge—an ornament—a charm—a propitiatory act? Was there any idea at all connected with it? It looked startling round his black neck, this bit of white thread from beyond the seas.

"Near the same tree two more bundles of acute angles sat with their legs drawn up. One, with his chin propped on his knees, stared at nothing, in an intolerable and appalling manner: his brother phantom rested its forehead, as if overcome with a great weariness; and all about others were scattered in every pose of contorted collapse, as in some picture of a massacre or a pestilence. While I stood horror-struck, one of these creatures rose to his hands and knees, and went off on all-fours[8] towards the river to drink. He lapped out of his hand, then sat up in the sunlight, crossing his shins in front of him, and after a time let his woolly head fall on his breastbone.

"I didn't want any more loitering in the shade, and I made haste towards the station.[9] When near the buildings I met a white man, in such an unexpected elegance of get-up[10] that in the first moment I took him for a sort of vision. I saw a high starched collar, white cuffs, a light alpaca jacket, snowy trousers, a clean necktie, and varnished boots. No hat. Hair parted, brushed, oiled, under a green-lined parasol held in a big white hand. He was amazing, and had a penholder behind his ear.

"I shook hands with this miracle, and I learned he was the Company's chief accountant, and that all the book-keeping was done at this station. He had come out for a moment, he said, 'to get a breath of fresh air.' The expression sounded wonderfully odd, with its suggestion of sedentary desk-life. I wouldn't have mentioned the fellow to you at all, only it was from his lips that I first heard the name of the man who is so indissolubly connected with the memories of that time. Moreover, I respected the fellow. Yes; I respected his collars, his vast cuffs, his brushed hair. His appearance was certainly that of a hairdresser's dummy; but in the great demoralization of the land he kept up his appearance. That's backbone. His starched collars and got-up shirt-fronts were achievements of character. He had been out nearly three years; and, later, I could not help asking him how he managed to sport[11] such linen. He had just the faintest blush, and said modestly, 'I've been teaching one of the native women about the station. It was difficult. She had a distaste for the work.' Thus this man had verily accomplished something. And he was devoted to his books, which were in apple-pie order.

"Everything else in the station was in a muddle—heads, things, buildings. Strings of dusty niggers with splay feet arrived and departed; a stream of manufactured goods, rubbishy cottons, beads, and brass-wire set into the depths of darkness, and in return came a precious trickle of ivory.

I had to wait in the station for ten days— an eternity. I lived in a hut in the yard, but to be out of the chaos I would sometimes get into the accountant's office. It was built of horizontal planks, and so badly put together that, as he bent over his high desk, he was barred from neck to heels with narrow strips of sunlight. There was no need to open the big shutter to see. It was hot there, too; big flies buzzed fiendishly, and did not sting, but stabbed. I sat generally on the floor, while, of faultless appearance (and even slightly scented), perching on a high stool, he wrote, he wrote. Sometimes he stood up for exercise. When a truckle-bed with a sick man (some invalid agent from upcountry[12]) was put in there, he exhibited a gentle annoyance. 'The groans of this sick person,' he said, 'distract my attention. And without that it is extremely difficult to guard against clerical errors in this climate.'

"One day he remarked, without lifting his head, 'In the interior you will no doubt meet Mr. Kurtz.' On my asking who Mr. Kurtz was, he said he was a first-class agent; and seeing my disappointment at this information, he added slowly, laying down his pen, 'He is a very remarkable person.' Further questions elicited from him that Mr. Kurtz was at present in charge of a trading-post, a very important one, in the true ivory-country, at 'the very bottom of there. Sends in as much ivory as all the others put together...' He began to write again. The sick man was too ill to groan. The flies buzzed in a great peace."

"Suddenly there was a growing murmur of voices and a great tramping of feet. A caravan had come in. A violent babble of uncouth sounds burst out on the other side of the planks. All the carriers were speaking together, and in the midst of the uproar the lamentable voice of the chief agent was heard 'giving it up' tearfully for the twentieth time that day. . . . He rose slowly. 'What a frightful row,' he said. He crossed the room gently to look at the sick man, and returning, said to me, 'He does not hear.' 'What! Dead?' I asked, startled. 'No, not yet,' he answered, with great composure. Then, alluding with a toss of the head to the tumult in the station-yard, 'When one has got to make correct entries, one comes to hate those savages—hate them to the death.' He remained thoughtful for a moment. 'When you see Mr. Kurtz' he went on, 'tell him from me that everything here'—he glanced at the deck—'is very satisfactory. I don't like to write to him—with those messengers of ours you never know who may get hold of your letter—at that Central Station.' He stared at me for a moment with his mild, bulging eyes. 'Oh, he will go far, very far,' he began again. 'He will be a somebody in the Administration before long. They, above—the Council in Europe, you know—mean him to be.'[13]

"He turned to his work. The noise outside had ceased, and presently in going out I stopped at the door. In the steady buzz of flies the homeward-bound agent was lying finished and insensible; the other, bent over his books, was making correct entries of perfectly correct transactions; and fifty feet below the doorstep I could see the still tree-tops of the grove of death.

"Next day I left that station at last, with a caravan of sixty men, for a two-hundred-mile tramp."

Notes

1. opened a reach—came into a part of the river.
2. detonation—explosion.
3. advanced in a file—walked forwards in a line.
4. by no stretch of imagination—it's very hard to imagine.
5. Inferno—Hell.
6. rapids—a dangerous part of a river which flows very fast because it is steep and sometimes narrow.
7. Another mine on the cliff went off—Another bomb exploded.
8. on all-fours—with one's hands and knees on the ground.
9. the station—the company's trading station.
10. get-up—clothes.
11. sport —wear.
12. upcountry—the country in the interior.
13. mean him to be—intend to make him to be, intend to give him a promotion.

For Study and Discussion

1. Why did the Captain mention the man who hanged himself to Marlow?
2. How does the author show the miserable sufferings of the African natives?
3. What is the function of the accountant?
4. What does the sick agent imply in this novel?

Chapter 4 E. M. Forster

E. M. Forster (1879 — 1970) is a novelist and essayist, social and literal critic and a notable figure in British literature. Foster's father, Edward Morgan Llewellyn Forster, was an architect, who died of consumption when the son was very young, leaving the little boy to be brought up by his mother and his paternal aunt. His mother, Alice Clara Whichelo (known as Lily to the family and the neighborhood), was kind-hearted and submissive.

Foster was born in London on 1 January 1879. He spent most of his childhood at Rooksnest, from which he got his inspirations for *Howards End*. He attended Tonbridge School as a dayboy, an important experience responsible for his later criticism of the English public school system. Then, he was educated at King's College, Cambridge, where he enjoyed a sense of freedom, got access to Mediterranean culture and civilization, and broadened his horizon and literary interests.

After graduating from the college, Forster went to travel with her mother. He visited Italy, Germany, Egypt and India, becoming quite familiar with India. Those travel experiences are significant and essential to his later novel creation. In 1905, Foster published his first novel, *Where Angels Fear to Tread*, which was adapted into a film by Charles Sturridge in 1991. Later, he published *The Longest Journey* (1907), *A Room with a View* (1908) and *Howards End* (1910) respectively. *Howards End* is Forster's first success in his literary career, which mainly focuses on the relationship between Schlegel sisters and Ruth Wilcox. Besides. After his journey in Italy, he wrote *A Passage to India*, which is the last novel published by him during his lifetime. Foster published two volumes of short stories, *The Celestial Omnibus* (1914) and *The Eternal Moment* (1924). In fact, Foster's fame lies mostly on *Howards End* and *A Passage to India*. He died in June of 1970 at the Coventry home of his good friends Bob and May Buckingham after a series of strokes.

Forster enjoys equal popularity with Joseph Conrad, D. H. Lawrence and Virginia Woolf. Partly as a late Victorian and an Edwardian and partly as modern, he witnessed radical social and cultural changes on an unprecedented scale. Yet it is his aesthetic response to such changes that makes him rare and special. He is a writer of great technical and intellectual significance, whose work is sufficiently complicated and dense to deserve close study and analysis.

A Passage to India was published on 4 June 1924. Forster was then forty-five years old and fourteen years had elapsed since the publication of his previous novels. Regarded as Forster's masterpiece, this novel was the result of his two trips to India, in 1912—13 and again in 1921. With the publication of the novel, Forster achieved international recognition.

The novel takes the relationship between East and West as its subject matter, with a touch of colonialism. The story takes place in an Indian town, Chandrapore, which is partly old and partly new. One night, when meeting with his friends, Aziz, an Indian doctor in the town, is sent for by his direct superior major Calendar, but on arrival he finds that the major has gone out. On his way back, Aziz enters a mosque where he meets an elderly English woman Mrs. Moore, with whom he talks in friendly atmosphere.

Mrs. Moore is the mother of the city Magistrate, Ronny Heaslop. She is accompanied by a young girl Adela Quested, who comes from England to explore the possibility of marrying Ronny. Both Mrs. Moore and Adela wish to see the real India, and Mr. Turton, the Collector, arranges a "Bridge Party" to enable them to meet the Indians. The party is not much of a success. However Cyril Fielding, the principle of the local government college, invites them to a tea at his house. The Tea Party is cordial but later is disturbed by Ronny's arrival.

During the Tea Party, Aziz has invited Mrs. Moore and Adela to visit the Marabar Caves, and the invitation is accepted. Aziz makes elaborate preparations for the Marabar expedition, however, accidents appear one after another. Fielding and Godbole are delayed and can't catch the train to the caves. When Mrs. Moore enters the first cave, something strikes her and she is greatly affected. Losing totally her beliefs, she sits down outside the caves while Adela and Aziz go on to visit the other caves. Like Mrs. Moore, Adela is also affected by the caves. In the state of confusion, she mistakenlyh believes Azis's attempt to molest her. She returns to Chandrapore to accuse Aziz.

After he has returned from the Marabar Caves to Chandrapre, Aziz is arrested at the station and taken to prison. The trial creates social and political tension in Chandrapore. Fielding is regarded as a renegade, for he believes that Aziz is not guilty. Mrs. Moore is arranged by her son to leave India ahead of time. At the trial Adela realizes and confesses her mistake, and bravely renounces her own people. It is a triumph for Aziz and the Indians. The Anglo-Indians are shocked by the strange turn of events.

Fielding escorts Adela to his house and he joins Aziz in his victory celebrations. Meanwhile the news of Mrs. Moore's death on her voyage to England is made known. Fielding persuades Aziz to give up his claim for damages from Adela for wrongly implicating him in the case. The engagement between Ronny and Adela is broken off, and Adela leaves for England.

Two years after the trial, the Hindus celebrate the Gokul Ashtami festival with great merriment at Mau, a small native state. Godbole now is the Education Minister and Aziz the personal physician of the Maharajah. Fielding comes to Mau for inspection of schools with his wife and her brother. Aziz meets Fielding but there is no intimacy between them because Aziz suspects that Fielding has married Adela and that he has been robbed of the compensation money. However, when he learns that Fieldinghas married Stella, Mrs. Moore's daughter, the misunderstanding is cleared up. Later when Aziz, Ralph, Fielding, and Stella join in the boating, their boats collide and they all fall into the water, only to realize the unity of all men.

Nevertheless, the unity is not the final one. Both Aziz and Fielding realize that only when Englishmen are driven out of India could they two become real friends.

Chapter 5 Virginia Woolf

Virginia Woolf (1882 —1941), one of the foremost modernist novelist and essayist in the twentieth century, was born in London on January 25, 1882, a descendant of one of Victorian England's most prestigious literary families. Her father, Sir Leslie Stephen, was a critic and the editor of the *Dictionary of National Biography*, who was married to Julia Prinsep Stephen, the daughter of the writer William Thackeray. Though denied the formal education allowed to males, the young Virginia was educated at home and able to take advantage of her father's abundant library and observe his writing talent.

Woolf began her literary career in 1905, initially for the *Times Literary Supplement* with a journalistic piece about Haworth, home of the Brontë family. Roger Fry as a critic of painting revolutionizing British taste by introducing the work of the Post-Impressionists, whose biography she wrote, was a close friend of hers. So were John Maynard Keynes, the economist; Lytton Strachey, the biographer; Bertrand Russell, the philosopher; and E. M. Forster, the novelist. Bound together by a common outlook, working and living in the Bloomsbury district of London, the Woolfs and some of their friends formed an intellectual circle known as the "Bloomsbury Group ".

Her first two novels, *The Voyage Out* published in 1915 by her half-brother's imprint, Gerald Duckworth and Company Ltd, and *Night and Day* (1919) were written in the conventional technique. Then Woolf began to try a new creative method as an experiment. She attacked and rebelled against the traditional method of realism adopted by such novelists as Arnold Bennett, John Galsworthy and H. G. Wells. In her experiment, she tried her best to reduce the element of plot in the novel, to adopt the stream-of-consciousness, or interior monologue in her novels, and to explore problems of human personality and personal relationships in a series of her maturer novels: *Jacob's Room* (1922), and the novel *Mrs. Dalloway* published in 1925, earned her reputation as an important psychological writer, a reputation made secure by later works, such as *To the Lighthouse* (1927), *Orlando* (1928), *The Waves* (1931), *The Years* (1931) and *Between the Acts* (1941).

Virginia Woolf also wrote two well-known volumes of critic essays, *The Common Reader* (1925) and *The Second Common Reader*(1932). She could make her essays read like short stories by recreating the personalities in a vivid and impressionistic way. She was a feminist in social and political attitude. Her long essay *A Room of One's Own* serves as an example of her concern with woman writer's plight facing a male-dominated society.

Virginia Woolf's poetic vision intensifies and elevates the ordinary, sometimes banal settings, often wartime environments, of most of her novels. *Mrs Dalloway* (1925) which centers on the efforts of Clarissa Dalloway, a middle-aged society woman, to organize a party, even as her life is paralleled with that of Septimus Warren Smith, a working-class veteran who has returned from the World War I bearing deep psychological scars.

To the Lighthouse (1927), one of her most experimental and remarkable works, is modulated by the consciousness of the characters instead of the passage of time. The plot centers around the Ramsay family's anticipation of and reflection upon a visit to a lighthouse. *To the Lighthouse* is a representative work which best exhibits Woolf's style and innovation. It is regarded as her autobiographical fictional record, for the characters are based on her own parents and siblings.

As a representative of modernism and a great creative writer of the twentieth century, Virginia Woolf's fame mainly lies in her special arts of story-telling. Her novels were reviewed extensively by editors and critics, which confirmed his position at the forefront of the modern British literary world, and have ensured her a niche in the British literary pantheon.

To the Lighthouse

To the Lighthouse is divided into three sections: "The Window", "Time Passes", and "The Lighthouse". Each section is fragmented into stream-of-consciousness contributions from various narrators.

"The Window" opens just before the start of World War I. Mr. Ramsay and Mrs. Ramsay bring their eight children to their summer home in the Hebrides (a group of islands west of Scotland). Across the bay from their house stands a large lighthouse. Six-year-old James Ramsay wants desperately to go to the lighthouse, and Mrs. Ramsay tells him that they will go the next day if the weather permits. James reacts gleefully, but Mr. Ramsay tells him coldly that the weather looks to be foul. James resents his father and believes that he enjoys being cruel to James and his siblings.

The Window

1

"Yes, of course, if it's fine tomorrow," said Mrs. Ramsay[1]. "But you'll have to be up with the lark," she added.

To her son these words conveyed an extraordinary joy, as if it were settled, the expedition were bound to take place, and the wonder to which he had looked forward, for years and years it seemed, was, after a night's darkness and a day's sail, within touch. Since he belonged, even at the age of six, to that great clan[2] which cannot keep this feeling separate from that, but must let future prospects, with their joys and sorrows, cloud what is actually at hand, since to such people even in earliest childhood any turn in the wheel of sensation has the power to crystallise and transfix the moment upon which its gloom or radiance rests, James Ramsay[3], sitting on the floor cutting out pictures from the illustrated catalogue of the Army and Navy stores, endowed the picture of a refrigerator, as his mother spoke, with heavenly bliss. It was fringed[4] with joy. The wheelbarrow, the lawnmower, the sound of poplar trees, leaves whitening before rain, rooks cawing, brooms knocking, dresses rustling—all these were so coloured and distinguished in his mind that he had already his private code, his secret language, though he appeared the image of stark and uncompromising severity, with his high forehead and his fierce blue eyes, impeccably[5] candid and pure, frowning slightly at the sight of human frailty, so that his mother, watching him guide his scissors neatly round the refrigerator, imagined him all red and ermine on the Bench or directing a stern and momentous enterprise in some crisis of public affairs.

"But," said his father, stopping in front of the drawing-room window, "it won't be fine."

Had there been an axe handy, a poker, or any weapon that would have gashed a hole in his father's breast and killed him, there and then, James would have seized it. Such were the extremes of emotion that Mr Ramsay[6] excited in his children's breasts by his mere presence; standing, as now, lean as a knife, narrow as the blade of one, grinning sarcastically, not only with the pleasure of disillusioning his son and casting ridicule upon his wife, who was ten thousand times better in every way than he was (James thought), but also with some secret conceit at his own accuracy of judgement. What he said was true. It was always true. He was incapable of untruth; never tampered with a fact; never altered a disagreeable word to suit the pleasure or convenience of any mortal being, least of all of his own children, who, sprung from his loins, should be aware from childhood that life is difficult; facts uncompromising; and the passage to that fabled land where our brightest hopes are extinguished, our frail barks founder in darkness (here Mr Ramsay would straighten his back and narrow his little blue eyes upon the horizon), one that needs, above all, courage, truth, and the power to endure.

"But it may be fine—I expect it will be fine," said Mrs. Ramsay, making some little twist of the reddish brown stocking she was knitting, impatiently. If she finished it tonight, if they did go to the Lighthouse after all, it was to be given to the Lighthouse keeper for his little boy, who was threatened with a tuberculous[7] hip; together with a pile of old magazines, and some tobacco, indeed, whatever she could find lying about, not really wanted, but only littering the room, to give those poor fellows, who must be bored to death sitting all day with nothing to do but polish the lamp and trim the wick and rake about on their scrap of garden, something to amuse them. For how would you like to be shut up for a whole month at a time, and possibly more in stormy weather, upon a rock the size of a tennis lawn? she would ask; and to have no letters or newspapers, and to see nobody; if you were married, not to see your wife, not to know how your children were,—if they were ill, if they had fallen down and broken their legs or arms; to see the same dreary waves breaking week after week, and then a dreadful storm coming, and the windows covered with spray, and birds dashed against the lamp, and the whole place rocking, and not be able to put your nose out of doors for fear of being swept into the sea? How would you like that? she asked, addressing herself particularly to her daughters. So she added, rather differently, one must take them whatever comforts one can.

"It's due west," said the atheist Tansley[8], holding his bony fingers spread so that the wind blew through them, for he was sharing Mr Ramsay's evening walk up and down, up and down the terrace. That is to say, the wind blew from the worst possible direction for landing at the Lighthouse. Yes, he did say disagreeable things, Mrs. Ramsay admitted; it was odious of him to rub this in, and make James still more disappointed; but at the same time, she would not let them laugh at him. "The atheist," they called him; "the little atheist." Rose[9] mocked him; Prue[10] mocked him; Andrew[11], Jasper[12], Roger[13] mocked him; even old Badger without a tooth in his head had bit him, for being (as Nancy[14] put it) the hundred and tenth young man to chase them all the way up to the Hebrides[15] when it was ever so much nicer to be alone.

"Nonsense," said Mrs. Ramsay, with great severity. Apart from the habit of exaggeration which they had from her, and from the implication (which was true) that she asked too many people to stay, and had to lodge some in the town, she could not bear incivility to her guests, to young men in particular, who were poor as churchmice, "exceptionally able," her husband said, his great admirers, and come there for a holiday. Indeed, she had the whole of the other sex under her protection; for reasons she could not explain, for their chivalry and valour, for the fact that they negotiated treaties, ruled India, controlled finance; finally for an attitude towards herself which no woman could fail to feel or to find agreeable, something trustful, childlike, reverential; which an old woman could take from a young man without loss of dignity, and woe betide the girl —pray Heaven it was none of her daughters! —who did not feel the worth of it, and all that it implied, to the marrow of her bones!

She turned with severity upon Nancy. He had not chased them, she said. He had been asked.

They must find a way out of it all. There might be some simpler way, some less laborious way, she sighed. When she looked in the glass and saw her hair grey, her cheek sunk, at fifty, she thought, possibly she might have managed things better—her husband; money; his books. But for her own part she would never for a single second regret her decision, evade difficulties, or slur over duties. She was now formidable to behold, and it was only in silence, looking up from their plates, after she had spoken so severely about Charles Tansley, that her daughters, Prue, Nancy, Rose—could sport with infidel ideas which they had brewed for themselves of a life different from hers; in Paris, perhaps; a wilder life; not always taking care of some man or other; for there was in all their minds a mute questioning of deference and chivalry, of the Bank of England and the Indian Empire, of ringed fingers and lace, though to them all there was something in this of the essence of beauty, which called out the manliness in their girlish hearts, and made them, as they sat at table beneath their mother's eyes, honour her strange severity, her extreme courtesy, like a queen's raising from the mud to wash a beggar's dirty foot, when she admonished them so very severely about that wretched atheist who had chased them—or, speaking accurately, been invited to stay with them—in the Isle of Skye.

"There'll be no landing at the Lighthouse tomorrow," said Charles Tansley, clapping his hands together as he stood at the window with her husband. Surely, he had said enough. She wished they would both leave her and James alone and go on talking. She looked at him. He was such a miserable specimen, the children said, all humps and hollows. He couldn't play cricket; he poked; he shuffled. He was a sarcastic brute, Andrew said. They knew what he liked best—to be for ever walking up and down, up and down, with Mr. Ramsay, and saying who had won this, who had won that, who was a "first rate man" at Latin verses, who was "brilliant but I think fundamentally unsound," who was undoubtedly the "ablest fellow in Balliol[16]," who had buried his light temporarily at Bristol or Bedford, but was bound to be heard of later when his Prolegomena, of which Mr. Tansley had the first pages in proof with him if Mr. Ramsay would like to see them, to some branch of mathematics or philosophy saw the light of day. That was what they talked about.

She could not help laughing herself sometimes. She said, the other day, something about "waves mountains high." Yes, said Charles Tansley, it was a little rough. "Aren't you drenched to the skin?" she had said. "Damp, not wet through," said Mr Tansley, pinching his sleeve, feeling his socks.

But it was not that they minded, the children said. It was not his face; it was not his manners. It was him—his point of view. When they talked about something interesting, people, music, history, anything, even said it was a fine evening so why not sit out of doors, then what they complained of about Charles Tansley was that until he had turned the whole thing round and made it somehow reflect himself and disparage[17] them—he was not satisfied. And he would go to picture galleries they said, and he would ask one, did one like his tie? God knows, said Rose, one did not.

Disappearing as stealthily as stags from the dinner-table directly the meal was over, the eight sons and daughters of Mr and Mrs. Ramsay sought their bedrooms, their fastness in a house where there was no other privacy to debate anything, everything; Tansley's tie; the passing of the Reform Bill; sea birds and butterflies; people; while the sun poured into those attics, which a plank alone separated from each other so that every footstep could be plainly heard and the Swiss girl sobbing for her father who was dying of cancer in a valley of the Grisons, and lit up bats, flannels, straw hats, ink-pots, paint-pots, beetles, and the skulls of small birds, while it drew from the long frilled strips of seaweed pinned to the wall a smell of salt and weeds, which was in the towels too, gritty with sand from bathing.

Strife, divisions, difference of opinion, prejudices twisted into the very fibre of being, oh, that they should begin so early, Mrs. Ramsay deplored. They were so critical, her children. They talked such nonsense. She went from the dining-room, holding James by the hand, since he would not go with the others. It seemed to her such nonsense—inventing differences, when people, heaven knows, were different enough without that. The real differences, she thought, standing by the drawing-room window, are enough, quite enough. She had in mind at the moment, rich and poor, high and low; the great in birth receiving from her, half grudging, some respect, for had she not in her veins the blood of that very noble, if slightly mythical, Italian house, whose daughters, scattered about English drawing-rooms in the nineteenth century, had lisped so charmingly, had stormed so wildly, and all her wit and her bearing and her temper came from them, and not from the sluggish English, or the cold Scotch; but more profoundly, she ruminated[18] the other problem, of rich and poor, and the things she saw with her own eyes, weekly, daily, here or in London, when she visited this widow, or that struggling wife in person with a bag on her arm, and a note-book and pencil with which she wrote down in columns carefully ruled for the purpose wages and spendings, employment and unemployment, in the hope that thus she would cease to be a private woman whose charity was half a sop to her own indignation, half a relief to her own curiosity, and become what with her untrained mind she greatly admired, an investigator, elucidating the social problem.

Insoluble questions they were, it seemed to her, standing there, holding James by the hand. He had followed her into the drawing-room, that young man they laughed at; he was standing by the table, fidgeting[19] with something, awkwardly, feeling himself out of things, as she knew without looking round. They had all gone—the children; Minta Doyle[20] and Paul Rayley[21]; Augustus Carmichael; her husband—they had all gone. So she turned with a sigh and said, "Would it bore you to come with me, Mr. Tansley?"

She had a dull errand in the town; she had a letter or two to write; she would be ten minutes perhaps; she would put on her hat. And, with her basket and her parasol, there she was again, ten minutes later, giving out a sense of being ready, of being equipped for a jaunt[22], which, however, she must interrupt for a moment, as they passed the tennis lawn, to ask Mr. Carmichael[23], who was basking with his yellow cat's eyes ajar, so that like a cat's they seemed to reflect the branches moving or the clouds passing, but to give no inkling of any inner thoughts or emotion whatsoever, if he wanted anything.

For they were making the great expedition, she said, laughing. They were going to the town. "Stamps, writing-paper, tobacco?" she suggested, stopping by his side. But no, he wanted nothing. His hands clasped themselves over his capacious paunch[24], his eyes blinked, as if he would have liked to reply kindly to these blandishments (she was seductive but a little nervous) but could not, sunk as he was in a grey-green somnolence which embraced them all, without need of words, in a vast and benevolent lethargy of well-wishing; all the house; all the world; all the people in it, for he had slipped into his glass at lunch a few drops of something, which accounted, the children thought, for the vivid streak of canary-yellow in moustache and beard that were otherwise milk white. No, nothing, he murmured.

He should have been a great philosopher, said Mrs. Ramsay, as they went down the road to the fishing village, but he had made an unfortunate marriage. Holding her black parasol very erect, and moving with an indescribable air of expectation, as if she were going to meet some one round the corner, she told the story; an affair at Oxford with some girl; an early marriage; poverty; going to India; translating a little poetry "very beautifully, I believe," being willing to teach the boys Persian or Hindustanee[25], but what really was the use of that? —and then lying, as they saw him, on the lawn.

It flattered him; snubbed as he had been, it soothed him that Mrs. Ramsay should tell him this. Charles Tansley revived. Insinuating, too, as she did the greatness of man's intellect, even in its decay, the subjection of all wives—not that she blamed the girl, and the marriage had been happy enough, she believed—to their husband's labours, she made him feel better pleased with himself than he had done yet, and he would have liked, had they taken a cab, for example, to have paid the fare. As for her little bag, might he not carry that? No, no, she said, she always carried THAT herself. She did too. Yes, he felt that in her. He felt many things, something in particular that excited him and disturbed him for reasons which he could not give. He would like her to see him, gowned and hooded, walking in a procession. A fellowship, a professorship, he felt capable of anything and saw himself—but what was she looking at? At a man pasting a bill. The vast flapping sheet flattened itself out, and each shove of the brush revealed fresh legs, hoops, horses, glistening reds and blues, beautifully smooth, until half the wall was covered with the advertisement of a circus; a hundred horsemen, twenty performing seals, lions, tigers ... Craning forwards, for she was short-sighted, she read it out ... "will visit this town," she read. It was terribly dangerous work for a one-armed man, she exclaimed, to stand on top of a ladder like that—his left arm had been cut off in a reaping machine two years ago.

"Let us all go!" she cried, moving on, as if all those riders and horses had filled her with childlike exultation and made her forget her pity.

"Let's go," he said, repeating her words, clicking them out, however, with a self-consciousness that made her wince. "Let us all go to the circus." No. He could not say it right. He could not feel it right. But why not? she wondered. What was wrong with him then? She liked him warmly, at the moment. Had they not been taken, she asked, to circuses when they were children? Never, he answered, as if she asked the very thing he wanted; had been longing all these days to say, how they did not go to circuses. It was a large family, nine brothers and sisters, and his father was a working man. "My father is a chemist, Mrs. Ramsay. He keeps a shop." He himself had paid his own way since he was thirteen. Often he went without a greatcoat in winter. He could never "return hospitality" (those were his parched stiff words) at college. He had to make things last twice the time other people did; he smoked the cheapest tobacco; shag[26]; the same the old men did in the quays. He worked hard—seven hours a day; his subject was now the influence of something upon somebody—they were walking on and Mrs. Ramsay did not quite catch the meaning, only the words, here and there ... dissertation ... fellowship ... readership ... lectureship. She could not follow the ugly academic jargon, that rattled itself off so glibly, but said to herself that she saw now why going to the circus had knocked him off his perch, poor little man, and why he came out, instantly, with all that about his father and mother and brothers and sisters, and she would see to it that they didn't laugh at him any more; she would tell Prue about it. What he would have liked, she supposed, would have been to say how he had gone not to the circus but to Ibsen with the Ramsays. He was an awful prig[27]—oh yes, an insufferable bore. For, though they had reached the town now and were in the main street, with carts grinding past on the cobbles, still he went on talking, about settlements, and teaching, and working men, and helping our own class, and lectures, till she gathered that he had got back entire self-confidence, had recovered from the circus, and was about (and now again she liked him away on both sides, they came out on the quay, and the whole bay spread before them and Mrs. Ramsay could not help exclaiming, "Oh, how beautiful!" For the great plateful of blue water was before her; the hoary Lighthouse, distant, austere, in the midst; and on the right, as far as the eye could see, fading and falling, in soft low pleats, the green sand dunes with the wild flowing grasses on them, which always seemed to be running away into some moon country, uninhabited of men.

That was the view, she said, stopping, growing greyer-eyed, that her husband loved.

She paused a moment. But now, she said, artists had come here. There indeed, only a few paces off, stood one of them, in Panama hat and yellow boots, seriously, softly, absorbedly, for all that he was watched by ten little boys, with an air of profound contentment on his round red face gazing, and then, when he had gazed, dipping; imbuing[28] the tip of his brush in some soft mound of green or pink. Since Mr Paunceforte had been there, three years before, all the pictures were like that, she said, green and grey, with lemon-coloured sailing-boats, and pink women on the beach.

But her grandmother's friends, she said, glancing discreetly as they passed, took the greatest pains; first they mixed their own colours, and then they ground them, and then they put damp cloths to keep them moist.

So Mr Tansley supposed she meant him to see that that man's picture was skimpy, was that what one said? The colours weren't solid? Was that what one said? Under the influence of that extraordinary emotion which had been growing all the walk, had begun in the garden when he had wanted to take her bag, had increased in the town when he had wanted to tell her everything about himself, he was coming to see himself, and everything he had ever known gone crooked a little. It was awfully strange.

There he stood in the parlour[29] of the poky little house where she had taken him, waiting for her, while she went upstairs a moment to see a woman. He heard her quick step above; heard her voice cheerful, then low; looked at the mats, tea-caddies, glass shades; waited quite impatiently; looked forward eagerly to the walk home; determined to carry her bag; then heard her come out; shut a door; say they must keep the windows open and the doors shut, ask at the house for anything they wanted (she must be talking to a child) when, suddenly, in she came, stood for a moment silent (as if she had been pretending up there, and for a moment let herself be now), stood quite motionless for a moment against a picture of Queen Victoria wearing the blue ribbon of the Garter; when all at once he realised that it was this: it was this:—she was the most beautiful person he had ever seen.

With stars in her eyes and veils in her hair, with cyclamen and wild violets—what nonsense was he thinking? She was fifty at least; she had eight children. Stepping through fields of flowers and taking to her breast buds that had broken and lambs that had fallen; with the stars in her eyes and the wind in her hair—He had hold of her bag.

"Good-bye, Elsie," she said, and they walked up the street, she holding her parasol erect and walking as if she expected to meet some one round the corner, while for the first time in his life Charles Tansley felt an extraordinary pride; a man digging in a drain stopped digging and looked at her, let his arm fall down and looked at her; for the first time in his life Charles Tansley felt an extraordinary pride; felt the wind and the cyclamen[30] and the violets for he was walking with a beautiful woman. He had hold of her bag.

"No going to the Lighthouse, James," he said, as trying in deference to Mrs. Ramsay to soften his voice into some semblance of geniality at least.

Odious little man, thought Mrs. Ramsay, why go on saying that?

Notes

1. Mrs. Ramsay—Mr. Ramsay's wife. She is a dutiful and loving wife but often struggles with her husband's difficult moods and selfishness.
2. clan—A large group of relatives, friends, or associates.
3. James Ramsay—A young, single painter who befriends the Ramsays on the Isle of Skye.
4. fringe—A decorative border or edging of hanging threads, cords, or strips, often attached to a separate band.
5. impeccable—Having no flaws; perfect.
6. Mr. Ramsay—Mrs. Ramsay's husband, and a prominent metaphysical philosopher. Mr. Ramsay loves his family but often acts like something of a tyrant.
7. tuberculous—Of, relating to, or having tuberculosis.
8. Tansley—Charles Tansley, a young philosopher and pupil of Mr. Ramsay who stays with the Ramsays on the Isle of Skye.
9. Rose—One of the Ramsays' daughters. Rose has a talent for making things beautiful. She arranges the fruit for her mother's dinner party and picks out her mother's jewelry.
10. Prue—The oldest Ramsay girl, a beautiful young woman. Mrs. Ramsay delights in contemplating Prue's marriage, which she believes will be blissful.
11. Andrew—The oldest of the Ramsays' sons. Andrew is a competent, independent young man, and he looks forward to a career as a mathematician.
12. Jasper—One of the Ramsays' sons. Jasper, to his mother's chagrin, enjoys shooting birds.
13. Roger—One of the Ramsays' sons. Roger is wild and adventurous, like his sister Nancy.
14. Nancy—One of the Ramsays' daughters. Nancy accompanies Paul Rayley and Minta Doyle on their trip to the beach. Like her brother Roger, she is a wild adventurer.
15. Hebrides—An island group of western and northwest Scotland in the Atlantic Ocean.
16. Balliol—One of the most famous colleges of Oxford.
17. disparage—To speak of in a slighting way; belittle.
18. ruminate—To turn a matter over and over in the mind.
19. fidget—To behave or move nervously or restlessly.
20. Minta Doyle—A flighty young woman who visits the Ramsays on the Isle of Skye. Minta marries Paul Rayley at Mrs. Ramsay's wishes.
21. Paul Rayley— A young friend of the Ramsays who visits them on the Isle of Skye. Paul is a kind, impressionable young man who follows Mrs. Ramsay's wishes in marrying Minta Doyle.
22. jaunt—A short trip or excursion, usually for pleasure; an outing.
23. Mr Carmichael—Augustus Carmichael, an opium-using poet who visits the Ramsays on

the Isle of Skye. Carmichael languishes in literary obscurity until his verse becomes popular during the war.

24. paunch—The belly, especially a protruding one; a potbelly.
25. Hindustanee—Of or relating to India or its peoples, languages, or cultures.
26. shag—A tangle or mass, especially of rough, matted hair; to make shaggy; roughen.
27. prig—A person who demonstrates an exaggerated conformity or propriety, especially in an irritatingly arrogant or smug manner.
28. imbuing—To inspire, permeate, or invade; to stain or dye deeply.
29. parlour—A room in a private home set apart for the entertainment of visitors.
30. cyclamen—Any of various plants of the genus Cyclamen, especially a Mediterranean species widely cultivated as a houseplant, having decorative leaves and showy, variously colored flowers with reflexed petals.

For Study and Discussion

1. *To the Lighthouse* opens with a portrayal of the oedipal struggle between James and Mr. Ramsay. This conflict resounds throughout the book. How does the family drama shape the book as a whole?
2. Conventional gender roles—and more broadly, conventional social roles—present a major subject of exploration in *To the Lighthouse*. Choose three characters and describe how each approaches this subject. Do gender roles play a part in the lives of the younger children?
3. What are some of the main symbols in *To the Lighthouse*, and what do they signify? How does Woolf's use of symbolism advance her thematic goals?
4. As the novel begins, how does young James Ramsay occupy himself?
5. Compare and contrast Mr. and Mrs. Ramsay. How are they alike? How are they different?
6. What effect does the ocean have on different characters in the novel? Why, for example, do the waves make Mrs. Ramsay sad?

Chapter 6 James Joyce

James Joyce (1882—1941) was born at Rathgar, Dublin, the capital of Ireland. His mother in succession gave birth to fifteen children. His father John Joyce was a tax-gatherer, and had in turn been a policeman, a small landlord, a small investor, somebody's secretary, and so on. His family, therefore, could not settle down, and was gradually reduced to poverty. From the age of six to the age of nine James Joyce studied at Congowes

Wood College run by the Society of Jesus, receiving rigorous education of classic culture and the religion, and from eleven to sixteen he was educated to become a Catholic priest at Belvedere College, Dublin, also a Jesuit institution. Later he went to study courses of modern languages at University College, Dublin.

Joyce went to Paris after graduation, was recalled to Dublin by his mother's fatal illness, had a short spell there as a school teacher, and then returned to the Continent in 1904 to teach English at Trieste and then at Zurich. He took with him Nora Barnacle, an uneducated Galway girl with no interest in literature; her native vivacity and peasant wit charmed Joyce, and the two lived in devoted companionship until Joyce's death, though they were not married until 1931. In 1920 Joyce settled in Paris, where he lived until December 1940, when the war forced him to take refuge in Switzerland; he died in Zurich a few weeks later, in 1941.

Although he spent most of his adult life outside Ireland, Joyce's psychological and fictional universe is firmly rooted in his native Dublin, the city which provides the settings and much of the subject matter for all his fictions. In particular, his tempestuous early relationship with the Irish Roman Catholic Church is reflected through a similar inner conflict in his recurrent alter ego Stephen Dedalus. As the result of his minute attentiveness to a personal locale and his self-imposed exile and influence throughout Europe, notably in Paris, Joyce became paradoxically one of the most cosmopolitan yet one of the most regionally-focused of all the English language writers of his time.

Joyce's Irish experiences constitute an essential element of his writings, and provide all of the settings for his fiction and much of their subject matter. His early volumes of short stories, *Dubliners*, is a penetrating analysis of the stagnation and paralysis of Dublin society. The final and most famous story in the collection, "The Dead," was made into a feature film in 1987, directed by John Huston (it was Huston's last major work). *A Portrait of the Artist as a Young Man* is a nearly complete rewrite of the abandoned novel *Stephen Hero*, the original manuscript of which Joyce partially destroyed in a fit of rage during an argument with Nora, who asserted that it would never be published. *A Künstlerroman*, or story of the personal development of an artist, it is a biographical coming-of-age novel in which Joyce depicts a gifted young man's gradual attainment of maturity and self-consciousness; the main character, Stephen Dedalus, is in many ways based upon Joyce himself. Some hints of the techniques Joyce was to employ frequently in later works—such as the use of interior monologue and references to a character's psychic reality rather than his external surroundings—are evident in this novel. Joseph Strick directed a film of the book in 1977 starring Luke Johnston, Bosco Hogan, T. P. McKenna and John Gielgud.

Ulysses is Joyce's masterpiece. The book consists of 18 chapters, each covering roughly one hour of the day, beginning around about 8 a. m. and ending sometime after 2 a. m. the following morning. Each of the 18 chapters of the novel employs its own literary style. Each chapter also refers to a specific episode in Homer's Odyssey and has a specific colour, art or science and bodily organ associated with it. This combination of kaleidoscopic writing with an extreme formal, schematic structure represents one of the book's major contributions to the development of 20th century modernist literature. Others include the use of classical mythology as a framework for his book and the near-obsessive focus on external detail in a book in which much of the significant action is happening inside the minds of the characters.

Joyce's method of stream of consciousness, literary allusions and free dream associations was pushed to the limit in *Finnegans Wake*, which abandoned all conventions of plot and character construction and is written in a peculiar and obscure language, based mainly on complex multi-level puns.

Joyce also published a number of books of poetry. His first mature published work was the satirical broadside "*The Holy Office*" (1904), in which he proclaimed himself to be the superior of many prominent members of the Celtic revival. His first full-length poetry collection *Chamber Music* (referring, Joyce explained, to the sound of urine hitting the side of a chamber pot) consisted of 36 short lyrics. This publication led to his inclusion in the *Imagist Anthology*, edited by Ezra Pound, who was a champion of Joyce's work. Other poetry Joyce published in his lifetime includes "*Gas From A Burner*" (1912), *Pomes Penyeach* (1927) and "*Ecce Puer*" (written in 1932 to mark the birth of his grandson and the recent death of his father). It was published in *Collected Poems* (1936).

EVELINE

Eveline is a story from Dubliners. A young woman of about nineteen years of age sits by her window, waiting to leave home with her boy fiend, Frank. Who is taking her to live in Buenos Ayres. When she meets him at the station and they are set to board the ship, Eveline suddenly decides she cannot go with Frank, because "he would drown her" in "all the seas of the world". Eveline's rejection of Frank is not just a rejection of love, but also a rejection of a new life abroad and escape from her hard life at home. Like many of the stories in Dubliners, moving eastward in "Eveline" is associated with new life. But for Eveline, sailing eastward with Frank is as much an escape as a promise of something better.

SHE sat at the window watching the evening invade[1] the avenue. Her head was leaned against the window curtains and in hernostrils was the odour of dusty cretonne. She was tired.

Few people passed. The man out of the last house passed on his way home; she heard his footsteps clacking along the concrete pavement and afterwards crunching on the cinder path before the new red houses. One time there used to [2] be a field there in which they used to play every evening with other people's children. Then a man from Belfast bought the field and built houses in it—not like their little brown houses but bright brick houses with shining roofs. The children of the avenue used to play together in that field —the Devines, the Waters, the Dunns, little Keogh the cripple, she and her brothers and sisters. Ernest[3], however, never played: he was too grown up. Her father used often to hunt them in out of the field with his blackthorn stick; but usually little Keogh used to keep nix[4] and call out when he saw her father coming. Still they seemed to have been rather happy then. Her father was not so bad then; and besides, her mother was alive. That was a long time ago; she and her brothers and sisters were all grown up her mother was dead. Tizzie Dunn was dead, too, and the Waters had gone back to England. Everything changes. Now she was going to go away like the others, to leave her home.

Home! She looked round the room, reviewing all its familiar objects which she had dusted once a week for so many years, wondering where on earth all the dust came from. Perhaps she would never see again those familiar objects from which she had never dreamed of being divided[5]. And yet during all those years she had never found out the name of the priest whose yellowing photograph hung on the wall above the broken harmonium beside the coloured print of the promises made to Blessed Margaret Mary Alacoque. He had been a school friend of her father. Whenever he showed the photograph to a visitor her father used to pass it with a casual word: "He is in Melbourne now."[6]

She had consented to go away, to leave her home. Was that wise? She tried to weigh each side of the question. In her home anyway she had shelter and food; she had those whom she had known all her life about her. Of course she had to work hard, both in the house and at business. What would they say of her in the Stores when they found out that she had run away with a fellow? Say she was a fool, perhaps; and her place would be filled up by advertisement. Miss Gavan would be glad. She had always had anedge on her[7], especially whenever there were people listening.

"Miss Hill, don't you see these ladies are waiting?"

"Look lively, Miss Hill, please."

She would not cry many tears at leaving the Stores[8].

But in her new home, in a distant unknown country, it would not be like that. Then she would be married—she, Eveline. People would treat her with respect then. She would not be treated as her mother had been. Even now, though she was over nineteen, she sometimes felt herself in danger of her father's violence. She knew it was that that had given her the palpitations. When they were growing up he had never gone for her like he used to go for Harry and Ernest, because she was a girl but latterly he had begun to threaten her and say what he would do to her only for her dead mother's sake. And no she had nobody to protect her. Ernest was dead and Harry, who was in the church decorating business, was nearly always down somewhere in the country. Besides, the invariable squabble for money on Saturday nights[9] had begun to weary her unspeakably. She always gave her entire wages—seven shillings—and Harry always sent up what he could but the trouble was to get any money from her father. He said she used to squander the money, that she had no head, that he wasn't going to give her his hard-earned money to throw about the streets, and much more, for he was usually fairly bad on Saturday night. In the end he would give her the money and ask her had she any intention of buying Sunday's dinner. Then she had to rush out as quickly as she could and do her marketing, holding her black leather purse tightly in her hand as she elbowed her way through the crowds and returning home late under her load of provisions. She had hard work to keep the house together and to see that the two young children who had been left to her charge went to school regularly and got their meals regularly. It was hard work—a hard life—but now that she was about to leave it she did not find it a wholly undesirable life.

She was about to explore another life with Frank. Frank was very kind, manly, open-hearted. She was to go away with him by the night-boat to be his wife and to live with him in Buenos Ayres[10] where he had a home waiting for her. How well she remembered the first time she had seen him; he was lodging in a house on the main road where she used to visit. It seemed a few weeks ago. He was standing at the gate, his peaked cap pushed back on his head and his hair tumbled forward over a face of bronze. Then they had come to know each other. He used to meet her outside the Stores every evening and see her home. He took her to see The Bohemian Girl[11] and she felt elated as she sat in an unaccustomed part of the theatre with him. He was awfully fond of music and sang a little. People knew that they were courting and, when he sang about the lass that loves a sailor, she always felt pleasantly confused. He used to call her Poppens[12] out of fun. First of all it had been an excitement for her to have a fellow and then she had begun to like him. He had tales of distant countries. He had started as a deck boy at a pound a month on a ship of the Allan Line[13] going out to Canada. He told her the names of the ships he had been on and the names of the different services. He had sailed through the Straits of Magellan and he told her stories of the terrible Patagonians. He had fallen on his feet in Buenos Ayres, he said, and had come over to the old country just for a holiday. Of course, her father had found out the affair and had forbidden her to have anything to say to him.

"I know these sailor chaps,[14]" he said.

One day he had quarrelled with Frank and after that she had to meet her lover secretly.

The evening deepened in the avenue. The white of two letters in her lap grew indistinct. One was to Harry; the other was to her father. Ernest had been her favourite but she liked Harry too. Her father was becoming old lately, she noticed; he would miss her. Sometimes he could be very nice. Not long before, when she had been laid up for a day, he had read her out a ghost story and made toast for her at the fire. Another day, when their mother was alive, they had all gone for a picnic to the Hill of Howth. She remembered her father putting on her mothers bonnet to make the children laugh.

Her time was running out but she continued to sit by the window, leaning her head against the window curtain, inhaling the odour of dusty cretonne. Down far in the avenue she could hear a street organ playing. She knew the air Strange that it should come that very night to remind her of the promise to her mother, her promise to keep the home together as long as she could. She remembered the last night of her mother's illness; she was again in the close dark room at the other side of the hall and outside she heard a melancholy air of Italy. The organ-player had been ordered to go away and given sixpence. She remembered her father strutting back into the sickroom saying:

"Damned Italians! coming over here!"[15]

As she mused the pitiful vision of her mother's life laid its spell on the very quick of her being—that life of commonplace sacrifices closing in final craziness. She trembled as she heard again her mother's voice saying constantly with foolish insistence:

"Derevaun Seraun! Derevaun Seraun!"[16]

She stood up [17] in a sudden impulse of terror. Escape! She must escape! Frank would save her. He would give her life, perhaps love, too. But she wanted to live. Why should she be unhappy? She had a right to happiness. Frank would take her in his arms, fold her in his arms. He would save her.

She stood among the swaying crowd in the station at the North Wall. He held her hand and she knew that he was speaking to her, saying something about the passage over and over again. The station was full of soldiers with brown baggages. Through the wide doors of the sheds she caught a glimpse of the black mass of the boat, lying in beside the quay wall, with illumined portholes. She answered nothing. She felt her cheek pale and cold and, out of a maze of distress, she prayed to God to direct her,[19] to show her what was her duty. The boat blew a long mournful whistle into the mist. If she went, tomorrow she would be on the sea with Frank, steaming towards Buenos Ayres. Their passage had been booked. Could she still draw back after all he had done for her? Her distress awoke a nausea in her body and she kept moving her lips in silent fervent prayer.

A bell clanged upon her heart. She felt him seize her hand:

"Come!"

All the seas of the world tumbled about her heart. He was drawing her into them: he would drown her. She gripped with both hands at the iron railing.[20]

"Come!"

No! No! No! It was impossible. Her hands clutched the iron in frenzy. Amid the seas she sent a cry of anguish.

"Eveline! Evvy!"

He rushed beyond the barrier and called to her to follow. He was shouted at to go on but he still called to her. She set her white face to him, passive, like a helpless animal. Her eyes gave him no sign of love or farewell or recognition.

Notes

1. invade—in the first paragraph, this is the only word that indicates action. "evening",

"dusty" and " tired" set a depressing tone.

2. used to—notice that "used to" is used five times in this paragraph to show that everything is bygone and not be regained.
3. Ernest—Eveline's brother.
4. keep nix—be alert.
5. divided—this word shows Eveline's feeling of oneness with the objects around her.
6. "He is in Melbourne now. "—People left Ireland, even the priest.
7. had an edge on her—dominated her.
8. She would not cry many tears at leaving the Stores—It doesn't mean she would cry a little. The sentence's meaning is negative, indicating she would not feel sorry or sad to leave the Stores.
9. on Saturday nights—At that time, workers were paid by the week. So they got paid on Saturday when they left work. The father was not willing to give his wages to Eveline for housekeeping.
10. Buenos Ayres—the capital city of Argentina.
11. The Bohemian Girl—an opera composed by the Irish composer Michael William Balfe.
12. Poppens—female swans.
13. Allan Line—the Allan Shipping Company.
14. "I know these sailor chaps"—I know what kind of people sailors are, fooling around with girls at every port of call.
15. "Damned Italians! coming over here!"—the father's attitude towards the Italians v indicates the narrow-mindedness of the Irish that Joyce resented.
16. "Derevaun Seraun! Derevaun Seraun!"—Gaelic for " the end of pleasure is pain".
17. stood up—this is the first time Eveline actually moved in this story.
18. Escape—the central theme of the story is the desire to escape and the inability of action, which, to Joyce, is symbolic of the situation of Ireland at his own time.
19. she prayed to God to direct her—when she didn't know what to do, she turned to God, a detail which shows how strong the influence of religion was.
20. the iron railing—image of a cage or a prison. Eveline gripped with both hands at the iron railing, incapable of escape.

For Study and Discussion.

1. How many people had there been in Eveline's family? How many were there now? What happened to them?
2. What job did she have? Did she find it pleasant?
3. What work did she do at home?
4. How did her father treat her?
5. Who was Frank?

6. What did Frank ask her to do?
7. Why was she in two minds about leaving home?
8. What made her suddenly decide to go to the boat station?
9. How do you feel after reading through the story?

Chapter 7 D. H. Lawrence

David Herbert (D. H.) Lawrence was born in 1885 and died in 1930. He is a versatile and influential English writer, poet, playwright, essayist and literary critic of the 20th century. He is best known for his novels, and good at short and travel stories.

He was born in the small coal-mining village of Eastwood, Nottinghamshire, in central England. Lawrence's father, Arthur, was a miner, and his mother Lydia was a well-educated schoolmistress. Lawrence's early unhappy family life provides the raw material for his literary creation. Spurred on by his mother, Lawrence escaped through education from the mining world of his father; he went to school to receive education. He won a scholarship to Nottingham high school and later, after working first as a clerk and then as an elementary schoolteacher, studied for two years at Nottingham University College, where he obtained his teacher's certificate in 1908. Still, he excelled in his work, and upon graduation in 1908 received a job at the Davidson Road Boys' School near London. During his time in college, he had begun his writing career. He did not enjoy the collegiate atmosphere and spent most of his time there writing and learning about socialism. His first published work was a group of poems, which appeared in the *English Review* for November, 1909. The following February the same periodical published his first short story. He was now regarded in London literary circles as a promising young writer; his first novel, *The White Peacock* (1910), was received with respect. From 1908 to 1912 he did school teaching in Croydon, a southern suburb of London, but he gave this up after falling in love with Frieda von Richthofen, the German wife of a Professor of French at Nottingham. They went to Germany together and got married in 1914, after Frieda had been divorced by her first husband.

Lawrence is a versatile writer, and in his short life span of 45 years, he wrote more than 40 books, including novels, short stories, poems, essays, plays, travel books, reviews and letters. His collected works represent an extended reflection upon the dehumanizing effects of modernity and industrialization. In them, Lawrence confronts issues on emotional health and vitality, spontaneity, human sexuality and instinct.

Lawrence is perhaps best known for his novels *Sons and Lovers*, *The Rainbow*, *Women in Love* and *Lady Chatterley's Lover*. In these works, Lawrence explores the possibilities for life and living within an industrial setting. Particularly, Lawrence is concerned with the nature of relationships that can be had within such settings. Though often classified as a realist, Lawrence's life philosophy is reflected in his description of his characters. His use of sexual activity, though shocking at the time, has its roots in this highly personal way of thinking being.

Lawrence leaves many good works to the people. He published a number of novels, essays, and poems including *The White Peacock* (1911), *The Prussian Officer* (1914), *Sons and Lovers* (1913), *The Lost Girl* (1920), *Women in Love* (1921), *Aaron's Rod* (1922), *Birds, Beasts and Flowers* (1923), *Studies in Classic American Literature* (1923), *The Plumed Serpent* (1926), and *Lady Chatterley's Lover* (1928). *The Rainbow* was published in November 1915. He won the James Tait Black Memorial prize for *The Lost Girl*.

Lawrence was a gifted poet, painter and novelist, although some of his works may be considered pornographic. Editors cut out highly sexually-charged scenes in *Sons and Lovers*. In 1929, some of his paintings in the Warren Gallery in London were prohibited because they were too obscene. Whether or not Lawrence's fascinations and fixations were too sexual for the general audience, his appeal to the human mind and soul remains unchanged. He is one of the few writers whose reputation is equally staked on novels, short stories, and poetry, and though his initially censored work now seems tame, he opens up a new road to the sensuality for countless writers after him. We can proudly say Lawrence is a great literary genius.

Chapter 8 George Orwell

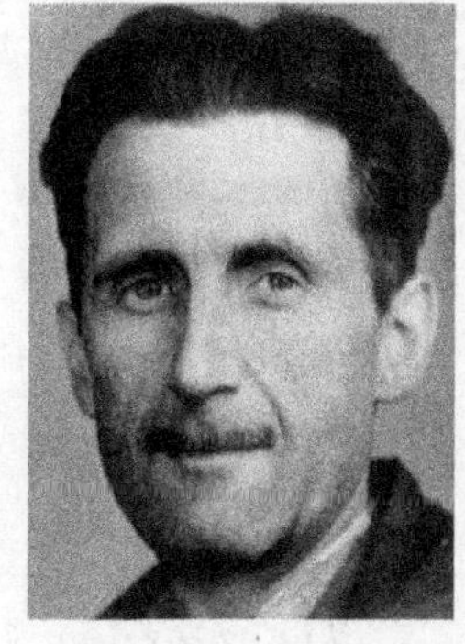

George Orwell (1903—1950) is the pen name of Eric Arthur Blair: essayist, novelist, literary critic, advocate and fighter for political change, and man of contradictions. Blair was born on June 25, 1903, in the Bengal region of Eastern India, which was a British territory. He was the son of Richard Walmesley Blair, a civil servant, and Ida Mabel Blair. He moved to England with his mother and sisters at the age of one. He displayed academic talent from a young age, so his mother took pains to send him into a well-known boarding school called St. Cyprian's. His family was neither poor nor wealthy, and Blair attended St. Cyprian's on a scholarship.

Orwell received his education at a series of private schools, including Eton, an elite school in England. Blair's academic prowess remained strong there. After his graduation, despite his intelligence, he could not afford to attend college. In 1922, he joined the Indian Imperial Police in Burma. He had spent the first year of his life in a British colony, and this time, he got a thorough experience of British colonial life and despised what he saw. His experiences made him a champion of the poor and downtrodden, a role in which he would continue for the rest of his life. Moreover, he could not stand the fact that his job put him directly in the position of a privileged oppressor. He resigned from the Indian Imperial Police five years later while on leave in England. Blair tried his luck in Paris briefly but found he could not make a living there as a writer. He returned to England in 1929, where he published essays and continued his fascination with and incorporation into the dregs of society.

His painful experiences with snobbishness and social elitism at Eton, as well as his intimate familiarity with the British imperialism in India, made him deeply suspicious of the entrenched class system in English society.

Considered "perhaps the 20th century's best chronicler of English culture", he wrote works in many different genres including novels, essays, polemic journalism, literary reviews, and poetry. His most famous works are the satirical novel *Animal Farm* (1945) and the dystopian novel *Nineteen Eighty-Four* (1949). His work is marked by a profound consciousness of social injustice, an intense dislike of totalitarianism, and a passion for clarity in language.

Animal Farm is a dystopian novel published in England in 1945. It was Orwell's first highly successful novel (the second being 1984), which helped him to become famous over night. It is an allegory or fable, a fairy tale for adults. Orwell uses animal characters in order to draw the reader away from the world of current events into a fantasy space where the reader can grasp ideas and principles more crisply. At the same time, Orwell personifies the animals in the tradition of allegory so that they symbolize real historical figures. Deception, mistreatment, and violence are embodied in the characters.

Animal Farm is also a powerful satire. Orwell uses irony to expose the folly of totalitarianism, and the harm of abuse of power of authoritarian government and human stupidity generally.

Time Magazine chose the book as one of the 100 best English-language novels (1923 to 2005), at number 31 on the Modern Library List of Best 20th-Century Novels. It won a Retrospective Hugo Award in 1996 and is also included in the Great Books of the Western World.

ANIMAL FARM (an excerpt)

The following is Chapter I of Animal Farm. In this chapter, the owner of Manor Farm, Mr. Jones has just gone to bed. The animals began to gather for a meeting called by Old Major to discuss a strange dream that he had the previous night. The three dogs,

Bluebell, Jessie, and Pincher, arrived the earliest, followed by the pigs, hens, pigeons, sheep, and cows along with the horses, Boxer and Clover. Muriel, the white goat, and the donkey Benjamin. Old Major addresses the animals, explaining that he wishes to impart his wisdom, because he is getting old and may die soon. Old Major later relates his dream to the animals. In his dream life, Old Major uncovered an old animal anthem that has lain dormant for generations. It is called "Beasts of England", which glorifies the freedom and joy that will follow "Tyrant Man's" overthrow, and he urges all animals to "toil for freedom's sake," even if they die before the cause is won.

Chapter I

MR JONES[1], of the Manor Farm, had locked the hen-houses for the night, but was too drunk to remember to shut the pop-holes. With the ring of light from his lantern dancing from side to side he lurched across the yard, kicked off his boots at the back door, drew himself a last glass of beer from the barrel in the scullery, and made his way up to bed, where Mrs Jones was already snoring.

As soon as the light in the bedroom went out there was a stirring and a fluttering all through the farm buildings. Word had gone round during the day that old Major, the prize Middle White boar, had had a strange dream on the previous night and wished to communicate it to the other animals. It had been agreed that they should all meet in the big barn as soon as Mr Jones was safely out of the way. Old Major[2] (so he was always called, though the name under which he had been exhibited was Willingdon Beauty) was so highly regarded on the farm that everyone was quite ready to lose an hour's sleep in order to hear what he had to say.

At one end of the big barn, on a sort of raised platform, Major was already ensconced[3] on his bed of straw, under a lantern which hung from a beam. He was twelve years old and had lately grown rather stout, but he was still a majestic-looking pig, with a wise and benevolent appearance in spite of the fact that his tushes[4] had never been cut. Before long the other animals began to arrive and make themselves comfortable after their different fashions. First came the three dogs, Bluebell, Jessie and Pincher[5], and then the pigs, who settled down in the straw immediately in front of the platform. The hens perched themselves on the window-sills, the pigeons fluttered up to the rafters, the sheep and cows lay down behind the pigs and began to chew the cud. The two cart-horses, Boxer and Clover, came in together, walking very slowly and setting down their vast hairy hoofs with great care lest there should be some small animal concealed in the straw. Clover was a stout motherly mare approaching middle life, who had never quite got her figure back after her fourth foal[6]. Boxer[7] was an enormous beast, nearly eighteen hands high, and as strong as any two ordinary horses put together. A white stripe down his nose gave him a somewhat stupid appearance, and in fact he was not of first-rate intelligence, but he was universally respected for his steadiness of character and tremendous powers of work. After the horses came Muriel, the white goat, and Benjamin the donkey. Benjamin was the oldest animal on the farm, and the worst tempered. He seldom talked, and when he did it was usually to make some cynical remark—for instance he would say that God had given him a tail to keep the flies off, but that he would sooner have had no tail and no flies. Alone among the animals on the farm he never laughed. If asked why, he would say that he saw nothing to laugh at. Nevertheless, without openly admitting it, he was devoted to Boxer; the two of them usually spent their Sundays together in the small paddock beyond the orchard, grazing side by side and never speaking.

The two horses had just lain down when a brood of ducklings which had lost their mother filed into the barn, cheeping feebly and wandering from side to side to find some place where they would not be trodden on. Clover made a sort of wall round them with her great foreleg, and the ducklings nestled down inside it and promptly fell asleep. At the last moment Mollie, the foolish, pretty white mare who drew Mr Jones's trap[8], came mincing daintily[9] in, chewing at a lump of sugar. She took a place near the front and began flirting her white mane, hoping to draw attention to the red ribbons it was plaited[10] with. Last of all came the cat, who looked round, as usual, for the warmest place, and finally squeezed herself in between Boxer and Clover; there she purred[11] contentedly throughout Major's speech without listening to a word of what he was saying.

All the animals were now present except Moses[12], the tame raven, who slept on a perch behind the back door. When Major saw that they had all made themselves comfortable and were waiting attentively he cleared his throat and began:

'Comrades, you have heard already about the strange dream that I had last night. But I will come to the dream later. I have something else to say first. I do not think, comrades, that I shall be with you for many months longer, and before I die I feel it my duty to pass on to you such wisdom as I have acquired. I have had a long life, I have had much time for thought as I lay alone in my stall, and I think I may say that I understand the nature of life on this earth as well as any animal now living. It is about this that I wish to speak to you.

'Now, comrades, what is the nature of this life of ours? Let us face it, our lives are miserable, laborious and short. We are born, we are given just so much food as will keep the breath in our bodies, and those of us who are capable of it are forced to work to the last atom of our strength; and the very instant that our usefulness has come to an end we are slaughtered with hideous cruelty. No animal in England knows the meaning of happiness or leisure after he is a year old. No animal in England is free. The life of an animal is misery and slavery: that is the plain truth.

'But is this simply part of the order of Nature? Is it because this land of ours is so poor that it cannot afford a decent life to those who dwell upon it? No, comrades, a thousand times no! The soil of England is fertile, its climate is good, it is capable of affording food in abundance to an enormously greater number of animals than now inhabit it. This single farm of ours would support a dozen horses, twenty cows, hundreds of sheep—and all of them living in a comfort and a dignity that are now almost beyond our imagining. Why then do we continue in this miserable condition? Because nearly the whole of the produce of our labour is stolen from us by human beings. There, comrades, is the answer to all our problems. It is summed up in a single word—Man. Man is the only real enemy we have. Remove Man from the scene, and the root cause of hunger and overwork is abolished for ever.

'Man is the only creature that consumes without producing. He does not give milk, he does not lay eggs, he is too weak to pull the plough, he cannot run fast enough to catch rabbits. Yet he is lord of all the animals. He sets them to work, he gives back to them the bare minimum that will prevent them from starving, and the rest he keeps for himself. Our labour tills the soil, our dung[13] fertilises it, and yet there is not one of us that owns more than his bare skin. You cows that I see before me, how many thousands of gallons of milk have you given during this last year? And what has happened to that milk which should have been breeding up sturdy calves? Every drop of it has gone down the throats of our enemies. And you hens, how many eggs have you laid in this last year, and how many of those eggs ever hatched into chickens? The rest have all gone to market to bring in money for Jones and his men. And you, Clover, where are those four foals you bore, who should have been the support and pleasure of your old age? Each was sold at a year old—you will never see one of them again. In return for your four confinements and all your labour in the fields, what have you ever had except your bare rations and a stall[14]?

'And even the miserable lives we lead are not allowed to reach their natural span. For myself I do not grumble, for I am one of the lucky ones. I am twelve years old and have had over four hundred children. Such is the natural life of a pig. But no animal escapes the cruel knife in the end. You young porkers who are sitting in front of me, every one of you will scream your lives out at the block within a year. To that horror we all must come-cows, pigs, hens, sheep, everyone. Even the horses and the dogs have no better fate. You, Boxer, the very day that those great muscles of yours lose their power, Jones will sell you to the knacker[15], who will cut your throat and boil you down for the foxhounds. As for the dogs, when they grow old and toothless Jones ties a brick round their necks and drowns them in the nearest pond.

'Is it not crystal clear, then, comrades, that all the evils of this life of ours spring from the tyranny of human beings? Only get rid of Man, and the produce of our labour would be our own. Almost overnight we could become rich and free. What then must we do? Why, work night and day, body and soul, for the overthrow of the human race! That is my message to you, comrades: Rebellion! I do not know when that Rebellion will come, it might be in a week or in a hundred years, but I know, as surely as I see this straw beneath my feet, that sooner or later justice will be done. Fix your eyes on that, comrades, throughout the short remainder of your lives! And above all, pass on this message of mine to those who come after you, so that future generations shall carry on the struggle until it is victorious.

'And remember, comrades, your resolution must never falter. No argument must lead you astray. Never listen when they tell you that Man and the animals have a common interest, that the prosperity of the one is the prosperity of the others. It is all lies. Man serves the interests of no creature except himself. And among us animals let there be perfect unity, perfect comradeship in the struggle. All men are enemies. All animals are comrades.'

At this moment there was a tremendous uproar. While Major was speaking four large rats had crept out of their holes and were sitting on their hindquarters, listening to him. The dogs had suddenly caught sight of them, and it was only by a swift dash for their holes that the rats saved their lives. Major raised his trotter[16] for silence:

'Comrades,' he said, 'here is a point that must be settled. The wild creatures, such as rats and rabbits-are they our friends or our enemies? Let us put it to the vote. I propose this question to the meeting: Are rats comrades?'

The vote was taken at once, and it was agreed by an overwhelming majority that rats were comrades. There were only four dissentients[17], the three dogs and the cat, who was afterwards discovered to have voted on both sides. Major continued:

'I have little more to say. I merely repeat, remember always your duty of enmity towards Man and all his ways. Whatever goes upon two legs is an enemy. Whatever goes upon four legs, or has wings, is a friend. And remember also that in fighting against Man, we must not come to resemble him. Even when you have conquered him, do not adopt his vices. No animal must ever live in a house, or sleep in a bed, or wear clothes, or drink alcohol, or smoke tobacco, or touch money, or engage in trade. All the habits of Man are evil. And above all, no animal must ever tyrannise over his own kind. Weak or strong, clever or simple, we are all brothers. No animal must ever kill any other animal. All animals are equal.

'And now, comrades, I will tell you about my dream of last night. I cannot describe that dream to you. It was a dream of the earth as it will be when Man has vanished. But it reminded me of something that I had long forgotten.

'Many years ago, when I was a little pig, my mother and the other sows used to sing an old song of which they knew only the tune and the first three words. I had known that tune in my infancy, but it had long since passed out of my mind. Last night, however, it came back to me in my dream. And what is more, the words of the song also came back-words, I am certain, which were sung by the animals of long ago and have been lost to memory for generations. I will sing you that song now, comrades. I am old and my voice is hoarse, but when I have taught you the tune you can sing it better for yourselves. It is called "Beasts of England".'

Old Major cleared his throat and began to sing. As he had said, his voice was hoarse, but he sang well enough, and it was a stirring tune, something between 'Clementine' and 'La Cucaracha[18]'. The words ran:

Beasts of England, beasts of Ireland,
Beasts of every land and clime,
Hearken to my joyful tidings
Of the golden future time.

Soon or late the day is coming,
Tyrant Man shall be o'erthrown,
And the fruitful fields of England
Shall be trod by beasts alone.

Rings shall vanish from our noses,
And the harness from our back,
Bit and spur shall rust forever,
Cruel whips no more shall crack.

Riches more than mind can picture,
Wheat and barley, oats and hay,
Clover, beans and mangel-wurzels[19]
Shall be ours upon that day.

Bright will shine the fields of England,
Purer shall its waters be,
Sweeter yet shall blow its breezes
On the day that sets us free.

For that day we all must labour,
Though we die before it break;
Cows and horses, geese and turkeys,
All must toil for freedom's sake.

Beasts of England, beasts of Ireland,
Beasts of every land and clime,
Hearken well and spread my tidings[20]
Of the golden future time.

The singing of this song threw the animals into the wildest excitement. Almost before Major had reached the end, they had begun singing it for themselves. Even the stupidest of them had already picked up the tune and a few of the words, and as for the clever ones, such as the pigs and dogs, they had the entire song by heart within a few minutes. And then, after a few preliminary tries, the whole farm burst out into 'Beasts of England' in tremendous unison. The cows lowed it, the dogs whined it, the sheep bleated it, the horses whinnied it, the ducks quacked it. They were so delighted with the song that they sang it right through five times in succession, and might have continued singing it all night if they had not been interrupted.

Unfortunately the uproar awoke Mr Jones, who sprang out of bed, making sure that there was a fox in the yard. He seized the gun which always stood in a comer of his bedroom, and let fly a charge of Number 6 shot into the darkness. The pellets buried themselves in the wall of the barn and the meeting broke up hurriedly. Everyone fled to his own sleeping-place. The birds jumped onto their perches, the animals settled down in the straw, and the whole farm was asleep in a moment.

Notes

1. Mr Jones—The owner of Manor Farm and a drunkard. His animals overthrow him in the Rebellion. Mr. Jones dies in a home for alcoholics in another part of the country. He represents the kind of corrupt and fatally flawed government. More specifically, Jones represents the latter days of imperial Russia and its last leader, the wealthy but ineffective Czar Nicholas II.
2. old Major—A prize Middle White boar that the Joneses exhibited under the name "Willingdon Beauty." He is, "stout ... But still a majestic-looking pig, with a wise and benevolent appearance".
3. ensconce—to settle securely or snugly.
4. tush—An elongated pointed tooth, usually one of a pair, extending outside of the mouth in certain animals such as the walrus, elephant, or wild boar.
5. Bluebell, Jessie, Pincher—The dogs. When Bluebell and Jessie give birth to puppies, Snowball confiscates them and secludes them in a loft, where he transforms them into fierce, elitist guard dogs.
6. foal—bringing forth young, as an animal of the horse kind.
7. Boxer—The male of the two horses on the farm. He is "an enormous beast, nearly eighteen hands high, and as strong as any two ordinary horses put together".
8. trap—*Chiefly British*. a carriage, esp. a light, two-wheeled one.
9. daintily—overly particular.
10. plait—to fold or arrange in pleats.
11. purr—to utter a low, continuous, murmuring sound expressive of contentment or pleasure, as a cat does.
12. Moses—A tame raven that is Mr. Jones's "especial pet." He is a spy, a gossip, and a "clever talker".
13. dung—excrement, esp. of animals; manure.
14. stall—a stable or shed for horses or cattle.

15. knacker—a person who buys animal carcasses or slaughters useless livestock for a knackery or rendering works.
16. trotter—the foot of an animal, esp. of a sheep or pig.
17. dissentient—a person who dissents.
18. Clementine and La Cucaracha—titles of two songs. They are childish ditties used here to ridicule the seriousness of the situation.
19. mangel-wurzel—The mangelwurzel has a history in England of being used for sport (mangold hurling), for celebration, for animal fodder and for the brewing of a potent alcoholic beverage.
20. tiding—A piece of information or news. Often used in the plural: tidings of great joy; sad tidings.

For Study and Discussion

1. What role does Mr. Jones perform in the novel? What does he represent?
2. What does Old Major represent?
3. What is the only way out for the animals according to Old Major?
4. How does the author establish idealism upon which the whole book is based in the first chapter?
5. The narrator describes "Beasts of England" as " a stirring tune, something between 'Clementine' and 'La Cucaracha'". What effect does it have?

Drama

Part Twelve
Major English Dramatists and Selected Plays

Chapter 1 General View of the English Drama

The Definition of Drama. The word "drama" is of Greek origin "dram", meaning "to do" or "to act". Aristotle defined it as "a criticism of life, on a stage, with action, characters and dialogue." According to *Webster's Dictionary*, drama is a composition, in prose or poetry, accommodated to action, and intended to exhibit a picture of human life, or to depict a series of grave or humorous actions of more than ordinary interest, tending toward some striking results. It is commonly designed to be spoken and represented by actors on the stage. In a simpler way, drama can be defined as a dramatic work designed for performance by actors on stage.

Genres of Drama. Drama can be categorized into tragedy, comedy and tragicomedy and melodrama.

Tragedy originates from the Greek "tragos", meaning "song of the goat". In Aristotle's *Poetics*, he offers the earliest definition of tragedy: "Tragedy, then, is an imitation of an action that is serious, complete, and of a certain magnitude; in language embellished with each kind of artistic ornament, the several kinds being found in separate parts of the play; in the form of action, not of narrative; with incidents arousing pity and fear, wherewith to accomplish its *katharsis* of such emotions." Tragedy must tell of a person who is "highly renowned and prosperous" and who falls as a result of some "error, or frailty" because of external or internal forces, or both. In general, tragedy is a story that presents courageous individuals who confront powerful forces within or outside themselves with a dignity that reveals the breadth and depth of the human spirit in the face of failure, defeat, and even death. Through a series of events, these dignified individuals, also known as tragic heroes, are brought to their final tragic downfall. A tragic hero possesses the potentiality for greatness but is destined to fail because he is trapped in a situation where he cannot win. There may be various and uncertain causes of a tragic hero's downfall. In traditional dramas, it might be the character's fate, flaw or an error in judgment; in modern dramas, it might range from moral or psychological weakness to the evils in the society. The tragic hero, though defeated or fallen, usually wins a moral victory or self-awareness.

Comedy, coming from Greek "komos" with the meaning "songs of merrymakers", presents human beings as "worse than they are" in life, in order to demonstrate a different type of imitation than in a classical tragedy. Aristotle thinks: "Comedy are an imitation of characters of a lower type,—not, however, in the full sense of the word bad, the ludicrous being merely a subdivision of the ugly." In a modern sense, comedy is a literary work intended to interest, involve, and amuse the reader or audience, in which no terrible disaster occurs and that ends happily for the main characters. Comedy is distinct from tragedy, which is generally concerned with a protagonist who meets an unhappy or disastrous end. A comic protagonist may be a person of ordinary character and ability, and need not achieve the heroic stature of the protagonist in a tragedy. Comedies are often concerned, at least in part, with exposing human folly, and frequently depict the overthrow of rigid social fashions and customs. A sense of wit, humor, and festivity are easily identified in comedies.

Tragicomedy, as the name indicates, is a type of drama that combines certain elements of both tragedy and comedy, usually with the tragic predominating. The play's plot tends to be serious, leading to a terrible catastrophe, until an unexpected turn in events leads to a reversal of circumstance, and the story ends happily. Tragicomedy often employs a romantic, fast-moving plot dealing with love, jealousy, disguises, treachery, intrigue, and surprises, all moving toward a melodramatic resolution.

Melodrama is from the French "melodrama" derived from the Greek "melos", meaning "song". It is a type of play that intensifies sentiment, exaggerates emotions, and relates sensational and thrilling action with four basic sharply contrasted and simplified characters: the hero, the heroine, their comic ally, and a villain. The hero always wins and the villain is always punished. The object of melodrama is to keep the audience thrilled by the arousal of strong feelings of pity, horror, or joy.

Elements of Drama. Aristotle, in his *Poetics*, outlines the six elements of drama: plot, character, thought, diction, music, and spectacle.

Aristotle thinks "plot is the first principle, ... and the soul of a tragedy". He defines plot as "the arrangement of the incidents": i. e., not the story itself but the way the incidents are presented to the audience, the structure of the play. According to Aristotle, tragedies where the outcome depends on a tightly constructed cause-and-effect chain of actions are superior to those that depend primarily on the character and personality of the protagonist. Plots that meet this criterion will have the following features: 1) being "a whole", with a beginning, middle, and end. A beginning is that which does not itself follow anything by casual necessity, but after which something naturally is or comes to be; a middle is that which follows something as some other thing follows it; an end is that which itself naturally follows come other thing, either by necessity, or as a rule, but has nothing following it. 2) being "complete", having "unity of action". 3) being "of a certain magnitude". 4) being either simple or complex.

Gustav Freytag, a German writer and critic, in his book *Technique of the Drama* (1863), proposed a method of analyzing plots derived from Aristotle's concept of unity of action. It is later known as Freytag's Triangle or Freytag's Pyramid.

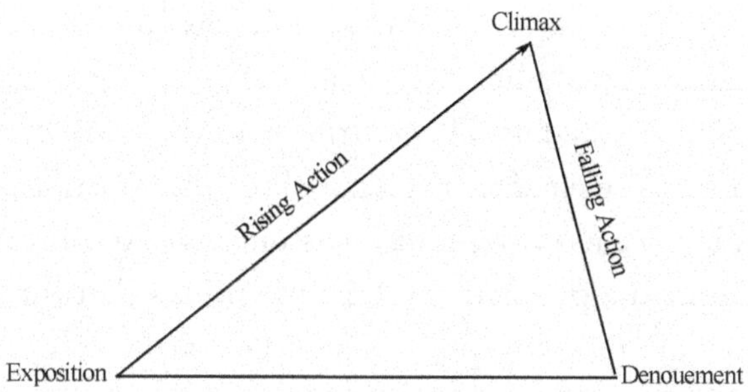

Freytag's pyramid

Exposition means exposing of the facts. It is usually the first thing that the playwright has to do with the intention to establish what is going on, what has happened, and who is involved. The playwright, in his exposition, should inform his audience clearly and slowly of the necessary information in order to relate it to subsequent scenes.

In the rising action, complication creates some sort of conflict for the protagonist. The playwright unfolds complications and conflicts between the "wants" and "haves" of the characters. The complication provides the conflict with its depth and breadth; conflict is the struggle within the plot among opposing forces, such as the conflict between man and man, man and nature, man and society, even man and self.

After the complication, the plot develops to the climax, the moment of the greatest emotional tension, usually marking a turning point in the plot at which the rising action reverses to become the falling action characterized by diminishing tensions and then the play heads toward the resolution, or denouement (a French term meaning "unraveling" or "unknotting"), in which the aftermath of falling actions is revealed.

Character, according to Aristotle, holds the second place. They are the people presented in a play that are involved in the pursuing plot. Characters in tragedy are characterized by the following qualities: 1) good or fine; 2) fitness of character; 3) true to life; 4) consistency; 5) necessary or probable; 6) true to life and yet more beautiful. To create his characters the playwright usually employ the following four methods, which are called characterization: 1) describing the character's appearance, clothes, and personal belongings; 2) reporting the character's speech and behavior; 3) describing the reactions of other characters to the individual; 4) revealing the character's thoughts and feelings. The first is regarded as the direct characterization, the other three as the indirect characterization.

Thought, Aristotle says, is third in importance, and is found "where something is proved to be or not to be, or a general maxim is enunciated". Therefore, thought refers to the reasoning aspect of drama associated with the themes of a play.

After thought comes diction, which means, in Aristotle's own explanation, "the expression of the meaning in words". They should be proper and appropriate to the plot, characters, and the denouement of the tragedy.

Song, Aristotle thinks, holds the chief place among embellishments. Music refers to all of the auditory aspect of a play, such as sound, rhythm, and melody of the speech. Aristotle argues that music should be fully integrated into the play like an actor, should be more than "mere interludes", and should contribute to the unity of the plot.

The spectacle is the last element, involving all of the visual aspects of the production of a play, for example, scenery, lighting, costume, maker-up, the movement of the actors, and special effects in a production. Aristotle thinks that the spectacle has, indeed, an emotional attraction of its own, but, of all the parts, it is the least artistic, and connected least with the art of poetry.

The Origin of English Drama. English drama originated from religious ritual and pantomimes of the Middle Ages. Before Elizabethan Period, English drama had experienced three periods of development: religious period, moral period and artistic period.

Religious Period. English drama, during this period, can be divided into two groups. One is the Liturgical drama, the other is the Miracle play.

The Liturgical drama grew out of the Church liturgy. During the early centuries, the Church forbade the faithful to attend the dissipated representations of decadent paganism. But once this immoral theatre had disappeared, the church itself played a part in the gradual development of a new drama, whose subjects were taken from the Scripture focused on Christ's death and resurrection. These plays intended to moralize, edify and revere.

Out of the Liturgical drama evolved by degrees the Miracle play, which is also known as Saint or Mystery play, founded on legends of the saints, performed first in churches, afterwards in public places. For four centuries during the Middle Ages, the Miracle play increased steadily in number and popularity, very common in England from the 12th century. But later it became corrupt through the introduction of grotesque indecorous comicalities. Due to this, priests forbade plays altogether on Church ground. Then the Miracle play was got out of the priests' hands and adopted by the town guild. It was presented as a cycle of short, inter-related scenes. The cycles were named after the city in which they were performed. The best-known example of the Miracle play is *The Second Shepherd Play* (c. 1385). Mak steals a sheep and brings it home. His wife Gill, in order to hide the sheep, pretends that she has given birth once again. She wraps the sheep in swaddling clothes and lays it in a cradle. One of the shepherds insists on peeking into the cradle and eventually the stolen sheep is discovered. This play portrays the adoration of Jesus, a symbol of hope and social justice, by the shepherds who represent the poor, meek, and downtrodden. Different from biblical shepherds, shepherds in the play complain about their sufferings from the cold winter and hunger, which reveal the typical social problems of the 15th century poor peasants.

The Miracle play reached their height in the 15th and 16th century and had a great influence on subsequent English playwrights.

Moral Period. This period was shown by the increasing prevalence of the Morality play, an allegorical drama, flourished especially during the 15th and 16th centuries, in which the characters personify virtues and vices (such as Charity, Mercy, Fellowship, Truth, Hate and Conscience) or abstractions (such as Death or Youth) and in which moral lessons are taught. The good and evil are involved in a struggle for a man's soul. The greatest English morality play is *Everyman* (c. 1509—1519), in which the hero, Everyman, is summoned by Death to the God's court to make an accounting for the life which was lent him. Everyman finds all his friends (Fellowship, Beauty, Strength, Knowledge, etc.) refuse to accompany him for the dangerous journey except Good Deed who offers to be his guide into the grave. In this play, Everyman represents all mankind. The moral is: how every man should meet death and how every man should live.

Springing from the Morality plays, the Interludes developed quickly and significantly as a transition from early English literature to the Elizabethan drama. In general, an interlude was a type of short and brief stage entertainment performed during the interval of a long play. The chief concern of the interludes shifted from the religious theme to realistic and comic incidents of the daily life. The best-known example is Henry Medwall's *Fulgens and Lucres* (c. 1497). The story centers on the heroine, Lucres, who hesitates to make a choice between two suitors. Eventually, she is determined to choose one whom she loves in spite of his poverty.

Artistic Period. The final stage in the development of the English drama is the artistic period, whose chief purpose was to represent human life. The plays of this period began to be divided into acts and scene. It was also at this period that comedies and tragedies emerged. Since these comedies and tragedies followed the structure and style of Greek and Latin drama, they paved the way for the flourishing of English drama in the Elizabethan Period.

One of the famous early English comedies is *Ralph Royster Doyster*, acted in 1553, written by Nicholas Udall, master of Eton College. The story takes place in London. The principle characters are Dame Custance, a rich and pretty widow, and Royster Doyster, an irrepressible suitor. Royster Doyster covets Dame Custance's "thousande pounde" rather than herself, so he woos her confidently. But out of his expectation, he is refused by the lady. The play ends with the return of the favored lover from a voyage, which he had undertaken, in a momentary pique. The play portrays a picture of the middle class's life in the 16th century London in an animated and natural way.

One of the famous early English tragedies is *Gorboduc*, acted in 1562, written by Thomas Norton and Thomas Sackville. Gorboduc, the legendary king of Britain, divided his kingdom between his sons Ferrex and Porrex. The elder son, Ferrex, aggrieved at being denied half his inheritance and suspicious of her younger brother's ambitions, set about raising soldiers to defend himself against his brother. On hearing of Ferrex's military preparations, Porrox sent his own troops against Ferrex and had him killed. Queen Videna, to avenge the death of her favorite elder son Ferrex, brought about the murder of his younger son Porrox. Then people rose in rebellion and slay both King and Queen. In the vacuum of power, the nobility united to destroy the rebels, and finally they fought each other. The whole country at last fells in anarchy. This play is important because it is the first English blank verse tragedy.

English Drama during the Elizabethan Age The growth of miracle plays, morality plays and interludes paved way for the the flourishing of the English drama during the Elizabethan Period. In the late 16th century appeared a group of well-educated Oxford and Cambridge graduates, including John Lyly (c. 1554—1606), George Peele (1556 — c. 1597), Thomas Lodge (c. 1558—1625), Thomas Kyd (1558—1594), Robert Greene (c. 1560—1592), Thomas Nashe (1567—1601), and Christopher Marlowe (1564—1593), among which Marlowe is the most outstanding one. They are later known as "the University Wits." This group came to London with the ambition to become professional playwrights. They chose to write for the public stage, taking over native traditions by transforming the native interludes and chronicle plays with their plays of quality and diversity. In this way, they brought new coherence in structure, real wit and poetic power to the language. Therefore, they helped to free English tragedy from artificial restrictions imposed by classical authority and developed a comedy tradition that is more close to life. Their plays exerted great influence upon many of William Shakespeare's masterpieces.

The forerunner of the University Wits is John Lyly, who is famous for his comedies with vaguely allegorical, philosophical, satirical and romantic coloring. Lyly wrote mainly for an aristocratic audience and his plays are almost accurate reflections of that audience's taste. His best-known plays are *Campaspe* (1584), *Endymion* (1588), and *Love's Metamorphosis* (between 1588 and 1598). Characterized by witty dialogue, interpolated songs, and artificiality of plot, Lyly's plays formed the basis of the later and greater achievement of Shakespeare.

George Peele, by nature more a poet than playwright, began his career by non-dramatic writing. His plays were in a courtly fantasy in the tradition of John Lyly. His best play is *The Old Wives Tale* (1593), which furnished John Milton with the groundwork of *Comus*.

Thomas Kyd is the only member of the Wits not trained in the University. He made use of the native English dramatic forms inherited from the miracle and morality plays of the Middle Ages. He followed the tradition of the Roman dramatist Seneca and adopted in *The Spanish Tragedy* the theme of revenge, the murder of a relative, the appearance of ghosts, the elements of lunacy and a play within a play. His outstanding contribution to the English drama lies in the influence of *The Spanish Tragedy and Ur-Hamlet* (c. 1588) upon Shakespeare's *Hamlet*. The type of these two plays came to be called "the tragedy of blood".

Robert Greene was chiefly marked by his talent for innovation. His best plays are *James IV of Scotland* (c. 1591) and *Friar Bacon and Friar Bungay* (c. 1590). *James IV of Scotland* has a clear and coherent development, unusual at this stage of the drama. One of its motifs, that of the persecuted woman who flees to the forest in the disguise of a page, was destined to become immensely popular in the later romantic drama, and to be used over and over again with endless variation by Shakespeare and other playwrights.

Elizabethan drama reached its summit with the appearance of Shakespeare's plays. After Shakespeare, the English drama underwent a process of decline. Ben Jonson, best known for his *Volpone* (1606), became the most important dramatist of his age after Shakespeare. He was the first English dramatist to publish plays, thereby encouraging the public to view them as literature instead of simply temporary entertainment.

English Drama during the Restoration Period The Restoration period began in 1660 during which a new type of drama, for example, heroic drama and comedy of manners, became prevalent while the Elizabethan drama with the romantic tendencies gradually disappeared out of people's sight. This new type continued to exist in the 18th century.

The heroic drama, also called heroic tragedy or heroic romance, is a genre of English drama composed in heroic couplets and generally characterized by exotic settings, bombastic rhetoric, highly stylized poetic dialogue, larger-than-life heroes and idealized heroines. This type became dominant because it was uniquely suited to the tumultuous era after the Civil War. English people at that time needed the spirit of heroism and moral behaviors needed to be praised. John Dryden, the dominant playwright and dramatic theorist of his time, wrote extensively in support of the heroic genre. His *The Conquest of Granada* (1670) extols heroic values such as ideal, love and valor. The heroic drama served as a significant phase in the development of the English drama and the evolution of English cultural ideology.

Comedy of manners is a dramatic genre that flourished in the late 17th century England. The best-known examples include *The Man of Mode* (1676) by Beorge Etherege, *The Plain Dealer* (1675) by William Wycherley, and *The Way of the World* by William Congreve. This type of plays is generally, for comic effect, a satire upon the falseness of decorum and the emptiness of social form, most often attacking superficiality and materialism. So the tone was usually lighter, defter, and more vivacious. Congreve is regarded as the best comedy playwright of the Restoration period.

The Restoration also saw the appearance of perhaps the first professional English woman writer Aphra Behn. After John Dryden, she was the most prolific dramatist of the age. Her major play is *The Forced Marriage* (1670), sharing some features with the comedies of manners but relied more on complex plots.

English Drama in the 18th Century. English drama in the first half of the 18th century, on the whole, lost its vitality. Though it continued to be very active in appearance, it lost originality and talent, for the genius of the century had turned from drama to novel. It was the novel in this period that became truly representative. Of the chief dramatic works in the first two decades of the century, there were, in the field of comedy, the sentimental comedies represented by Richard Steele and moralized comedies represented by Colley Cibber, while in the field of tragedy, there was Joseph Addison's *Cato*, which is significant for its theme of liberty, its implied political satire, and its strict observance of the dramatic rules of neo-classicism.

The second half of the 18th century appeared the greatest English playwright after Shakespeare, Richard Brinsley Sheridan, whose dramatic works such as *The School for Scandal* marked the highlight of the 18th century drama. The major contribution of the century to serious drama was the innovation of tragedies that portrayed people in everyday life, a form pioneered in English drama with *The London Merchant* by George Lillo.

English Drama in the 19th Century. From the death of Sheridan on, few English plays written in the 19th century succeeded both on the stage and with the readers, since the 19th century was an age of blossom in poetry and novel which produced many distinguished poets and excellent novelists. Toward the end of the century, under the influence of the theatrical revolution in Europe, especially the Norwegian dramatist Henrik Isben (1828—1906) and the Russian playwright Anton Chekhov (1860—1904), English drama began to change its silent state and there appeared many prominent dramatists including Oscar Wilder (1854—1900), George Bernard Shaw (1856—1950), John Galsworthy (1867—1933), John Millington Synge (1871—1909), Sean O'Casey (1880—1964), and Thomas Stearns Eliot (1888—1965).

English Drama in the 20th Century. The two world wars produced major shifts of English people in attitudes towards Western myths of progress and civilization.

In 1914, nearly a quarter of the earth's territory and more than a quarter of its population were under British dominion. But after World War II, Britain lost its most colonies. The 20th century witnessed the emergence of internationally acclaimed voices from the former imperial dominions. During World War II, in order to prevent a possible invasion of the Nazis, all the English people voluntarily and enthusiastically participated in the war to fight for their common cause. Their participation revealed that every one was important to his country and every one was equal in his social position. But what happened after the war? Their sense of importance and equality totally disappeared, since the class distinction became sharper and sharper. The common people could not see the hope of changing their social and financial condition, they became dissatisfied, and to some extent, they became angry. They felt a sense of hopelessness and meaninglessness in their life, even worse, they thought life, to them, was absurd.

The two world wars also exerted enormous influence upon people's mind, especially those intellectuals. Freud's psychoanalysis changed understandings of rationality and personal development, the influence of organized religion became weakened, and Jean Paul Sartre's existentialism was widely accepted. Sartre, in his *Being and Nothingness* (1943), defined the term "existentialism" as "existence precedes essence". Sartre thought "...man first of all exists, encounters himself, surges up in the world—and defines himself afterwards. If man as the existentialist sees he is not definable, it is because to begin with he is nothing. He will not be anything until later, and then he will be what he makes of himself." This understanding of human existence goes against most philosophical and theological traditions. According to prominent religious teachings, for example, God created human beings with a purpose in mind—to serve God's will, for example, or to live a certain kind of life. Sartre said: "God makes man according to a procedure and a conception, exactly as the artisan manufactures a paper-knife, following a definition and a formula. Thus each individual man is the realization of a certain conception which dwells in the divine understanding." People have their own choice to behave and perform and it is not something predetermined by some divine being or by nature. They realize that their life is not fixed in a stable state of being but rather in an active process of becoming.

Another prominent philosophical thinker is Albert Camus. Although he did not admit that he himself was an existentialist, his works shared many themes with that of existentialists. In his *The Myth of Sisyphus*, Camus, by describing Sisyphus, a tragic character in Greek mythology who was punished for all eternity to roll a rock up a mountain only to have it roll back down to the bottom when he reaches the top, expressed his central concern being called by himself "the absurd". According to Camus, Sisyphus is the ideal absurd hero and that his punishment is representative of the human condition: Sisyphus must struggle perpetually and without hope of success. Human beings are in the similar situation with Sisyphus. They try to create meaning in a world that has no meaning

Existentialism transformed the 20th century philosophy with its impassioned argument for the value of life in a world without religious meaning. Therefore, it immensely influenced the 20th century playwrights in their dramatic creation. A widespread sense of the utter meaninglessness of human existence was expressed in the body of plays that have come to be known collectively as the Theater of the Absurd represented by Eugene Ionesco, Samuel Beckett, and Harold Pintern. They thought that human beings cannot communicate. "Absurdist Theatre" discards traditional plot, characters, and action to assault its audience with a disorienting experience. Characters often engage in seemingly meaningless dialogue or activities, and, as a result, the audience senses what it is like to live in a universe that doesn't "make sense". In their plays human beings are often portrayed as dupes, clowns who, although not without dignity, are at the mercy of forces that are inscrutable. The most characteristic play in this style was Beckett's *Waiting for Godot*. The theater of absurd had only a limited impact in England, but several playwrights did adopt its approaches and principles, for instance, N. F. Simpson in his *The*

Resounding Tinkle, and Tom Stoppard in his *Resencrantz and Guiildenstern are Dead*.

In the mid-1950s and earlier 1960s there appeared a group of young novelists and playwrights with lower-middle-class or working-class background. They were known as "the Angry Young Men", a term originally taken from the title of Leslie Allen Paul's autobiography, *Angry Young Man* (1951). It became current with the production of John Osborne's play *Look Back in Anger* (1956). The works of the "Angry Young Men" were characterized by outspoken dissatisfaction with the status quo, particularly by their discontent with the staid, hypocritical institutions of English establishment. They betrayed disillusionment with itself and with its own achievements. Their impatience and resentment were especially aroused by what they perceived as the hypocrisy and mediocrity of the upper and middle classes. Included among the angry young men were the playwrights John Osborne, John Arden, Arnold Wesker, and Edward Bond. In the 1960s these writers turned to more individualized themes and were no longer considered a group.

Many British and Irish plays of this period demonstrated an interest in social and political issues, represented by Joan Littlewood's *Oh What a Lovely War*! and Brendan Behan's *The Hostage*.

The social upheavals of the 1960s, 70s, and 80s—particularly the civil rights and women's liberation movement, gay liberation, and the AIDS crisis—provided impetus for new plays that explored the lives of minorities and women. One of the most Significant figures of feminist playwrights was Caryl Churchill with her *Top Girls*. In the works of gay playwrights, gay subjects were presented and explored more explicitly and frequently with greater variety and openness, notably in Lillian Hellman's *The Children's Hour*, Robert Anderson's *Tea and Sympathy*, Martin Sherman's *Bent* and Peter Gill's *Mean Tears*.

The final decades of the 20th century saw more emphasis placed upon the work of directors than on that of dramatists. Some of the most prominent figures enjoyed both roles. During the 1990s Ireland maintained one of the strongest continuing traditions of new drama in not only England but Europe.

Chapter 2 Major English Dramatists

Christopher Marlowe(1564—1593)

Life. Christopher Marlowe, the eldest son of a Canterbury shoemaker, was born on February 6, 1564. He was christened at St. George's Church, Canterbury, on the 26th of February, 1564, some two months before Shakespeare's baptism at Stratford-on-Avon.

Marlowe received education at Cambridge and in 1584 he took a degree of B. A. Instead of continuing in Cambridge, he left his studies to carry out a secret mission for the government. In 1587 he took the degree of M. A. At first, the university authority did not agree to gramt him the degree for two reasons: one is that they believed he had been converted to Catholicism, the other is that he had been absent too long from his studies. The controversy was not settled until the Queen's Privy Council intervened on behalf of Marlowe.

Marlowe had been arrested and put into prison for several times, but each time he could be acquitted. These facts led to suspicion that Marlowe was a secret agent of the government. On May, 30, 1593, he was stabbed to death in a quarrel over either money or love in a tavern, and buried at St. Nicholas, Deptford. His mysterious death aroused many scholars' research. Now some believe that Marlowe was the victim of a political murder.

Major Works. In 1584 Marlowe came to London and took up play writing as his profession. Anything was hardly known of Marlowe's career in London, apart from his four great theatrical successes between 1585 and 1593, among them *Tamburlaine* (1587—1588), *The Tragical History of Dr Faustus* (1589?), *The Jew of Malta* (1590?), *Edward the Second* (1592—1593).

Tamburlaine contains two parts of five acts each written in blank verse. The story is about the rise and fall of Timur, the Tartar king of the 14th-century central Asia. Part I is a play of conquest, dealing with Tamburlaine's rise to power from a shepherd chief. He defeats Mycetes, king of Persia and became the king of Persia. Then he conquers the Turkish emperor, Bajazet. And finally he captured Damascus from the Soldan of Egypt. Intoxicated by his success, he rushes like a tempest over the East. Seated on his chariot drawn by captive kings, with a caged emperor before him, he boasts of his power. His victories were a triumph of immense natural energy and of ruthlessness over equally cruel but weak and decadent civilization. His ferocity was softened only by his passionate love for Zenocrate, the daughter of the Soldan. Part II deals with the continuation of his conquests, which includes victories over kings and princes both Christian and Mohammedan, until he reached Babylon. Then, Tamburlain is forced to face the truth of death. Though he feels that his energy is inexhaustible, he cannot triumph over death—first that of Zenocrate, and then that of his own.

This play is therefore a tragedy about a man who thinks he can control his own fate but falls nonetheless into its hands. The central figure Tamburlain represents the Renaissance desire for infinite power and authority. He is a product of Marlowe's Renaissance imagination. He is not only ruthlessly cruel and brutal in punishing his enemies, but also violently passionate in love.

The Tragical History of Dr Faustus is generally considered as Marlowe's best play. It is based on the medieval German legend of the bargain with Devil. Bored with the scholastic study of the four subjects of medieval knowledge, that is, Theology, Philosophy, Medicine and Law, the great scholar Doctor Faustus turns to magic book. With the aid of black magic, he calls up Mephistopheles, the Devil's servant with whom he makes a compact to sell his soul to the devil on the condition that he may have the service of Mephistopheles and satisfy every demand of his for a period of 24 years. Then a series of adventures and romances follow the signing of the contract. First his romances with a woman, then his visit to Alexander the Great, king of Macedonia and later a visit from Helen of Troy. In the meantime, D. Faustue undergoes endless spiritual struggle with a Good and Bad Angel. The play ends with Faustus' forced surrender of his soul to the devil after a lapse of 24 years.

This play is a sort of companion to *Tamburlain* in reflecting the Renaissance desire for infinite power through knowledge. It celebrates the human passion for knowledge, power and happiness, and reveals man's frustration in realizing the high aspiration in a hostile moral order.

The Jew of Malta is a tragedy and parody of Niccolo Machiavelli (1469—1527). Machiavelli—or Machiavel as Marlowe calls him—is portrayed as the embodiment of political manipulator. The hero of the play, Barabas, is a worshipper and owner of infinite wealth. He plays all sorts of tricks for gaining and preserving his wealth. His only philosophy is the art of gaining advantage. He ruthlessly makes his daughter's two Christian suitors kill each other and then poisons her for loving one of them. He first betrays Malta to the Turks and then tries to betray the Turks too, but he himself is betrayed and falls through a collapsible floors into a caldron prepared by him for the Turkish commander

This play is another expression of the spirit of the renaissance, the desire for infinite wealth, as it is also a satire on money-worship and Machiavellianism in the age of rising capitalism. The theme of the play is the satire on greed and evil deeds that naturally come with greed. This play significantly anticipated Shakespeare's *The Merchant of Venice*.

Edward the Second, Marlowe's last play in blank verse, is a tragic study of a king's weakness and misery. Edward II is described as a decadent sensual prince in Renaissance style. There is nothing heroic about Marlowe's Edward. He is a hopeless ruler, an impossible husband, a pathetic wreck of a man. This play can be regarded as a worthy predecessor of Shakespeare's historical plays, for there is resemblance in the blank verse used here to that in some of Shakespeare's history plays, particularly in *Richard II*.

Literary Comments. Marlowe's dramatic career lasted for only six years, but he is regarded as the father of English tragedy, instaurator of dramatic blank verse, the teacher and the guide of William Shakespeare. Marlowe's greatest literary achievement lies in that he perfected the blank verse and made it the principal medium of English drama. He brought vitality and grandeur into the blank verse with his "mighty lines" which carry strong emotions. Marlowe's second achievement is his creation of the Renaissance hero for English drama. Such hero is always individualistic and full of ambition, facing bravely the challenge from both gods and men. Such a hero embodies Marlowe's humanistic ideal of human dignity and capacity. With the endless aspiration for power, knowledge, and glory, the hero embodies the true Renaissance spirit.

William Shakespeare(1564—1616)

Life. William Shakespeare was born in April 1564 in Stratford-on Avon, a small but important country market town. Very little is known about Shakespeare early life. His father was a well-to-do glove maker and later became an alderman of the town. He attended the local grammar school, where he picked up some "small Latin and less Greek", but his schooling was cut short as a result of his father's financial decline. He did not receive any college education. In 1582, at the age of 18, he married Anne Hathaway, a local girl, who was eight years older. In 1586 Shakespeare was prosecuted by a big landlord for hunting illegally on his estate and that might be the direct reason for him to leave his native town.

About 1588 Shakespeare went to London, where he first did some odd jobs such as keeping horses for the audience outside the play house, then he became an actor and later a rather successful playwright by 1592. His career as an actor and playwright stretched for more than twenty years. About 1610 Shakespeare retired from London and went back to his birthplace, where he died on April 23 (his birthday), 1616, and was buried in Holy Trinity Church, Stratford.

Major Works. Shakespeare's dramatic career may be roughly divided into four periods:

1. The period of his apprenticeship, dating from 1590 to 1595

In the first period, Shakespeare wrote four early history plays and four comedies. The four history plays are: *Henry Ⅵ*, *Parts* Ⅰ, Ⅱ (1591), and Ⅲ (1592), and *Richard* Ⅲ

(1593). The four comedies are: *The Comedy of Error*(1590); *The Taming of the Shrew* (1591); *The Two Gentleman of Verona*(1593); *Love's Labour's Lost*(1593). The first is a period of experimentation. It is marked by the imitation of existing plays, by the spirit of youthfulness and rich imagination, by exaggerated language and by the frequent use of rhymed couplets.

2. The period of rapid growth and development, dating from 1595 to 1600

In the second period, Shakespeare wrote five history plays, six comedies and two tragedies. The four history plays are: *King John* (1595), *Richard II* (1595), *Henry IV in two parts* (1597), *Henry V* (1598); six comedies are: *A Midsummer Might's Dream* (1595), *The Merchant of Venice* (1596), *As You Like It* (1598), *Much Ado About Nothing* (1599), *The Merry Wives of Windsor* (1599), *Twelfth Night* (1600); two tragedies are: *Romeo and Juliet* (1595) and *Julius Caesar*(1599). The plays written in this period show more careful and artistic work, better plot, and a marked increase in the knowledge of human nature. Shakespeare's style and approach became highly individualized. The plays in the first and second period reflected Shakespeare's spirit of optimism.

3. The period of gloom and depression, dating from 1600 to 1608

The third is a period of Shakespeare's greatest tragedies and some tragic-comedies. The tragedies are: *Hamlet* (1600), *Troilus and Cressida*(1602), *Othello* (1604), *King Lear* (1605), *Macbeth* (1605), *Antony and Cleopatra* (1606), *Timon of Athens* (1606), *Coriolanus*(1608). The two comedies of this period are also dark in mood and are sometimes called problem plays because they do not fit into clear categories or present easy resolution. They are: *All's Well That Ends Well*(1603) and *Measure for Measure*(1604). This period marks the full maturity of his power. In depth of thought, in searching analysis of human motive, in the expression of the profoundest feelings, his tragedies make one of the most magnificent creations of the human mind.

4. The period of restored serenity, dating from 1608 to 1612

The final is a period of calm after storm, in which Shakespeare wrote a number of plays that are often called romances or tragicomedies. They had neither the lightness of the beginning nor the somber violence of the middle period. Instead, they had a spirit of serenity and optimism. In these tragic-comedies, Shakespeare experimented with a new way to end a play that could easily develop into a tragedy. The tragic facts of human existence are fully acknowledged but reassuring patterns of reconciliation and harmony can be seen finally to shape the action. However, plays written in this period weakened the elements of realism but increased the elements of illusion and compromise. His major plays include: *Pericles, Prince of Tyre* (1607), *Cymbeline*(1609), *The Winter's Tale* (1610), *The Tempest*(1611), *Henry* Ⅷ(1613), *The Two Noble Kinsmen*(1613).

Literary Comments. Shakespeare is considered to be the greatest dramatist of all time. During his whole life, Shakespeare wrote 37 plays, some of which, such as *Hamlet* and

Romeo and Juliet, are among the most famous literary works of the world.

Shakespeare's greatness depends upon his penetrating exposure of human nature, his lively paintings of human life and his truthful reflections of human reality. He is a genius of character portrayal. In his plays he has created a variety of life-like characters with strong and distinct personalities, who are representatives of the people of his age.

Usually there are two groups of characters in Shakespeare's comedies. The first group is composed of characters of young men and young women. They live in the world of youth and dreams and laughter, and fight for their happiness. The second group consists of simple and shrewd clowns and other common people. These characters make the play full of humor and laughter. Shakespeare puts women characters at a prominent place in his comedies. He shows great respect for the dignity, honesty, wit, courage, determination and resourcefulness of women who are of a new type: witty, bold, loving, laughing and faithful. The more important thing is that these new women characters carry their destinies in their own hands. In speaking, thinking and feeling they are equals or even superiors of men.

Each of Shakespeare's great four tragedies *Hamlet*, *Othello*, *King Lear* and *Macbeth* describes some noble hero, who faces the injustice of human life, who is caught in a difficult situation, and whose fate is closely connected with the fate of the whole nation. Therefore, these tragedies express a profound dissatisfaction with life, showing the conflicts between good and evil, justice and injustice. Shakespeare explores with extraordinary brilliance some of the deepest moral problems and ambiguities involved in human experience.

Shakespeare's historical plays reflect the horrors of civil war, convey the theme of the necessity for national unity under one sovereign, and advocate the importance of legitimate succession to the throne of an efficient ruler. Shakespeare's treatment of the ideal English kings is extremely critical. For example, Richard II is condemned for his vanity, political blindness and inability to subdue the feudal lords; Richard III is presented as a king strong willed and vicious; Henry IV is criticized for his participation in the murder of Richard II and his treacherous arrest of the rebels after the truce; Henry V, being the only ideal king, is portrayed as a symbol of English glory in the eye of the well-to-do citizens of England.

Shakespeare is also a genius of plot construction. He is good at plotting his plays with a pattern of five-act structure: Act I: Conflict is established; Act II: Suspense is built up as both the protagonist and the antagonist make preliminary moves against one another; Act III: Things begin to look as if the antagonist might win and thus make audience worried; Act IV: The act closes with everything prepared for the final victory, but just short of it; Act V: There may be a "surprise", but the victory of the side which wins nevertheless follows a kind of "logic". Obviously, Shakespeare places a play within the play so as to make the play within which the play appears seem real in comparison to the play within the play. Therefore, the structure of his plays is usually well-organized, with harmony and order disbalanced at the beginning, social conflicts sharpened in the middle and harmony and order restored at the end. It is worthy to notice that Shakespeare seldom invents plots for his own plays, instead, he often wisely borrows plot from Greek and Roman dramas, ancient myth, historical chronicles or old plays, and then instills into the old materials a new spirit that gives new life to his plays. Shakespeare skillfully interweaves several threads running through the play with the combination of tragic and comic elements. In addition, by using the dramatic irony, comparison and contrast, Shakespeare brings vividness to his characters and interest to his audience.

Shakespeare is a master of the English language with tremendous vocabulary. Many of his quotations and phrases have been absorbed into the English language. He is especially successful in handling the different meanings of the same word, or words having the same sound but different meanings, and in forming very new and striking expressions out of rather common words. The language of each of his characters not only fits his position but also reveals his peculiarities. His mastery of poetic language and of the techniques of drama enabled him to combine multiple viewpoints, human motives, and actions to produce a uniquely compelling theatrical experience.

Shakespeare is a realistic dramatist. His plays can be regarded as the mirrors of his age, reflecting the major contradictions of that time. He describes the decaying of the feudal society and the rising of the bourgeois spirit. His comedies reflect the young men and women who just free themselves from the fetters of feudalism and who are striving for individual emancipation. In his tragedies Shakespeare depicts the life and death struggle between the humanists, who represent the newly emerging forces, and the corrupted king and his feudal followers, who represented the dark power of that time. He shows his sympathy to the poor, discloses the greed and cruelty of the rich, exposes religious persecution, racial discrimination and social inequality. His plays communicate a profound knowledge of the wellsprings of human behavior.

Ben Jonson (1572 —1637)

Life. Ben Jonson was born around June 11, 1572 at Westminster, the posthumous son of a clergyman. He was educated at Westminster School where he learned the classics of ancient Greece and Rome. Later, he worked in his stepfather's trade, bricklaying. The trade did not please him in the least, so he run away from this, and went with the English army to fight Spaniards in the Low Countries. These gave him broad experience in the wide world. About 1592 he returned to England and married Anne Lewis on November 14, 1594. Misfortune dogged him in his new profession, and Jonson was arrested for acting in a seditious satire called *The Isle of Dogs*. In 1598 Jonson killed an actor named Gabriel Spencer in a duel, and he was arrested and tried at the Old Bailey on a charge of murder. He escaped hanging only by claiming benefit of clergy, and was imprisoned. It was after his release from prison that Jonson's first play was performed at the Globe Theatre.

Jonson became practically the first poet-laureate in 1616 and was granted a pension by King James, but he died poverty-stricken on August 6, 1637 and was buried in Westminster Abbey under a plain slab on which was later carved the words, "O Rare Ben Jonson!"

Major Works. Jonson's plays fall roughly into three groups: the realistic comedies, the tragedies, and the masques.

The play *Every Man in His Humour* (1598) inaugurated the school of realistic comedy. This is Ben Jonson's first play. It is said that Shakespeare acted one of the parts and that might have been the beginning of their long friendship. The play deals with the misunderstanding among people of different temperaments. In this play and another play *Every Man Out Of His Humor*, Jonson made the declaration of his theory of "comedy of humors", according to which each character in the drama has some dominating passion or prevailing eccentricity such as jealousy, greed, or credulity. He insisted on an adherence to the unity of time, place and action. He rejected the mixture of comedy and tragedy and thought romantic comedy and chronicle history are full of absurdities. The word "humor" in Jonson's age stood for some characteristic whim or quality of society. To his leading characters Jonson gave some prominent humor, exaggerated it that all other qualities are lost sight of. The special aim of the play was to ridicule the humors of the city, lash the variously-exaggerated caprices of people, and disclose the vanity of society.

Volpone is often regarded as Jonson's masterpiece. The scene of this comedy is laid in Venice. The hero Volpone (Italian word for "the fox") is an old and childless rich Venetian gentleman governed by an overwhelming love of money for its own sake. His method of increasing his wealth is to play upon avarice(greed; great eagerness to get) of men by pretending to be at the point of death and thus inveigles his false friends to bring him magnificent gifts.. His "suitors" who know his love of gain and the fact that he has no heir, endeavor hypocritically to sweeten his last moments by giving him rich presents, so that he will leave them all his wealth. But Volpone, wishing to enjoy a general disappointment to the full, draws up a will, in which he bequeaths(arrange to give at death) all his property to his servant Mosca (Italian word for "the fly"). Mosca, also a cunning fellow, avails himself of the will, proclaims his master dead, and as his heir, claims possession of Volpone's wealth. Then a quarrel arises between Volpone and Mosca, in the end both knaves are exposed and receive due punishment: Volpone is imprisoned and his property confiscated, while Mosca is condemned to penal servitude in the galleys.

Volpone, one of the great comic masterpieces of the English stage, is written in blank verse with a bitter satire on greed as the predominant trait in the age of the rising bourgeois society. It is a thorough and merciless exposure of the corruption wrought by greed on those obsessive and fantastic creatures whose cunning scheme for getting money makes gold itself of a parody religion.

The Alchemist tells the story that with the aid of two rascals, a servant who is left in charge of a big house sets himself up as an alchemist, and cheats a number of people by promising them the philosopher's stone. It is an exposure of dupers(cheater) and duped(cheated). It satirizes those people who let themselves cheated by the hope of sudden riches.

Jonson wrote two tragedies *Sejanus, His Fall* (1603) and *Catiline, His Conspiracy* (1611). *Sejanus* is based on Roman history and offering an astute view of dictatorship. This tragedy got Jonson into trouble with the authorities. Jonson was called before the Privy Council on charges of "popery and treason". Jonson did not, however, learn a lesson, and was again briefly imprisoned for controversial views. These two incidents jeopardized his emerging role as court poet to King James I.

After 1603 Jonson began to write masques for the entertainment of the court of King James I. Masque is defined as an elaborate form of court entertainment, a mixture of drama, music, song and dance. It developed in the Renaissance Italy, transported to England during Elizabethan times and became popular among the English aristocracy in the late 16th and early 17th centuries. The speaking characters were often courtiers wore masks. *Comus* by John Milton is probably the most important masque in English literature. Jonson's masques, including *The Satyr* (1603), *Masque of Beauty* (1608), and *Masque of Queens* (1609), displayed his erudition, wit, versatility and contained some of his best lyric poetry.

Literary Comments. Ben Jonson is best known for his satiric comedies. As a dramatist, he was resourceful in the creation of character and in the invention of comic situations. While for the most part he confined himself to laugh at the more obvious absurdities of society, yet his wit was so keen and his humor so robust as to make a lasting impression upon English drama. He influenced nearly all the writers of the 17th century, and his peculiar type of play has persisted on the English speaking stage to the present time. An enormously learned man with an irascible and domineering personality, he was, next to Shakespeare, the greatest dramatic genius of the English Renaissance.

John Dryden (1631—1700)

Life. John Dryden was born on August 9, 1631 at Aldwinkle, Northamptonshire. On both his father's and mother's sides Dryden's family were of the Parliamentary party. He received his early education as a king's scholar at Westminster, then to Cambridge where he took his B. A. in 1654. Making excellent use of his opportunities Dryden studied eagerly and became one of the best-educated men of his age.

Dryden gained notice in 1658 with his *Heroic Stanzas on the Death of Oliver Cromwell*. His attachment to Cromwell's principles seems not to have gone very deep, however, for two years later he was celebrating in verse *Astroea Redux* (1660) the return of Charles II. When James II, a Roman Catholic, was made king in 1685, Dryden was converted to Catholicism. These shifts of allegiance have led some to question the sincerity of his beliefs. After James's abdication and the accession of the Protestant William and Mary in 1688, Dryden lost the poet laureateship, with the accompanying pension, that he had held under Charles and James.

In 1662 Dryden began his dramatic career with *The Wild Gallant*, a prose comedy of humors, which was not well received by the public. In 1664, he produced *The Rival Ladies*, a tragic comedy, from a Spanish model. During his life time Dryden wrote about 27 plays. In his last ten years he turned his attention to translate many of the Latin classics: Virgil, Ovid, Lucretius, Horace, Theocritus, and others, and modernized Chaucer. In 1700, he died of inflammation caused by gout, and was buried in "Poets' Corner" Westminster Abbey, near to Chaucer.

Major Works. Dryden introduced a new type of drama, known as the "heroic play". Modeled after French Neoclassical tragedy, the heroic play was written in rhyming pentameter couplets. Such plays presented characters of almost superhuman stature, and their predominant themes were exalted ideals of love, honor, and courage. This type of play became the most prevalent form of dramatic writing in Restoration England between the 1660s and 1670s. Dryden was the chief writer of this kind of play. The two most successful of Dryden's heroic play were *Almanzor* and *Almahide*, or *The Conquest of Granade* (in two parts, 1670—1672) and *Aureng-Zebe* (1675).

All for Love or *The World Well Lost* (1678), a new version of William Shakespeare's *Antony and Cleopatra*, acclaimed as Dryden's best tragedy, and that was written in blank verse. Dryden treats of the story of *Antony and Cleopatra* in a totally different way from that in Shakespeare's play, by relating only the last part of Antony's life and confining the dramatic conflict to the hero's internal struggle between love for Cleopatra and worldly ambitions for himself. If in Shakspeare's tragedy, Antony is more of a Renaissance man who has the powerful passion of love, while Antony in Dryden's *All for Love* is no more than a sophisticated nobleman of the Restoration who indulges in his passion for a woman at the sacrifice of all his earthly ambitions. There is more psychological analysis of the major characters in Dryden's *All for Love* in which Dryden kept the three unities: unity of action, unity of place, and unity of time more exactly. According to the classical principles of dramatic structure, the setting of a good play should be one location, the action should represent the passage of no more than one day, no action or scene in the play was to be a digression; all were to contribute directly in some way to the plot. Dryden, accordingly, trimmed Shakespeare's plot and changed it into a personal drama, but the theme is much less significant.

Marriage A-la-Mode (1672) is regarded as Dryden's best tragic-comedy. The play has two plots. The "tragic" plot primarily involves Polydamas and Leonidas and the struggle to find a rightful heir to the throne. The "comic" plot, centered around two couples: one is Rhodophil and Doralice, and the other Palamede and Melantha. Both couples have their own marriage problem, so the two couples change partners. However, through a series amusing incidents, each of the two couples bring about reconciliation. The play takes questions of royalist loyalty and provisional morality as its themes.

Literary Comments. Dryden is the great representative figure in the literature of the latter part of the 17th century. He exemplifies in his work most of the main tendencies of the time. His enormous literary significance is threefold. He established succeeding ages the heroic couplet as one of the principal English verse form, clarified English prose and made it concise and flexible. His contribution to English literature, besides his poems and plays, was the invention of a direct and simple style for literary criticism. He also enjoyed the advantage of being able to bring his knowledge of the drama of Spain and France to bear on his criticism of English dramatists.

Richard Brinsley Sheridan(1751—1816)

Life. Richard Brinsley Sheridan was born in Dublin on October 30, 1751. He attended **Harrow School** in London. In 1773 he married Miss Linley, an accomplished singer. In 1775 he brought out *The Rivals*, a comedy, which, though it proved a failure on the first performance, was afterwards very successful. Sheridan was educated for the bar, but the success of *The Rivals* led him into close relations with the theatre. Then he became manager of the Theatre Royal, Drury Lane, after buying the large part of David Garrick's stake of the theatre. In 1777 he wrote *The School for Scandal*, a model of wit-comedy. At the proposal of Samuel Johnson, Sheridan, at the age of 28, was elected a member of the Literary Club. In 1779 he wrote *The Critic*, one of the wittiest farces in the language.

After 1780, Sheridan's playwriting career was cut short by his interests and activities in politics. He was returned to parliament for Stafford. When the Rockingham party came into power he was made one of the under-secretaries; and in the coalition administration he was appointed secretary to the treasury. Sheridan became the most renowned orator of his age, and counted the Prince of Wales, the radical philosopher William Godwin, and the young Lord Byron among his friends.

In 1806 Sheridan was defeated in the general election of 1807 but soon afterwards found a seat at Ilchester. In 1812 he attempted to win his old seat of Stafford, but unable to raise the money to pay the normal fee of five guineas per voter, he was defeated. After the burning of the Drury Lane Theater, Sheridan was troubled by serious financial problems and finally he was arrested for debt. On 7th July 1816 he died in great poverty and was buried in Poets' Corner, Westminster Abbey.

Major Works. Sheridan is chiefly known as writer of two famous comedies: *The Rivals* (1775) and *The School for Scandal* (1777).

The Rivals is a prose comedy of five acts dealing with two stories. The main plot has to do with the love affair between Captain Absolute, the son of a baronet, and Lydia Languish, a girl with romantic and sentimental fancies. Lydia is interested in reading romantic and sentimental novels and wants a love affair like those in her romance stories. In order to win the girl's heart, Absolute has to disguise himself as Ensign Beverley, a poor lieutenant. However, obstacles to their romance come in the shape of Lydia's aunt, Mrs Malaprop, without whose consent to marry she would lose half her fortune. Meanwhile a rival suitor, Bob Acres, is persuaded to challenge Beverly to a duel even though he is terrified of being killed. Everything is resolved when Acres discovers that Beverly is really Absolute. Lydia agrees to give up her romantic dream and decides that she will marry the captain, even though he is not a poor ensign.

The secondary plot involves the relationship between Lydia's friend Julia and her jealous and mistrustful lover Faulkland. After much torture at the game of love, they are finally united.

The Rivals, a comedy about romantic, generational and social identities, satirizes sentimentalism and sophisticated pretensions without the typical 18th century moralizing. Due to its complex plot and subtle characterization of stock comic caricatures of human folly, the play continues to be produced to this day.

The School for Scandal is usually considered Sheridan's masterpiece. Sheridan juxtaposes the character of Joseph, a portrait of hypocrisy hidden behind a mask of sentiment, with his prodigal but good-natured brother, Charles Joseph. Charles is in love with Maria, the ward of Sir Peter Teazle, who has married a very young girl from the countryside. After entering the big city, Lady Teazle becomes attracted and corrupted by the fashionable society epitomized by a group of scandal-mongers led by the malicious Lady Sneerwell, who loves Charles and instigates Joseph t pursue Maria. Joseph, while making advances to Maria, secretly tries to seduce Lady Teazle. Owing to the fabrications of Lady Sneerwell and Joseph, Sir Peter Teazle believes Charles to be the person flirting with his young wife. One day, Lady Teazle foolishly pays Joseph a visit in his own room. Joseph is on the point of corrupting her when Sir Peter Teazle arrives unexpectedly. Lady Teazle is forced to hide behind a screen. Just at that time, Charles turns up. Sir Peter Teazle also has to take cover. The climax comes when Charles knocks over the screen and reveals Lady Teazle. Thus Sir Peter Teazle finds out that it is not Charles but Joseph who has been carrying an intrigue with his wife.

When Sir Oliver JOSEPH, the wealthy uncle of Charles and Joseph , returns from India, he assumes disguise in order to assess the true characters of his nephews. First he goes to visit Charles in the guise of a usurer. Charles sells all the family portraits to him but refuses to part with his uncle's portrait. Then disguising as a poor relative, he goes to see Joseph, begging for aid. With a fine manner Joseph refuses to give him even a penny, and says some dirty words about his uncle. In this way Joseph's villainy and hypocrisy are revealed. Charles is chosen to be the heir of Sir Oliver Joseph and is free to marry Maria. At the same time, Sir Peter Teazle and his wife are reconciled.

In this play, Sheridan carried the comedy of manners to the highest point it has reached in England. He lampoons English society for its materialism, gossip, vanity, and hypocrisy. The play has been a great success on the stage and is regarded as the best English comedy since Shakespeare.

Literary Comments. Although his career as a dramatist was short, lasting from 1773 to 1780, Sheridan was undoubtedly the greatest playwright of his age. He mainly wrote comedies that are permeated with amusing scenes, clever situation, epigrammatic wit, satiric character portrayal, and sophisticated dramatic irony. In his dramatic works, the artificial comedy reaches their climax, and the anti-sentimental movement reaches its culmination. It is Sheridan who brings the comedy of manners to the highest perfection.

Oscar Wilde(1854—1900)

Life. Oscar Wilde was born in Dublin, Ireland, on October 16, 1854. His father was a well-known surgeon and his mother a respected poet. Because of his mother's literary successes, Wilde enjoyed a cultured and privileged childhood. He attended from 1871 to 1874 at Trinity College, Dublin, where he won a scholarship to Magdalene College in Oxford which he entered in 1875. The biggest influences on his development as an artist at this time were Swinburne, Walter Pater and John Ruskin. During 1875—1876 he published poetry in several literary magazines. By 1880's Wilde would establish himself as a writer, poet, and lecturer, but above all as a "Professor of Aesthetics". In late 1881, after publishing the volume *Poems* at his own expense, he began a lecture tour of the United States and Canada in 1882, and in the following year he lives in Paris. Between the years 1883 and 1884 he lectured in Britain. On May 29, 1884 Oscar married Constance Lloyd in London. From the mid-1880s he was a regular contributor to *Pall Mall Gazette and Dramatic View*. From 1887 to 1889 Wilde edited the magazine *Woman's World*. In 1890 he published his now well-known novel *The Picture of Dorian Gray*.

In the summer of 1891 Wilde first met Lord Alfred Douglas, an undergraduate at Oxford. Their meeting altered the course of the rest of Wilde's life. On May 25, 1895 Oscar Wilde was convicted of homosexuality and sentenced to two years imprisonment with hard labor. After his release, Wilde immediately moved to France, living pennilessly and sinking into drug addiction. He died in a cheap Paris hotel on November 30 at the age of 46.

Major Works. The early 1890's were the most productive and fruitful time for Wilde. Between 1892 and 1895 he was an active dramatist, writing what he identified as "trivial comedies for serious people." He produced some of his most familiar plays such as *Lady Windemere's Fan* (1892), dealing with a blackmailing divorcée driven to self-sacrifice by maternal love; *A Woman of No Importance* (1893), describing that an illegitimate son is torn between his father and mother; *An Ideal Husband* (1895), involving blackmail, political corruption and public and private honor; and *The Importance of Being Earnest* (1895), talking about two fashionable young gentlemen and their eventually successful courtship.

Literary Comments. Oscar Wilde was the representative among the writers of aestheticism and decadence. The English aesthetic movement spanned from the 1860s to the end of the 19th century with the trial of Oscar Wilde. It was influenced by the French symbolism, presenting to the reader with symbols an ideal world of which the real world is but a shadow. This movement was dedicated to the doctrine of "art for art's sake", namely, art as a self-sufficient entity concerned solely with beauty and not with any moral or social purpose. In Ralph Fox's words:" Art for Art's Sake is only the hopeless answer of the artist to the slogan art for money's sake." The main characteristics of the movement were: suggestion rather than statement, sensuality, massive use of symbols, and synaesthetic effects—that is, correspondence between words, colors and music. It belonged to the anti-Victorian reaction, had post-Romantic roots, and anticipated modernism.

Oscar Wilde was closely linked with the Aesthetic movement. He, being one of the major advocates of art for art's sake", claimed: "The artist is the creator of beautiful things. To reveal art and conceal the artist is art's sake.... There is no such thing as a moral or an immoral book. Books are well written, or badly written. That is all." His aestheticism led him to decadence, and he gave a curious definition: "Classicism is the subordination of the parts to the whole; decadence is the subordination of the whole to the parts." The nation-wide depression of the late 1870's in England provided the background for the appearance of the decadent literature, which reflected the crisis of bourgeois culture, opposed the democratic and socialist ideals, upheld bourgeois individualism. Writers of this kind thought that the world was suffering from an incurable disease and their writings were just like the groans of the desperate patients.

Wilde's reputation rests mainly on his comic masterpieces. His plays were popular because their dialogue was baffling, clever, and often short and clear, relying on puns and elaborate word games for their humorous effect.

George Bernard Shaw (1856—1950)

Life. George Bernard Shaw was born in Dublin, Ireland, on July26, 1856 in a lower-middle class family of Scottish-Protestant ancestry. He had a troubled childhood. His father was a drunkard and his mother left them when he was less than 16 years old. Shaw remained with his father, completing his schooling and working as a clerk for an estate office. In 1876, Shaw left Dublin and his father and moved to London, joining with his mother and sister. He did not return to Ireland for nearly 30 years. From 1879 to 1883, he finished five novels but none of them were successful. His main interest during the period was political propaganda, and in 1884, he joined the Fabian Society, a socialist political organization dedicated to transforming Britain into a socialist state, not by revolution but by systematic progressive legislation, bolstered by persuasion and mass education.

The outbreak of the WWI in 1914 changed Shaw's life. For Shaw, the war represented the bankruptcy of the capitalist system, the last desperate gasp of the 19th century empires, and a tragic waste of young lives, all under the guise of patriotism. He wrote a series of anti-war newspaper articles entitled "*Common Sense About the War*", which proved to be a disaster for Shaw's public stature: he was treated as an outcast in his adopted country, and there was even rumor of his being tried for treason. After the war, Shaw's dramatic reputation was rebuilt, and in 1925, he was awarded the Nobel Prize for Literature. Shaw lived the rest of his life as an international celebrity, traveling the world, continually involved in local and international politics. He died at the age of 94 on November 2, 1950.

Major Works. Shaw began his literary career as a novelist, but being a fervent advocate of the new theatre of Ibsen, he decided to write plays in order to illustrate his criticism of the English stage. Shaw's most productive period of the dramatic career from 1893 to 1939 can be categorized into three cycles. The first is named "Plays Unpleasant", including two plays: *Widower's Houses* (1892) and *Mrs. Warren's Profession* (1893); the second cycle called "Plays Pleasant" contains *Arms and Man* (1894), *A Man of Destiny* (1897), and *Candida* (1897). The final cycle named "Three Plays for Puritans" consists of *The Devil's Disciple* (1901) and *Caesar and Cleopatra* (1901). Besides the plays in these three cycles, Shaw also wrote *Man and Superman* (1903), *Major Barbara* (1907), *Pygmalion* (1912), *Back to Methuselah* (1921), *Saint Joan* (1923), etc.

Widower's Houses, Shaw's first comedy, tells the story of Harry Trench, a young English doctor, and Blanche Sartorius, the daughter of an English businessman. Harry falls in love with Blanche. But when Harry gets to know that Blanche's father is a slum owner, he wants to break his engagement to her. Mr. Sartorius reveals to him that his houses arebuilt on land belonging to his aunt and that he lives to his aunt and he lives on the interest of the mortgage. Thus Trench proves to be no better than the girl's father. This puts an end to the young man's revolt and he marries Blanche. Trench's change of attitude indicates that one individual's rebellion seems too fragile in face of the strong social system. This play savagely attacks the hypocrisy of society and slum owners.

In *Mrs. Warren's Profession*, the protagonist is Vivie Warren, a Cambridge student with intelligence, comes to visit her mother in Surrey. Accidentally, she discovers that her mother, Mrs. Warren, is the owner of several brothels throughout Europe. Then she breaks off with her mother and goes to London and hopes to earn her own living by finding an "honest" job. An older friend of Mrs. Warren, Sir George Crofts, falls in love with Vivie, who, however, is attached to the worthless young son of the parish rector, Frank Gardner. When Crofts gets to know that Frank's father was once a lover of Mrs. Warren, he breaks up the match between Vivie and Frank by telling them they are half-brother and sister. Frank does not believe Crofts, but when he learns of Mrs. Warren's true profession, he determines that he cannot marry Vivie.

Obviously, these two plays in the first cycle possess the similar theme: to satirize bourgeois businessmen whose ill-gotten money was squeezed out of the poor and suffering people.

In *Candida*, Morell, a clergyman, is married to Candida, a brilliant woman. She returns from a vacation with her children. Marchbanks, a young poet, falls in love with Candida and comes back with her to her home. He wants to rescue her from her dull family life. Thus the conflict rises between the two men. Morell demands his wife choose one between them. Candida decides that she must choose the man who needs her most, her husband. In this play Shaw satirizes the liberal talks and preachers of "Christian socialism."

The Devil's Disciple derides puritan piety and touches upon the independent movement of the American colonies against British rule. *Caesar and Cleopatra* assails bourgeois morality and English aggressive policy upon other countries.

Major Barbara evolves chiefly round the central character Major Barbara, the daughter of rich industrialist and owner of a munitions factory, who is an officer in the Salvation Army. Barbara and her fiancé Cusins share the same idea to improve the workers' conditions. So there arises the conflict between the girl's father and the young lovers. Finally, both of Barbara and Cusins enter her father's business, because they believe that only under the condition that one has "power", one can fight successfully. Money and power can be better weapons against evil than love.

Pygmalion was originally written for the actress Mrs. Patrick Campbell. It tells the story of how Higgins, a linguist, turns Eliza, a flower girl in the street, into a graceful lady. This play is not only a poignant satire on high life and artificiality but also a witty study and clever treatment of middle-class morality and class distinction. It is a combination of the dramatic, the comic, and the social corrective that gives Shaw's comedies their special flavour.

Saint Joan is regarded as Shaw's masterpiece. Shaw rewrites the well-known story of the French maiden and extends it from the Middle Ages to the present. In Shaw's play, Joan of Arc is not portrayed as a heroine or martyr, but as a stubborn young woman. She acts out of her conscience rather than any political motivation. And as in classic tragedies, her flaw is fatal and brings about her downfall.

Literary Comments. It was from George Bernard Shaw on that English plays began to touch upon serious social issues. Shaw was strongly against the credo of "art for art's sake" held by those decadent aesthetic artists. He firmly claimed that art should serve social purpose by reflecting human life, revealing social contradictions and educating the common people. In his plays, Shaw was concerned with war, religion, morality, economics, health, slum poverty, prostitution, and so on. He portrays the situations in a frank and honest way with the intention to shock the audience with a new view of society. Therefore, from a thematic point of view, Shaw is a critical realistic playwright with the aim to reveal the characters' interior mind instead of their emotions and physical sensations. His plays are filled with humor with which Shaw managed to produce amusing and laughable effect. He delighted in ridiculing, unsetting, scandalizing and astonishing his public.

Samuel Beckett (1906—1989)

Life. Samuel Beckett was born on April 13, 1906 in Foxrock, south of Dublin, into a prosperous Protestant family. His father was a quantity surveyor and his mother worked as a nurse. He attended Portora Royal School in Enniskillen, excelling at sport and languages, and later studied French and Italian at Trinity College Dublin, where he took a B. A. Beckett once worked as a teacher in Belfast and lecturer in English in Paris in 1926. During this time he became a friend of James Joyce. In 1931 Beckett returned to Dublin and received his M. A. in 1931. He taught French at Trinity College until 1932, when he resigned to devote his time entirely to writing.

When the WWII broke out, Beckett was in Ireland, but he hastened to Paris and joined a Resistance network. Sought by the Nazis, he fled to Southern France, where he remained hidden in a village for two and half years. He only returned in 1945 after Paris was liberated from the Germans. After the war Beckett worked briefly with the Irish Red Cross in St. Lo in Normandy. Between 1946 and 1949 he produced the major prose narrative trilogy, *Molloy* (1951), *Malone Dies* (1951), and *The Unnamable* (1953), which is among the greatest prose writings of the century, and these books mark out in their pages a very grim but ridiculously circuitous and labored path of human life.

Fame and accolades began to come in the 1960s. Beckett returned to Dublin in 1959 to receive an honorary doctorate from Trinity College, and two years later he won, with Jorge Luis Borges, the Prix International des Editeurs. In 1969 he received the Nobel Prize for Literature "for his writing, which—in new forms for the novel and drama—in the destitution of modern man acquires its elevation". He continued to write until his death in 1989, but towards the end he remarked that each word seemed to him "an unnecessary stain on silence and nothingness". Beckett died, following respiratory problems, in a hospital in Paris on December 22, 1989.

Major Works. Samuel Becket is mostly known for his *Waiting for Godot*, written in 1949 and published in English in 1954. This play brought Beckett international fame and established him as one of the leading names of the theater of the absurd. Originally written in French in 1948, Beckett personally translated the play into English.

Waiting for Godot is a two-act play that consists of five characters: Estragon, Vladimir, Lucky, Pozzo, and a boy. Estragon and Vladimir are two tramps, Lucky, the servant of Pozzo who is the master ruling over Lucky, the boy is the servant of Mr. Godot. The play tells about two tramps Vladimir and Estragon, who are waiting in the evening on a country road by a tree for the arrival of a mysterious man named Godot. It appears they do not remember Godot very well, but they think he is going to give them an answer. They cannot remember the question. They are homeless and penniless, traveling from one place to another. Now they simply wait for Godot. The sun sets and the moon rises. They get the message that Godot will not come today, but will try to come tomorrow. They decide to move on, but they do not move.

Waiting for Godot has been known as one of the masterpieces of tragicomedy. It revolutionized the 20th century theatre and had a profound influence on generations of succeeding dramatists, including such renowned contemporary playwrights as Harold Pinter and Tom Stoppard. The entire play is pervaded by a sense of despair and tragedy. It conveys the idea that human condition is a dismal and distressful state. The derelict man struggles to live or rather exist, in a hostile and uncaring world. A sense of stagnancy and bareness captivates man, and whenever he tries to assert himself, he is curbed. The play has often been viewed as fundamentally existentialist in its interpretation of life and elements of the Theater of the Absurd.

Literary Comments. Samuel Beckett is generally regarded as one of the first absurdist playwrights to win international fame. His work has extended the possibilities of drama and fiction in unprecedented ways, bringing to the theatre and the novel an acute awareness of the absurdity of human existence, for example, human being's desperate search for meaning, individual isolation, and the gulf between human desires and the language in which they find expression. Many of Becket's work have been intensely and internationally studied by critics, performed on stage and TV, and continue to be greeted with more or less equal proportions of fascination, devotion and horror.

John Osborne(1929 —1994)

Life. John Osborne was born in London on December 12, 1929, the year of the stock market crash, and brought up during the Depression of the 1930s. Much of his childhood was spent in near poverty, and he suffered from frequent extended illnesses. His father, a commercial artist and copywriter, died when Osborne was in his teens. He and his mother lived together through the WWII in Fulham, southern west of London. Osborne attended St. Michael's College, in Barnstaple, Devon. He was expelled at the age of 16 after the headmaster slapped Osborne's face and Osbone hit him back. Thereafter he received no other formal education. After spending some time at home, he took a series of jobs writing copy for various trade journals, a tutor for child actors in a theatrical company, an assistant stage manager, and an actor. Osborne made his acting debut in March 1948, and at the same time, he began to write plays on his own. Osborne received several awards for his work, including the *Evening Standard* Drama Award, the Best Play of the Year Award, the Tony Award for Best Play, and the Macallan Award for Lifetime Achievement, and an Academy Award for best adapted screenplay. He died of heart failure December 24, 1994.

Major Plays. Osborne started his theatrical career as an actor and playwright in provincial English repertory theaters in the 1950s. His first commercial success was *Look Back in Anger* (1956), which made him gain international fame. After the success of *Look Back in Anger*, Osborne continued to have a highly successful career as playwright. Among Osborne's other plays are *The Entertainer* (1957), *Luther* (1961), *Inadmissible Evidence* (1964), *A Patriot for Me* (1965), *The End of Me Old Cigar* (1974), *Watch It Come Down* (1976), and *Déjà vu* (1991). Besides his plays, Osborne also wrote the screenplay for the Oscar winning *Tom Jones* (1964), a two volume autobiography, *A Better Class of Person* (1981, televised 1985) and *Almost a Gentleman* (1991).

Look Back in Anger is written in the form of a three-act realistic play. The play is set in a one-room attic apartment in the Midlands of England. The hero Jimmy Porter is a 25 year-old candy-shop owner with a university degree, but he is embittered and alienated by his inability to advance socially. Then he shifts his frustration and anger onto his wife Alison. He engages in a vindictive affair with his best friend's wife Helena Charles. He treats his wife and his mistress boorishly and insults them cruelly. In this way, Jimmy rebels against the establishment and strikes back at the world with explosive intensity.

Look Back in Anger established Osborne as a leading writer of the British theater. It became the seminal work for the so-called "Angry Young Men". Jimmy Porter is a character of psychological complexity and interest. He operates out of a deep well of anger. His anger is directed at those he loves because they refuse to express strong feelings, at a society that did not fulfill promises of opportunity, and at those who smugly assume their places in the social and power structure and who do not care for others. He lashes out in anger because of his deeply felt helplessness. Therefore, Jim Porter becomes a symbol of a generation of young people who were rebellious, disillusioned and hysterically mad at social injustice. In Osborne's words, Jim is "a disconcerting mixture of sincerity and cheerful malice, of tenderness and freebooting cruelty; restless, importunate, full of pride, a combination which alienates the sensitive and insensitive alike".

Literary Comments. Osborne's *Look Back in Anger* is credited with having a great influence on British theater and culture. It helps open a new era in British theater, emphasizing aggressive social criticism, authentic portrayals of working-class life, and anti-heroic characters. It is often regarded as an insightful commentary on England's social and political situation during the 1950s. By using a fresh, unadorned working-class language, Osborne condemns the contemporary social evils angrily, violently and unrelentingly. With an entirely new sense of reality, he brought vitality to the English theater and became known as the first "Angry Young Man."

Harold Pinter(1930 —)

Life. Harold Pinter was born on October 10, 1930 in North East London. He grew up as the only child of working-class Jewish immigrant parents. Pinter received his education at a London grammar school and studied briefly at London's Royal Academy of Dramatic Arts. From 1949 to 1957 he published several poems and began working as a professional actor. He did not gave himself over full-time to playwriting until 1959. In his later years Pinter has been active in human rights issues. His interest in politics is a very public one. Over the years he has spoken out forcefully about the abuse of state power around the world.

Major Works. Harold Pinter has written 29 plays including: *The Birthday Party* (1958), *The Caretaker* (1960), *The Homecoming* (1965), *Betrayal* (1979), and *A Kind of Alaska* (1982). He is also the author of a number of screenplays, including *The Servant* (1963), *The Accident* (1967), *The Go-Between* (1971), *The French Lieutenant's Woman* (1981), *Turtle Diary* (1985), *Reunion* (1989), *The Handmaid's Tale* (1990), *The Comfort of Strangers* (1990), and *The Trial by Franz Kafka* (1990).

The Homecoming is perhaps Pinter's greatest play. The story takes place in a North London house under the control of Max, a nagging and aggressive ex-butcher. He abuses his chauffeur brother Sam, alternatively laments and condemns his late wife. Two of his three sons Lenny, a snide pimp, and Joey, a possible boxer, live at home together with him. His estranged son, Teddy, a lecturer in philosophy at an American university, arrives home from North America with his wife Ruth. She's beautiful, civilized, and seems sexually charged even in the way she moves. Her presence creates a sexual tension. At the end of the play Teddy returns alone to his university job in America, while Ruth stays as a sexual consort and money-earning prostitute.

The Homecoming remains a challenging work of theatre. It is endlessly debatable and offers itself to analysis from diverse perspectives. One critic once notes: "You can never say with Pinter that one interpretation is wholly right or another wholly wrong. What you can say, with reasonable certainty, is that the play continues to get under our collective skins..." The play is complex, confrontational, and casually brutal about human nature. It is also linguistically rich, laden with levels of personal and social criticism and characterization, darkly funny, and frequently disturbing.

The Caretaker was the first of Pinter's plays to bring him artistic and commercial success as well as national recognition. The setting is a single room cluttered by junk. There are only three characters: the brothers Mick and Aston and Davies. Aston has suffered from mental illness and saves Davies, an old tramp, when he is about to be beaten up. Mick, a builder, has difficulty to communicate with Aston. He is unwilling to accept the coming of Davies. He even jeers at and terrorizes Davies. However, Davies eventually gets a job as caretaker in the house. But his selfish and inconsiderate behavior towards Aston results in his being told to leave. An attempt to gain the support of Mike fails. Disillusioned and shattered, the wretched tramp creeps back to his original benefactor, hoping for a reconciliation; but it is impossible.

Pinter has been awarded the Shakespeare Prize, the European Prize for Literature, the Pirandello Prize, the David Cohen British Literature Prize, the Laurence Olivier Award, the Legion d'Honneur and the Moliere D'Honneur for lifetime achievement. In 1999 the Royal Society of Literature made him a Companion of Literature; in 2005, Pinter was awarded the Nobel Prize for literature.

Literary Comments. The Swedish Academy's citation noted Pinter's position as "the foremost representative of British drama in the second half of the 20th century", and recognized that his opposition to imperialist war and his dedication to freedom of speech and democratic rights "can be seen as a development of the early Pinter's analyzing of threat and injustice". He is now acclaimed to be one of the most challenging and influential English playwrights after WWII. His plays are noted for their use of silence to increase tension, understatement, and cryptic small talk. Equally recognizable are the "Pinteresque" themes—nameless menace, erotic fantasy, obsession and jealousy, family hatred and mental disturbance. Characteristically, Pinter's plays are not symbolic or distorted; they are instead prosaic, recognizable, but inexplicable.

Chapter 3 Selected Plays
William Shakespeare

(Act III, Scene I)

HAMLET:

To be, or not to be,[1] that is the question:
Whether 'tis nobler in the mind, to suffer
The slings and arrows[2] of outrageous fortune;
Or to take arms against a sea of troubles,
And, by opposing, end them? To die: to sleep;
No more;[3]—and, by a sleep, to say we end
The heart-ache, and the thousand natural shocks
That flesh is heir to, 'tis a consummation[4]
Devoutly to be wish'd. To die, to sleep;
To sleep: perchance[5] to dream: ay, there's the rub[6];
For in that sleep of death what dreams may come
When we have shuffled off this mortal coil[7]
Must give us pause: there's the respect,
That makes calamity of so long life;
For who would bear the whips and scorns of time,
The oppressor's wrong, the proud man's contumely[8],
The pangs of despis'd love, the law's delay,
The insolence of office and the spurns
That patient merit of the unworthy takes,
When he himself might his quietus make
With a bare bodkin? who would fardels bear,
To grunt and sweat under a weary life,
But that the dread of something after death,
The undiscover'd country from whose bourn
No traveller returns,[9] puzzles the will
And makes us rather bear those ills we have
Than fly to others that we know not of?
Thus conscience does make cowards of us all;
And thus the native hue of resolution
Is sicklied o'er with the pale cast of thought,

And enterprises of great pith and moment,
With this regard, their currents turn awry[10],
And lose the name of action.

Notes

1. To be, or not to be—To live or to die; to suffer or to take actions.
2. slings and arrows—sling: an instrument for throwing stones or others missiles. This phrase here refers to attacks.
3. To die...No more—To die is to sleep; to die is to exist no more.
4. a consummation—a final settlement of everything.
5. Perchance—perhaps.
6. ay there's the rub—"rub" is a figure from the game of bowls, referring to an obstacle which divested the bowl from its course. Here it refers to an obstacle hindrance, difficulty, or impediment.
7. this mortal coil—this turmoil of mortality.
8. contumely—insolent treatment; haughty and contemptuous rudeness.
9. No traveller returns—refers to the world after death.
10. heir currents turn awry—deviate from their original purpose.

Por Study and discussion

1. Throughout the play, Hamlet claims to be feigning madness, but Shakespeare's description of a mad man is so intense and so convincing that many readers believe that Hamlet actually slips into insanity at certain parts in the play. Do you think this is true, or is Hamlet merely play-acting insanity? What evidence can you find for either claim?
2. How does Hamlet think about death?
3. This passage is one of the famous monologues of Hamlet. Please try to recite it.

Richard Brinsley Sheridan
The School for Scandal

(Act IV Scene 3)

Excerpt

(A library in Joseph surface's house. Enter Joseph surface's and Servant)

JOSEPH. No letter from Lady Teazle?

SERVANT. No Sir.

JOSEPH. (Aside) I am surprised she hasn't sent, if she is prevented from coming. Sir Peter certainly does not suspect me. Yet I wish I may not lose the heiress, through the scrape I have drawn myself in with the wife; however, Charles's imprudence and bad character are great points in my favor[1].

(knocking without)

SERVANT. Sir, I believe that must be Lady Teazle.

JOSEPH. Hold! See whether it is or not before you go to the door: I have a particular message for you if it should be my brother.

SERVANT. 'Tis[2] her ladyship Sir; She always leaves her chair at the milliner's in the next street.

JOSEPH. Stay, stay: draw that Screen before the window—that will do; my opposite neighbour is a maiden lady of so curious a temper.

(SERVANT draws the screen and exit.)

I have a difficult hand to play in this affair. Lady Teazle has lately suspected my views on Maria; but she must by no means be let into that secret, —at least, till I have her more in my power.

(Enter LADY TEAZLE)

LADY TEAZLE. What sentiment in soliloquy now? Have you been very impatient now? O Lud! Don't pretend to look grave. I vow I couldn't come before.

JOSEPH. O madam, punctuality is a species of constancy, a very unfashionable quality in a lady.

(Places chairs, and sits after Lady Teazle is seated)

LADY TEAZLE. Upon my word, you ought to pity me. Do you now Sir Peter is grown so ill-tempered to me of late, and so jealous of Charles too —that's the best of the story, isn't it?

JOSEPH. I am glad my scandalous friends keep that up. (Aside)

LADY TEAZLE. I am sure I wish He would let Maria marry him, and then perhaps he would be convinced; don't you, Mr. Surface?

JOSEPH. (Aside) Indeed I do not. —(Aloud.) Oh, certainly I do! for then my dear Lady Teazle would also be convinced how wrong her suspicions were of my having any design on the silly girl.

LADY TEAZLE. Well, well, I'm inclined to believe you, besides, I really never could perceive why she should have so any admirers.

JOSEPH. O for her fortune, nothing else.

LADY TEAZLE. I believe so for tho' she is certainly very pretty, yet she has no conversation in the world and is so grave and reserved that I declare I think she'd have made an excellent wife for Sir Peter.

JOSEPH. So she would.

LADY TEAZLE. Then, one never hears her speak ill of anybody which you know is mighty dull.

JOSEPH. Yet she doesn't want understanding.

LADY TEAZLE. No more she does, yet one is always disappointed when one hears (her) speak, for though her eyes have no kind of meaning in them. She very seldom talks nonsense.

JOSEPH. Nay, nay, surely. She has very fine eyes.

LADY TEAZLE. Why so she has tho' sometimes one fancies there' s a little sort of a squint.

JOSEPH. A squint? O fie, Lady Teazle.

LADY TEAZLE. Yes, yes. I vow now, come there is a left-handed Cupid in one eye—that's the truth on't.

JOSEPH. Well, his aim is very direct however, but Lady Sneerwell has quite corrupted you.

LADY TEAZLE. No indeed. I have not opinion enough of her to be taught by her, and I know that she has lately rais'd many scandalous hints of me, which you know one always hears from one common friend, or other.

JOSEPH. Why to say truth? I believe you are not more obliged to her than others of her acquaintance.

LADY TEAZLE. But isn't (it) provoking to hear the most ill-natured things said to one and there's my friend Lady Sneerwell has circulated I don't know how many scandalous tales of me, and all without any foundation, too; that' s what vexes me.

JOSEPH. Ay, madam, to be sure, that is the provoking circumstance—without foundation; yes, yes, there's the mortification, indeed; for, when a slanderous story is believed against one, there certainly is no comfort like the consciousness of having deserved it.

LADY TEAZLE. No to be sure, then I'd forgive their malice; but to attack me, who am really so innocent, and who never say an ill-natured thing of anybody—that is, of any friend; and then Sir Peter, too, to have him so peevish, and so suspicious, when I know the integrity of my own heart—indeed 'tis monstrous!

JOSEPH. But, my dear Lady Teazle, 'tis your own fault if you suffer it. When a husband entertains a groundless suspicion of his wife, and withdraws his confidence from her, the original compact is broke, and she owes it to the honour of her sex to endeavour to outwit him.

LADY TEAZLE. Indeed! So that, if he suspects me without cause, it follows, that the best way of curing his jealousy is to give him reason for't?

JOSEPH. Undoubtedly—for your Husband should never be deceived in you: and in that case it becomes you to be frail in compliment to his discernment.

LADY TEAZLE. To be sure, what you say is very reasonable, and when the consciousness of my own innocence—

JOSEPH. Ah: my dear madam, there is the great mistake; 'tis this very conscious innocence that is of the greatest prejudice to you. What is it makes you negligent of forms, and careless of the world's opinion! Why, the consciousness of your own innocence. What makes you thoughtless in your conduct, and apt to run into a thousand little imprudences? Why, the consciousness of your own innocence. What makes you impatient of Sir Peter's temper, and outrageous at his suspicions? Why, the consciousness of your own innocence.

LADY TEAZLE. 'Tis very true!

JOSEPH. Now, my dear Lady Teazle, if you would but once make a trifling *faux pas*[3], you can't conceive how cautious you would grow, and how ready to humour and agree with your husband.

JOSEPH. Then, by this hand, which he is unworthy of—(Taking her hand)

(Re-enter SERVANT)

'Sdeath, you blockhead—what do you want?

SERVANT. I beg your pardon, sir, but I thought you wouldn't choose Sir Peter to come up without announcing him.

JOSEPH. Sir Peter! —Oons—the devil!

LADY TEAZLE. Sir Peter! O Lud! I'm ruined! I'm ruined!

SERVANT. Sir, 'twasn't I let him in.

LADY TEAZLE. O I'm quite undone! What will become of me? Now, Mr. Logic—Oh! mercy, sir, he's on the stairs—I'll get behind here—and if ever I'm so imprudent again—(Goes behind the screen)

Notes

1. great points in my favor—to my great advantage.
2. 'Tis—It is.
3. *faux pas*—false step, a social blunder.

For Study and discussion

1. What is your impression on Joseph Surface?
2. Please summarize the plot of this excerpt.

Harold Pinter
The Caretaker

Excerpt

A ROOM. A window in the back wall, the bottom half covered by a sack. An iron bed along the left wall. Above it a small cupboard, paint buckets, boxes containing nuts, screws, etc. More boxes, vases, by the side of the bed. A door, up right. To the right of the window, a mound: a kitchen sink a step-ladder, a coal bucket, a lawn-mower, a shopping trolley, boxes, sideboard drawers. Under this mound an iron bed. In front of it a gas stove. On the gas stove a statue of Buddha. Down right, a fireplace. Around it a couple of suitcases, rolled carpet, a blow-lamp, a wooden chair on its side, boxes, a number or ornaments, a clothes horse, a few short planks of wood, a small electric fire and a very old electric toaster. Below this a pile of old newspapers. Under ASTON'S bed by the left wall, is an electrolux, which is not seen till used. A bucket hangs from the ceiling.

Act One

Mick is alone in the room, sitting on the bed. He wears a leather jacket.

Silence.

He slowly looks about the room looking at each object in turn. He looks up at the ceiling, and stares at the bucket. Ceasing, he sits quite still, expressionless, looking out front.

Silence for thirty seconds.

A door bangs. Muffled voices are heard.

Mick turns his head. He stands, moving silently to the door, goes out, and closes the door quietly.

Silence.

Voices are heard again. They draw nearer, and stops. The door opens. ASTON and DEVIES enter, ASTON first, DEVIES following, shambling, breathing heavily.

ASTON. wears an old tweed overcoat, and under it a thin shabby dark-blue pinstripe suit, single-breasted, with a pullover and faded shirt and tie. DEVIES wears a worn brown overcoat, shapeless trousers, a waistcoat, vest, no shirt, and sandals. ASTON puts the key in his pocket and closes the door. DEVIES looks about the room.

ASTON. Sit down.

DEVIES. Thanks. (Looking about.) Uuh. ...

ASTON. Just a minute.

ASTON. *looks around for a chair, sees one lying on its side by the rolled carpet at the fireplace, and starts to get it out.*

DEVIES. Sit down? Huh... I haven't had a good sit down... I haven't had a proper sit down...well, I

ASTON. (*placing the chair*). Here you are.

DEVIES. Ten minutes off for a tea-break in the middle the night in that place and I couldn't find a seat, not one. All them Greeks had it, Poles, Greeks, Blacks, the lot of them, all them aliens had it. And they had me working there... They had me working...

ASTON. *sits on the bed, takes out a tobacco tin and papers, and begins to roll himself a cigarette. DEVIES watches him.*

All them blacks had it. Blacks, Greeks, Poles, the lot of them, that's what, doing me out of a seat, treating me like dirt. When he come at me tonight I told him.

Pause.

ASTON. Take a seat.

DEVIES. Yes, but what I got to do first, you see, what I got to do, I got to loosen myself up, you see what I mean? I could have got done in down there.

DAVIES *exclaims loudly, punches downward with closed fist, turns his back to ASTON and stares at the wall.*

Pause. ASTON lights a cigarette.

ASTON. You want to roll yourself one of these?

DEVIES. (*turning*). What? No, no, I never smoke a cigarette. (*Pause. He comes forward.*) I'll tell you what, though. I'll have a bit of that tobacco there for my pipe, if you like.

ASTON. (*handing him the tin*). Yes. Go on. Take some out of that.

DEVIES. That' kind of you, minster. Just enough to fill my pipe, that's all. (*He takes a pipe from his pocket and fills it.*) I had a tin, only... only a while ago. But it was knocked off. It was knocked off on the Great West Road. (*He holds out the tin.*) Where shall I put it?

ASTON. I'll take it.

DEVIES. (*handing the tin.*) When he come at me tonight I told him. Didn't I? You heard me tell him, didn't you?

ASTON. I saw him have a go at you.

DEVIES. Go at me? You wouldn't grumble. The filthy skate, an old man like me, I've had dinner with the best.

Pause.

ASTON. Yes, I saw him have a go at you.

DEVIES. All them toe-rags[1], mate, got the manners of pigs. I might have been on the road a few years but you can take it from me I'm clean. I keep myself up. That's why I left my wife. Fortnight after I married her, no, not so much as that, no more than a week, I took the lid off a saucepan, you know what was in it? A pile of her underclothing, unwashed. The pan for vegetables, it was. The vegetable pan. That's when I left her and I haven't seen her since.

DEVIES. *turns, shambles across the room, comes face to face with a statue of Buddha standing on the gas stove, looks at it and turns.*

I've eaten my dinner off the best of plates. But I'm not young any more. I remember the days I was as handy as any of them. They didn't take any liberties with me. But I haven't been so well lately. I've had a few attacks.

Pause.

(*Coming closer.*) Did you see what happened with that one?

ASTON. I only got the end of it.

DEVIES. Comes up to me, parks a bucket of rubbish at me tells me to take it out the back. It's not my job to take out the bucket! They got a boy there for taking out the bucket. I wasn't engaged to take out buckets. My job's cleaning the floor, clearing up the tables, doing a bit of washing-up, nothing to do with taking out buckets!.

ASTON. Uh.

He crosses down right, to get the electric toaster.

DEVIES. (following). Yes, well say I had! Even if I had! Even if I was supposed to take out the bucket, who was this git[2] to come up and give me orders? We got the same standing . He's not my boss. He's nothing superior to me.

ASTON. What was he, a Greek?

DEVIES. Not him, he was a Scotch. He was a Scotchman.

(ASTON *goes back to his bed with the toaster and stars to unscrew the plug.*

DEVIES. follows him.) You got an eye of him, did you?

ASTON. Yes.

DEVIES. I told him what to do with his bucket. Didn't I? You heard. Look here, I said, I'm an old man, I said, where I was broughtup we had some idea how to talk to old people with the proper respect, we was brought up with the right ideas, if I had a few years off me I'd··· I'd break you in half. That was after the guvnor give me the bullet. Making too much commotion, he says. Commotion, me! Look here, I said to him, I got my rights. I told him that. I might have been on the road but nobody's got more rights than I have. Let's have a bit of fair play, I said. Anyway, he give me the bullet. (*He sits in the chair*). That's the sort of place.

Pause.

If you hadn't come out and stopped that Scotch git I'd be inside the hospital now. I'd have cracked my head on that pavement if he'd have landed. I'll get him. One night I'll get him. When I find myself around that direction.

ASTON. *crosses to the plug box to get another plug.*

I wouldn't mind so much but I left all my belongings in that place, in the back room there. All of them, the lot there was, you see, in this bag. Every lousy blasted bit of all my bleeding belongings I left down there now. in the rush of it. I bet he's having a pike around in it now this very moment.

ASTON. I'll pop down sometime and pick them up for you.

ASTON. *goes back to his bed and starts to fix the plug on the toaster.*

DEVIES. Any way, I'm obliged to you, letting me... letting me have a bit of a rest, like... for a few minutes. (*He looks about.*) This is your room?

ASTON. Yes.

DEVIES. You got a good bit of stuff here.

ASTON. Yes.

DEVIES. Must be worth a few bob[3], this...put it all together.

Pause.

There's enough of it.

ASTON. There's a good bit of it, all right.

DEVIES. You sleep here, do you?

ASTON. Yes.

DEVIES. What, in that?

ASTON. Yes.

DEVIES. Yes, well, you'd be well out of the draught there.

ASTON. You don't get much wind.

DEVIES. You'd be well out of it. It'd different when you're kipping out.

ASTON. Would be.

DEVIES. Nothing but wind then.

Pause.

ASTON. Yes, when the wind gets up it...

Pause.

DEVIES. Yes...

ASTON. Mmmm...

Pause.

DEVIES. Gets very draughty.

ASTON. Ah.

DEVIES. I'm very sensitive to it.

ASTON. Are you?

DEVIES. Always have been.

Pause.

You got any more rooms then, have you?

ASTON. Where?

DEVIES. I mean, along the landing here...up the landing there.

ASTON. They're out of commission.

DEVIES. Get away.

ASTON. They need a lot of doing to.

Slight pause.

DEVIES. What about downstairs?

ASTON. That's closed up. Needs seeing to... The floors...

Pause.

DEVIES. I was lucky you come into that caff. I might have been done by that Scotch git. I been left for dead more than once.

Pause.

I noticed that there was someone was living in the house next door.

ASTON. What?

DEVIES. (gesturing). I noticed...

ASTON. Yes. There's people living all along the road.

DEVIES. Yes, I noticed the curtains pulled down there next door as we came along.

ASTON. They're neighbours.

Pause.

DEVIES. This your house then, is it?

Pause.

ASTON. I'm in charge.

DEVIES. You are landlord, are you?

He puts a pipe in his mouth and puffs without lighting it.

Yes, I noticed them heavy curtains pulled across next door as we came along. I noticed them heavy big curtains right across the window down there. T thought there must be someone living there.

ASTON. Family of Indians live there.

DEVIES. Blacks?

ASTON. I don't see much of them.

DEVIES. Blacks, eh? (*DEVIES stands and moves about.*) Well you've got some knick-knacks[4] here all right, I'll say that. I don't like a bare room. (*ASTON joins DEVIES upstage center*). I'll tell you what, mate, you haven't got a spare pair of shoes?

ASTON. Shoes?

ASTON *moves downstage right.*

DEVIES. Them bastards at the monastery let me down again.

ASTON. (*going to his bed.*) Where?

DEVIES. Down in Luton. Monastery down at Luton... I got a mate at Shepherd's Bush, you see...

ASTON. (*looking under his bed*). I might have a pair.

DEVIES. I got this mate at Shepherd's Bush. In the convenience. Well, he was in the convenience. Run about the best convenience they had. (*He watches ASTON.*) Run about the best one. Always slipped me a bit of soap. Any time I went in there. Very good soap. They have to have the best soap. I was never without a piece of soap, whenever I happened to be knocking about the Shepherd's Bush area.

ASTON. (*emerging from under the bed with shoes*). Pair of brown.

DEVIES. He's gone now. Went. He was the one who put me on to this monastery. Just the other side of Luton. He'd heard they give away shoes.

ASTON. You've got to have a good pair of shoes.

DEVIES. Shoes? It's life and death to me. I had to go all the way to Luton in these.

ASTON. What happened when you got there, then?

Pause.

You know what that bastard monk said to me?

Pause.

How many more Blacks you got around here then?

ASTON. What?

DEVIES. You got any more Blacks around here?

ASTON. (*holding out the shoes*). See if these are any good.

DEVIES. You know what that bastard monk said to me? (*He looks over to the shoes.*) I think those'd be a bit small.

ASTON. Would they?

DEVIES. No, don't they look the right size.

ASTON. Not bad trim.

DEVIES. Can't wear shoes that don't fit. Nothing worse. I said to this monk, here, I said, look here, mister, he opened the door, big door, he opened it, look here, mister, I said, I come all the way down here, look, I said, I showed him these, I said, you haven't got a pair of shoes, have you, a pair of shoes, I said, enough to keep me on my way. Look at these, they're nearly out, I said, they're no good to me. I heard you got a stock of shoes here. Piss off[5], he said to me. Now look here, I said, I'm an old man, you can't talk me like that, I don't care who you are. If you don't piss off, he says, I'll kick you all the way to the gate. Now look here, I said, now wait a minute, all I'm asking for is a pair of shoes, you don't want to start taking liberties with me, it's taken me three days to get here, I said to him, three days without a bite, I'm worth a bite to eat, en I? Get out round the corner to the kitchen, he says, get out round the corner, and when you've had your meal, piss off out of it. I went round to this kitchen, see? Meal they give me! A bird, I tell you, a little bird, a little tiny bird, he could have ate it in under two minutes. Right, they said to me, you've had your meal, get off out of it. Meal? I said, what do you think I am, a dog? Nothing better than a dog. Hat do you think I am, a wild animal? What about them shoes I come all the way here to get I heard you was giving away? I've a good mind to report you to your mother superior. One of them, an Irish hooligan[6], come at me. I cleared out. I took a short cut to Watford and picked up a pair there. Go onto the North Circular, just past Hendon, the sole come off, right where I was walking. Lucky I had my old ones wrapped up, still carrying them, otherwise I'd have been finished, man. So I've had to stay with these, you see, they're gone, they're no good, all the good's gone out of them.

ASTON. Try these.

DAVIES. *takes the shoes, takes off his sandals and tries them on.*

DAVIES. Not a bad air of shoes. (*He trudges round the room.*) They're strong, all right. Yes. Not a bad shape of shoe. This leather's hardy, en't? Very hardy. Some bloke tried to flog me some suede the other day. I wouldn't wear them. Can't beat leather, for wear, Suede goes off, it creases, it stains for life in five minutes. You can't beat leather. Yes. Good shoe this.

ASTON. Good.

DAVIES. *waggles his feet.*

DAVIES. Don't fit though.

ASTON. Oh?

DAVIES. No. I got a very broad foot.

ASTON. Mmnn.

DAVIES. These are too pointed, you see.

ASTON. Ah.

DAVIES. They'd cripple me in a week. I mean these ones I got on, they're no good but at least they're comfortable. Not much cop, but I mean they don't hurt. (*He takes them off and gives them back*). Thanks anyway, mister.

ASTON. I'll see what I can look out for you.

DAVIES. Good luck. I can't go on like this. Can't get from one place to another. And I'll have to be moving about, you see, try to get fixed up.

ASTON. Where you going to go?

DAVIES. Oh, I got one or two things in mind. I'm waiting for the weather to break.

Pause.

ASTON. (*attending to the toaster*). Would ... would you like to sleep here?

DAVIES. Here?

ASTON. You can sleep here if you like.

DAVIES. Here? Oh, I don't know about that.

Pause.

How long for?

ASTON. Till you... get yourself fixed up.

DAVIES. (*sitting*). Ay well, that...

ASTON. Get yourself sorted out...

DAVIES. Oh, I'll be fixed up... pretty soon now...

Pause.

Where would I sleep?

ASTON. Here. The other rooms would... would be no good to you.

DAVIES. (*rising, looking about*). Here? Where?

ASTON. (*rising, pointing upstage right*). There's a bed behind all that.

DAVIES. Oh, I see. Well, that's handy. Well, that's ... I tell you what, I might do that... just till I get myself sorted out. You got enough furniture here.

ASTON. I picked it up. Just keeping it here for the time being. Thought it might come in handy.

ASTON. *goes out and closes the door.*

DAVIES. *stands still. He waits a few seconds, then goes to the door, opens it, looks out, closes it, stands with his back to it, turns swiftly, opens it, looks out, comes back, closes the door, finds the keys in his pocket, tries one, tries the other, looks the door. He looks about the room. He then goes quickly to ASTON'S bed, bends, brings out the pair of shoes and examines them.*

Not a bad pair of shoes. Bit pointed.

He puts them back under the bed. He examines the area by ASTON'S bed, picks up a vase and looks into it, then picks up a box and shakes it.

Screws!

He sees paint buckets at the top of the bed, goes to them, and examines them.

Paint. What's he going to paint?

He puts the bucket down, comes to the center of the room, looks up at bucket, and grimaces[7].

I'll have to find out about that. (He crosses right, and picks up a low-lamp). He's got some stuff in here. (He picks up the Buddha and looks at it.) Hull of stuff. Look at all this. (His eye falls on the piles of papers.) What's he got all those papers for? Damn pile of papers.

He goes to a pile and touches it. The pile wobbles[8]. *He steadies it.*

Hold it, hold it!

He holds the pile and pushes the papers back unto place.

The door opens.

MICK. *comes in, puts the key in his pocket, and closes the door silently. He stands at the door and watches DAVIES.*

MICK. What's the game?

Notes

1. toe-rag—(BrE spoken) an offensive word for someone you dislike.
2. git—(BrE slang) an unpleasant and annoying person.
3. bob—a shilling (=coin used in the past in Britain).
4. knick-knacks—a small object used as a decoration.
5. Piss off—an offensive expression meaning to go away.
6. hooligan—a noisy violent person who causes trouble by fighting.
7. grimace—To make a sharp contortion of the face.

8. wobbles—to move unsteadily from side to side.

For Study and Discussion

1. Please describe the scene of this play.
2. Please make a brief analysis of Aston and Davies in the play.

Essays

Part Thirteen
Major Essayists and Selected Essays

Chapter 1 General View of the English Essays

The Definition of Essay. The word "essay"originates from the word "*essai*", a French word invented by Michel de Montaigne, originally intended to mean an attempt or a try at something. Montaigne used this word to describe his prose reflections on commonplace topics and occurrences with the publication entitled *Essais* in 1580. Influenced by Montaigne, Francis Bacon, in 1597, published his *Essays*, which is described as "grains of salt which will rather give an appetite than offend with satiety". It is generally accepted that it is Francis Bacon who introduced and popularized essay in the English-speaking world. Nowadays the signification of the term "essay" has been greatly extended. It applies to long treatises in prose, short pieces of moralizing exposition, personal observations and comprehensive, informative articles. To be more exact, essay, being a literary form, is a relatively short piece of expository prose on a specific subject with an attempt to persuade the reader to accept a particular point of view. It is a complete piece of writing that can stand alone—it must make sense to the reader "in itself".

The purpose of the essay is different from that of the story. The essay is to inform or explain whereas the story is to dramatize or create an experience. The essay achieves its effects by direct statement rather than by imaginary characters acting out a situation. Therefore, the essay must be brief, readable, interesting and well-structured. In this way, the reader can easily and clearly find and follow the idea about the literary texts. Furthermore, the essay should have a self-contained unity which expository work usually cannot maintain.

The Types of Essays The essay can be generally classified into two categories: formal and informal. A formal essay focuses on a particular idea free from the author's feelings, casual musings or experiences. It is generally characterized by a serious purpose, logical organization and formality of the vocabulary. So the formal essay is dogmatic, impersonal, systematic, and expository. It is usually dignified in style, serious and objective in tone. And its main idea is frequently introduced at the very beginning of the essay for the sake of engaging the reader's interest and attention. In order to make the idea clearly expressed, the writer makes effort to arrange the development of details logically with various transitions. In addition, he has the tendency to employ alternative ways such as illustration, definition, comparison and contrast, analogy, etc. to make his point more explicit and easily acceptable. The representatives of this type are Francis Bacon, Joseph Addison, Samuel Johnson, and Matthew Arnold.

An informal essay, also named personal or familiar essay, is usually personal, intimate, relaxed, conversational, and humorous as if the writer is talking or even chatting to the reader about some topic. It is characterized by its brief and discursive style, personal or humorous tone. The writer might digress from the topic at hand, or express some amusing, startling, or absurd opinions. In general, an informal essay reveals as much about the personality of its author as it does about its subject. There is no effort to objectify his thoughts and no concealment that this is his opinion. The distinguished writers of the informal essay include Jonathan Swift, Charles Lamb, William Hazlitt and Thomas De Quincey.

Two distinctions exist between formal and informal essay. Firstly, an informal essay is usually loosely structured with a humorous tone, whereas a formal essay is tightly organized with a serious tone. The result is that the reader feels difficult to catch the development of an informal essay although it develops with a certain form of the beginning, middle and end. Secondly, an informal essay is flatly assertive, more suggestive than a formal essay. After reading, the reader might keep the state of profound meditation.

The Development of the English Essays. The English essay has experienced quite a long history of the development with the illustration of a large number of distinguished authors.

English Essays before the 15th Century. It was not until the 8th century that English prose literature showed its appearance. The famous writers included Venerable Bede (673—735), Alfred the Great (849—899), and Aelfric (955—1023). Venerable Bede wrote in Latin his *The Ecclesiastical History of the English People*, which earned him the title of the Father of English History. The book is of great significance because it covers the whole length of early English history from the invasion by Julius Caesar to the year 731. In addition, it not only describes how religion was introduced and spreaded in England but also recounts some historical events of the period and Anglo-Saxon mythological legends.

Alfred the Great, the king of Wesses Kingdom, has been described as the greatest Englishman who ever lived. He was a wise leader and a well-known translator as well. He translated *Consolation of Philosophy*, a Latin work written by Boethius of the sixth century. *The Anglo-Saxon Chronicle* was compiled under his guidance. He possessed a free and natural way of writing style to achieve clearness and conciseness. This exerted great influence on the improvement of the writing style of the Old English prose.

Aelfric wrote a large number of religious works in Greek and Latin. Into his works he introduced a lighter, clearer and more musical prose. His works demonstrated that the Old

English prose possessed high quality in writing style and using language.

In the 15th century the only prose writer was Thomas Malory (1405—1471), the author of the most famous work of Arthurian literature, *Le Morte D'Arthur*. Being not a professional writer, Malory's composition grew in power throughout its length, while his style remained simple and informal. He saw his romances as the chronicles of an historical Arthur perhaps with a moralistic slant and expressed the religious and chivalric ideas of his age.

English Essays in the 16th Century. The 16th century had nothing in its prose to match the excellence of the drama, yet writers had been preparing the way for the acceptance of English as the standard medium of the expression. The major works of prose in the 16th century remained translation, chronicle, and history. It was John Foxe's (1516—1587) religious writings that helped to make English prose more popular to the general public. John Foxe is remembered as the author of Foxe's *Acts and Monuments of the Christian Church*, more commonly known as Foxe's *Book of Martyrs*, which is to this day the only exhaustive reference work on the persecution and martyrdom of Early Christians and Protestants from the first century up to the mid-16th century. He revealed his indignation towards the persecution and oppression of the religious saints.

One of the best examples of the 16th century prose was represented by John Lyly's (1554—1606) *Euphues, or the Anatomy of Wit* (1578) and its sequel *Euphues and His England* (1580). The works were characterized with abundant, even excessive use of elaborate sentence structure based upon parallel figures drawn from history, geography, pseudoscience and the author's imagination. Lyly's reputation had depended largely on his highly affected and ornate style, being later called "euphuism", which exerted the immense impact on the prose of the time. Euphuism achieved its height of popularity in the 1580s and imitated by many writers.

English Essays in the 17th Century. The 17th century in English literature was a great age of prose with a number of great prose writers, including Francis Bacon (1561—1626), Robert Burton(1577—1640), Thomas Hobbes(1588—1679), Izaak Walton(1593—1683), Thomas Browne(1605—1682), John Locke(1632—1704) and Samuel Pepys(1633—1703), among whom Francis Bacon, Thomas Browne and Samuel Pepys were the greatest. The social and political background was the first reason to provide the century with the arrival of the heyday of English prose. During the Civil War, political pamphlets and treatises became popular to involve the public in the revolution. Thus the writings possessed the characteristics of a plain style with strong persuasive power. The typical examples were Thomes Hobbes' *Leviathan*, which attacked the Puritans' political ideas boldly and directly, and John Milton's(1608—1674) *Areopagitica*, which defended the freedom of publication. The second reason was religious education which was resulted in the Civil War by which English people had gradually got the sense of freedom of the press. The Bible could be read only by clergymen in the past, but now the common folks were encouraged to read the Bible by themselves due to the religious reformation of Martin Luther. Several new translations appeared, for example, William Tyndale's (c. 1494—1536) version, Miles Coverdale's (1488—1568) version, which was later revised and known as *The Great Bible*, and finally became the Bishop's Bible under the direction of Archbishop Parker in 1568. The most successful version was The King James Version which was published in 1611 and regarded as "the noblest monument of English Prose". It was characterized by its simple style, brilliant language, concrete terms and images, straightforward phrases and sentences, elaborate balance and parallelism. Therefore, the appearance of The King James Version exerted a dramatic influence upon English literature, English people and their life.

English Essays in the 18th Century. The 18th century was a prosperous age of prose which , for the first time in English history, occupied a literary position with the birth of many great prose writers such as Sir Richard Steele(1672—1729), Joseph Addison(1672—1719), Samuel Johnson(1709—1784), and Edward Gibbon(1737—1794).

The 18th century England was known as the Age of Enlightenment, or the Age of Reason. After the civil war in the 17th century, English people were fed up with religious fanaticism as practiced by the Puritans. The dramatic development of science played a vital role in making people think more about the rationality of their behavior. The result was that reason became the only standard to evaluate everything. Therefore, the 18th century was an age of reason without passion. This explained why the age did not produce the classic poetry; instead it was an age of argumentative prose. The public reacted positively to this new literary genre, which could best reflect the world and life around them. So the individual voice could be heard through prose discussing the intimate details.

The essayists in the 18th century tended to compose the periodical paper. Sir Richard Steele and Joseph Addison enjoyed their fame in English literature because of their joint production in journalism, particularly in *The Tatler* (1709—1711) and *The Spectator* (1711—1712 and 1714), both of which offered the best essays of the time, greatly influencing the taste and opinion of the 18th century English public. It can be said that Steele and Addison inaugurated a tradition of light essay, because their essays were a successful combination of entertainment with enlightenment, characterized by an informal, witty, humorous, relaxed, easy style, by the creation of character, and by well-intentioned satire to criticize the follies and foibles of society.

The Tatler was brought out by Steele under the pseudonym of Isaac Bickerstaff. The first issue, a triweekly journal, was published on April 12, 1709. According to Steele the journal would contain "accounts of gallantry, pleasure and entertainment". So *The Tatler* , in a lofty and sympathetic tone, ridiculed and denounced old-fashioned ideals of gallantry and self-indulgence, the evils of dueling and gambling, the disguises of cunning, vanity, and affectation. It emphasized that only kindness and self-suppression could constitute good breeding. Although *The Tatler* appealed to the public without distinction of political parties, it was colored by Steele's Whig views. Accordingly, when the authors wished to avoid politics altogether they abandoned *The Tatler*, replacing it by *The Spectator*.

The Spectator, an influential literary magazine, claims to be the oldest continuously-published magazine in the English language. As a daily publication, it was founded on March 1, 1711 with the collaboration of Addison and Steele. *The Spectator*, along with *The Tatler*, started the tradition of the daily periodical whose subject was not news, but literature and manners, and they adapted the gentlemanly culture of polite letters to a wide print audience. Steele played a larger part than Addison did in *The Tatler* but it was Addison who wrote most of the best essays for *The Spectator*.

The Spectator was supposed to be edited by a small club headed by Mr. Spectator, a man of travel and learning, who offered his comments and criticism on the manners of what was then the new age. The best-known portion of magazine consists of a series of essays known as the Sir Roger de Coverley papers. Sir Roger de Coverley is a country gentleman of good humor and old-fashioned manners. His foibles make a setting for his virtues that point an example to the world of fashion. Readers come to know him on his estate, in church, wooing his neighbor the widow, or visiting the strange sights of the city. His singularities, however, did not offend people; on contrary, they liked this character. The series of essays on Sir Roger de Coverley almost make a novel; at all events they create a character.

Steele and Addison have been remembered chiefly as editors and contributors of *The Tatler* and *The Spectator*, the English periodical literature of the early 18th century. Their essays provide a new code of social morality for the rising bourgeoisie, and give a true picture of the social life of England at that time. In their hands, English essay has completely established itself as a literary genre. Using it as a form of character sketching and story-telling, they ushered in the flourishing of literary periodicals and the arrival of modern English novels.

Samuel Johnson was another important essayist who made his contribution to the founding of his own periodicals, *The Rambler* (1750—1752) and *The Idler* (1758—1760). He himself also contributed to *The Gentleman's Magazine*, often considered the first modern magazine in England. Johnson's style of his essays, for the most part, was didactic, lapidary, eloquent and insightful. However, his reputation rested mainly on his compilation of *The Dictionary of the English Language*, which became the foundation of all the subsequent English dictionaries. His last influential work is *The Lives of the English Poets*, which comprises the biographies of 52 poets and literary criticism.

English Essays in the 19th Century. The year 1784 was the year of Samuel Johnson's death and marked the end of the Age of Reason. During the 18th century, the writings of neoclassic poets and some essayists had exerted their great influence upon the change of the English language. Essayists such as Richard Steele, Joseph Addison and Samuel Johnson once attempted to formalize English and to make English more dignified and precise.

Contrary to their expectation, what they tried did not stimulate the purification and standardization of English but put a temporary end to the spirit of variety and experimentation that had contributed much to making English more vivid and fresh.

The coming of the new age became one of revolution in literature, of rebellion against the old standards of classicism, and the establishment of individual freedom in the world of the imagination. From 1802 to 1820, three modern magazines, *The Edinburgh Review*, *The Quarterly Review*, and *The London Magazine*, were established.

In the first decades of the 19th century essayists like Charles Lamb (1775—1834), William Hazlitt (1778—1830), and Thomas De Quincy (1785—1859) gave up the style to write in accordance with rules and models, thus began to attempt a style to entertain themselves and to express their own personality. This new genre is known as the familiar essay, which is characterized by its brevity and discursive style with a more personal and intimate tone. The subjects and characters of the familiar essays are quite extensive: from the concerns of the leisure class to every aspect of life, from ordinary clerks to opium smokers, from chimney-sweepers to murderers.

The middle and late 19th century, known as the Victorian era, was the great age of the serious or formal essays. The rise of industrialism contributed to the increased wealth and leisure of the middle class, which, together with free creation, produced an increased interest in books and magazines. Simultaneously, industrialism generated many despicable social conditions that deeply troubled responsible citizens. Many authors found the serious essay best suited to the expression of their concern over these issues. Perhaps the most famous were Thomas Carlyle (1795—1881), Mathew Arnold (1822—1888), and John Ruskin (1819—1900).

English essays in the 19th century developed to its climax. The essayists with different styles further promoted the genre and made it an artistic classic with beautiful language, delicate structure and distinctive style.

English Essays in the 20th Century. During the 20th century the tradition of English essays had been inherited by some essayists who were skillful at writing the short and relaxed essays, for example, E. V. Lucas (1868—1938), Hilaire Belloc (1870—1953), G. K. Chesterton (1874—1936), Rob Lynd (1879—1949), Virginia Woolf (1882—1941), Aldous Huxley (1894—1963), and J. B. Priestley (1894—1984). On the other hand, the formal essay in the literary criticism also developed quickly. The notable essayists of this kind include A. N. Whitehead (1861—1947), Bertrand Russell (1872—1970), W. S. Maugham (1874—1965), A. S. Neil (1883—1973) and George Orwell (1903—1950). Although many essayists appeared and essay remained popular, it cannot be denied that the English essays had fallen unavoidably. This fact was even worsened by the two world wars, the high development of economy, and the appearance of radio and television.

English essays have developed through a long history with different forms and styles, but they share some common characteristics: short and lively to be more readable, didactic with direct or indirect intention, clear and brief in style, relaxed and humorous tone with personality expressed.

Chapter 2 Major Essayists

Francis Bacon(1561—1626)

Life. Francis Bacon, the youngest son of Sir Nicholas Bacon, Lord Keeper, was born at York House in the Strand on January 22, 1561. He was educated at Trinity College, Cambridge and Gray's Inn in London. It was at Trinity College that he first met the Queen, who was impressed by his precocious intellect, and was accustomed to call him "the young Lord Keeper". From 1577 to 1578 the young Bacon accompanied Sir Amias Paulet, the English ambassador, on his mission in Paris; but he returned when his father died. In 1584 he was elected to the House of Commons and he remained a Member of Parliament for thirty-seven years. With the ascension of James his political career rose quickly. Knighted in 1603, he was then steadily promoted to a series of offices, including Solicitor General (1607), Attorney General (1613), and eventually Lord Chancellor (1618). While serving as Chancellor, he was accused of bribery and sentenced to a fine of £40,000. In September 1621, he was remitted by the King but prohibited to be holding office or sitting in parliament. He then retired to his estate where he devoted himself full time to his continuing literary, scientific, and philosophical work. He died in London on April 9, 1626, leaving behind a cultural legacy.

Major Works. Bacon was a man with a wide range of knowledge. His works can be mainly divided into three types: philosophical, literary and professional.

The two best known of Bacon's philosophical works are *The Advancement of Learning* (1605) and *Novum Organum* (1620). *The Advancement of Learning* is a report on the deficiencies of learning in the 17th century along with possible approaches for overcoming them. It offers the first description of science as a tool to improve human condition and summarizes the accomplishments of science up to his time. Therefore, it is generally considered as the first philosophical work written in English. *Novum Organum* exerted great influence on the acceptance of accurate observation and experimentation in science. Bacon regarded himself as the inventor of a scientific method, induction, which involved the collection of data, judicious interpretation, the carrying out of experiments, thus to learn the secrets of nature by organized observation of its regularities. By advocating his inductive reasoning, Bacon reveals a fresh empirical attitude toward truth about nature.

Bacon's famous literary works are his collection of essays, *The Essays*, which is generally regarded as the first collection of essays as such in the English language. His essays, covering a variety of subjects such as love, truth, friendship, marriage, beauty, studies, garden, death, are characterized by formal and compact in style, clear and concise in expression, profound and forceful in thoughts, balanced and well-ordered in sentence structure.

His professional works include *Maxims of the Law* (1630) and *Reading on the Statute of Uses* (1642).

Literary Comments. Bacon, being an important English prose writer in the early 17th century, is a key figure in the transition from the intellectual world of the late Middle Ages to that of Modern Europe. Bacon, a representative of the Renaissance in England, is a well-known philosopher, scientist and essayist. He lays the foundation for modern science with his insistence on scientific way of thinking and fresh observation rather than authority as a source for knowledge. His *Essays* is the first example of that genre in English literature, which has been recognized as the important landmark in the development of English prose. Bacon recognized his unique position, calling himself "the trumpeter of a new age".

Charles Lamb(1775 —1834)

Life. Charles Lamb was born on February 10, 1775 in London in a family of lawyer's clerk. He was the youngest of the seven children, of whom only three survived into adulthood. Lamb went to school at Christ's Hospital, where began his lifelong friendship with Samuel Taylor Coleridge. Unfortunately, Lamb's family had a hereditary disease. At 20, Lamb suffered a period of insanity. His sister, Mary Ann Lamb, had similar problems and in 1796 attacked and wounded their father, stabbed and killed their mother in a fit of temporary madness. Mary was confined to an asylum but was eventually released into the care of her brother. In order to take care of Mary, Lamb never got married and they lived together after 1799. Mary was an intelligent and affectionate girl. She and her brother co-worked on several books for children, among which *Tales from Shakespeare* (1807) was the most famous. From 1792 to 1825, Lamb was a clerk in the accounting department of the East India Company in London, and he remained there till his retirement in 1825. At the same time he managed to contribute articles to journals and newspapers. Although burdened with terrible hereditary disease and life, he had an easy-going personality. He frequently gathered at his home a group of literary men, including Coleridge, William

Wordsworth, Robert Southey, and William Hazlitt. His generosity and good humor won him many friends. After his death on December 12th, 1834, Hazllit expressed Lamb was "the most delightful, the most provoking, the most witty and sensible of men". De Quincy summed up his feeling: Lamb was "the very noblest of human beings ... [he had] the habit of hoping cheerfully and kindly on behalf of those who were otherwise objects of moral blame" . Wordsworth wrote: "O, he was good, if e'er a good Man lived!" Mary Lamb survived her brother nearly thirteen years, dying at the ripe age of 82, in 1847; she was buried beside her brother in the churchyard of All Saint's Church, Edmonton.

Major Works. Lamb's works can also be categorized into three: the works of poetry, the works of literary criticism, and the works of essays.

His poetic works include his four sonnets contributed to *Coleridge's Poems on Various Subjects* (1796), a sentimental romance *A Tale of Rosamund Gray and Old Blind Margaret* (1798), *Blank verse* (1798), and *The King and Queen of Hearts* (children's verses 1805).

His first successful literary venture is generally regarded as *Tales from Shakespeare* (1807), a book retelling Shakespeare's tragedies and comedies intended to familiarize English children with Shakespeare's plays. His dramatic essays, *Specimens of English Dramatic Poets, Who Lived about the Time of Shakespeare* (1808), include selections from the plays of Elizabethan and Jacobean dramatists. Since many of the works and playwrights were previously unobtainable to the early nineteenth-century readers, Lamb's compilation became both an important reference source with supplemented explanatory notes and his most significant critical work. It was this work that laid the foundation of Lamb's reputation as a critic. At the same time, he played a considerable part in reviving the dramatic writers of the Elizabethan Age.

The establishment of Lamb's literary success was based upon his essays entitled *Essays of Elia* (1823) and *Last Essays of Elia* (1833) to the *London Magazine* from 1820 to 1825. They were written under the pseudonym narrator Elia, a fanciful and old-fashioned character with whimsical and eccentric qualities. Through the persona of "Elia", Lamb developed a highly personal narrative technique known as the familiar essay characterized by a relaxed style, conversational tone and diverse subjects. Lamb wrote about his personal reminiscences on his childhood, school days, family, about his whimsies and fantasies. The most popular examples include "Christ's Hospital", "Old Child", "Dissertation upon Roast Pig", "The Old Familiar Faces", "A Farewell to Tobacco", and "Dream Children".

Literary Comments. Charles Lamb is a well-known literary figure in the 19th-century England. He is entitled to a position as an essayist beside Francis Bacon, Richard Steele and Joseph Addison. So Lamb and Bacon are often compared. Bacon is the first to invent the literary genre in his *The Essays* in the English literature. His essays cover a variety of subjects concerning with nearly every aspect of life. They are marked by formal and compact in style, clear and concise in expression, profound and forceful in thoughts, balanced and well-ordered in sentence structure. These qualities have earned Bacon the father of the English essay. Lamb, in his famous *Essays of Elia*, developed a style peculiar to his own. The essays also cover a variety of subjects and maintain throughout an intimate, familiar and humorous tone. His close-knit, subtle organization, his self-revealing observations on life, his humor, fantasy, and pathos combine to make him one of the great masters of the English essay. Lamb, therefore, is regarded as the Shakespeare of the English essay.

William Hazlitt(1778 —1830)

Life. William Hazlitt, the son of an Irish Unitarian clergyman, was born in Maidstone, Kent, on 10th April, 1778. His mother was from an English dissenting family who were friendly with Godwin's family. Both Hazlitt's father and mother were enthusiastic supporters of the American Revolution. As a result, his family was forced to leave their hometown and live in Ireland. His family background had a deep influence on Hazlitt whose writings drew strongly on the culture of radical dissent between Britain and Ireland. In 1787, they returned to England. When Hazlitt was 15 years old, he was trained for the ministry in London at New Unitarian College at Hackney, which had a reputation for producing free thinkers. Four years later, his interest in being a Unitarian minister completely lost and thus he left college. In 1799, he took up the study of painting, and he did not give up the dream of becoming a painter until 1812. While in London Hazlitt got acquainted with a group of writers with radical political ideas, including William Wordsworth, Samuel Taylor Coleridge, Charles Lamb, Thomas Barnes, Henry Brougham, Leigh Hunt, Robert Southey, Mary Wollstonecraft, Percy Bysshe Shelley, Lord Byron, and William Godwin. He hated monarchy, despised aristocracy, and made his prose sing of liberty. Hazlitt never wavered in his commitment to the values of the French Revolution and remained always an impoverished member of the radical intelligentsia. He acted as parliamentary reporter and drama critic for the London *Morning Chronicle* and later a frequent contributor to Leigh Hunt's *Examiner*, the *Edinburgh Review*, the *London Magazine*, and the *New Monthly*. Hazlitt died in poverty of stomach cancer on 18th September 1830.

Hazlitt's life and career had been greatly influenced by the rise and fall of the French Revolution. After the defeat of Napoleon, Hazlitt was the only old Romantic who never wavered in his devotion to the Revolution. All his life, he remained loyal to the principles of liberty, equality, and fraternity. For this reason he estranged himself from most of his former friends.

Major Works. His major collections of essays include: *An Essay on the Principles of*

Human Action (1805), *Free Thoughts on Public Affairs* (1806), *The Round Table* (1817), *Political Essays with Sketches of Public Characters*(1819), *Table Talk* (1821—1822), *The Spirit of the Age: Contemporary Portraits* (1825), and *The Plain Speaker* (1826). His penetrating literary criticism is collected in *Characters of Shakespeare's Plays* (1817), *Lectures on the English Poets* (1818), *Lectures on the English Comic Writers* (1819), and *Dramatic Literature of the Age of Elizabeth* (1820). His most notable single essays include "On Going a Journey," "My First Acquaintance with Poets", "On the Feeling of Immortality in Youth", and "Going to a Fight".

Literary Comments. Hazlitt, best remembered for his humanistic essays and literary criticism, is one of the great masters of the miscellaneous essays, displaying a keen intellect, sensibility, and wide scope of interest and knowledge. He is one of the great masters of a lucid and confident prose style, which make many of his essays like conversation poems—witty, profound and fresh. His radical essays are written in a fast, hard-hitting prose being aptly called "literary-colloquial English": it gives the effect of good talk but heightened. No study of the Romantic Movement can be complete without reading his essays. For too long he has been regarded as a marginal figure, instead of being seen as the supreme genius of Romantic prose.

Hazlitt is distinguished from Charles Lamb in several aspects. Firstly, in political attitude, Lamb is more mild and neutral while Hazlitt more radical and persistent; secondly, in personality, Lamb is a kind man with generosity while Hazlitt a bitter man difficult to get along with; lastly, in language style, Lamb likes to play with words, while Hazlitt prefers to use a fast, hard-hitting prose.

Thomas De Quincy(1785—1859)

Life. Thomas De Quincy was born in Manchester on 15 August 1785, the second son and fifth of eight children born to a successful and wealthy linen merchant, Thomas Quincy, a man of literary tastes. At the age of fifteen, he was sent to Manchester Grammar School. But 18 months later he ran away from it wandering in Wales and returned to London finally. After his reconciliation with his family he went to Oxford, where he was a very solitary student who read widely and absorbed the Classics readily. During this period he began taking opium to relieve his toothache. Because he was not satisfied with the pressure of examination, he left the school without taking a degree. In 1807 he got to know Coleridge through whom he met Wordsworth. Then he made a decision to spend the rest of his life in the Lake Country near Wordsworth and Coleridge. He died on 8 December 1859 and was buried in the West Church-yard of Edinburgh with his wife.

Major Works. In order to earn his living, De Quincy was obliged to take up writing.

His literary career really started with writings mainly for journals and magazines at the age of 36. His reputation rested upon *Confessions of an English Opium Eater* (1822), *Blackwood's* (1826), including his famous essay, "Murder Considered as One of the Fine Arts".

Literary Comments. De Quincey, a versatile essayist and accomplished literary critic, is recognized as one of the foremost prose writers of the Romantic Age. Compared with Charles Lamb, De Quincey's essays are marked by an acute psychological awareness, which put him within the realm of modernity. His ornate, clear and precise style owes much to his vivid imagination and subjective desire to recreate his own intense personal experiences. Charles Lamb's essays are marked by genuine love and profound nostalgia for the past time and fancied world. His familiar essays cover a wide range of subjects, even including the most trivial things in daily life.

Mathew Arnold(1822 —1888)

Life. Mathew Arnold was born on 24 December 1822. His father Thomas Arnold was a historian and great headmaster of Rugby. After graduating from Oxford, Arnold became an inspector of schools and remained in this position for 35 years. He died of a sudden heart attack on 15 April 1888.

Major Works. Arnold was both a poet and literary critic. His literary career began in 1849 with the publication of *The Strayed Reveller and Other Poems*. Many of his poetic works express a tone of regret, disillusion and melancholy. Comparing to his essays, his output of poems is relatively small. Now the best remembered and anthologized is his *Dover Beech*.

Arnold started his career as a critic with the *Preface to the Poems* being issued in 1853. But the bulk of his literary criticism appeared after 1860, among which the most influential include *Essays in Criticism* (1865), *Essays in Criticism: Second Series* (1888), *Culture and Anarchy* (1889). The majority of his prose works deal with, practically, the entire fabric of English civilization and culture in his day; and they are all directed by one clear and consistent critical purpose, i. e. to "cure the great vice of our intellect, manifesting itself in our incredible vagaries in literature, in art, in religion, in morals; namely, that it is *fantastic*, and wants *sanity*".

In *Essays in Criticism* (1865 and 1888) Arnold points out the social function and responsibility of an artist. He observes that literary criticism is not only a simple book reviewing, instead it is "a disinterested endeavor to learn and propagate the best that is known and thought in the world, and thus to established a current of fresh and true ideas". Therefore, the responsibility of a literary critic is to make the public "see the object as in itself it really is".

In *Culture and Anarchy*, Arnold thinks that English society of his time was composed of "barbarians, philistines and populace". To Arnold, barbarians refer to the aristocratic class, whom he thought to be essentially crude in soul in spite of their good clothes and superficial graces; philistines refer to the middle class, whom he regarded as narrow-minded and self-conceited; Populace refer to the lower class, whom he dismissed as an ineffectual, inchoate mass. Both barbarians and philistines are opposed to "sweetness and light", a phrase (borrowed from Jonathan Swift) suggesting reasonableness of temper and intellectual insight. Arnold argues that as the middle class gradually assumed control of English politics, they must be transformed from their unpolished state into a sensitive, sophisticated, intellectual community. He hopes to see a society "permeated by though, sensible to beauty, intelligent and alive". He asserts "knowledge and truth, in the full sense of the words, are not attainable by the great mass of the human race at all". To Arnold, culture includes the political, social and religious aspects of life. It is culture not class struggle or violent revolution that can effectively cure the ills of English society. Obviously he places hopes on moral education and open-mindedness.

Literary Comments. Arnold's integration of social criticism and literary analysis is accepted now by critics as his most significant and lasting achievement. His writings can be regarded as the representation of tensions of modern literature, particularly his remarks on aesthetic judgment, and his attempts to formulate a theory of the role of criticism in culture. As a prose writer, Arnold is distinguished by his clear and polished style, by his sober and scientific spirit, by his enlivened and forceful humor. He is gifted at inventing memorable phrases to add attraction to his thought and concept. He becomes a significant figure in the intellectual field of the 19th century England.

John Ruskin(1819 —1900)

Life. John Ruskin was born in London on 8 February 1819 in a wealthy, cultured and religious family. At the age of 17, he was educated at the University of Oxford, where he was awarded a prize for poetry. His evangelical parents prepared their son for the ministry. It was his stay at Oxford (1836—1840) that resulted in his determining not to enter the ministry. But his mother's over protectiveness undoubtedly contributed to his later psychological breakdown. The following two years he traveled in Europe, studying nature, painting and architecture. During these trips, Ruskin formed his own aesthetic thought and gained materials for his book *Modern Painters*. After 1960, Ruskin turned his attention to social problems, and his literary career witnessed a transition from art criticism to social criticism. He lectured to workers and wrote articles on social reforms. Upon the death of his father (who was a wealthy wine merchant), Ruskin declared that it was not possible to be a rich socialist and gave away most of his inheritance to educational organizations. Ruskin became a great friend of his contemporary writers such as Rossetti, Burne-Jones and Millais. In his later years, he suffered further attacks of madness. On 20 January 1900 Ruskin died at Brantwood of influenza, and was buried in the churchyard of St Andrew's Church in Coniston.

Major Works. Ruskin's major works of art criticism are *Modern Painters* (5 volumes, 1843—60), *The Seven Lamps Of Architecture* (1849), *The Stones Of Venice* (1851), *Sesame and Lillies* (1865), *The Crown Of Wild Olives* (1866), and *Fors Clavigera* (1871—74). Throughout his works, he expounds that the main purpose of art is not to delight a few cultured people but to serve the practical ends of people's daily life. The object of art is to find and express the truth in nature, and art, in order to express the truth, must copy nature and abandon the old conventions and set rules. He states that art is allied with morality, and there exists a close relation between goodness and wickedness, beauty and ugliness. He feels that the imperfections of modern art are closely related to the ugliness of modern capitalist civilization. Ruskin's social criticism provoked a great stir among the ruling class in England.

Literary Comments. Ruskin was one of the greatest figures of the Victorian age, poet, artist, environmentalist, philosopher, social theorist, and, importantly here, the pre-eminent art critic of his time. His view on art was influential but not difficult to understand. Ruskin's transformation to social criticism caused a change in his style from gorgeous and rhythmical to simple and eloquent.

Thomas Henry Huxley(1825—1895)

Life. Thomas Henry Huxley was born near London on May 4, 1825, the seventh of eight children in his family. Due to the family financial embarrassment, Huxley received no formal education, but he read voraciously in science, history, and philosophy, and taught himself German. When he was 15, he began a medical apprenticeship; soon he won a scholarship to study at Charing Cross Hospital. At the age of 21, Huxley signed on as assistant surgeon on the H. M. S. *Rattlesnake*, a Royal Navy frigate assigned to chart the seas around Australia and New Guinea. This experience provided him with rich materials. After coming back to England in October 1850, he found that his research results, which he had mailed back to England from each port, had won him acceptance into the ranks of the English scientific establishment.

Major Works. Huxley was an outspoken defender and the principal exponent of Darwinism in England. His major works include *Evidence as to Man's Place in Nature* (1863), *Evolution and Ethics* (1893), *Collected Essays* (9 vol., 1893—1894), *Scientific Memoirs* (4 vol., 1898—1902), and an autobiography (1903).

Evidence on Man's Place in Nature, published only five years after Darwin's *Origin of Species*, was a comprehensive review of what was known at the time about primate and human paleontology and ethology. More than that, it was the first attempt to apply evolution explicitly to the human race.

Huxley later invented the term "agnosticism". In 1889 he explained: "Agnosticism is not a creed but a method, the essence of which lies in the vigorous application of a single principle ... Positively the principle may be expressed as in matters of intellect, do not pretend conclusions are certain that are not demonstrated or demonstrable." His views on religion, education, philosophy, and on man's newly conceived place in nature had a deep and great influence on his contemporaries.

Literary Comments. Huxley, an English biologist and educator, is a man of astonishing energy and prodigious talent. He had a sharp wit and a brilliant, questioning mind. Because of his lucid and popular lectures, he was warmly accepted by his audience.

Chapter 3 Selected Essays

Francis Bacon
Of Studies

Studies serve for delight[1], for ornament, and for ability. Their chief use for delight, is in privateness and retiring[2]; for ornament, is in discourse; and for ability, is in the judgment, and disposition of business; for expert men can execute, and perhaps judge of particulars, one by one; but the general counsels, and the plots and marshalling of affairs[3] come best from those that are learned. To spend too much time in studies, is sloth[4]; to use them too much for ornament, is affectation; to make judgment wholly by their rules, is the humor of a scholar. They perfect nature, and are perfected by experience: for natural abilities are like natural plants, that need pruning[5] by study; and studies themselves do give forth directions too much at large, except they be bounded in by experience. Crafty men[6] contemn[7] studies, simple men admire them, and wise men use them, for they teach not their own use; but that is a wisdom without them, and above them, won by observation. Read not to contradict and confute, nor to believe and take for granted, nor to find talk and discourse, but to weigh and consider. Some books are to be tasted, others to be swallowed, and some few to be chewed and digested; that is, some books are to be read only in parts; others to be read but not curiously; and some few to be read wholly, and with diligence and attention. Some books also may be read by deputy[8], and extracts made of them by others; but that would be only in the less important arguments and the meaner sort of books; else distilled books are like common distilled waters, flashy things[9]. Reading maketh a full man; conference[10] a ready man; and writing an exact man; and therefore, if a man write little, he had need have[11] a great memory; if he confer[12] little, he had need have a present wit[13]; and if he read little, he had need have much cunning, to seem to know that he doth not[14]. Histories make men wise; poets, witty; the mathematics, subtile[15]; natural philosophy, deep; moral[16], grave; logic and rhetoric, able to contend. *Abeunt studia in mores*[17]; nay, there is no stond[18] or impediment in the wit[19], but may be wrought out[20] by fit studies; like as[21] diseases of the body may have appropriate exercises; bowling is good for the stone and reins[22], shooting for the lungs and breast, gentle walking for the stomach, riding for the head, and the like. So if a man's wit be wandering, let him study the mathematics; for in demonstrations, if his wit be called away never so little[23], he must begin again; if his wit be not apt to distinguish or find differences, let him study the school men[24]; for they are *cumini sectores*[25]. If he be not apt to beat over matters, and to call up one thing to prove and illustrate another, let him study the lawyers' cases: so every defect of the mind may have a special receipt[26].

Notes

1. delight—personal satisfaction.
2. in privateness and retiring—in privacy and retirement.
3. the plots and marshalling of affairs—the plans and arrangement of affairs.
4. sloth—laziness; idleness.
5. pruning—cultivation; trim.
6. Crafty men—man of skill.
7. contemn—despise.
8. be read by deputy—read with the assistance of others.
9. flashy—brilliant but empty or meaningless.
10. conference—conversation.
11. had need have—would need to have.
12. confer—converse.
13. present wit—ready wit.
14. that he doth not—that he does not.
15. subtile—This is the old spelling for "subtle", which means to be able to distinguish.
16. moral—moral philosophy.
17. *Abeunt studia in mores*—This line is taken from Heroides written by Ovid, meaning "Studies translate themselves into character".
18. stond—obstacle.
19. in the wit—in the mind.
20. wrought out—eliminate.
21. like as—as.
22. the stone and reins—testicles and kidneys.

23. never so little —ever so little; no matter how little.
24. the school men—scholastic scholars, who cling to the method or subtleties of the Medieval schools.
25. *cumini sectores*—(Latin) splitters of cumin seeds; hair-splitters.
26. receipt—recipe; prescription.

For Study and Discussion

1. What are the three functions of study?
2. What is the writer's purpose in writing this essay?
3. Please try to memorize the following sentences:
   1) Studies serve for delight, for ornament, and for ability.
   2) Some books are to be tasted, others to be swallowed, and some few to be chewed and digested.
   3) Reading maketh a full man; conference a ready man; and writing an exact man.
   4) Histories make men wise; poets, witty; the mathematics, subtile; natural philosophy, deep; moral, grave; logic and rhetoric, able to contend.

Charles Lamb
Dream Children: A Reverie

Children love to listen to stories about their elders, when they were children; to stretch their imagination to the conception of a traditionary great-uncle or grandame[1], whom they never saw. It was in this spirit that my little ones[2] crept about me the other evening to hear about their great-grandmother Field[3], who lived in a great house in Norfolk[4] (a hundred times bigger than that in which they and papa lived) which had been the scene—so at least it was generally believed in that part of the country—of the tragic incidents which they had lately become familiar with from the ballad of the Children in the Wood[5]. Certain it is that the whole story of the children and their cruel uncle was to be seen fairly carved out in wood upon the chimney-piece of the great hall, the whole story down to the Robin Redbreasts[6], till a foolish rich person pulled it down to set up a marble one of modern invention in its stead, with no story upon it. Here Alice[7] put out one of her dear mother's looks, too tender to be called upbraiding. Then I went on to say, how religious and how good their great-grandmother Field was, how beloved and respected by everybody, though she was not indeed the mistress of this great house, but had only the charge of it (and yet in some respects she might be said to be the mistress of it too) committed to her by the owner, who preferred living in a newer and more fashionable mansion which he had purchased somewhere in the adjoining county; but still she lived in it in a manner as if it had been her own, and kept up the dignity of the great house in a sort while she lived, which afterward came to decay, and was nearly pulled down, and all its old ornaments stripped and carried away to the owner's other house, where they were set up, and looked as awkward as if some one were to carry away the old tombs they had seen lately at the Abbey[8], and stick them up in Lady C.'s tawdry gilt drawing-room. Here John[9] smiled, as much as to say, "that would be foolish indeed." And then I told how, when she came to die, her funeral was attended by a concourse of all the poor, and some of the gentry too, of the neighborhood for many miles round, to show their respect for her memory, because she had been such a good and religious woman; so good indeed that she knew all the Psaltery[10] by heart, aye, and a great part of the Testament besides. Here little Alice spread her hands[11]. Then I told what a tall, upright, graceful person their great-grandmother Field once was; and how in her youth she was esteemed the best dancer—here Alice's little right foot played an involuntary movement, till upon my looking grave, it desisted—the best dancer, I was saying, in the county, till a cruel disease, called a cancer, came, and bowed her down with pain; but it could never bend her good spirits, or make them stoop, but they were still upright, because she was so good and religious. Then I told how she was used to sleep by herself in a lone chamber of the great lone house; and how she believed that an apparition of two infants[12] was to be seen at midnight gliding up and down the great staircase near where she slept, but she said "those innocents would do her no harm"; and how frightened I used to be, though in those days I had my maid to sleep with me, because I was never half so good or religious as she—and yet I never saw the infants. Here John expanded all his eyebrows and tried to look courageous. Then I told how good she was to all her grand-children, having us to the great house in the holidays, where I in particular used to spend many hours by myself, in gazing upon the old busts of the Twelve Cæsars[13], that had been Emperors of Rome, till the old marble heads would seem to live again, or I to be turned into marble with them; how I never could be tired with roaming about that huge mansion, with its vast empty rooms, with their worn-out hangings, fluttering tapestry, and carved oaken panels, with the gilding almost rubbed out—sometimes in the spacious old-fashioned gardens, which I had almost to myself, unless[14] when now and then a solitary gardening man would cross me—and how the nectarines and peaches hung upon the walls, without my ever offering to pluck them, because they were forbidden fruit, unless now and then,—and because I had more pleasure in strolling about among the old melancholy-looking yew trees, or the firs, and picking up the red berries, and the fir apples, which were good for nothing but to look at—or in lying about upon the fresh grass, with all the fine garden smells around me—or basking in the orangery, till I could almost fancy myself ripening, too, along with the oranges and the limes in that grateful warmth—or in watching the dace that darted to and fro in the fish pond, at the bottom of the garden, with here and there a great sulky pike hanging midway down the water in silent state, as if it mocked at their impertinent friskings,—I had more pleasure in these busy-idle diversions than in all the sweet flavors of peaches, nectarines, oranges, and such like common baits of children. Here John slyly deposited back upon the plate a bunch of grapes, which, not unobserved by Alice, he had mediated dividing with her, and both seemed willing to relinquish them for the present as irrelevant. Then, in somewhat a more heightened tone, I told how, though their great-grandmother Field loved all her grand-children, yet in an especial manner she might be said to love their uncle, John L-[15], because he was so handsome and spirited a youth, and a king to the rest of us; and, instead of moping about[16] in solitary corners, like some of us, he would mount the most mettlesome horse he could get, when but an imp no bigger than themselves, and make it carry him half over the county in a morning, and join the hunters when there were any out—and yet he loved the old great house and gardens too, but had too much spirit to be always pent up within their boundaries —and how their uncle grew up to man's estate as brave as he was handsome, to the admiration of everybody, but of their great-grandmother Field most especially; and how he used to carry me upon his back when I was a lame-footed boy—for he was a good bit older than me—many a mile when I could not walk for pain; and how in after life[17] he became lame-footed too, and I did not always (I fear) make allowances enough for him when he was impatient, and in pain, nor remember sufficiently how considerate he had been to me when I was lame-footed; and how when he died, though he had not been dead an hour, it seemed as if he had died a great while ago, such a distance there is betwixt life and death; and how I bore his death as I thought pretty well at first, but afterward it haunted and haunted me; and though I did not cry or take it to heart as some do, and as I think he would have done if I had died, yet I missed him all day long, and knew not till then how much I had loved him. I missed his kindness, and I missed his crossness, and wished him to be alive again, to be quarreling with him (for we quarreled sometimes), rather than not have him again, and was as uneasy without him, as he their poor uncle must have been when the doctor took off his limb. Here the children fell a crying, and asked if their little mourning which they had on was not for uncle John, and they looked up and prayed me not to go on about their uncle, but to tell them some stories about their pretty dead mother. Then I told them how for seven long years, in hope sometimes, sometimes in despair, yet persisting ever, I courted the fair Alice W—n[18]; and, as much as children could understand, I explained to them what coyness, and difficulty, and denial meant in maidens when suddenly, turning to Alice, the soul of the first Alice looked out at her eyes with such a reality of re-presentment, that I became in doubt which of them stood there before me, or whose that bright hair was; and while I stood gazing, both the children gradually grew fainter to my view, receding, and still receding till nothing at last but two mournful features were seen in the uttermost distance, which, without speech, strangely impressed upon me the effects of speech: "We are not of Alice, nor of thee, nor are we children at all. The children of Alice call Bartrum father. We are nothing; less than nothing, and dreams. We are only what might have been, and must wait upon the tedious shores of Lethe[19] millions of ages before we have existence, and a name"—and immediately awaking, I found myself quietly seated in my bachelor armchair, where I had fallen asleep, with the faithful Bridget[20] unchanged by my side—but John L. (or James Elia[21]) was gone forever.

Notes

1. grandame—grandmother.
2. my little ones—Lamb's dream children.
3. Field—Lamb's grandmother, Mary Field, who was a house keeper for more than fifty years at Blakesware in Hertfordshire, the seat of the Plumers.
4. Norfolk—Blakesware is meant here.
5. the ballad of the Children in the Wood—This is a popular ballad given in Bishop Percy's *Reliques*, a story about the little brother and sister, who were left with a considerable fortune in the care of an uncle. He, in order to secure the property, hired two men to murder the children. But one of them relented and killed his companion and then committed suicide. The little ones were, however, left in the wood, where they perished at night of cold and terror.
6. to the Robin Redbreasts—the robins which at the end of the ballad covered the bodies of the children with leaves.
7. Alice—Lamb's dream daughter.
8. the Abbey—referrin to the West Minster Abbey.
9. John—Lamb's dream son.
10. Psaltery—the Book of Psalms.
11. spread her hands—a gesture showing her surprise.
12. an apparition of two infants—There was a legend in the Plumer family about the mysterious disappearance of two children in the 17th century.
13. the old busts of the Twelve Cæsars—These were among the things removed by Mr. Plumer from Blakesware.
14. unless—excerpt.
15. John L—John Lamb, brother of Charles, who died in October, 1821.
16. moping about—going about aimlessly and listlessly.
17. in after life—in the latter part of life.
18. Alice W—n—Alice Winterton in Lamb's key, but it is a feigned name, it probably refers to Ann Simmons, who was the sweetheart of Lamb in his boyhood. She later got married to William Bartrum, a London pawnbroker; and thus "the children of Alice call Bartrum father".
19. Lethe—In Greek mythology, Lethe is one of the several rivers that flow through the realm of Hades: those who drank from it experienced complete forgetfulness of their past lives on earth.
20. Bridget—the name given by Lamb to his sister in *My Relations*.

21. James Elia—the name given by Lamb to his brother in *My Relations*.

For Study and Discussion

1. What is the tone of the writer in this essay?
2. Charles Lamb, in this essay, repeats the sentence "Then I told" with some variations several times. What is Lamb's intention in his deliberate use of this repetition?
3. Try to recite the final part of the essay:

   when suddenly, turning to Alice, the soul of the first Alice looked out at her eyes with such a reality of re-presentment, that I became in doubt which of them stood there before me, or whose that bright hair was; and while I stood gazing, both the children gradually grew fainter to my view, receding, and still receding till nothing at last but two mournful features were seen in the uttermost distance, which, without speech, strangely impressed upon me the effects of speech: "We are not of Alice, nor of thee, nor are we children at all. The children of Alice call Bartrum father. We are nothing; less than nothing, and dreams. We are only what might have been, and must wait upon the tedious shores of Lethe millions of ages before we have existence, and a name"—and immediately awaking, I found myself quietly seated in my bachelor armchair, where I had fallen asleep, with the faithful Bridget unchanged by my side—but John L. (or James Elia) was gone forever.

William Hazlitt
On Familiar Style[1]

It is not easy to write a familiar style. Many people mistake a familiar for a vulgar style, and suppose that to write without affectation is to write at random. On the contrary, there is nothing that requires more precision, and, if I may so say, purity of expression, than the style I am speaking of. It utterly rejects not only all unmeaning pomp[2], but all low, cant phrases[3], and loose, unconnected, slipshod allusions[4]. It is not to take the first word that offers[5], but the best word in common use; it is not to throw words together in any combinations we please, but to follow and avail ourselves of the true idiom of the language. To write a genuine familiar or truly English style, is to write as any one would speak in common conversation who had a thorough command and choice of words, or who could discourse with ease, force, and perspicuity[6], setting aside all pedantic and oratorical flourishes. Or, to give another illustration, to write naturally is the same thing in regard to common conversation as to read naturally is in regard to common speech. It does not follow that it is an easy thing to give the true accent and inflexion to the words you utter, because you do not attempt to rise above the level of ordinary life and colloquial speaking. You do not assume, indeed, the solemnity of the pulpit, or the tone of stage declamation; neither are you at liberty to gabble on at a venture[7], without emphasis or discretion, or to resort to a vulgar dialect or clownish pronunciation. You must steer a middle course. You are tied down to a given and appropriate articulation, which is determined by the habitual associations between sense and sound, and which you can only hit by entering into the author's meaning, as you must find the proper words and style to express yourself by fixing your thoughts on the subject you have to write about. Any one may mouth out a passage with a theatrical cadence, or get upon stilts[8] to tell his thoughts; but to write or speak with propriety and simplicity is a more difficult task. Thus it is easy to affect a pompous style, to use a word twice as big as the thing you want to express: it is not so easy to pitch upon the very word that exactly fits it. Out of eight or ten words equally common, equally intelligible, with nearly equal pretensions, it is a matter of some nicety and discrimination to pick out the very one the preferableness of which is scarcely perceptible but decisive. The reason why I object to Dr. Johnson's style is that there is no discrimination, no selection, no variety in it. He uses none but "tall, opaque words," taken from the "first row of the rubric"—words with the greatest number of syllables, or Latin phrases with merely English terminations. If a fine style depended on this sort of arbitrary pretension, it would be fair to judge of an author's elegance by the measurement of his words and the substitution of foreign circumlocutions (with no precise associations) for the mother-tongue. How simple is it to be dignified without ease, to be pompous without meaning! Surely, it is but a mechanical rule for avoiding what is low, to be always pedantic and affected. It is clear you cannot use a vulgar English word if you never use a common English word at all. A fine fact is shown in adhering to those which are perfectly common, and yet never falling into any expressions which are debased by disgusting circumstances, or which owe their signification and point to technical or professional allusions. A truly natural or familiar style can never be quaint or vulgar, for this reason, that it is of universal force and applicability, and that quaintness and vulgarity arise out of the immediate connection of certain words with coarse and disagreeable, or with confined ideas. The last form what we understand by *cant* or *slang* phrases. —To give an example of what is not very clear in the general statement. I should say that the phrase *To cut with a knife, or To cut a piece of wood*, is perfectly free from vulgarity, because it is perfectly common; but to *cut an acquaintance* is not quite unexceptionable, because it is not perfectly common or intelligible, and has hardly yet escaped out of the limits of slang phraseology. I should hardly, therefore, use the word in this sense without putting it in italics as a license of expression, to be received *com grano salis*[9]. All provincial or bye-phrases come under the same mark of reprobation —all such as the writer transfers to the page from his fireside or a particular *coterie*[10], or that he invents for his own sole use and convenience. I conceive that words are like money, not the worse for being common, but that it is the stamp of custom alone that gives them circulation or value. I am fastidious in this respect, and would almost as soon coin the currency of the realm as counterfeit the King's English[11]. I never invented or gave a new and unauthorized meaning to any words but one single one (the term *impersonal* applied to feelings), and that was in an abstruse metaphysical discussion to express a very difficult distinction. I have been (I know) loudly accused of reveling in vulgarisms and broken English. I cannot speak to that point; but so far I plead guilty to the determined use of acknowledged idioms and common elliptical expressions. I am not sure that the critics in question know the one from the other, that is can distinguish any medium between formal pedantry and the most barbarous solecism[12]. As an author I endeavour to employ plain words and popular modes of construction, as, were I a chapman and dealer, I should common weights and measures.

The proper force of words lies not in the words themselves, but in their application. A word may be a find-sounding word, of an unusual length, and a very imposing from its learning and novelty, and yet in the connecxion in which it is introduced may be quite pointless and irrelevant. It is not pomp or pretension, but the adaptation of the expression to the idea, that clinches a writer's meaning[13]:—as it is not the size of glossiness of the materials, but their being fitted each to its place, that gives strength to the arch; or as the pegs and nails are as necessary to the support of the building as the larger timber, and more so than the mere showy, unsubstantial ornaments[14]. I hate anything that occupies more space than it is worth. I hate to see a load of band-boxes[15] go along the street, and I hate to see a parcel of big words without anything in them. A person who does not deliberately dispose of all his thoughts alike in cumbrous draperies and flimsy disguises, may strike out twenty varieties of familiar every-day language, each coming somewhat nearer to the feeling he wants to convey, and at last not hit upon that particular and only one which may be said to be identical with the exact impression in his mind. This would seem to show that Mr Cobbet[16] is hardly right in saying that the first word that occurs is always the best. It may be a very good one; and yet a better may present itself on reflection or from time to time. It should be suggested naturally, however, and spontaneously, from a fresh and lively conception of the subject. We seldom succeed by trying at improvement, or by merely substituting one word for another that we are not satisfied with, as we cannot recollect the name of a place or person by merely plaguing ourselves about it. We wander farther form the point by persisting in a wrong scent[17]; but it start up accidentally in the memory when we least expect it, by touching some link in the chain of previous association.

There are those who hoard up and make a cautious display of nothing but rich and rare phraseology—ancient medals, obscure coins, and Spanish pieces of eight[18]. They are very curious to inspect, but I myself would neither offer not take them in the course of exchange. A sprinkling of archaisms is not amiss, but a tissue of obsolete expressions is more fit *for keep than wear*. I do not say I would not use any phrase that had been brought into fashion before the middle or the end of the last century, but I should be shy of using any that had not been employed by any approved author during the whole of that time. Words, like clothes, get old-fashioned, or mean and ridiculous, when they have been for some time laid aside. Mr. Lamb[19] is the only imitator of old English style I can read with pleasure; and he is so thoroughly imbued with the spirit of his authors that the idea of imitation is almost done away. There is an inward unction, a marrowy vein, both in the thought and feeling, an intuition, deep and lively, of his subject, that carries off any quaintness or awkwardness arising from an antiquated style and dress. The matter is completely his own, though the manner is assumed. Perhaps his ideas are altogether so marked and individual as to require their point and pungency to be neutralised by the affectation of a singular but traditional form of conveyance. Tricked out in the prevailing costume, they would probably seem more startling and out of the way. The old English authors, Burton[20], Fuller[21], Coryate [22], Sir Thomas Browne [23], are a kind of mediators between us and the more eccentric and whimsical modern, reconciling us to his peculiarities. I do not, however, know how far this is the case or not, till he condescends to write like one of us. I must confess that what I like best of his papers under the signature of Elia[24] (still I do no presume amidst such excellence, to decide what is most excellent) is the account of "Mrs Battle's Opinions on Whist[25]," which is also the most free from obsolete allusions and turns of expression —

A well of native English undefiled[26]

To those acquainted with his admired prototypes, these *Essays* of the ingenious and highly gifted author have the same sort of charm and relish that Erasmus's *Colloquies*[27] or a fine piece of modern Latin have to the classical scholar. Certainly, I do not know any borrowed pencil[28] that has more power or felicity of execution than the one of which I have here been speaking.

It is as easy to write a gaudy style without ideas as it is to spread a pallet of showy colours or to smear in a flaunting transparency. "What do you read?" "Words, words, words."—"What is the matter?" "Nothing," it might be answered. The florid style is the reverse of the familiar. The last is employed as an unvarnished medium to convey ideas; the first is resorted to as a spangled veil to conceal the want of[29] them. When there is nothing to be set down but words, it costs little to have them fine. Look through the dictionary and cull out a *florilegium*, rival the *tulippomania*. Rouge high enough, and never mind the natural complexion. The vulgar, who are not in the secret, will admire the look of preternatural health and vigour; and the fashionable, who regard only appearances, will be delighted with the imposition. Keep to your sounding generalities, your tinkling phrases, and all will be well. Swell out an unmeaning truism to a perfect tympany[30] of style. A thought, a distinction is the rock on which all this brittle cargo of verbiage splits at once. Such writers have merely *verbal* imaginations, that retain nothing but words. Or their puny thoughts have dragon-wings, all green and gold. They soar far above the vulgar failing of the *Sermo humi obrepens*[31]—their most ordinary speech is never short of an hyperbole, splendid, imposing, vague, incomprehensible, magniloquent[32], a cento of sounding common-places. If some of us, whose "ambition is more lowly," pry a little too narrowly into nooks and corners to pick up a number of "unconsidered trifles," they never once direct their eyes or lift their hands to seize on any but the most gorgeous, tarnished, threadbare, patchwork set of phrases, the left-off finery of poetic extravagance, transmitted down through successive generations of barren pretenders. If they criticize actor and actresses, a huddled phantasmagoria[33] of feathers, spangles, floods of light, and oceans of sounds float before their morbid sense, which they paint in the style of Ancient Pistol[34]. Not a glimpse can you get of the merits of defects of the performers: they are hidden in a profusion of barbarous epithets and wilful rhodomontade[35]. Our hypercritics are not thinking of these little fantoccini[36] beings—

That strut and fret their hour upon the stage[37]—

but of tall phantoms of words, abstractions, genera and species, sweeping clauses, periods that unite the Poles, forced alliterations, astounding antitheses—

And on their pens Fustian sits plumed

If they describe kings and queens, it is an Eastern pageant. The Coronation at either House is nothing to it[38]. We get at four repeated images—, a curtain, a throne, a sceptre, and a footstool. These are with them the wardrobe of a lofty imagination; and they turn their servile strains to servile uses. Do we read a description of pictures? It is not a reflection of tones and hues which "nature's own sweet and cunning hand laid on," put piles of precious stones, rubies, pearls, emeralds, Golconda's[39] mines, and all the blazonry of art. Such persons are in fact besotted with words, and their brains are turned with the glittering but empty and sterile phantoms of things. Personifications, capital letters, seas of sunbeams, visions of glory, shining inscriptions the figures of a transparency, Britannia with her shield[40], or Hope[41] leaning on an anchor, make up their stock-in-trade. They may be considered *hieroglyphical*[42] writers. Images stands out in their minds isolated and important merely in themselves, without any ground-work of feeling—there is no context in their imaginations. Words affect them in the same way, by the mere sound, that is, by their possible, not by their actual application to the subject in hand. They are fascinated by first appearances, and have no sense of consequences. Nothing more is meant by them than meets the ear: they understand or feel nothing more than meet their eye. The web and texture of the universe, and of the heart of man, is a mystery to them: they have no faculty that strikes a chord in unison with it. They cannot get beyond the daubings of fancy, the varnish of sentiment. Objects are not linked to feelings, words to things, but images revolve in splendid mockery, words represent themselves in their strange rhapsodies[43]. The categories of such a mind are pride and ignorance—pride in outside show, to which they sacrifice everything, and ignorance of the true worth and hidden structure both of words and things. With a sovereign contempt for what is familiar and natural, they are the slaves of vulgar affectation—of a routine of high-flown phrases. Scorning to imitate realities, they are unable to invent anything, to strike out one original idea. They are not copyists of nature, it is true; but they are the poorest of all plagiarists, the plagiarists of words. All is far-fetched, dear bought, artificial, oriental in subject and allusion; all is mechanical, conventional, vapid, formal, pedantic in style and execution. They startle and confound the understanding of the reader by the remoteness and obscurity to their illustrations; they sooth the ear by the monotony of the same everlasting round of circuitous metaphors. They are the *mock-school* in poetry and prose. They flounder about between fustian in expression and bathos in sentiment. They tantalize the fancy, but never reach the head nor touch the heart. Their Temple of Fame is like a shadow structure raised by Dulness to Vanity, or like Cowper's[44] description of the Empress of Russia's palace of ice, "as worthless as in show 'twas glittering"—

"It smiled, and it was cold!"[45]

Notes

1. Hazlitt's "On Familiar Style" is to be found in *Table Talk*, *Essays on Men and Manners* (1822).
2. pomp—This is a formal word meaning all the impressive clothes, decorations, music etc that are traditional for an important official or public ceremony.
3. cant phrases—special phrases.
4. slipshod allusions—allusions used too quickly, carefully and frequently.
5. It is not to take the first word that offers—It does not mean to use the first word that comes into your mind.
6. perspicuity—having a good judgment and understanding of people and situation.
7. to gabble on at a venture—to say quickly without careful consideration.
8. upon stilts—referring to the use of a pompous style.
9. *com grano salis*—Latin for "with a grain of salt". According to the OED, to accept a statement "with a grain of salt" is to accept it "with a certain amount of reserve".
10. *coterie*—a small group of people who enjoy doing the same things together, and do not like including others.
11. the King's English—the standard English.
12. solecism—something deviating from the proper, normal, or accepted order.
13. that clinches a writer's meaning—that grasps firmly the writer's meaning.
14. and more so than the mere showy, unsubstantial ornaments—and are more necessary than ornaments that are simply and lacking in solid value.
15. a load of band-boxes—a carriage carrying bandboxes.
16. Mr Cobbet—referring to William Cobbet (1762—1835), a popular political writer, and in his last years a member of Parliament.

17. persisting in a wrong scent—persisting in the following a wrong path (for recollecting the name of a place or person, as mentioned above).
18. ancient medals, obscure coins, and Spanish pieces of eight—Here the author compares the rich and rare phraseology with such antiquities as ancient medals, obscure coins, and Spanish pieces of eight. Obscure coins refer to the ancient coins which have been so long out of use that the designs and numbers inscribed on them have become indiscernible. Spanish pieces of eight refer to Spanish dollars.
19. Mr. Lamb—referring to Charles Lamb (1773—1834), a well-known English essayist and Hazlitt's contemporary.
20. Burton—Robert Burton (1577—1640), English philosopher and author, known chiefly for his book *The Anatomy of Melancholy*.
21. Fuller—Thomas Fuller (1608—1661), English preacher and author, known chiefly for his book *The Worthies of England*.
22. Coryate—Thomas Coryate (1577—1617), English traveler and author.
23. Sir Thomas Browne—(1605—1682), English physician and author, known chiefly for his book *Religio Medici* (*The Religion of a Medical Doctor*).
24. Elia—Lamb wrote his essays under the pseudonym of "Elia" (*Essays of Elia* and *Last Essays of Elia*).
25. Mrs Battle's Opinions on Whist—an essay written by Lamb and published in his *Essays of Elia*.
26. *A well of native English undefiled*—A line, taken from *The Faerie Queen* written by Edmund Spenser (1552? —1599), was to glorify Geoffrey Chaucer (c. 1343—1400), who is regarded as the father of English literature for his *Canterbury Tales*. undefiled: not corrupted.
27. Erasmus's *Colloquies*—a book written by Desiderius Errasmus (1446? —1536), a well-known Dutch scholar and written in the age of Renaissance.
28. any borrowed pencil—any way of writing that is borrowed from some other writer.
29. the want of—the lack of.
30. tympany—a resonant sound heard in percussion (as of the abdomen). Here it means swelling.
31. *Sermo humi obrepens*—Latin for idiom on the ground.
32. magniloquent—speaking in or characterized by a high-flown often bombastic style or manner.
33. phantasmagoria— A fantastic sequence of haphazardly associative imagery, as seen in dreams or fever.
34. Ancient Pistol—a character under Falstaff in Shakespeare's *Henry the Fourth*, who likes to quote verses improperly.
35. rhodomontade=rodomontade—a bragging speech.
36. fantoccini—A show using puppets animated by moving wires or mechanical means.

37. That strut and fret their hour upon the stage—This line is taken from Shakespeare's *Macbeth* Act V Scene V. that=who.
38. The Coronation at either House is nothing to it—The ceremony of Coronation at both the House of Commons and the House of Lords can not b compared with it.
39. Golconda—The legendary Golconda was the Indian El Dorado, a fabled outpost whose streets, so to say, were paved with precious stones. Here it is metaphorically to mean treasure.
40. Britannia with her shield—referring to the goddess of Britannia who is wearing shield.
41. Hope—referring to the goddess of Hope.
42. *hieroglyphical*—being a system of writing, such as that of ancient Egypt, in which pictorial symbols are used to represent meaning or sounds or a combination of meaning and sound.
43. rhapsodies—exalted or excessively enthusiastic expression of feeling in speech or writing.
44. Cowper—William Cowper (1731—1800), an English poet famous for his *The Task* published in 1785.
45. It smiled, and it was cold—a line taken from Cowper's *The Task*.

For Study and Discussion

1. Why does the author object to Dr. Johnson's style?
2. What is a truly familiar style?
3. Please memorize the following sentences:
   1) To write a genuine familiar or truly English style, is to write as any one would speak in common conversation who had a thorough command and choice of words, or who could discourse with ease, force, and perspicuity, setting aside all pedantic and oratorical flourishes. Or, to give another illustration, to write naturally is the same thing in regard to common conversation as to read naturally is in regard to common speech.
   2) The proper force of words lies not in the words themselves, but in their application. A word may be a find-sounding word, of an unusual length, and a very imposing from its learning and novelty, and yet in the connection in which it is introduced may be quite pointless and irrelevant. It is not pomp or pretension, but the adaptation of the expression to the idea, that clinches a writer's meaning:—as it is not the size of glossiness of the materials, but their being fitted each to its place, that gives strength to the arch; or as the pegs and nails are as necessary to the support of the building as the larger timber, and more so than the mere showy, unsubstantial ornaments.

Thomas De Quincy
On the Knocking at the Gate in Macbeth

From my boyish days I had always felt a great perplexity on one point in *Macbeth*. It was this: the knocking at the gate, which succeeds to the murder of Duncan[1], produced to my feelings an effect for which I never could account. The effect was that it reflected back upon the murderer a peculiar awfulness and a depth of solemnity; yet, however obstinately I endeavoured with my understanding to comprehend this, for many years I never could see why it should produce such an effect.

Here I pause for one moment, to exhort the reader never to pay any attention to his understanding, when it stands in opposition to any other faculty of his mind. The mere understanding, however useful and indispensable, is the meanest faculty in the human mind, and the most to be distrusted; and yet the great majority of people trust to nothing else—which may do for ordinary life, but not for philosophical purposes...

But to return from this digression, —my understanding could furnish no reason why the knocking at the gate in Macbeth should produce any effect, direct or reflected. In fact, my understanding said positively that it could not produce any effect. But I knew better; I felt that it did; and I waited and clung to the problem until further knowledge should enable me to solve it. — At length, in 1812, Mr. Williams made his debut[2] on the stage of Ratcliffe Highway[3], and executed those unparalleled murders which have procured for him such a brilliant and undying reputation. On which murders, by the way, I must observe, that in one respect they have had an ill effect, by making the connoisseur in murder very fastidious in his taste, and dissatisfied by anything that has been since done in that line. All other murders look pale by the deep crimson of his; and, as an amateur once said to me in a querulous tone, "There has been absolutely nothing *doing since* his time, or nothing that's worth speaking of." But this is wrong; for it is unreasonable to expect all men to be great artists, and born with the genius of Mr. Williams. Now it will be remembered, that in the first of these murders (that of the Marrs), the same incident (of a knocking at the door soon after the work of extermination was complete) did actually occur, which the genius of Shakespeare has invented; and all good judges, and the most eminent dilettanti[4], acknowledged the felicity of Shakespeare's suggestion, as soon as it was actually realized. Here, then, was a fresh proof that I was right in relying on my own feeling, in opposition to my understanding; and I again set myself to study the problem. At length I solved it to my own satisfaction; and my solution is this: Murder, in ordinary cases, where the sympathy is wholly directed to the case of the murdered person, is an incident of coarse and vulgar horror; and for this reason—that it flings the interest exclusively upon the natural but ignoble instinct by which we cleave to life: an instinct which, as being indispensable to the primal law of self-preservation, is the same in kind (though different in degree) amongst all living creatures. This instinct, therefore, because it annihilates all distinctions, and degrades the greatest of men to the level of "the poor beetle that we tread on[5]", exhibits human nature in its most abject and humiliating attitude. Such an attitude would little suit the purposes of the poet. What then must he do? He must throw the interest on the murderer. Our sympathy must be with *him* (of course I mean a sympathy of comprehension, a sympathy by which we enter into his feelings, and are made to understand them—not a sympathy of pity or approbation). In the murdered person, all strife of thought, all flux and reflux of passion and of purpose, are crushed by one overwhelming panic; the fear of instant death smites him "with its petrific mace[6]." But in the murderer, such a murderer as a poet will condescend to, there must be raging some great storm of passion—jealousy, ambition, vengeance, hatred—which will create a hell within him; and into this hell we are to look. In *Macbeth*, for the sake of gratifying his own enormous and teeming faculty of creation, Shakespeare has introduced two murderers: and, as usual in his hands, they are remarkably discriminated; but, though in Macbeth the strife of mind is greater than in his wife, the tiger spirit not so awake, and his feelings caught chiefly by contagion from her,—yet, as both were finally involved in the guilt of murder, the murderous mind of necessity is finally to be presumed in both. This was to be expressed; and on its own account, as well as to make it a more proportionable antagonist to the unoffending nature of their victim, "the gracious Duncan[7]," and adequately to expound "the deep damnation of his taking off[8]," this was to be expressed with peculiar energy. We were to be made to feel that the human nature—i. e. , the divine nature of love and mercy, spread through the hearts of all creatures, and seldom utterly withdrawn from man,—was gone, vanished, extinct, and that the fiendish nature had taken its place. And, as this effect is marvelously accomplished in the *dialogues* and *soliloquies* themselves, so it is finally consummated by the expedient under consideration; and it is to this that I now solicit the reader's attention. If the reader has ever witnessed a wife, daughter, or sister in a fainting fit, he may chance to have observed that the most affecting moment in such a spectacle is *that* in which a sigh and a stirring announce the recommencement of suspended life. Or, if the reader has ever been present in a vast metropolis on the day when some great national idol was carried in funeral pomp to his grave, and chancing to walk near the course through which it passed, has felt powerfully, in the silence and desertion of the streets, and in the stagnation of ordinary business, the deep interest which at that moment was possessing the heart of man—if all at once he should hear the death-like stillness broken up by the sound of wheels rattling away from the scene, and making known that the transitory vision was dissolved, he will be aware that at no moment was his sense of the complete suspension and pause in ordinary human concerns so full and affecting as at that moment when the suspension ceases, and the goings-on of human life are suddenly resumed. All action in any direction is best expounded, measured, and made apprehensible, by reaction. Now, apply this to the case in *Macbeth*. Here, as I have said, the retiring of the human heart and the entrance of the fiendish heart was to be expressed and made sensible. Another world has stepped in; and the murderers are taken out of the region of human things, human purposes, human desires. They are transfigured: Lady Macbeth is "unsexed[9];" Macbeth has forgot that he was born of woman; both are conformed to the image of devils; and the world of devils is suddenly revealed. But how shall this be conveyed and made palpable? In order that a new world may step in, this world must for a time disappear. The murderers, and the murder must be insulated—cut off by an immeasurable gulf from the ordinary tide and succession of human affairs—locked up and sequestered in some deep recess; we must be made sensible that the world of ordinary life is suddenly arrested, laid asleep, tranced, racked into a dread armistice; time must be annihilated; relation to things without abolished; and all must pass self-withdrawn into a deep syncope and suspension of earthly passion. Hence it is that, when the deed is done, when the work of darkness is perfect, then the world of darkness passes away like a pageantry in the clouds: the knocking at the gate is heard; and it makes known audibly that the reaction has commenced; the human has made its reflux upon the fiendish; the pulses of life are beginning to beat again; and the re-establishment of the goings-on of the world in which we live first makes us profoundly sensible of the awful parenthesis that had suspended them.

O Mighty poet! Thy works are not as those of other men, simply and merely great works of art, but are also like the phenomena of nature, like the sun and the sea, the stars and the flowers; like frost and snow, rain and dew, hail-storm and thunder, which are to be studied with entire submission of our own faculties, and in the perfect faith that in them there can be no too much or too little, nothing useless or inert, but that the farther we press in our discoveries, the more we shall see proofs of design and self-supporting arrangement where the careless eye had seen nothing but accident!

Notes

1. Duncan—King of Scotland, being killed by Macbeth.
2. debut—a first public appearance, as of a performer.
3. Ratcliffe Highway—referring to John Williams, a sailor, who had thrown London into a panic in December 1811 by murdering the Marr family and twelve days late, the Williamson family.
4. dilettanti—an amateur who engages in an activity without serious intentions and who pretends to have knowledge; a connoisseur.
5. the poor bettle we tread on—a line taken from Shakespeare's *Measure for Measure* III. i. 79.
6. its petrific mace—a phrase taken from Milton's Paradise Lost X. 294. petrific: turning into stone. Mace: a ceremonial staff as the symbol of a public official's authority.
7. the gracious Duncan—a phrase taken from Shakespeare's Macbeth III. I. 66.

8. the deep damnation of his taking off—a phrase taken from Shakespeare's Macbeth I. vii. 20. taking off: murdering.
9. unsexed—a word taken from Shakespeare's Macbeth I. v. 42.

For Study and Discussion

1. Read the last paragraph loudly. Please memorize the similes used by the writer.
2. Please read as widely as you can about Shakespeare's great tragedies *Hamlet*, *Othello*, *Macbeth*, and *King Lear*. Try to understand the significance of Shakespeare's tragedies.

Virgina Woolf
Professions as Women

When your secretary invited me to come here, she told me that your Society is concerned with the employment of women and she suggested that I might tell you something about my own professional experiences. It is true that I am a woman; it is true I am employed; but what professional experiences have I had? It is difficult to say. My profession is literature; and in that profession there are fewer experiences for women than in any other, with the exception of the stage—fewer, I mean, that are peculiar to women. For the road was cut many years ago—by Fanny Burney[1], by Aphra Behn[2], by Harriet Martineau[3], by Jane Austen[4], by George Eliot[5]—many famous women, and many more unknown and forgotten, have been before me, making the path smooth, and regulating my steps. Thus, when I came to write, there were very few material obstacles in my way. Writing was a reputable and harmless occupation. The family peace was not broken by the scratching of a pen. No demand was made upon the family purse. For ten and sixpence one can buy paper enough to write all the plays of Shakespeare—if one has a mind that way. Pianos and models, Paris, Vienna, and Berlin, masters and mistresses, are not needed by a writer. The cheapness of writing paper is, of course, the reason why women have succeeded as writers before they have succeeded in the other professions.

But to tell you my story—it is a simple one. You have only got to figure to yourselves a girl in a bedroom with a pen in her hand. She had only to move that pen from left to right—from ten o'clock to one. Then it occurred to her to do what is simple and cheap enough after all—to slip a few of those pages into an envelope, fix a penny stamp in the corner, and drop the envelope into the red box at the corner. It was thus that I became a journalist; and my effort was rewarded on the first day of the following month—a very glorious day it was for me—by a letter from an editor containing a check for one pound ten shillings and sixpence. But to show you how little I deserve to be called a professional woman, how little I know of the struggles and difficulties of such lives, I have to admit that instead of spending that sum upon bread and butter, rent, shoes and stockings, or butcher's bills, I went out and bought a cat—a beautiful cat, a Persian cat, which very soon involved me in bitter disputes with my neighbors.

What could be easier than to write articles and to buy Persian cats with the profits? But wait a moment. Articles have to be about something. Mine, I seem to remember, was about a novel by a famous man. And while I was writing this review, I discovered that if I were going to review books I should need to do battle with a certain phantom. And the phantom was a woman, and when I came to know her better I called her after the heroine of a famous poem, *The Angel in the House*[6]. It was she who used to come between me and my paper when I was writing reviews. It was she who bothered me and wasted my time and so tormented me that at last I killed her. You who come off a younger and happier generation may not have heard of her—you may not know what I mean by The Angel in the House. I will describe her as shortly as I can. She was intensely sympathetic. She was immensely charming. She was utterly unselfish. She excelled in the difficult arts of family life. She sacrificed herself daily. If there was chicken, she took the leg; if there was a draft she sat in it—in short she was so constituted that she never had a mind or a wish of her own, but preferred to sympathize always with the minds and wishes of others. Above all—I need not say it—she was pure. Her purity was supposed to be her chief beauty—her blushes, her great grace. In those days—the last of Queen Victoria—every house had its Angel. And when I came to write I encountered her with the very first words. The shadow of her wings fell on my page; I heard the rustling of her skirts in the room. Directly, that is to say, I took my pen in my hand to review that novel by a famous man, she slipped behind me and whispered: "My dear, you are a young woman. You are writing about a book that has been written by a man. Be sympathetic; be tender; flatter; deceive; use all the art and wiles of our sex. Never let anybody guess that you have a mind of our own. Above all, be pure." And she made as if to guide my pen. I now record the one act for which I take some credit to myself, though the credit rightly belongs to some excellent ancestors of mine who left me a certain sum of money—shall we say five hundred pounds a year? —so that it was not necessary for me to depend solely on charm for my living. I turned upon her and caught her by the throat. I did my best to kill her. My excuse, if I were to be had up in a court of law, would be that I acted in self-defense. Had I not killed her she would have killed me. She would have plucked the heart out of my writing. For, as I found, directly I put pen to paper, you cannot review even a novel without having a mind of your own, without expressing what you think to be the truth about human relations, morality, sex. And all these questions, according to the Angel of the House, cannot be dealt with freely and openly by women; they must charm, they must conciliate, they must—to put it bluntly—tell lies if they are to succeed. Thus, whenever I felt the shadow of her wing or the radiance of her halo upon my page, I took up the inkpot and flung it at her. She died hard. Her fictitious nature was of great assistance to her. It is far harder to kill a phantom than a reality. She was always creeping back when I thought I had dispatched her. Though I flatter myself that I killed her in the end, the struggle was severe; it took much time that had better have been spent upon learning Greek grammar; or in roaming the world in search of adventures. But it was a real experience; It was an experience that was bound befall all women writers at that time. Killing the Angel in the House was part of the occupation of a woman writer.

But to continue my story. The Angel was dead; what then remained? You may say that what remained was a simple and common object—a young woman in a bedroom with an inkpot. In other words, now that she had rid herself of falsehood, that young woman had only to be herself. Ah, but what is "herself"? I mean, what is a woman? I assure you, I do not know. I do not believe that you know. I do not believe that anybody can know until she has expressed herself in all the arts and professions open to human skill. That indeed is one of the reasons why I have come here—out of respect for you, who are in process of showing us by your experiments what a woman is, who are in process of providing us, by your failures and succeeded, with that extremely important piece of information.

But to continue the story of my professional experiences. I made one pound ten and six by my first review; and I bought a Persian cat with the proceeds. Then I grew ambitious. A Persian cat is all very well, I said; but a Persian cat is not enough. I must have a motorcar. And it was thus that I became a novelist—for it is a very strange thing that people will give you a motorcar if you will tell them a story. It is a still stranger thing that there is nothing so delightful in the world as telling stories. It is far pleasanter than writing reviews of famous novels. And yet, if I am to obey your secretary and tell you my professional experiences as a novelist, I must tell you about a very strange experience that befell me as a novelist. And to understand it you must try first to imagine a novelist's state of mind. I hope I am not giving away professional secrets if I say that a novelist's chief desire is to be as unconscious as possible. He has to induce in himself a state of perpetual lethargy. He wants life to proceed with the utmost quiet and regularity. He wants to see the same faces, to read the same books, to do the same things day after day, month after month, while he is writing, so that nothing may break the illusion in which he is living—so that nothing may disturb or disquiet the mysterious nosings about, feelings round, darts, dashes, and sudden discoveries of that very shy and illusive spirit, the imagination. I suspect that this state is the same both for men and women. Be that as it may, I want you to imagine me writing a novel in a state of trance. I want you to figure to yourselves a girl sitting with a pen in her hand, which for minutes, and indeed for hours, she never dips into the inkpot. The image that comes to my mind when I think of this girl is the image of a fisherman lying sunk in dreams on the verge of a deep lake with a rod held out over the water. She was letting her imagination sweep unchecked round every rock and cranny of the world that lies submerged in the depths of our unconscious being. Now came the experience that I believe to be far commoner with women writers than with men. The line raced through the girl's fingers. Her imagination had rushed away. It had sought the pools, the depths, the dark places where the largest fish slumber. And then there was a smash. There was an explosion. There was foam and confusion. The imagination had dashed itself against something hard. The girl was roused from her dream. She was indeed in a state of the most acute and difficult distress. To speak without figure, she had thought of something, something about the body, about the passions which it was unfitting for her as a woman to say. Men, her reason told her, would be shocked. The consciousness of what men will say of a woman who speaks the truth about her passions had roused her from her artist's state of unconsciousness. She could write no more. The trace was over. Her imagination could work no longer. This I believe to be a very common experience with women writers—they are impeded by the extreme conventionality of the other sex. For though men sensibly allow themselves great freedom in these respects, I doubt that they realize or can control the extreme severity with which they condemn such freedom in women.

These then were two very genuine experiences of my own. These were two of the adventures of my professional life. The first—killing the Angel in the House—I think I solved. She died. But the second, telling the truth about my own experiences as a body, I do not think I solved. I doubt that any woman has solved it yet. The obstacles against her are still immensely powerful—and yet they are very difficult to define. Outwardly, what is simpler than to write books? Outwardly, what obstacles are there for a woman rather than for a man? Inwardly, I think, the case is very different; she has still many ghosts to fight, many prejudices to overcome. Indeed it will be a long time still, I think, before a woman can sit down to write a book without finding a phantom to be slain, a rock to be dashed against. And if this is so in literature, the freest of all professions for women, how is it in the new professions which you are now for the first time entering?

Those are the questions that I should like, had I time, to ask you. And indeed, if I have laid stress upon these professional experiences of mine, it is because I believe that they are, though in different forms, yours also. Even when the path is nominally open—when there is nothing to revert a woman from being a doctor, a lawyer, a civil servant—there are many phantoms and obstacles, as I believe, looming in her way. To discuss and define them is I think of great value and importance; for thus only can the labor be shared, the difficulties be solved. But besides this, it is necessary also to discuss the ends and the aims for which we are fighting, for which we are doing battle with these formidable obstacles. Those aims cannot be taken for granted; they must be perpetually questioned and examined. The whole position, as I see it—here in this hall surrounded by women practicing for the first time in history I know not how many different professions—is one of extraordinary interest and importance. You have won rooms of your own in the house hitherto exclusively owned by men. You are able, though not without great labor and effort, to pay the rent. You are earning your five hundred pounds a year. But this freedom is only a beginning; the room is your own, but it is still bare. It has to be furnished; it has to be decorated; it has to be shared. How are you going to furnish it, how are you going to decorate it? With whom are you going to share it, and upon what terms? These, I think are questions of the utmost importance and interest. For the first time in history you are able to ask them; for the first time you are able to decide for yourself what the answers should be. Willingly would I stay and discuss those questions and answers—but not tonight. My time is up; and I must cease.

Notes

1. Fanny Burney (1572—1840)—an English novelist, diarist, and playwright. Totally she wrote 4 novels, 8 plays, 1 biography and 20 volumes of journals and letters. Her writings deals with the lives of English aristocrats and satirizes their social pretensions and personal foibles.
2. Aphra Behn (1640—1689)—an English dramatist of the Restoration. She was one of the first English professional female writers, famous for her two novels: *Love-Letters Between a Nobleman and His Sister* (1684), *Oroonoko* (1688).
3. by Harriet Martineau (1802—1876)—an English writer and philosopher. She mainly writes a series of stories concerning politics and religion.
4. by Jane Austen (1775—1817)—An English novelist, often regarded as the greatest of English women novelists. Her major novels include: *Sense and Sensibility* (1811), *Pride and Prejudice* (1813), *Mansfield Park* (1814) *and Emma* (1815).
5. by George Eliot (1819—1880)—an English novelist, one of the leading writers of the Victorian era. Her major novels include: *Adam Bede* (1859), *The Mill on the Floss* (1860), *Silas Marner* (1861), *Romola* (1863), *Middlemarch* (1871).
6. *The Angel in the House*—a poem by Coventry Patmore (1823—1896), an English poet and critic. The poem is an account of Patmore's wife, Emily, whom he believed to be the perfect Victorian wife and head of the home. The poem was largely ignored upon its publication, but it became enormously popular during the 19th century and its influence well into the 20th century.

For Study and Discussion

1. What are the distinctive qualities of a Victorian woman described by the writer?
2. In what way does the writer express her main idea in Paragraph 3?